Ecology and Management
of Forest Insects

Ecology and Management of Forest Insects

Martin R. Speight
Lecturer in Agricultural and Forest Entomology,
Department of Zoology,
University of Oxford
and
Fellow of St Anne's College, Oxford

and

David Wainhouse
Principal scientific officer
Forestry Commission Research Station
Farnham, Surrey

CLARENDON PRESS · OXFORD

1989

Oxford University Press, Walton Street, Oxford OX2 6DP
Oxford New York Toronto
Delhi Bombay Calcutta Madras Karachi
Petaling Jaya Singapore Hong Kong Tokyo
Nairobi Dar es Salaam Cape Town
Melbourne Auckland
and associated companies in
Berlin Ibadan

Oxford is a trade mark of Oxford University Press

Published in the United States
by Oxford University Press, New York

British Library Cataloguing in Publication Data
Speight, M.R.
Ecology and management of forest insects.
1. Forests. Insects. Ecological aspects
I. Title II. Wainhouse, David
595.7'052'642
ISBN 0–19–854162–7
ISBN 0–19–854161–9 (pbk.)

Library of Congress Cataloging in Publication Data
Speight, Martin R.
Ecology and management of forest insects / Martin R. Speight and David Wainhouse
p.   cm.   Bibliography: p.
Includes index.
1. Forest insects—Ecology. 2. Forest insects—Control.
3. Forest insects—Host plants. I. Wainhouse, David. II. Title.
SB761.S68 1989   634.9'—dc19   88–27273
ISBN 0–19–854162–7
ISBN 0–19–854161–9 (pbk.)

Set by Footnote Graphics, Warminster, Wilts
Printed and bound in Great Britain by
Biddles Ltd, Guildford and King's Lynn

Preface

Forest entomology as a distinct discipline can trace its origins back to the practices of central European foresters in the eighteenth century. This strong European tradition has been maintained since that time, and a number of classic German texts such as *Die Forstinsekten Mitteleuropas* by K. Escherich (4 vols 1914–42) and *Die Waldkrankheiten* by F. Schwerdtfeger (3 edns 1944–70) are still invaluable sources of information on the biology and control of forest insects. Only two European books written in English address the topic of forest entomology; *Insects of the British Woodlands*, published in 1937 by Neil Chrystal, and much more recently *Forest Insects* by Dermot Bevan (1987, HMSO, London). These books are an admirable guide to the identification of forest insects and the damage they cause, but they have not addressed in detail the vital question of the integration of insect ecology with management.

We must emphasize that the present book does not attempt to describe in detail the taxonomy and biology of all major forest pests; such information is available elsewhere. Northern Europe is very well covered by *Forest Insects* by Dermot Bevan, *Ecologie des insectes forestiers* by Roger Dajoz (1980, Gaulthier-Villars) and *Die Forstschadlinge Europas* by Wolfgang Schwenke (1972, 5 volumes, Paul Parey). Useful books on North American forest insects include *Insects that feed on trees and shrubs* by Warren Johnson and Howard Lyon (1976, Cornell University Press), and *Insects harmful to forest trees* by R. Martineau (1984, Multiscience Publications). We aim instead to bring together the wealth of new material on the ecology of forest insects and recent advances in insect control, and place them in the context of the more traditional aspects of the subject, in which are rooted the principles of integrated pest management.

The text is written mainly for those familiar with temperate forest ecosystems, with particular emphasis on plantation forestry. An understanding of the important role played by climate, food, and other insects in the ecology of insect herbivores is fundamental to an understanding of pest population dynamics and hence management, and the first part of this book (Chapters 1, 2, and 3) presents a synthesis of these complex interactions. Chapter 4 is an appraisal of the life history characteristics of forest insects that contribute to their status as pests and provides a basis for understanding their impact on host trees and the consequent need for control. This chapter concentrates mainly—although not exclusively—on the pests of European forests, many of which, however, will be familiar to entomologists in the New World as introduced pests. The last part of the book (Chapters 5–10) is a critical assessment of the various strategies available to the forester or pest manager to control forest pests and minimize economic damage to forest trees. In these chapters we have drawn freely on examples from both the New and the Old World, and the principles of management discussed should be applicable to forest pests in most parts of the world, including the tropics.

There can be no doubt that modern cost-effective pest management cannot be accomplished without a sound knowledge of the biotic and abiotic factors that influence insect population dynamics. Throughout the book, we have attempted to highlight those characteristics of insect ecology that can be exploited in their management and have tried to illustrate the theory and practice of insect control with particular examples which are then critically discussed.

A great number of colleagues and friends have helped us during the writing of this book and it would have been impossible to produce a balanced discussion of the various topics without the benefit of their critical appraisal and personal experiences. We would like to thank in particular: Alf Bakke, Alan Berryman, Erik Christiansen, Dermot Bevan, Hermann Bogenschutz, John Borden, Jean-Claude Grégoire, John Gibbs, Nick Mills, Fernando Robredo, John Stoakley, and Richard Waring.

We are indebted to Keith Day who read the whole book and to the following who read one or more chapters: David Barbour, Alan Berryman, Martin Birch, John Borden, Alistair Burn, Clive Carter, Tom Coaker, Mick Crawley, Philip Entwistle, Hugh Evans, Julian Evans, Charles Godfray, Jean-Claude Grégoire, Ralph Harmer, Owen Jones, Colin King, Peter Konowski, Jack Lattin, John Lawton, Don Reynolds, Peter Savill, Phil Sterling, John Stoakley, and Tim Winter. We are also grateful to a host of undergraduate and postgraduate students in the Zoology and Plant Sciences Departments of Oxford University, and the Oxford Forestry Institute who appraised various drafts.

Finally we would like to express deep gratitude to our wives Wendy and Valmai whose patience and support has seen us through a process that seemed so straightforward at the outset.

September 1988   M.R.S.
                                                                              D.W.

Acknowledgements

All photographs were taken by Martin Speight, except the following:
Fig. 7.6 Anon; Fig. 4.26. Don Barrett; Fig. 9.4 (a), (b) & (c); John Borden; Fig. 4.5. Robin Buxton; Fig. 8.6. (a), (b) & (c) copyright Canadian Entomologist, with permission; Figs 4.9(b), 6.2. Clive Carter; Figs. 3.8, 4.11(b), & 4.12. Eric Christiansen; Fig. 8.9. Jenny Cory; Fig. 4.25. Paul Embden; Fig. 7.3(a). George Gradwell; Figs 3.5, 4.16, 4.18 (a), (b) & (c), 4.22(b), 4.33, 5.11, 5.18, 6.2, 7.3(c), 7.7, 9.6 (c) & (d), copyright Forestry Commission, with permission; Fig. 4.14. Mark Hunter; Fig. 7.13. copyright Institute of Horticultural Research, by permission; Fig. 7.9. copyright Institute of Virology, by permission; Fig. 3.7. Cathy Kennedy; Fig. 2.26. Peter Savill; Fig. 7.10. Philip Sterling; Fig. 4.20. Andrew Storer; Figs. 3.4, 4.10, 5.17, 6.3, 10.1. David Wainhouse.

All diagrams were reproduced by permission of the author(s) and/or publisher as cited in the Bibliography, except the following:—

Figs 2.7, 2.8, 3.1 & 3.22, copyright Ecological Society of America, reprinted by permission; Fig. 2.33. copyright © 1987 Macmillan Magazines Ltd., reprinted by permission; Fig. 5.6. Crown Copyright, reprinted by permission of the Forestry Commission; Fig. 8.8. copyright 1984 American Chemical Society, reprinted by permission; Fig. 9.1. copyright 1971 American Association for the Advancement of Science, reprinted by permission; Figs. 3.19, 7.11, & 8.2. copyright 1978, 1985 & 1983 Pergamon Press PLC, reprinted by permission.

Contents

1

Introduction

This book is primarily concerned with the insect pests of temperate forests, how their ecology is shaped by the habitat in which they live, and how different aspects of their life history contribute to their status as forest pests. These life history characteristics, discussed in Chapter 4, also determine to some extent how these insects are managed and this important aspect of forest entomology is considered in the second part of the book in Chapters 5–10. The first part of this introductory chapter sets temperate forests and particularly plantations in perspective by briefly discussing the extent and character of forest ecosystems and the ways in which they are exploited. Of the many insect species that inhabit temperate forests only a few compete directly with man by damaging or killing trees. Outbreaks of these insect pests differ in extent and intensity as well as in frequency of occurrence, and classification of outbreak patterns, discussed later in the chapter, helps to focus attention on the underlying causes, an understanding of which is an essential background to the management of forest pests. Some of these aspects are discussed in detail in Chapters 2 and 3.

1.1 FORESTS AS A RENEWABLE RESOURCE

Forests cover about a third of the land surface of the earth producing more biomass than all the other major terrestrial biomes put together (Whittaker 1975; Begon *et al* 1986). Since much of this biomass is stored as wood, it can, at least in theory, be exploited as a renewable natural resource. The extent of forest cover varies considerably between countries with most of the world's closed forest growing in the Americas and the USSR and relatively little of it, a mere 4 per cent, occurring in Europe (Table 1.1). The kinds of forest that grow naturally in these geographical regions are determined largely by differences in climate and climatic stability. Complex communities dominated by broad-leaved species grow in the tropics which have equable temperatures throughout the year and seasons usually only delimited by rainfall patterns. In contrast, ecologically simple communities are characteristic of the mainly temperate higher latitudes where about 90 per cent of coniferous forests grow.

These forest ecosystems are exploited in many different ways. In tropical

Table 1.1. *The approximate world distribution of forest land*

Country	%
Europe	4
USSR	22
North America	16
South America	23
Asia	10
China	3
Africa	17
Other countries	3

Data from Anon 1986.

areas for example, selective removal of high value hardwoods on a non-sustainable basis results in considerable destruction of natural forest but the impact of local agriculture in the form of slash and burn cultivation and clearance for grazing land or other agricultural settlement has had a greater impact. In Europe, where the process of forest clearance began many centuries ago, little truly natural forest now remains. Here, the forest resource consists largely of semi-natural forest and plantations, often of exotic species and usually managed on a sustained yield basis to provide wood and wood products. In the densely populated areas of western Europe, there is now an increasing emphasis on multiple-use forests managed not only for timber production but also for recreation and amenity.

1.1.1 Wood production

Forest ecosystems provide a range of products that can be exploited by man, of which wood is by far the most important. In the tropics about 80 per cent of wood harvested is burnt as fuel or has other domestic uses, but in Europe and other developed regions, it is used mainly for structural and decorative purposes and for conversion into pulp for paper making.

The amount of wood produced in forests is influenced by a number of factors including species composition, age and, importantly, extent of management. As forest ecosystems mature, their biomass increases, but net productivity (i.e. the rate of storage of organic matter by trees which is not used in respiration nor consumed by herbivores) declines, and is close to zero in 'climax' forests where production roughly equals losses through death and decay. It is partly for this reason that the average productivity of the world's closed forests is only about 1 m^3 ha^{-1} $year^{-1}$ (Evans 1982). One of the principal aims of forest management, therefore, is to harvest the accumulated biomass and maintain productivity by encouraging the development of younger more vigorous stands. The extent to which the

productivity of natural or plantation forests can be increased and maintained depends largely on the local climate, site fertility, stand density, and
species composition. The average productivity of managed forests in
Canada and Siberia, for example, is only around 1 m^3 ha^{-1} $year^{-1}$ but
productivity is much higher for plantations of conifers in the UK (11 m^3
ha^{-1} $year^{-1}$) and of pines in New Zealand (18–30 m^3 ha^{-1} $year^{-1}$). In some
tropical areas on the other hand, extremely high productivity can be
achieved; eucalypt plantations, for example, may produce up to 60 m^3 ha^{-1}
$year^{-1}$ (Evans 1982; Savill and Evans 1986).

In general, by establishing plantations of fast growing pioneer species
which can tolerate the conditions of dense monocultures, productivity can
be much higher than that achieved from managed natural forests. Such
plantations are becoming increasingly important in temperate forestry and
have the advantage that by allowing the manipulation of species composition, planting pattern and density, they give the forester greater control over
yield and quality of the timber produced (Savill and Evans 1986). It is also
much easier to estimate current growth and future yields from plantations
because they are usually even-aged and composed of a single species. A
typical growth curve for an even-aged conifer plantation is shown in Fig.
1.1a in which growth, conventionally measured as the volume of stemwood
over 7 cm diameter, is expressed as the current annual increment (c.a.i.),
i.e. the rate at which the trees are growing in m^3 ha^{-1} (Johnston 1975).
Typically, growth increases rapidly after an initial establishment period,
reaches a maximum, and then declines as trees approach maturity. When
growth is expressed as the mean annual increment (m.a.i.), which is the
average rate of increase in volume since planting, the curve rises more
slowly and eventually culminates at the point where it intercepts the curve
of c.a.i. This point represents the maximum rate of volume increment that
can be achieved by a particular tree species on a given site, so that for
maximum productivity, plantations should be felled and replanted once
they have reached this stage of growth.

The maximum m.a.i. expressed in m^3 ha^{-1} forms the basis of the 'yield
class' system which is used as a measure of stand productivity in the UK
(Hamilton and Christie 1971). Yield class varies not only between tree
species but also between different stands of the same species growing on
different sites. In temperate regions conifers usually grow more rapidly
than broad-leaved species, such as oak; thus they reach their maximum
m.a.i. earlier and so they can usually be grown more profitably. However,
some broad-leaved species such as poplars and willows also grow quickly
(Fig. 1.1b) and when coppiced can be extremely productive, yielding up to
12 t ha^{-1} $year^{-1}$. These broad-leaved species are sometimes established in
'energy' or 'biomass' plantations harvested on very short rotations of up to
6 years.

1.1.2 Non-timber products

Plantations established to yield non-timber products are important in many countries. Christmas trees are a familiar example, and seed orchards are needed all over the world to sustain plantation forestry. Other important products include the bark of the cork oak, *Quercus suber*, which is periodically harvested from the living tree to provide cork, and conifer bark, a by-product of timber harvesting, is used as a soil conditioner after suitable treatment to reduce the concentration of phytotoxic chemicals (Aaron 1976). Edible seeds are obtained from the stone pine, walnut, and sweet chestnut in southern Europe, and in North America the sap of sugar maple provides the raw material for maple syrup.

Biochemicals from trees are also an important resource especially in tropical areas where forest trees produce a wealth of pharmacologically active chemicals. In Russia, pines are tapped to produce resin and in Spain and Portugal, *Eucalyptus* plantations have been established for the production of essential oils (Savill and Evans 1986).

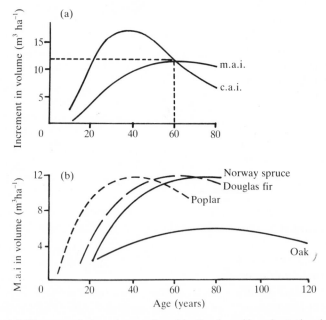

Fig. 1.1. (a) The growth in volume of an idealized conifer plantation in Britain. Increment in m³ per hectare is expressed as the current annual increment (c.a.i.) and the mean annual increment (m.a.i.) (b) The mean annual increment of two conifers and two broad-leaved trees. (after Johnston 1975).

1.1.3 Amenity and conservation

Forests have traditionally been used for hunting and fishing but other leisure and recreation activities such as walking and camping are becoming increasingly important in developed countries. Such activities are not incompatible with plantation forestry and even dense conifer plantations can have considerable aesthetic appeal (Cooper 1976), especially when established along natural contours with broad-leaved trees breaking up boundaries between compartments. Many forest areas deserve conservation in their own right, but those that support rare or unusual plants and animals need special attention and conservation of the habitat may be the prime objective of management in such areas. On the other hand, the establishment of new forests can change the nature of the local wildlife dramatically, mainly by eliminating, at least temporarily, most of the flora and fauna associated with open areas (NCC 1986).

The management of forests for amenity and conservation as well as timber production (multiple-use forests) may require some changes in practice from those in forests run on strictly commercial lines. For example, the conservation value of woodland may be greatly enhanced by the presence of dying and dead timber, but such trees are usually removed from production forests and plantations to prevent their harbouring pests which may subsequently damage living trees. Where conservation is the most important aspect of management, as in the diminishing areas of ancient woodland in Europe, disturbance needs to be kept to a minimum to ensure the survival of the plant and animal species that occur there. Although conservation is usually associated with less intensive management, in some cases existing intensive management techniques need to be continued in order to preserve the habitat. An example of this is the coppicing of broad-leaved species such as ash and hazel, a practice that has created a habitat suitable for rare woodland plants (Peterken 1981).

1.2 FORESTRY IN DIFFERENT COUNTRIES

The economic importance of productive forestry in different countries will depend largely on the extent and character of the forests that grow there. But national and regional differences in the scale, species composition, and management intensity of forests also influence the approach to management and control of forest insects and these important aspects are discussed in later chapters.

The tree species native to different regions are determined largely by characteristics of the climate, especially rainfall, but the establishment of

Table 1.2. *Extent of forests in Europe*

Country	Total closed forest 10⁶ ha	Per cent forest cover	Total plantations 10⁶ ha
Northern Europe			
Finland	19.8	76	0.003
Norway	7.6	28	
Sweden	24.4	68	5.00
Denmark	0.5	11	0.03
Central Europe			
Belgium/Luxembourg	0.7	23	
France	13.9	28	
Ireland	0.3	6	0.3
Netherlands	0.3	10	
UK	2.2	10	2.0
W. Germany	6.9	30	
Eastern Europe			
Bulgaria	3.3		0.3
Czechoslovakia	4.4		
E. Germany	2.7		
Hungary	1.6		
Poland	8.6		
Romania	6.3		
Southern Europe			
Greece	5.8	45	
Italy	6.3	27	0.7
Portugal	2.7	35	
Spain	11.9	25	
Yugoslavia	9.1		0.06

Modified from Savill and Evans 1986; Forestry Commission 1987.

plantations of exotic species can significantly modify the natural vegetation pattern (see Allsop (1973); Barrett (1980); Larsen (1980); Young (1982); Carron (1985); Savill and Evans (1986); and Zobel *et al.* (1987) for further details).

1.2.1 North America

The northern coniferous or boreal forests extend from Alaska to eastern Canada. This vast forest region is dominated by spruce but larch, fir and pine and broad-leaves such as birch, poplar and willow also grow there. The coastal areas of western Canada and western USA are of particular interest to European foresters because some of the trees that grow there, especially Sitka spruce, Douglas fir, and lodgepole pine grow well in temperate plantations.

In the USA, regional differences in climate have resulted in the development of distinct forest types in different parts of the country. The occurrence of fire has also had a major impact on the character of the forest community in some areas, for example in the maintenance of non-climax ponderosa pine in western forests and of southern pines in south-eastern areas (Spurr and Barnes 1980). About two-thirds of forests in the USA are exploited commercially (Collins and White 1981), many of them natural or semi-natural, having reverted to forest after clearance for agriculture by early European settlers.

Temperate mixed forests are typical of the north-eastern USA, with beech, birch, maple, aspen, and oak occurring together with coniferous species including pine and hemlock. In the central region, forests are dominated by broad-leaved species among which are oak, hickory, beech, elm, maple, and ash. In the commercially important southern region, which comprises about a third of all forests in the USA, pine is the major genus and is widely grown in plantations. Broad-leaves growing in this region include maple, black tupelo, oak, and poplar. In the west of the country, the Rocky Mountain forests, which extend from Canada to Mexico, are dominated by conifers, such as spruce, Douglas fir, larch, and especially pine, but the broad-leaved aspen is also a significant species. In the Pacific coast region, famous for its giant redwoods, conifers such as Douglas fir, true firs, pine, hemlock, and spruce are the predominant species although some broad-leaves such as alder, maple, and oak also occur. The commercially unimportant tropical or sub-tropical forests are confined to southern Florida and south-eastern Texas.

1.2.2 Europe and the USSR

The northern coniferous forests of the Old World occur mostly within the Soviet Union and extend from parts of Scandinavia across to Sakhalin and Hokkaido in the Pacific. Larch, spruce, fir, and pine are the main conifers, with the broadleaved component made up of a number of species including birch, poplar, and willow.

Within Europe, as in North America, differences in climate have influenced the distribution and dominance of particular tree species. Most of western Europe lies within the central broad-leaved forest region in which oak, beech, and birch together with spruce, pine, and fir grow abundantly. In general, however, this region is less rich in native tree species than the comparable broad-leaved forests of eastern North America. In southern Europe, with its dry Mediterranean climate, pine is a major conifer but there are many broad-leaved trees as well, including chestnut and the evergreen holm and cork oaks.

Although western Europe contains relatively little forest on a world scale (Table 1.1), some European countries have a high percentage of forest cover (Table 1.2) and in the region as a whole there are many millions of hectares.

Scandinavian countries

In timber-rich countries such as Finland and Sweden, forestry makes a major contribution to the national economy. In northern parts of the region, Norway spruce and Scots pine are the most important commercial species in the natural forest, but in the more maritime southern areas, Sitka spruce has been established in plantations. Denmark is notable for its lack of native conifers of commercial significance but a number of exotic species have been planted, principally Norway and Sitka spruce, larch, and Douglas fir. Birch, which can grow rapidly on relatively poor soils, is the dominant species in some parts of Scandinavia.

Ireland and the UK

These are timber-poor countries in which most of the natural forest has long since disappeared and only 10 per cent or less of the land is now forested. In the UK, the natural tree flora is relatively poor and Scots pine is the only native conifer of economic significance. Productive forestry therefore depends to a large extent on plantations of introduced trees, predominantly Sitka spruce, lodgepole pine, and Douglas fir, species which have been selected for their ability to grow well in the local climatic and edaphic conditions (Johnston 1975; Matthews, J. D. 1983). About 2 million ha of plantations have been established in the UK (Table 1.2) with Sitka spruce (0.6 million ha) the most abundant species. Even so the UK still imports around 85 per cent of its timber.

Central and southern Europe

Broadleaved species are still dominant in many parts of central Europe where stands of oak and beech may be intensively managed to produce high-quality timber. In some areas, however, broad-leaved stands are being replaced with exotic spruces, firs, and larch. In western Germany for example, the percentage of conifers in the growing stock has increased from 30 per cent at the turn of the century to 60 per cent in 1960 (Zobel *et al.* 1987). In southern Europe, plantations are also becoming increasingly important, and in the Iberian peninsula for example, eucalypts and pines are now widely planted.

1.2.3 New Zealand and Australia

In New Zealand, about a third of the land area is covered by forest. Species of *Nothofagus*, the southern beech, are an important part of the native flora and pure beech forests account for almost half of the 6.2 million ha of indigenous forest (Wardle 1984). Plantation forestry, however, is also important in New Zealand and is based largely on exotic trees. Predominant among these is radiata pine which is now planted over approximately 1 million ha (Lavery 1986). Interestingly, this tree grows naturally in only a small region of California and yet as well as being grown extensively in New Zealand, it is the principal plantation species in Chile, the Cape region of South Africa, and also in Australia.

Much of the interior of Australia is too dry to support tree growth and forests of commercial importance are restricted by and large to the eastern seaboard, with a smaller area in the south-western tip of the country. Only around 5 per cent of the land area is covered with indigenous forest, which, including Tasmania, is equivalent to around 41 million ha (Carron 1985). About 70 per cent of these indigenous forests are composed of various eucalypt species. The remaining areas are made up of rainforest or forests composed largely of species such as *Callitris*, *Casuarina*, and *Acacia*.

Fire has had a significant influence in shaping the natural forest communities in the drier parts of eastern and southern Australia where it also poses a serious threat to commercial forests. Many *Eucalyptus* species are fire tolerant and some highly inflammable eucalypt communities are classed as fire climaxes whose existence is maintained by more or less regular burning.

Only about a third of indigenous forests in australia are managed for timber production, most of the timber harvested coming from eucalypt forests. Plantations are of increasing importance, however, and these now extend to around 1 million ha. As in New Zealand, plantations are dominated by radiata pine, which is grown over an area of about 0.6 million ha (Lavery 1986).

Some eucalypt species have been established in plantations outside Australia, in the tropics, subtropics, and some Mediterranean countries. Together with pines they are the world's most widely planted exotic trees.

Plantation forests have clearly had a large impact on forestry in some countries. The higher productivity of plantation forests can make an essential contribution to current and future demands for timber as well as helping to relieve pressure on remaining areas of natural forest. Countries with extensive plantations of exotic trees, however, are clearly at risk from the accidental introduction of pests found in the native habitat of the trees and this subject is discussed in Chapter 5. But are these highly productive monocultures, like simple agricultural systems, inherently more susceptible to damage by insect pests?

1.3 SUSCEPTIBILITY OF PLANTATION MONOCULTURES TO INSECT OUTBREAKS

A parallel is often drawn between the use of plantations in forestry and the intensive management of agricultural crops. Because agricultural crops are vulnerable to pest outbreaks and frequently sustain high levels of damage in the absence of direct control measures, plantation monocultures are often considered to be more likely to suffer damage from insect pests than 'natural' forests. The assumption is that 'simple' systems are more vulnerable to pest outbreaks and this touches on one of the central themes of community ecology, that of the relationship between stability (absence of large-scale fluctuations in population density) and diversity (the number and relative abundance of different species) (see Price 1984 for discussion). In fact, many forest trees exist naturally either in monocultures or in association with only a few species as, for example, in temperate coniferous forests and the *Nothofagus* forests of New Zealand (Chapman 1958). The establishment of such species in plantations is therefore not a radical departure from the natural vegetation pattern and should not automatically make them more vulnerable to insect pests (but see Chapter 5). There are, nevertheless, some obvious differences between natural and plantation forests. For example, in natural forest monocultures, a mixed age structure is often maintained as old trees die and seedlings become established. Such forests would obviously be more resistant to pests that attack trees at a particular stage of growth. Another important factor is the degree of genetic variability between individuals within the stand. Although plantation trees are genetically unrefined in comparison to agricultural crops, the gene base of natural forests is, nevertheless, usually broader than that of plantations and is maintained by outcrossing. Future development of selective breeding programmes to improve yields would narrow the gene base further and this could have important consequences for pest susceptibility (Chapter 6).

There is some evidence that tropical forest trees that normally occur at low density in diverse natural forests are much more likely to be affected by outbreaks when they are planted in monoculture (Gibson and Jones 1977). This suggests that while simple natural communities may not be more susceptible to pest outbreaks than complex ones, simplified communities may be.

1.4 CHARACTERISTICS OF INSECT OUTBREAKS

Most forest insects cause relatively little damage to growing trees and are not therefore regarded as pests. Some insects, however, may kill trees or significantly reduce their growth and may cause other changes in the forest ecosystem (Chapter 4). Most pests typically cause damage to trees during outbreaks when population density is very high and during which defoliation or other damage to the trees is often highly visible. However, outbreaks of different kinds of pest vary in their frequency, intensity, duration, and in the area affected and this has important implications for their management and control (Berryman and Stark 1985; Berryman 1986, 1987; see also McNamee *et al.* 1981, Nothnagle and Schultz 1987). Outbreaks can be broadly classified into one of three main kinds: gradients, cycles, and eruptions (Fig. 1.2).

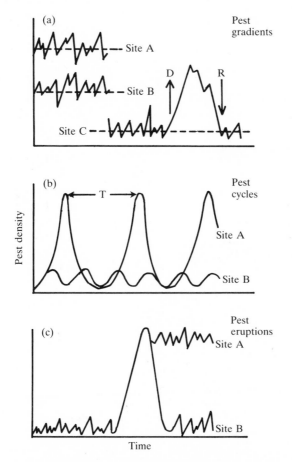

FIG. 1.2. Three major patterns of the population dynamics of forest insects (a) gradients (b) cycles, and (c) eruptions (D = disturbance in environmental conditions, R = return to normality, T = periodicity of population cycle) (see text) (from Berryman and Stark 1985).

Pest gradients

The abundance of some forest insects is largely determined by environmental factors which may vary from place to place and from season to season (Fig. 1.2a, sites A, B, and C). Population density of these insects is determined essentially by a graded response to local environmental conditions and when outbreaks develop they do not spread into surrounding less favourable areas. Typical environmental factors include local topography and climate, the number of susceptible trees or the amount of felled material available for breeding which can increase following disturbances (e.g. D at site C, Fig. 1.2a) such as windthrow or silvicultural operations such as felling. For example in managed forests, the abundance of the pine weevil, *Hylobius abietis*, is largely determined by the number of cut stumps in which it can breed and so populations increase in clearfelled areas and the adults then feed on the replanted crop. The outbreak subsides when environmental conditions return to normal; in this case when the stumps eventually become unsuitable for breeding (e.g. R at site C, Fig. 1.2a). Another example is the brown-tail moth, *Euproctis chrysorrhoea*, in Britain, which defoliates broad-leaved trees and shrubs only in certain coastal areas in the south and east and at some inland sites close to rivers (Sterling 1983). Other insects that typically have gradient outbreaks are 'non-aggressive' bark beetles, tip and shoot borers, and seed insects, species that feed in, rather than on, their host plant.

Pest cycles

The more or less regular cyclic outbreaks of some forest pests (Fig. 1.2b) have excited interest among generations of forest entomologists. Such outbreaks are typically confined to specific areas although cycles may sometimes be synchronized among different populations over relatively large areas. Population cycles are associated with time lags in negative feedback processes (action of natural enemies, response of the host plant to attack) that can regulate population growth. Characteristics of the cycle such as its periodicity (T) and amplitude (e.g. sites A and B Fig. 1.2b) are influenced by the extent of the time lag and local environmental conditions, and in some species genetic factors may also be important. Defoliating insects provide the best examples of population cycles and one of the most intensively studied is the larch budmoth, *Zeiraphera diniana*, in the Engadine valley in Switzerland in which the remarkably regular cycles of abundance have a periodicity of 8 or 9 years (Fig. 1.3). Mean population density may vary by 20 000 times within five generations, although locally 100 000-fold increases have been observed (Baltensweiler 1984). Other examples of cyclic population behaviour can be found in the Douglas fir tussock moth, *Orgyia pseudotsugata*, in North America (Brookes *et al.*

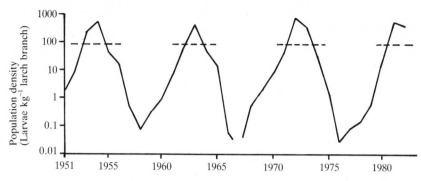

FIG. 1.3. Fluctuation in numbers of larvae of *Zeiraphera diniana* on larch at Sils in the Engadine Valley, Switzerland. Dotted line is the defoliation threshold (from Baltensweiler 1984).

1978), the autumnal moth, *Epirrita autumnata*, in Scandinavia (Haukioja 1980) and the pine looper moth, *Bupalus piniaria*, in The Netherlands (Klomp 1966).

Pest eruptions

Eruptive pests are amongst the most damaging of all forest insects. They often remain at low population densities for long periods but outbreaks can develop suddenly and they often spread out from local epicentres into the surrounding forests. Once outbreaks have developed, they may be sustained for a long time, causing considerable mortality of the host over large areas (Fig. 1.2c). Populations of eruptive pests are often kept at low density by scarce resources (e.g. few susceptible trees) or natural enemies. Outbreaks can develop when these natural regulating factors break down or when hosts are overwhelmed following changes in the environment that permit rapid reproduction of the pest (e.g. consecutive seasons of favourable weather) or through sudden increases in population density by immigration from other high density areas.

Introduced insects often cause eruptive outbreaks in a new favourable habitat which may often lack effective natural enemies and where host trees may not have evolved appropriate defences. Although such outbreaks may continue for long periods (Fig. 1.2c, site A) they cannot persist indefinitely at outbreak levels and populations eventually decline to a lower level determined by local conditions. Aggregating bark beetles which exhibit aggressive mass-attack behaviour such as the mountain pine beetle, *Dendroctonus ponderosae*, in western North America and the European spruce bark beetle, *Ips typographus*, are eruptive pests that have caused considerable damage in their native habitats. In a healthy forest, these insects are normally limited by the shortage of moribund trees in which to breed. But when such trees become more abundant, following drought or storm damage for example, beetle populations can rise dramatically. Pheromone-mediated mass-attack of healthy trees (positive feedback) may then be possible so that the outbreak can sustain itself and spread into the surrounding forest (Fig. 1.4). The tendency of such outbreaks to be self-sustaining means that they are relatively insensitive to subsequent environmental changes. Some Lepidoptera such as the nun moth, *Lymantria monacha*, in Europe and the gypsy moth, *L. dispar*, and spruce budworm, *Choristoneura fumiferana*, in North America also have widespread eruptive outbreaks.

In classifying the outbreak patterns of forest pests, it is important to emphasize that they are broad descriptive categories that focus attention on differences in the underlying causes of population change. They should not be regarded as rigid categories to which each pest species can be assigned, and some outbreaks may have characteristics of more than one pattern (e.g. cyclical eruptions). Furthermore, as the classic population studies of the pine looper moth, *Bupalus piniaria* (Schwerdtfeger 1941; Klomp 1966), the larch budmoth, *Zeiraphera diniana* (Baltensweiler 1968; Baltensweiler *et al.* 1977), and the winter moth, *Operophtera brumata*, (Varley and Gradwell 1968; Varley *et al.* 1973) show, the dynamic behaviour of the same species can vary from place to place and with it the

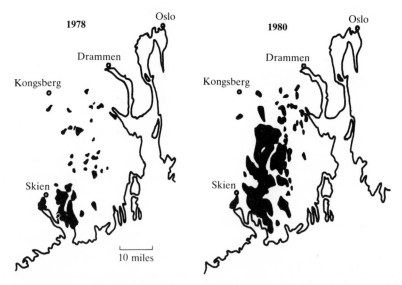

FIG. 1.4. Areas severely affected by eruptive outbreaks of *Ips typographus*. The outbreak rapidly spread from a number of epicentres (1978) seriously to damage large areas of forest (1980) (after Worrell 1983).

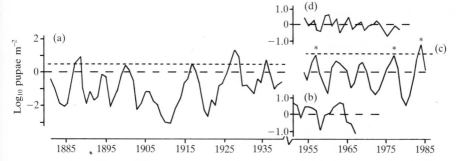

FIG. 1.5. Annual pupal counts of *Bupalus piniaria* in (a) Letzlingen, Germany, 1881–1940, (b) de Hoge Veluwe, Netherlands, 1951–67, (c) Tentsmuir Forest, Scotland, 1954–85, and (d) Sherwood Forest, England, 1954–78. The approximate forest average outbreak threshold for Letzlingen and Tentsmuir is shown by a dotted line. Chemical control operations in the UK are indicated by asterisks. Only certain forest compartments were treated (from Varley 1949; Klomp 1968; Barbour 1985, 1987 and personal communication).

pest status of these insects. Fluctuations from year to year in the abundance of *B. piniaria*, have been studied at Letzlingen in Germany (Varley 1949), at de Hoge Veluwe in The Netherlands (Klomp 1966), and at several sites in Britain (Barbour 1985, 1988) (Fig. 1.5). At Letzlingen, pupal density in the soil fluctuates widely from year to year and five major outbreaks were recorded between 1881 and 1940. In The Netherlands, 'average' population density for the years 1951–67 was higher than in Germany but the amplitude of fluctuations was smaller and outbreaks did not occur. In Britain, pupal densities in some forests such as Sherwood are fairly stable with relatively small fluctuations about an equilibrium density of 1 pupa m^{-2} and outbreaks have not been recorded at this or other similar sites. In Tentsmuir forest on the other hand, populations appear to be cyclic with a periodicity of 6–7 years and three outbreaks have required chemical control during the period of study. These regional differences emphasize the importance of interactions between the insect, its environment, natural enemies, and the host tree itself in ultimately determining the population dynamics of insect pests and these aspects are discussed in the following two chapters.

2

Forests as a habitat for insects

The unique character of forests as a habitat owes much to the longevity and structural complexity of individual trees and their tendency to occupy large contiguous areas either as a monoculture or in mixture with other species. The number of different kinds of insects that occur in forests, their distribution, average levels of abundance, and tendency of some species to cause outbreaks are all influenced to a greater or lesser extent by the biotic and abiotic characteristics of the forest habitat, the most important of which are considered in this chapter.

2.1 THE COMMUNITY OF INSECTS ON TREES

Forest entomologists are usually concerned with the ecology of those relatively few forest insects that damage or kill forest trees. But these pests share their habitat with an enormous variety of other species, among which may be potential competitors as well as natural enemies. The different feeding groups or 'guilds' of insects found on trees have been studied by Moran and Southwood (1982) who collected insects from 10 species of trees among six genera in South Africa and Britain. Birch, oak, and *Robinia* (introduced to both Britain and South Africa) were the only three species sampled in both countries. Given the differences in climate, habitat, and range of species studied, they found a remarkable similarity in the proportions of insects in the seven major guilds studied during the late summer sampling period and the combined data are shown in Fig. 2.1. The herbivorous insects, which made up about one-quarter of the species, constituted about two-thirds of the individuals. Many of these individuals were sap-feeding insects but being fairly small they were less dominant in terms of biomass. The parasitoids showed an interesting pattern. They were clearly a diverse group in terms of species but were represented by relatively few individuals.

Although the proportional composition of the communities is broadly similar on these and probably many other tree species, the total number of insect species on them can show marked variations. Herbivorous insects have attracted particular attention and the question of how many different kinds occur on different tree species is of more than academic interest

NOS. SPECIES

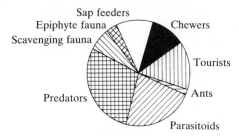

INDIVIDUALS

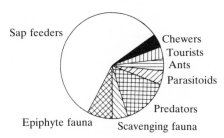

BIOMASS

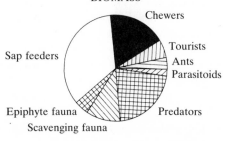

FIG. 2.1. The proportions of the major guilds of arthropods on trees sampled in Britain and South Africa. Ten species of tree were sampled, three of which were common to both countries, namely birch, oak and *Robinia* (from Strong *et al*. 1984; after Moran and Southwood 1982).

because of the increasingly widespread practice of planting forest trees outside their natural range where they are exposed to colonization by insects from native trees, among which may be potential pest species. Before going on to discuss the major ecological determinants of the diversity of herbivorous insects on different tree species, we will first consider briefly how trees differ from other kinds of plants because this has an important bearing on the number of species (i.e. species diversity or richness) associated with them.

2.1.1 The structural complexity of trees; the influence of plant architecture

The 'architecture' of trees (their size, shape, structure, and variety of feeding niches) is much more complex than that of other kinds of plants. On trees therefore there is a great variety of niches that insects can occupy and this is one of the main reasons why they support many more different kinds of insect than herbaceous plants and shrubs (Lawton 1978; Strong and Levin 1979; Strong *et al.* 1984). Trees are also long-lived and the permanence of the above-ground parts means that there are many over-wintering sites. Even in winter the surface area of a tree is roughly four times that of the soil below it and much more if bark epiphytes, which are present on many trees, are included in this calculation. The layered canopy of trees provides a range of microclimates which differ in exposure, insola-tion and in many other ways (section 2.2). Within the tree, insects may feed on bark which varies in age and thickness on different parts of the tree; heart and sapwood; twigs and shoots of different age classes; buds; leaves which in evergreen conifers comprise several age categories and also flowers and seeds. Even woody debris, such as fallen branches beneath the tree, is utilized by a variety of insects. The quality of the food itself varies both within and between these different parts and may require special adaptations by insects to exploit it, so encouraging speciation. Interestingly, feeding itself may change the shape of a tree and so alter the microclimate within it. For example, shoot mortality in pines caused by the pine shoot beetle, *Tomicus piniperda*, or the shoot moth, *Dioryctria albovitella*, can eventually produce flat-topped or even shrub-like trees (Whitham and Mopper 1985).

The insects associated with a given tree species will be characteristic of a particular geographical locality, but within that area all insects will not occur on all individuals and there will also be a distinctly seasonal pattern to the species diversity. A hypothetical pattern of seasonal change in insect diversity on a deciduous tree and a perennial herb is shown in Fig. 2.2. Trees increase markedly in complexity in spring, largely as a result of leaf flush and there is a corresponding increase in the number of herbivorous insect species actually feeding on the tree during this period. Birches and alders in Finland provide an exception to this generalized pattern because they have long shoot growth periods so that both new and old leaves are present later in the season when species richness may also be high (Niemela and Haukioja 1982). In generalizing about the role of plant architecture on

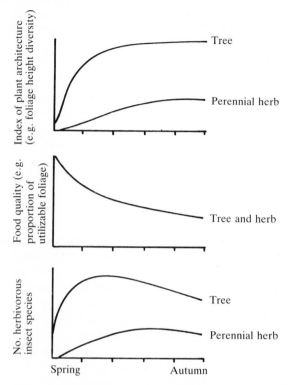

FIG. 2.2. Hypothetical seasonal changes in insect diversity on a deciduous tree and a perennial herb in response to seasonal changes in plant architecture and food quality (from Lawton 1978).

species richness it is important to remember that seasonal changes in food quality and architecture may be linked, so that the separate effects may be difficult to determine (Fig. 2.2) (Lawton 1978).

2.1.2 Insect species richness and the present distribution and abundance of trees

Many studies of species richness on plants have shown a convincing relationship between the number of insect species (S) and the geographical abundance or area (A) over which the plants occur. This relationship has been shown for many different kinds of plants from weeds to trees and for whole insect faunas as well as specific insect groups. These species–area relationships ($S = cA^z$, c and z are constants) have been widely used in studies of island biogeography and seem appropriate for the study of insect–plant relationships because host plants can be visualized as islands in a 'sea' of unsuitable vegetation (MacArthur and Wilson 1967; Jansen 1968, 1973). Difficulties arise if this analogy is pushed too far and it must not be assumed, for example, that dynamic equilibrium levels of insect species on trees arise from balanced immigration and extinction rates as it does for real islands (Connor and McCoy 1979; Southwood and Kennedy 1983). As an empirical relationship, however, it has proved of considerable value in the investigation of species richness on plants (see Strong *et al.* 1984 for a comprehensive review).

One of the most familiar species–area relationships is that for British trees (Opler 1974; Strong 1974*a*; Kennedy and Southwood 1984) (Fig. 2.3). It shows that more widely distributed and abundant tree species are host to more insect species than those with a more restricted distribution. Trees which have been introduced into Britain relatively recently such as sweet chestnut, holm oak, larch, horse chestnut, and sycamore also fit into the general pattern and are associated with the number of species expected from their current distribution. This suggests that introduced trees acquire their complement of herbivores relatively quickly, although their faunas may be impoverished during an initial colonization period of a few hundred years, a relatively short time span in ecological terms (Strong 1974*a*). Thus, insect species richness can be broadly predicted from a knowledge of the present abundance of a particular tree species. One consequence of this is that trees with a wide geographical range can have different numbers of insect species associated with them according to their relative abundance in

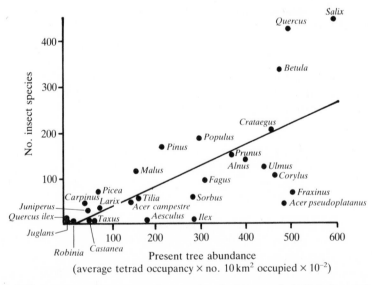

FIG. 2.3. The number of insect species associated with trees in Britain in relation to their estimated present abundance (from Kennedy and Southwood 1984).

the different regions. In Russia, the tree flora is dominated by conifers and pine and spruce support 2 and 3 times more insect species than they do in Britain where they are a much less prominent part of the tree flora (Table 2.1). In contrast, the oak, *Quercus robur*, supports many more insect species in Britain than in Russia, reflecting the relative importance of oak woodland in the two countries.

The simple correlation between species and area or abundance of trees says little about the underlying mechanisms although clearly, abundant and widespread trees present greater opportunities for potential insect colonists to find them; they are 'apparent' in the sense of Feeny (1976) (see Chapter 3). However, widespread trees are also likely to occupy a greater range of habitats (habitat heterogeneity) than trees with more restricted distributions and are thus more likely to be colonized by insects which themselves have a restricted geographical range (Strong *et al.* 1984). Some support for the importance of habitat heterogeneity comes from the study by Stevens (1986) on wood-boring insects. He found that within a given forest, trees with a wide geographical range do not support a richer

Table 2.1. *The number of insect species on broad-leaved and coniferous trees that occur in both Britain and Russia, showing differing relative abundance in the two countries*

Tree	Numbers of insect species	
	Britain	Russia
Broad-leaves		
Oak (*Quercus*)	284	150
Willow (*Salix*)	266	147
Birch (*Betula*)	229	101
Hawthorn (*Crataegus*)	149	59
Poplars (*Populus*)	97	122
Apple (*Malus*)	93	77
Alder (*Alnus*)	90	63
Elm (*Ulmus*)	82	81
Hazel (*Corylus*)	73	26
Beech (*Fagus*)	64	79
Ash (*Fraxinus*)	41	41
Lime (*Tilia*)	31	37
Hornbeam (*Carpinus*)	28	53
Holly (*Ilex*)	7	8
Conifers		
Pine (*Pinus*)	91	190
Spruce (*Picea*)	37	117
Larch (*Larix*)	17	44
Fir (*Abies*)	16	42

From Southwood 1961.

wood-boring fauna than co-occurring trees with a more limited range. This suggests that for this group of insects, the larger number of species on widespread trees results from the fact that they occupy a greater number of forest habitats and so acquire more 'host records'.

The amount of variation explained by species–area relationships for different tree species and insect groups is not constant (Table 2.2). For the leaf-mining Lepidoptera on American oaks, the relationship accounts for 90 per cent of the observed variation while explaining only 16 per cent for another taxonomically uniform group, the leafhoppers on British trees.

Table 2.2 *Some species–area relationships of insects on trees*

Herbivore group	Host type	$r^2 \times 100$	Reference
Leaf-mining Lepidoptera	American oaks	90	Opler 1974
Cynipid gall wasps	American oaks—		
	Atlantic region	41	Cornell and
	Californian region	72	Washburn 1979
Insects	British trees	61	Strong 1974*a,b*
Insects	British trees	58	Strong and Levin 1979
Leafhoppers	British trees	16	Claridge and Wilson 1981
Leafhoppers	British trees + *Nothofagus* sp.	12	Claridge and Wilson 1981
Leafminers	British trees	19	Claridge and Wilson 1982

After Price 1984; Strong *et al.* 1984.

Recently, attention has focused on the 50 per cent or more of unexplained variation in species richness between trees.

2.1.3 Other factors affecting insect species richness on trees

The use of multiple regression analysis instead of the straightforward species–area regression has allowed the inclusion of other factors that could influence species richness and this has usually considerably increased the amount of variation explained (Table 2.3). However, different factors have proved to be important in different studies. Abundance in geological time, 'evergreenness', taxonomic relatedness of the host and its structural complexity have all been shown to influence species richness. Some of these are considered below.

The abundance of trees in geological time
Southwood (1961) was the first to demonstrate the importance of historical abundance when he showed that insect species richness on British trees was

Table 2.3. *Multiple regressions of species richness on trees*

Herbivore group	Host type	$r^2 \times 100$	Reference
Macro-lepidoptera	Finnish trees and shrubs	71	Neuvonen and Niemela 1981
Insects	British trees	82	Kennedy and Southwood 1984
Lepidoptera, Hymenoptera, Homoptera, Diptera	British trees in family Rosaceae	83	Leather 1986

For variables see text and individual references.

correlated with the number of recorded remains of these trees during the Quaternary period, i.e. the most recent period of geological time (Fig. 2.4). There has been considerable debate over the interpretation of these data because the past and present abundance of trees is often highly correlated (Strong 1974*b*). Further difficulties arise because fossil records are at best fragmentary and only a very crude estimate of the abundance of trees in the geological past. It is possible to get round this to some extent because the time that a particular species has been present continuously in Britain, irrespective of its abundance, can be more reliably determined from the fossil record and studies of this aspect of a tree's geological history shows that it makes a small but significant contribution to the number of insect species colonizing trees in Britain (Birks 1980; Kennedy and South-wood 1984).

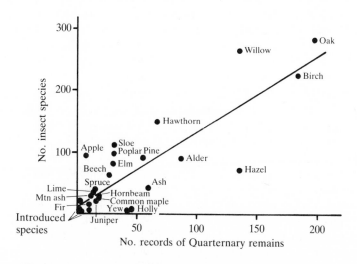

FIG. 2.4. The number of insect species associated with trees in Britain in relation to the number of records of Quarternary remains (from Southwood 1961).

Over long geological periods, co-evolutionary factors may be important in tree/insect associations and so we might expect numbers of insect 'specialists' to correlate better with tree abundance in time and 'generalists' to be better correlated with present-day abundance (Price 1984).

Taxonomy, chemistry, and introduced plants

Some native British trees such as ash, holly, and yew have few close relatives, i.e. they are 'taxonomically isolated' and have been found to have an impoverished fauna (Kennedy and Southwood 1984) (Fig. 2.3). Such effects may often be due to chemical distinctiveness rather than taxonomic affinity itself as appears to be the case for leafminers on British trees (Claridge and Wilson 1982). The distinctiveness of introduced trees has an important bearing on their colonization by native insects. *Eucalyptus* is chemically highly distinctive and is host to relatively few insects in southern Europe compared to its native Australia (Morrow 1977). Where introduced trees are related to native ones there should be a ready source of potential insect colonists with a 'predilection' for the introduced tree (Connor *et al.* 1980; Southwood and Kennedy 1983). A good example of this is provided by the southern beech, *Nothofagus*, which is native to South America and New Zealand and was introduced into Britain in the mid-nineteenth century. It has become more widely established in the last 30 years but the total area planted is still very small (Nimmo 1971). During this time *Nothofagus* has acquired an extensive insect fauna, most of the leaf-feeding Lepidoptera coming from the related oaks (Welch 1981). Thus, for *Nothofagus* the size of the potential pool of colonists seems to have been a major factor in species accumulation. *Nothofagus* also has a much richer leafhopper fauna than expected from its current distribution (Fig. 2.5) and since some of these insects were previously considered to be host-specific, Claridge and Wilson (1981) suggested that *Nothofagus* may lack feeding deterrents.

Colonists of introduced trees may sometimes come from unexpected sources. Winter (1974), for example, recorded a number of insect species attacking conifers for the first time in the UK which had transferred from unrelated native moorland plants at the plantation sites, and Stoakley (1985) has described outbreaks of the oak-feeding winter moth, *Operophtera brumata*, on Sitka spruce. Clearly there is an element of uncertainty in determining the likelihood of pest attacks on introduced trees based on their broad taxonomic relationship to native ones (Strong *et al.* 1984).

Of course, introduced trees run the additional risk of colonization by pests accidentally introduced from their native habitat and such pests have often proved extremely damaging to forest trees in their new habitat (Chapter 5). Introduced pines and eucalypts in central and South Africa have enjoyed freedom from pest attack for well over one rotation, largely

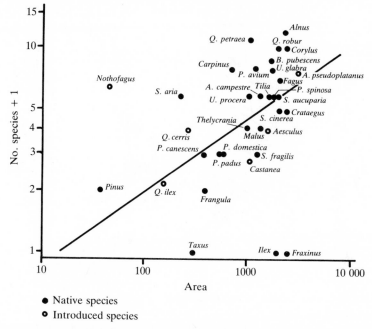

FIG. 2.5. The number of mesophyll-feeding leafhopper species in relation to the present range of the trees on which they feed. Points for *Pinus* and *Nothofagus* were not included in the regression. Circles with a white centre represent introduced trees (from Claridge and Wilson 1981).

due to the absence of close relatives in these regions, but recent problems have been associated with exotic pests introduced by accident.

Geographical isolation

The localized occurrence of introduced trees may reduce the rate at which they acquire an insect fauna, although even small isolated plantations will be located relatively quickly by highly mobile insects. It is, however, difficult to separate the effect of isolation from that of local climate on potential colonists. Spruce planted outside its natural range in north Norway was found to have an impoverished bark fauna (Nilssen 1978). The bark beetle, *Dryocoetes autographus*, which is tolerant of a wide range of climatic conditions was widely distributed in the spruce plantations whereas the less tolerant *Ips typographus*, which is a serious pest of spruce, occurred in only a few of them (Fig. 2.6).

In an experimental situation, Faeth and Simberloff (1981) were unable to detect an effect of isolation on the accumulation of leafmining species on small oak trees (Fig. 2.7). Non-isolated trees were planted near the

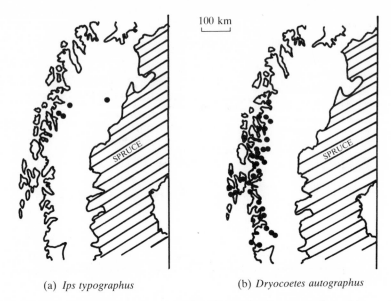

(a) *Ips typographus*   (b) *Dryocoetes autographus*

FIG. 2.6. The distribution of two bark beetle species in spruce planted beyond its natural range in northern Norway. The 'climatically tolerant' *Dryocoetes autographus* is much more widely distributed than the less tolerant *Ips typographus* (from Nilssen 1978).

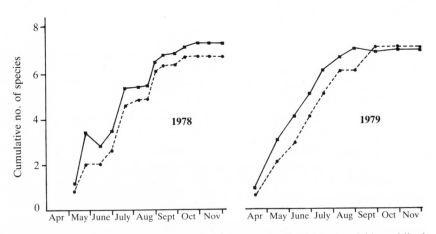

FIG. 2.7. Mean cumulative number of leaf-mining species on isolated (dotted line) and non-isolated (solid line) trees of three species of oak (after Faeth and Simberloff 1981).

edge of a field surrounded by mixed oak–pine forest and the 'isolated' ones were planted in the field 165 m away. However, they did observe higher levels of parasitism of leafminers on non-isolated trees which they assumed was caused by adult parasitoids restricting their searching behaviour to the vicinity of the resident mature oaks (Fig. 2.8). No discernible difference was found in the activities of generalist predators between isolated and

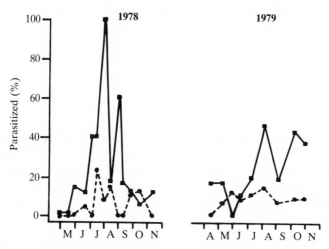

FIG. 2.8. Percentage parasitism of leafminers on isolated (dotted line) and non-isolated (solid line) trees of three species of oak (from Faeth and Simberloff 1981).

non-isolated trees. This raises the important point that by colonizing introduced trees, insect herbivores may temporarily escape from their natural enemies (Price 1976), especially those which locate their hosts by searching for particular tree species.

2.2 CLIMATE AND WEATHER IN THE ECOLOGY OF FOREST INSECTS

Among the insect herbivores that colonize trees will be some that are actual or potential pests and these species are usually characterized by periods of very high abundance, during which trees are damaged or killed by their feeding activities. The majority of insects, however, are not pests and so by definition their populations remain below some limit at which damage to the trees becomes important. In this and the following section, we look at two contrasting aspects of the forest environment that affects the abundance of insects; the physical environment of the forest and biotic environment of competitors and natural enemies.

Insects that inhabit different geographical regions have evolved appropriate behavioural and physiological mechanisms that adapt them to the rhythm of the seasons and the availability of their food. In temperate regions, conditions may range from the extreme winters and short growing season of Siberian forests to the long dry summers and cool moist winters characteristic of forests in southern Europe. Both diurnal and seasonal patterns of insect activity in these different forests will be determined by local weather and other environmental conditions, knowledge of which may be useful in predicting times of emergence or flight activity for incorporation into forest pest management programmes. For example, Jensen and Nielsen (1984) found that in Denmark, pheromone trapping of the nun moth, *Lymantria monacha*, gave a poor correlation with the female population in years with long periods of warm and dry weather. A better correlation was obtained when cold and wet weather terminated male flight early.

The most important environmental variables are temperature, humidity, precipitation, wind, light intensity, and daylength. But other factors can be important, barometric pressure, for example, appears to influence the responsiveness of some bark beetles to pheromones (Lanier and Burns 1978). As well as directly affecting insects, weather factors also influence the growth and development of trees and so can affect them indirectly by influencing the timing and perhaps the amount of food available for insects at different places and in different years (Dempster and Pollard 1981). Wherever they occur, forests provide a sheltered environment for insects, acting as a buffer to sudden changes in windspeed or temperature, and light intensity is usually lower and relative humidity higher than in adjacent open areas. In plantations and other managed forests, however, thinning operations periodically reduce tree density so that both insects and the remaining trees are more exposed to the elements and this may influence their subsequent growth and survival.

2.2.1 Seasonal development

Diapause

In temperate regions, insect development is not continuous but is interrupted by the need to avoid winter cold or lethal summer temperatures. Insects may have one or several generations per year (uni- or multi-voltine) partly depending on the length of the growing season but some insects such as the spruce bark beetle, *Dendroctonus micans*, and the pine weevil, *Hylobius abietis*, may need more than one season (semi-voltine) to complete development.

Many insects overwinter in a state of dormancy called diapause which can occur in any stage from egg to adult (Tauber *et al*. 1986). Diapause not only allows survival of unfavourable periods but also synchronizes the life cycle with the development of the host plant and the return of favourable conditions. It may also be important in the life cycle of natural enemies which must be synchronized with that of their insect prey. Diapause is induced by specific environmental cues that signal the onset of unfavourable conditions. In temperate regions, daylength is the main determining factor although temperature may have an important modifying influence (Tauber *et al*. 1986). It is terminated only after a period of 'diapause development' during which the insect is unresponsive to changes in ambient conditions and it thus differs from 'quiescence' in that development may not be resumed as soon as conditions become favourable. Eggs of the larch budmoth, *Zeiraphera diniana*, must spend 120–210 days at 2 °C or below before diapause development is complete and normal development is resumed (Baltensweiler *et al*. 1977).

In central Europe the pine sawfly, *Diprion pini*, provides a good example of the role of diapause in the ecology of forest insects. This sawfly has either one or two generations per year but up to four flight periods so that prediction of insect activity depends on detailed knowledge of the local populations (Dusaussoy and Geri 1971; Eichhorn 1978). In higher latitudes and in mountainous areas, development is always uni-voltine whereas in lowland areas it is often bi-voltine. The occurrence of a second generation is determined by the proportion of the 'sensitive' last larval instar that develops in the 'long-day' conditions allowing diapause-free development. This proportion will vary from year to year depending on climatic conditions.

In Fig. 2.9 the Liechtenstein population has diapause-free development if cocoons are formed by 5 July whereas about 70 per cent of those forming cocoons in the following week entered diapause. The Edlitz population on the other hand, which comes from a similar latitude but in an area with a more favourable climate, develops without diapause provided that cocoons are formed by 25 July but in the following week over 80 per cent enter diapause. Thus, insects in the Edlitz population are more likely to form a second generation. A complicating factor in predicting abundance of this pest is that not all diapausing individuals emerge at the same time in the spring and some may emerge in the following or subsequent years. Thus of the several flight waves that can occur each year, the third one in July/August may contain some individuals of the first generation as well as some of a true second generation. Completion of diapause development in this insect is indicated by the formation of a pupal eye which can be used to determine proportional emergence and thus the approximate size of the next flight (Eichhorn 1978).

The tendency of some individuals within insect populations to remain in

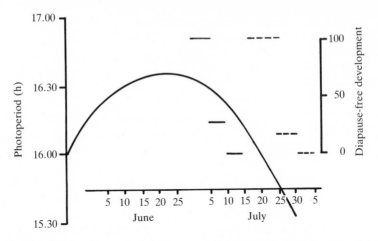

FIG. 2.9. The occurrence of diapause in two populations of *Diprion pini*. The percentage of the populations from Edlitz (dotted line) and Liechtenstein (solid line) with diapause-free development are shown in relation to photoperiod (after Eichhorn 1978).

extended diapause is a means of 'spreading the risk' especially where the amount of food available each year is variable. Seed-feeding insects such as the spruce-cone tortrix, *Cydia strobilella*, provide a good example of this mechanism. The extent of cone setting varies widely from year to year, apparently in response to summer temperatures and that occurring in part of southern Norway between 1941 and 1962 is shown in Fig. 2.10. Higher than average temperatures result in extensive coning in the following year and also appear to stimulate larvae of *C. strobilella* to break diapause. However, even larvae in the same cone do not all break diapause at the same time even in good flowering years (Bakke 1971).

Not only does the occurrence of extended diapause in these and other insects make it difficult to predict population size, but certain weather conditions can promote synchronized emergence of the whole population as observed in the spruce sawfly, *Cephalcia abietis*, in central Europe (Eichhorn and Pausch 1986). Such synchronized emergence could result in increased damage levels and perhaps precipitate a full scale outbreak.

Seasonal polymorphism

For multi-voltine insects such as aphids, polymorphic forms may appear in the population in response to changing environmental conditions. The development of alate individuals within aphid populations provides a ·familiar example. Indeed in adelgid species which alternate between two conifer hosts, two different alate morphs are formed (Carter and Barson

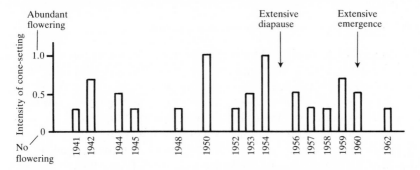

FIG. 2.10. The intensity of cone-setting on spruce in part of Norway from 1941–62. Studies of populations of *Cydia strobilella* in 1954–5 and 1959–60 showed extensive diapause in 1955 when flowers were largely absent. A large proportion of the population emerged in 1960 when, as in 1959, there was extensive flowering on the trees (from Bakke 1963).

1973). Aphid population density and host plant condition are probably the most important triggers for alate development but in some species, photoperiod can be more important. The green spruce aphid, *Elatobium abietinum*, disperses from its host tree in the early summer when the tree's nutritional quality begins to decline but daylength is the major factor inducing the development of migrants (Fig. 2.11).

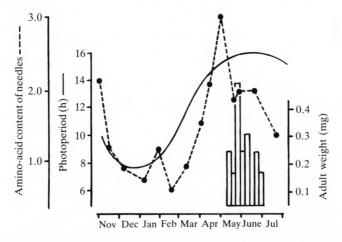

FIG. 2.11. The amino acid content of Sitka spruce foliage (dotted line), photoperiod at 52 degrees north (solid line), and the number of alate *Elatobium abietinum* (histogram) in weekly trap captures (from Fisher and Dixon 1986).

2.2.2 Temperature, insolation, and insect ecology

For insects, as with all poikilothermic animals, temperature is a critical environmental variable, affecting every aspect of their activity and development. In northern latitudes and in mountainous areas, temperatures may be too low or the summer season too short for many species to complete their development, and those that do need special adaptations to survive the harsh winter period. In more temperate areas, years that are warmer than normal may allow insects to produce more than one brood or even form additional generations. As well as these broad regional and temporal effects, local differences within and between forests also affect insect development and survival.

Variation in the forest

On calm sunny days the daily cycle of temperature change within forests lags behind that in open areas and it is cooler during the day and warmer at night, but on overcast days and in windy conditions, the differences are less pronounced. On sunny days there is a temperature inversion within the forest so that temperature increases with height up to the canopy (Fig. 2.20), with normal lapse conditions above it. Local topography can have an important influence on average temperatures and forests on sloping sites with a southerly aspect will be warmer than those on northern slopes. At night, cold air drains from hillsides and collects in valleys and low lying hollows which may be subject to unseasonable frosts, affecting development of both insects and trees. A striking illustration of this is provided by the pattern of defoliation of the autumnal moth, *Epirrita autumnata*, in relation to cold air sinks. In the sub-alpine birch forest of the Scandinavian mountain chain, outbreaks of this pest can cover several square kilometres. In 1955, areas of undefoliated forest contrasting with brown defoliated areas occurred along rivers and lakes where cold air collected and caused widespread mortality of the larvae (Tenow 1975).

Within the forest, temperatures vary widely among the different microhabitats that insects occupy. Insolation which causes local heating is one of the most important factors contributing to these local differences. Temperature fluctuations are highest in the outer canopy where leaves are exposed to direct sunlight during the day, but they cool rapidly at night. Insects in bark and wood on the other hand are likely to experience much lower amplitude fluctuations, but in forest stands of low density and around forest edges or following thinning, the sun can strike directly onto tree trunks, causing local heating. The temperatures within pine bark on the shaded north and non-shaded south sides of a tree in spring are shown in Fig. 2.12. Some tree species may be sensitive to direct heating of the bark of pre-

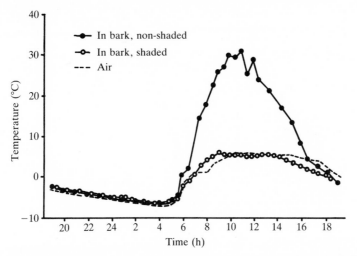

FIG. 2.12. Temperatures in the bark of pine on the south (non-shaded) and north (shaded) sides of the tree. Local air temperature is shown for comparison. Measurements were made 20 cm above the ground (from Bakke 1968).

viously shaded stems, and on beech trees in central Europe 'sunscorch' can damage or kill strips of bark following thinning of stands; this can result in attack by ambrosia beetles and fungi.

The amount of sunlight penetrating to the forest floor depends both on the tree species and its density and is generally much lower in plantations than in natural forests. In the early part of a rotation, light levels within a plantation are very low and insufficient to support a herb layer. Successive thinnings, however, increase average light intensity allowing a ground flora typical of the site to develop (Anderson 1979). Not only does this add to the intrinsic interest of a forest but flowers may be important sources of food for adult parasitoids (see Chapter 7).

Insect development

Above a lower threshold temperature, insect development rate increases linearly with temperature over a wide range. Towards an upper limit, the rate declines and very high temperatures are lethal (Fig. 2.13). Since development rate is proportional to temperature it is possible to predict the duration of development even under fluctuating temperatures in the field. Development rates may vary considerably as a direct result of the temperature variations discussed above. Studies in Scandinavia on the pine weevil, *Hylobius abietis*, showed that its development rate in billets buried in the soil varied according to the amount of exposure to sun. A comparison of open felled areas and shaded areas within the forest showed that genera-

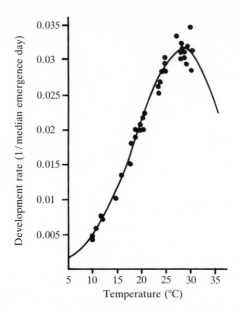

FIG. 2.13. The rate of development of *Tomicus piniperda* at constant temperatures (from Saarenmaa 1985).

tion time could vary from one to three years in the same locality (Bakke and Lekander 1965).

Under field conditions, units of development are usually expressed as 'day-degrees' determined for each day by calculating the difference in degrees between the developmental threshold (which may vary from species to species) and the daily mean temperature (Beck 1968). Thus, to predict the time of emergence of the overwintering stage of an insect an empirical relationship is established for the number of day-degrees accumulated from a given time, e.g. when overwintering stages are sampled, until emergence in the spring. An example is given for *Glypta fumiferanae*, a parasitoid of the spruce budworm, *Choristoneura fumiferana* (Fig. 2.14). For pests with a wide geographical range there will be considerable variation in time of emergence among different populations because average temperatures decrease with increasing latitude and altitude. Hopkins, in formulating his bioclimatic law (Hopkins 1920), estimated that development was retarded by about one day for each 30 m of elevation.

Saarenmaa (1985) has developed a model to predict the timing of emergence of the pine shoot beetle, *Tomicus piniperda*, from log stacks left in the forest. Timing is dependent mainly on temperature and so varies with geographical location, position in the stack and local conditions such as sun or shade. The predicted emergence in different parts of Finland is shown in

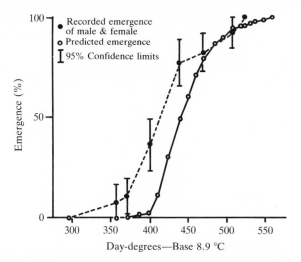

FIG. 2.14. The observed cumulative emergence of male plus female *Glypta fumiferanae* and the predicted emergence of females based on accumulated day degrees above 8.9 °C (from Nyrop and Simmons 1986).

Fig. 2.15. In general, these beetles prefer to attack the outer logs where development is faster. The biggest difference in development time in fact occurred between the sunny and shaded sides of the logs on the top of the stack. In the inner parts of the stack, brood development may not be completed in the short summer of northern areas. Although this model can predict the timing of emergence, the size of the population will depend, among other things, on the operation of mortality factors during development.

Insolation is an important factor in the distribution and development of the pine processionary moth, *Thaumetopoea pityocampa*. Larvae, which are active during the autumn and winter, spin a communal winter nest in exposed positions on attacked pine trees (Fig. 4.5). The nests are warmed by winter sun to several degrees above ambient and larvae may continue feeding even at low ambient temperatures. In France, the distribution of this insect is restricted by its minimum requirement of 1800 hours of sun exposure per year and average minimum January temperatures above −4 °C (Huchon and Demolin 1971).

Insect activity

Like insect development, insect movement is highly dependent on temperature. Temperature thresholds, however, vary widely between different species depending on the conditions to which they are adapted. For example, the flight threshold for the winter moth, *Operophtera brumata*,

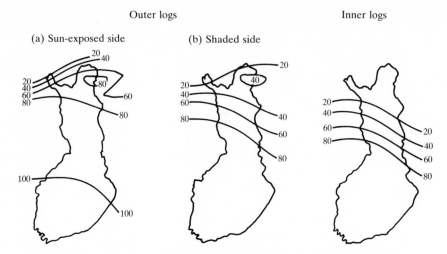

FIG. 2.15. Maps of the percentage of *Tomicus piniperda* emerging by 1 October in Finland for three different positions in pulpwood stacks. Data are based on an average year for stacks in sunlit conditions (from Saarenmaa 1985).

which flies during early winter, is as low as 6 °C (Alma 1970). Temperature thresholds for flight are an important factor in the ecology of bark beetles. The synchronization of mass flights on suitably warm days ensures a large aerial population that can respond to pheromones released to attract mates and co-ordinate mass-attack of trees (see Chapters 4 and 9). Flight intensity in the pine bark beetle, *Ips acuminatus*, is a function of both temperature and the length of time the temperature is above the threshold (Fig. 2.16). On most days the two variables are highly correlated but on two consecutive days with similar temperatures (arrows) the influence of the number of hours above the threshold can be seen. Maximum attacks by the spruce bark beetle, *Pityogenes chalcographus*, on logs occur when air temperatures ranged between 18 and 25 °C but no attacks occurred when air temperatures dropped below 14 °C (Zumr 1982). Figure 2.17 shows how the number of *I. typographus* re-emerging from attacked spruce trees is related to maximum temperature (Botterweg 1982). It is important to remember that in all these studies, the aerial population density of insects is not determined solely by temperature or other weather factors but also depends on the actual population size and the proportion of the population in flight (Johnson 1969).

The temperature inversion conditions that are commonly found within the forest may enhance both host location and response to pheromones by bark beetles since, under these stable air conditions, pheromone and presumably host tree odour is trapped under the canopy, aiding orientation

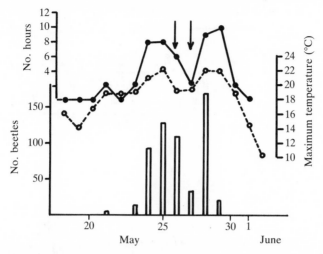

FIG. 2.16. The relationship between the daily trap catch of *Ips acuminatus* (histogram), maximum air temperature (dotted line), and the number of hours above 18 °C (solid line). Arrows indicate low beetle captures despite relatively high air temperatures. Threshold temperature was exceeded for 2 hours only on that day, as compared with 6 hours on the previous day (from Bakke 1968).

by beetles which also appear to be more active under inversion conditions (Fares *et al.* 1980).

Cold hardiness and overwintering

Not all insects enter diapause during the winter but have adopted other strategies for surviving cold weather. The main danger during severe cold is the formation of ice crystals within the tissues. Since cells contain complex organic molecules they have a natural ability to 'supercool', i.e. to avoid freezing and this ability increases by exposure to non-lethal 'conditioning' temperatures. This can be demonstrated experimentally by determining the temperature at which freezing occurs (the supercooling point) with and without previous exposure to low temperatures. About half the individuals of the green spruce aphid, *Elatobium abietinum*, reared at 0 °C for 5 days were able to survive temperatures of −14 °C whereas half those reared at 15 °C died at −9 °C (Fig. 2.18) (Carter 1972). Aphids which have recently been feeding are also more prone to freezing than starved ones. In continental Europe only the egg stage of *E. abietinum* is capable of surviving the harsh winters, but in the milder climate of Britain aphids may be found on the trees throughout the winter. However, mortality of these aphids can be high during winters which are generally mild but punctuated by periods of low temperature (less than −8 °C) (no preconditioning, some

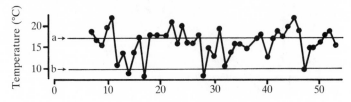

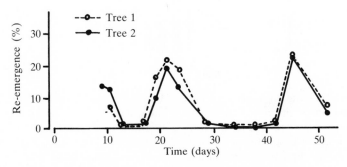

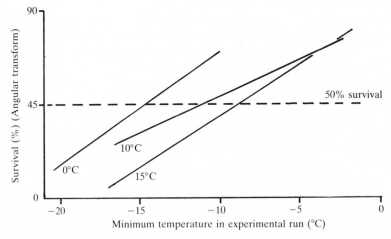

FIG. 2.17. The percentage of *Ips typographus* beetles re-emerging from two attacked trees on different days during May–June in relation to daily maximum air temperature. The mean maximum and minimum temperatures are also shown (after Botterweg 1982).

FIG. 2.18. Regression of survival of *Elatobium abietinum* on spruce foliage when exposed to low temperatures for 6 hours. Before exposure, aphids were preconditioned at 0, 10 or 15 °C for at least 5 days (from Carter 1972).

previous feeding) and this fact may be useful in estimating the risk of high spring populations which may damage spruce trees (Fig. 2.30).

The overwintering stages of some insects may be protected from rapid temperature changes or very low temperatures by an insulating blanket of snow. The temperatures recorded in overwintering sites for three species of pine bark beetle in Norway are shown in Fig. 2.19 (Bakke 1968). The pine shoot beetle, *Tomicus piniperda*, hibernates under the bark near the base of pine trees where the temperature is about −5 °C. In the soil, where the related *T. minor* hibernates, temperatures were above freezing at +2 °C. The most severe temperatures were experienced by *Ips acuminatus* which is found under the thinner bark higher up the stem and usually above the snow line where temperatures of −22 °C were recorded. Clearly *I. acuminatus* must withstand much lower temperatures than the other beetles and its ability to do so is revealed by the low supercooling point of the adult beetles (Table 2.4). Feeding larvae are less cold-hardy and may not survive the winter in northern areas.

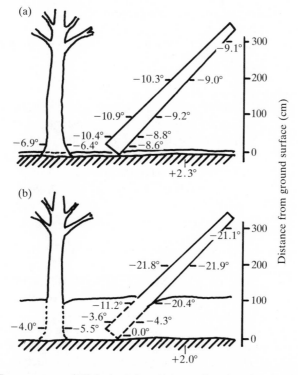

FIG. 2.19. Temperatures (°C) in bark beetle overwintering sites in pine trees and soil with a thin (a) and a thick (b) insulating layer of snow (from Bakke 1968).

Table 2.4. *Supercooling points (°C) of two species of pine bark beetle in various stages of development*

Species	Supercooling points (°C)			
	Larvae	Pupae	Adults	
			Newly emerged	In hibernation
Tomicus piniperda	−12.5	−18.2	−18.2	−18.4
Ips acuminatus	−16.6	−19.9	−19.0	−32.9

From Bakke 1968.

2.2.3 Patterns of wind movement in the forest

The strength of the wind blowing over and through forests will vary most notably with altitude and exposure. On open hill tops strong winds may stunt tree growth, cause wind rocking of established trees and so damage roots and, in stormy weather, trees in such locations are liable to be blown over. The stability of trees in exposed positions is an important consideration in the establishment of plantations because windthrow not only disrupts harvesting schedules but, by providing additional breeding sites for bark beetles, can precipitate outbreaks (Chapters 4 and 5). In forests which are not wind stable, thinning operations may be abandoned because they can precipitate windthrow of the remaining trees.

Within the forest itself, wind movement may be quite complex with vertical as well as horizontal components and wind direction can even deviate temporarily from that in surrounding open areas (Oliver 1975). The speed of the wind is generally lower in the forest but varies with height in a characteristic S-shaped profile (Fig. 2.20). Windspeed is low close to the ground and also in the canopy where the wind is slowed by branches and leaves. In the relatively unrestricted trunk zone, however, the speed of movement is normally higher, and it also increases rapidly with height above the canopy.

Wind and insect dispersal

Wind may contribute directly to insect mortality by dislodging them from their host tree and it has been shown to disturb aphid populations and reduce their fecundity (Dixon and McKay 1970). Most attention, however, has been focused on the role of wind in the dispersal of insects, a process which itself can be an important cause of mortality.

The occurrence of dispersal and its importance in the ecology of different insects depends on a number of life history characteristics. Insects which must seek out ephemeral host plants need to be effective dispersers, whereas for those in 'permanent' habitats such as temperate forests, dispersal tends to be a less prominent part of the life cycle (Southwood 1977).

Nevertheless, even within a permanent habitat, particular resources may be ephemeral or at least hard to find. Bark beetles, for example, exploit moribund or stressed trees, a resource which is usually scarce and certainly unpredictable and beetles may need to search large areas of forest to find them.

The relative importance of wind depends partly on the mode of dispersal. Insects which disperse in juvenile flightless stages such as scale insects and some larval Lepidoptera are entirely dependent on the wind for their dispersal. The first instar 'crawlers' of the beech scale, *Cryptococcus fagisuga*, disperse passively on air currents within the forest. Most dispersing crawlers impact on the ground only a few metres away from the host tree but some are deposited on nearby beech stems. However, a small proportion of this aerial population (around 1 per cent) is carried by vertical air movements into the faster winds above the canopy so that a longer range dispersal is possible for this insect (Fig. 2.20) (Wainhouse 1980).

Larvae of the gypsy moth, *Lymantria dispar*, are also adapted for passive dispersal. The larvae have very long setae and prior to dispersal they produce a long silken thread which further reduces their sinking speed and so they may be carried for some distance on the wind. Although most dispersal occurs as short hops within the canopy (Mason and McManus 1981), the larvae may also utilize winds blowing over the forest. In the ridge and valley system in Pennsylvania, larvae are lifted into the winds flowing over the valley and deposited near the top of the downwind ridge and this gives rise to a characteristic pattern of infestation in this region (Fig. 2.21).

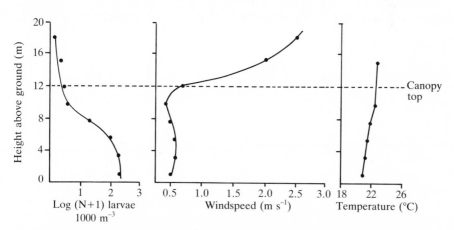

FIG. 2.20. The vertical distribution of dispersing crawlers of *Cryptococcus fagisuga*, windspeed and temperature in and above a beech forest in southern England (from Wainhouse 1980).

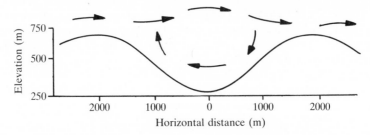

FIG. 2.21. Winds circulating over the ridge and valley system in Pennsylvania, USA. Larvae of *Lymantria dispar* are lifted into the winds flowing over the ridge and deposited by downdraughts as the wind passes over downwind ridges (from Mason and McManus 1981).

Flying insects are relatively independent of the wind within the forest but may be displaced for long distances downwind when they fly above the forest canopy. The spruce budworm, *Choristoneura fumiferana*, is an eruptive pest and dispersal plays an important part in its population dynamics (Fisher and Greenbank 1979). The adult moths are known to fly at night over considerable distances but the full extent of this dispersal has only recently been shown using a range of novel techniques including ground and airborne insect-detecting radar and airborne wind-finding radar (Schaefer 1976, 1979; Greenbank *et al.* 1980).

In New Brunswick, emigration of *C. fumiferana* is a regular nightly occurrence with moth take-off apparently stimulated by falling illumination around sunset (Fig. 2.22). The moths fly upwards above the forest canopy and concentrate in the warmest layers of air just above the temperature inversion (Fig. 2.23) although flight may occur at appreciably higher

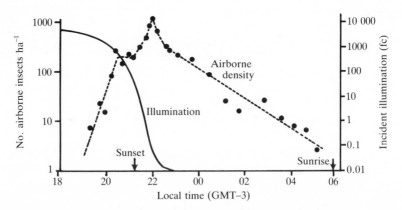

FIG. 2.22. Light intensity (solid line) in relation to take off and airborne density (dotted line) of *Choristoneura fumiferana* in New Brunswick (from Schaefer 1976).

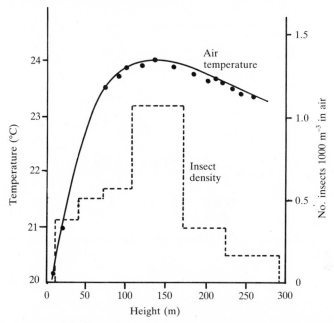

FIG. 2.23. Aerial density of flying *Choristoneura fumiferana* in relation to air temperature above the forest canopy (from Schaefer 1976).

altitudes in disturbed weather when a temperature inversion is not present. These airborne moths are then displaced downwind and under the right conditions some moths may be capable of crossing much of New Brunswick in a few hours (Dickison *et al.* 1986).

Flying moths are also concentrated in wind convergence zones such as sea breeze fronts (Greenbank *et al.* 1980) and storm cells associated with synoptic-scale cold fronts (Dickison *et al.* 1983, 1986). Rainey (1979), for example, describes a case where a concentration of budworm moths, detected as a line-echo on ground radar was associated with a meteorological front whose sharply defined wind-shift line had been located by aircraft wind-finding equipment (Fig. 2.24). Large numbers of settled moths, probably from this concentration were killed during spraying operations in the area the next day and indeed the appearance of large numbers of moths at ground level during rainstorms and thunderstorms associated with cold fronts is historically well documented (Greenbank 1957; Greenbank *et al.* 1980). Clearly, in the right weather conditions aerial concentrations can lead to high ground densities of moths and since migrating female *C. fumiferana* still carry 50 per cent of their eggs, deposition of large numbers of these moths in uninfested or lightly infested areas could be important in triggering or spreading outbreaks (Miller *et al.* 1978).

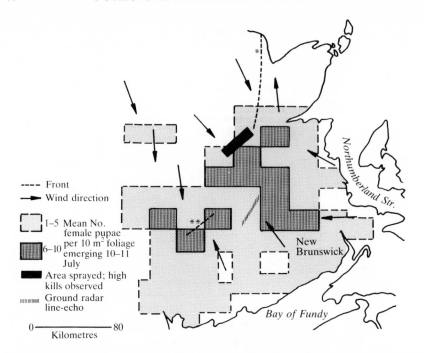

FIG. 2.24. The concentration of *Choristoneura fumiferana* in a zone of wind convergence. The direction of the wind (arrow) at selected points on the aircraft track and the position of the front (dotted line) at 21.10(*) and 23.39(**) on 12 July 1974 is shown. The position of the ground radar line-echo early on 13 July is shown (vertical bars) together with the area sprayed later the same day (shaded) that resulted in high kill of budworms (see text) (after Rainey 1979).

Dispersal of the larch budmoth, *Zeiraphera diniana*, in parts of the Swiss alps is similarly determined by wind patterns. In the alpine valleys there are predictable nightly windfields caused by cold air draining from upper regions of the mountains and creating laminar winds of up to 3 m s^{-1} which flow down slopes and valleys. The moths, which disperse at night in temperatures greater than 7 °C, tend to fly upwind (positively anemotactic) so that they arrive in the upper regions of the mountain valleys from which they disperse (Fig. 2.25). Long distance dispersal to new areas may help to synchronize outbreaks along the alpine arch (Baltensweiler and Fischlin 1979).

Wind and chemical communication

Many forest insects respond to chemicals emanating from their host trees or released by prospective mates and air movement in and around a forest is an integral part of the detection and response to these wind-borne

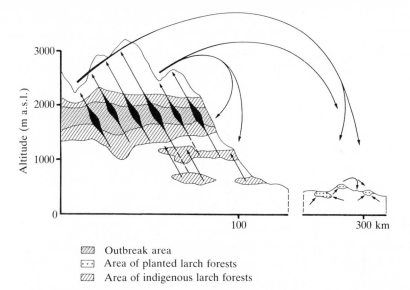

Outbreak area
Area of planted larch forests
Area of indigenous larch forests

FIG. 2.25. Upwind flight in Alpine valleys by *Zeiraphera diniana* followed by long range dispersal between mountains (from Baltensweiler and Fischlin 1979).

odours. Some aspects of host and mate finding are discussed in Chapters 3, 4 and 9.

2.2.4 Rain, snow, and relative humidity

The amount and seasonal distribution of precipitation will largely determine its impact on insect populations. Summer rain will have a greater direct effect on insects than winter rain or snow but unusually dry weather, for example, can indirectly affect insects through the host plant.

Rainfall is intercepted first by the outer forest canopy where some is deflected or lost by evaporation so that in light showers insects within or below the canopy are unaffected. During heavy rain many small insects such as scales, adelgids, and aphids that feed on the surface of leaves may be washed away. In broad-leaved trees, water 'collected' by the canopy during heavy rain is channelled towards and down the main trunk so that insects feeding on the surface of the bark can also be dislodged. An additional danger during periods of wet weather is that the high humidity may promote epizootics of insect pathogenic fungi which may decimate insect populations in some years (Chapter 7).

During the winter, heavy rainfall may cause waterlogging of the soil which can drown the overwintering stages of some species as shown for the larch sawfly, *Pristiphora erichsonii*, in Manitoba (Ives and Nairn 1966).

Winter snowfall on the other hand forms an insulating layer that, as we have seen, protects overwintering stages from severe cold. Heavy snowfall can also indirectly affect insects because conifers with a horizontal or even upward branching pattern collect so much snow that branches can break off and so provide breeding sites for bark beetles and perhaps increase the susceptibility of damaged trees to attack.

For many herbivorous insects that feed on the plant surface, the drying effects of sun and wind pose a greater threat than high humidity or the physical effects of rainfall (Southwood 1973). Some forest insects avoid this risk by completing the vulnerable stages of the life cycle within the tissues of the plant. Sawflies, for example, deposit eggs in wood or leaves, bark beetle larvae mine in the bark and there are also many leafminers and gall formers attacking trees. During particularly dry weather, trees may become stressed and this can indirectly affect secondary pests such as bark beetles which often attack these trees successfully. These aspects are discussed in Chapters 3 and 4.

2.2.5 Lightning

Forest fires started by lightning may destroy large areas of forest and by renewing the process of forest succession change the nature of the forest insect community. Lightning plays a less dramatic but nevertheless important role in the population dynamics of the southern pine beetle, *Dendroctonus frontalis*, in parts of the southern USA. Lightning strikes on trees during thunderstorms are a frequent occurrence in the southern pine forests and this bark beetle is able to locate and exploit these trees which can act as outbreak foci (Coulson *et al.* 1983).

2.2.6 Aerial pollution

Pollutants in the air are, unfortunately, becoming an increasingly important part of the abiotic environment of insects and are widely considered to be responsible for forest decline or 'Waldsterben' in central Europe (Fig. 2.26.) (Innes 1987). Like weather and climate, atmospheric pollutants can influence forest insects directly (e.g. as toxins), indirectly (e.g. induced changes in the host plant) or by influencing the activities of natural enemies (Fig. 2.27). However, unlike other environmental factors the extent of pollution is largely under man's control so, in theory, it should be possible to reduce the concentration of pollutants in the atmosphere and minimize their effect on insects and the environment.

There are many different types and sources of pollutants and a good review of the subject is provided by Kozlowski and Constantinidou (1986). Primary pollutants, such as sulphur dioxide from the burning of fossil fuels

FIG. 2.26. Forest trees in Europe killed or damaged by aerial pollution/acid rain.

and oxides of nitrogen from car exhausts, are toxic chemicals that are released directly into the air. Secondary pollutants such as ozone, which like sulphur dioxide is thought to cause widespread plant injury, are formed in the atmosphere by the action of sunlight on the products of fuel combustion. Dusts and soot and other particulates are another form of pollution and come mainly from industrial sources.

Like flying insects themselves, pollutants are not uniformly distributed in the air. Concentrations will be high close to point sources of primary pollutants but for diffuse sources, concentration can be affected by temperature inversions and the movement of discrete air masses, and pollutants

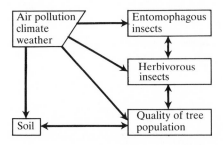

FIG. 2.27. The influence of air pollution on various levels within ecosystems (after Führer 1985).

can be deposited hundreds of miles from the source. There may also be diurnal and seasonal variations in the concentration of pollutants.

An early and particularly well-studied example of the effect of pollution on insect populations was that of industrial melanism in the peppered moth, *Biston betularia* (Kettlewell 1973). Pollution associated with the industrial revolution in western Europe resulted in the blackening of, among other things, tree trunks and walls on which the moths rest during the day. Against this dark background, the normal pale forms of the moth are highly visible and are taken in greater proportion by birds than the melanic form. Since its appearance in the mid-nineteenth century, the melanic form has become common throughout most urban areas of western Europe, although in Britain, the introduction of the clean air act in the mid-1950's has reduced the incidence of particulate pollution and with it the frequency of the melanic form of *B. betularia*. This example of the indirect effects of pollution on insects is also a vivid demonstration of the effects that predation can have on insect populations.

The impact of aerial pollutants on insects has often been determined from correlations between levels of pollution and changes in insect population density (Alstad *et al.* 1982). It is often not possible, therefore, to distinguish direct effects on the insects from those on natural enemies or the host tree itself. Direct effects on insects have been demonstrated in some cases. Fig. 2.28, for example, shows the effect of increasing fluoride concentration in spruce needles on mortality of larvae of the nun moth, *Lymantria monacha*. Trees can be damaged directly by pollutants such as sulphur dioxide and ozone, and also indirectly by the complex secondary pollutant 'acid rain', which causes changes in the chemical environment in the soil and so can affect the health and growth of trees and their susceptibility to pests (Führer 1985).

It is not possible at the moment to generalize about the effects of pollution on insect populations. Present observations have shown that the

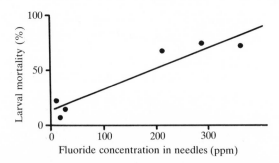

FIG. 2.28. Correlation between the mortality of larvae of *Lymantria monacha* and the fluoride concentration of spruce needles (from Führer 1985).

same pollutant can have positive or negative effects depending on the concentration or the insect species affected. Some examples are given in Table 2.5.

2.2.7 Weather, population dynamics, and the prediction of outbreaks

By affecting the activity, dispersal, and survival of insects, weather can play a significant role in their population dynamics and, for some species, it may be the key factor (see later) determining population change. By affecting insect populations over wide areas weather may even precipitate outbreaks of forest pests. The impact of weather on insects will depend among other things on the extent to which the insects are exposed on the plant surface to

Table 2.5. *Air pollutants and their effects on forest insect abundance or damage '+' indicates an increase; '−' indicates a decline*

Pollutant	Insect		Effect (+/−)	Apparent cause
Fluorides	*Rhyacionia buoliana*	Pine shoot moth	−	
Fluorides	*Pityokteines* spp.	Bark beetle	−	
Fluorides	*Exoteleia dodecella*	Pine bud moth	+	
Fluorides	*Lymantria monacha*	Nun moth	−	Toxic effect of fluoride in needles
Fluorides + sulphur dioxide	*Cryptococcus fagisuga*	Beech scale	+/−	Complex interaction
Sulphur dioxide	Scolytidae	Bark beetles	+	Damaged trees more vulnerable to attack
Sulphur dioxide	Diprionidae	Spruce sawflies	+	Increased food quality of needles
Sulphur dioxide	*Rhyacionia buoliana*	Pine shoot moth	+	Increased food quality of needles
Sulphur dioxide	*Exoteleia dodecella*	Pine bud moth	+	Increased food quality of needles
Ozone	*Dendroctonus ponderosae*	Mountain pine beetle	+	Damaged trees more vulnerable to attack
Ozone	*Lymantria dispar*	Gypsy moth	+/−	Acceptability of leaves affected by concentration
Dust	*Nuculaspis californica*	Pine needle scale	+	Parasitoids killed
Heavy metals and mixed air pollutants	*Aradus cinnamomeus*	Pine bark bug	+	

From Jeffords and Endress 1984, Führer 1985, Heliovaara and Vaisanen 1986, and references in Alstad *et al.* 1982.

the effects of wind and rain or are hidden within the plant tissues. But indirect effects on, for example, the amount of food or the time during which it is available, can be equally important. Because temperature thresholds and rates of development for insect and tree are likely to be different, normal temperature variations in the forest can lead to asynchrony between insects and the appropriate stage of the host. Thus in some years insects may starve or be forced to develop on food of reduced nutritional quality (Chapter 3).

In spruce, budburst phenology depends on accumulated temperature but winter chilling may advance the time of budburst so it occurs after a different period of accumulated spring temperatures (physiological time). The food quality of the needles declines after budburst so its timing can have an important influence on the population density of the spruce aphid, *Elatobium abietinum* (Day 1984). Aphid population density peaks shortly after budburst which, in the 3 years studied by Day, occurred at more or less the same time each year (Fig. 2.29). The same data plotted on a physiological time-scale (day °C), however, revealed that in 1983 less physiological time had passed during that cool spring before budburst and a subsequent decline in food quality occurred. Thus, despite the high overwintering population that year, peak aphid densities were less than might have been anticipated.

Geographical location of insect populations is also important in determining the impact of weather on population dynamics. At the margins of an insect's natural range and in extreme environments such as high latitudes and altitudes, weather is more likely to be a limiting factor in population growth. In northern Finland the short summers do not normally allow development of a full generation of the spruce bark beetle, *Ips typographus*, and larvae are unable to survive the winter. Although many of the spruce forests in these northern areas are overmature and thus highly susceptible to bark beetle attack, outbreaks only develop following a succession of warm summers (Saarenmaa 1985).

Because of its predictive value, special attention has been focused on the role of weather in the 'release' of outbreaks of forest pests (Schwerdtfeger 1935; Carpenter 1940; but see Martinat 1987). In deciduous forests in Europe, Carpenter concluded that outbreaks of different species tended to occur in the same groups of years and, therefore, proposed a climatic influence. In North America, dry sunny weather favours survival of the spruce budworm, *Choristoneura fumiferana*, especially if it occurs during the larval feeding period and populations may rise to outbreak densities after a succession of warm dry years (Wellington 1954; Greenbank 1963). In these and other cases it is not always possible to determine the relative importance of the direct effects of weather on insects from indirect effects via the host plant or perhaps factors associated with the site on which the

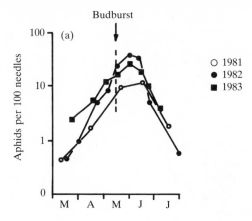

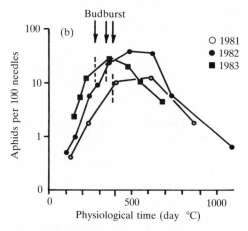

FIG. 2.29. (a) Population density of *Elatobium abietinum* on spruce trees during the spring–summer cycle for three consecutive years by Julian date. (b) The data for (a) plotted on a physiological time-scale (day °C above 4°C from 1 January) (from Day 1984).

forest grows. A straightforward example, however, is provided by the green spruce aphid, *Elatobium abietinum*. In Britain, adults of this aphid are present on the trees throughout the winter when the nutritional quality of the trees is high and in mild weather they will feed and reproduce. In the spring of 1971, outbreaks of this insect occurred in the western half of Britain where the winter had been continuously mild. However, in these mild conditions, the aphids do not become cold-hardened through exposure to gradually declining temperatures as would happen in a normal

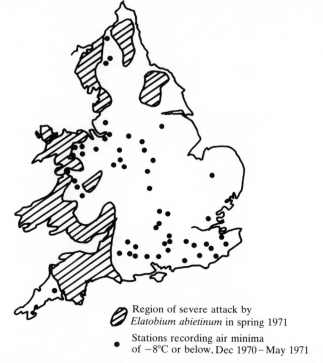

Region of severe attack by
Elatobium abietinum in spring 1971

Stations recording air minima
of −8°C or below, Dec 1970 – May 1971

FIG. 2.30. The approximate distribution of forests severely attacked by *Elatobium abietinum* in spring 1971. In the outbreak area in the west of the country, no climatological stations recorded air temperature minima of −8 °C or below, where-as in the east, such temperatures were widely recorded (from Carter 1972).

winter (Fig. 2.18) and so are susceptible to sudden cold snaps. While outbreaks developed in the western half of Britain in 1971, in the east a sudden air frost of −11 °C in an otherwise mild winter caused considerable aphid mortality preventing population build-up to outbreak levels in the spring (Fig. 2.30) (Carter 1972).

2.2.8 Weather and biological control

The most successful examples of biological control involve the release of natural enemies in new geographical areas in which their normal hosts have become established as serious pests. The success of these attempts at classical biological control (see Chapter 7) will depend on a number of factors directly or indirectly affected by the weather. Clearly, choosing natural enemies with the appropriate seasonal adaptations such as diapause is an essential requirement but the occurrence of diapause itself is one of the major problems limiting the successful use of natural enemies (Messenger 1970). It can cause problems of synchrony in the field and present considerable difficulties for continuous rearing of uni-voltine natural enemies for release (van den Bosch and Messenger 1973). Weather conditions at the time of release can affect the likelihood of establishment of natural enemies. The careful timing of release can minimize such effects and is essential where techniques such as mass or inundative release of such species as *Trichogramma* are contemplated (Smith *et al.* 1986).

Problems of asynchrony can also limit the effectiveness of native natural enemies attacking introduced pests. The pine sawfly, *Neodiprion sertifer*, an introduced species in North America, is attacked in the late larval stage by a native ichneumonid, *Exenterus canadensis*. Asynchrony appears to be a consequence of microclimatic temperature differences in the litter layer which have a pronounced effect on parasitoid pupal development so that emergence of some individuals in each generation does not coincide with the preferred stage of the host which is only present in the field for about 3 weeks (Griffiths 1969).

2.3 BIOTIC FACTORS IN THE ECOLOGY OF FOREST INSECTS

Weather is clearly an important factor in the development and survival of insects and thus in their population dynamics. But even in favourable environments, most insects remain at non-outbreak densities and do not cause conspicuous damage to their hosts. Their populations fluctuate about some average density which is often characteristic of the species in a particular locality and even quite similar species can have different average levels of abundance.

Populations of Lepidoptera, among which are many important pests, have been intensively studied and for a few species much is known about long-term variation in abundance. Changes in population density of the pine looper moth, *Bupalus piniaria* (Chapter 1), and two other pine defoliators, the pine beauty moth, *Panolis flammea*, and the pine hawk moth, *Hyloicus pinastri*, in Germany and Holland are shown in (Figs 2.31 and 2.32). In both these areas and in other parts of Europe, *B. piniaria* is, on average, the most abundant species, followed by *P. flammea* then *H. pinastri* (Klomp 1968); this is most clearly seen in the Dutch populations sampled as larvae on twigs (Fig. 2.31). The population densities of the three pine defoliators may be quite unrelated in any one year and, in general, fluctuate independently of one another. In Germany, for

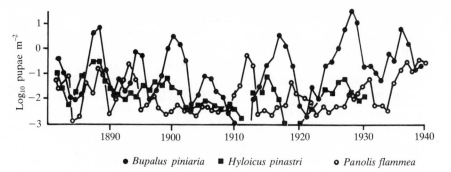

FIG. 2.31. The abundance of three pine defoliators at Letzlingen, Germany, from the late nineteenth century (from Varley 1949).

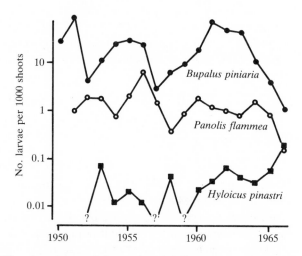

FIG. 2.32. The abundance of three pine defoliators at south Veluwe in Holland during the 1950s and 60s (from Klomp 1968).

example, all three species were very abundant in 1888 but in 1912 only *P. flammea* reached outbreak levels and the other two species were extremely scarce. Similarly in Holland in the mid-1960s, populations of *H. pinastri* were increasing while those of *P. flammea* and *B. piniaria* were decreasing.

This example shows that even important pests such as *B. piniaria* are at sub-outbreak densities most of the time. Determining which mortality factors are most important in limiting population growth is one of the principal aims of population dynamic studies. Although the abiotic environment can play an important part in determining levels of abundance, weather-induced mortality acts independently of insect density and so cannot 'regulate' a population, i.e. cause it to return to an equilibrium density after departure from it. Regulation can only occur through the operation of negative feedback or density-dependent mortality factors whose intensity is proportional to population density (Varley *et al*. 1973). Competition between individuals for some limiting resource such as food and the action of natural enemies, particularly predators and parasitoids, have been identified as the main components of the biotic environment capable of causing density-dependent mortality. Diseases can also be important causes of mortality, especially at high population density but discussion of this topic is deferred to Chapter 7.

2.3.1 The natural enemy community

Many different species of natural enemy are found in the insect community on trees (Fig. 2.1) and this is partly due to the variety of insect herbivores that are found there (section 2.1.1). But another important contributory factor is that tree-feeding insects on the whole support more kinds of parasitoids than herbivorous insects that occur on other plants. Part of the explanation for this appears to be that associations with tree-feeding insects are more likely to have evolved because they are an 'apparent' and predictable resource since the trees on which they feed are large and long-lived and more likely to be encountered by natural enemies (see Chapter 3) (Askew and Shaw 1986; Hawkins and Lawton 1987).

Individual herbivore species do, nevertheless, vary considerably in the number of natural enemies that attack them; some, for example, have a complex of 20 or more species whereas many others have only one or two (Askew and Shaw 1986; Hawkins and Lawton 1987). Indeed some highly specialized forest insects such as the balsam woolly aphid, *Adelges piceae*, are not attacked by parasitoids at all. These differences are partly explained by the influence of the host insect feeding niche on parasitoid species richness (Fig. 2.33). Data collected from a range of different kinds of host plant suggest that more sedentary insects, which are only partially protected by plant tissues, support more parasitoid species than either more mobile external feeders or those completely protected as, for example, those within galls or wood. Root-feeders seem to be the most difficult to locate and they support fewer parasitoids than other insects.

In general, however, it is not the richness of the natural enemy community itself that is important in population dynamics but whether it contains species that are able to kill an increasing proportion of their host population as its density increases and so have the potential to regulate it. The majority of natural enemies do not exert density-dependent mortality on their prey population (Strong *et al*. 1984) and to understand the reasons for this we need to look at the behaviour of predators and parasitoids. To

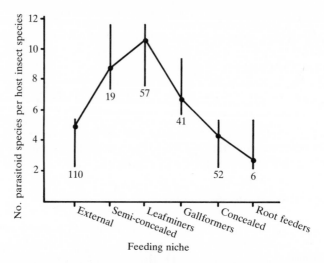

FIG. 2.33. Effect of host insects' feeding niche on parasitoid species richness. Data were collected from a range of different host plants and plotted as mean number of parasitoids per host insect on linear scales. Associated statistics are based on ANOVA of log transformed richness. Vertical bars delimit significantly different means, and numbers under them refer to sample size (from Hawkins and Lawton 1987).

simplify the following discussion we will refer mainly to predator/prey interactions to cover the activities of either predators or parasitoids except where it is necessary to make a clear distinction between these two kinds of natural enemy.

2.3.2 The characteristics of predators and parasitoids

Functional and numerical responses

Individual predators respond directly to the abundance of their prey through changes in behaviour, but the availability of prey also affects both survival and reproductive success so that predators can also respond indirectly to prey density and increase their numbers through reproduction. The terms 'functional' and 'numerical' response were originally proposed by Solomon (1949) to describe these effects and the concepts were later developed extensively by Holling (1959, 1965, 1966).

When prey is abundant it is encountered more frequently by individual searching predators who are thus able to consume more prey individuals within a given time. This functional response is ultimately limited, however, because predators require a certain minimum 'handling time' to pursue and capture, eat and digest individual prey and eventually they become satiated. Similarly, parasitoids must locate and oviposit in hosts and their fecundity ultimately sets an upper limit to the number of individuals that can be parasitized. A typical curve of this functional response called 'type 2' by Holling is shown in Fig. 2.34 for the parasitoid, *Pleolophus basizonus*, attacking the pine sawfly, *Neodiprion sertifer*. The maximum of about 3 eggs day^{-1} is only laid when density is around 30 hosts m^{-2} but there is little further response to increased host density. Clearly the rate of attack declines with increasing host density so that this kind of functional response causes mortality which is inversely density dependent. Such effects are inherently destabilizing, causing prey populations to fluctuate more rather than less violently in the absence of other density dependent mortality (Varley *et al.* 1973, but see Hassell 1985).

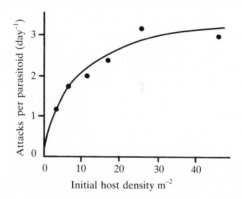

Fig. 2.34. A 'type 2' functional response of the ichneumonid *Pleolophus basizonus* in response to changes in the density of its host *Neodiprion sertifer*. The parasitoid lays one egg per attack (from Griffiths 1969).

A second type of functional response called, 'type 3', is sigmoid. At low prey density there is little predation but above a threshold density, predators switch their attention to this species from less abundant prey and the resulting increase in predation rate causes mortality which is directly density dependent. At higher population densities, however, the curve assumes a form reminiscent of the type 2 functional response and mortality becomes inversely density-dependent. Type 3 responses have been associated particularly with vertebrate predators such as birds which may spend more time in areas where more prey are found (Royama 1970) or perhaps may develop a specific 'searching image' for the most profitable prey (Tinbergen 1960). Type 3 responses may, in fact, occur more widely in invertebrate natural enemies than previously assumed (Hassell *et al.* 1977; see also Embree 1966.)

When predators respond to increased availability of prey through reproduction, i.e. a numerical response, the population of predators increases in the following generation. This time delay can have important consequences for population dynamics as discussed below. However, a local numerical response caused by aggregation in areas of abundant prey may occur and this can have an immediate impact on the prey population.

Generalists and specialists

Generalist or polyphagous natural enemies are typified by vertebrate and invertebrate predators which feed, often as both juveniles and adults, on many individuals of a number of different prey species (Chapter 7). This choice of prey items means that their survival and reproductive success is less dependent on fluctuations in the abundance of a single prey species. But an important difference between vertebrate and invertebrate predators is that when single prey species are abundant, as for example during incipient outbreaks, vertebrate predators have a much smaller capacity for a reproductive numerical response than their invertebrate counterparts.

At the other end of the spectrum there are the highly specialized natural enemies, such as many of the parasitic Hymenoptera, which are associated with one or a few closely-related hosts. The female parasitoids have highly specialized mechanisms for locating and ovipositing in their hosts (Vinson 1976) and their immature stages often develop on only a single host individual. The population density of such specialized parasitoids often tracks that of their host, sometimes leading to 'coupled' oscillations, the properties of which have been widely explored in the theoretical literature (Hassell 1978).

The emphasis on the use of specific natural enemies in biological control and the many theoretical studies of parasitoid–host interactions obscures the fact that highly specialized natural enemies are the exception rather than the rule. For example, Table 2.6 shows the degree of specificity of parasitoids attacking the winter moth, *Operophtera brumata*, in Europe and in Canada where it is an introduced pest. The majority of natural

Table 2.6. *Specificity of parasitoids attacking Operophtera brumata in Europe and Canada*

Parasitoid status	Europe	Canada	
	Native host	Introduced host	
	Native parasitoid	Native parasitoid	Introduced parasitoid
Widely polyphagous	16	19	1[a]
Moderately polyphagous	8	—	—
Fairly polyphagous	2	—	1[b]

[a] *Agrypon flaveolatum;* [b] *Cyzenis albicans.*
From Hassell 1978, after Zwolfer 1971.

enemies in its native habitat are polyphagous and there are relatively few specialists. Naturally, specialists are absent in Canada but a number of polyphagous parasitoids are able to attack it. Two effective parasitoids were introduced from Europe during attempts at biological control (Graham 1958; Embree 1965) and this is discussed in Chapter 7.

2.3.3 Population change and the measurement of mortality

Life tables

The relative importance of different kinds of mortality factor and the causes of population change from generation to generation can only be determined from detailed studies of insect populations in the field, ideally through the compilation of detailed life tables (Varley *et al.* 1973). For many insects, age-specific life tables can be used to follow the fate of members of a single discrete generation and only these are considered in the following discussion. For species with overlapping generations such as aphids and some bark beetles, time-specific life tables must be employed but these are more difficult to compile and interpret (Southwood 1978; Price 1984).

The size of a population is entirely determined by the number of births and deaths and the number of individuals dispersing into or out of it. In order to construct a life table, the population must be sampled at regular intervals as it passes through a generation, usually from adult to adult. At each 'stage' of the population, the average density before and after the operation of mortality factors can be estimated and so the magnitude of mortalities acting successively on the population can be determined. When populations are sampled for several consecutive years, it may be possible to determine the role of such factors in the overall pattern of population change. The life table approach to the study of population dynamics is best illustrated by Varley and Gradwell's (1960, 1968) classic study of the winter moth, *Operophtera brumata*, in Wytham Wood near Oxford.

Life tables of the number of *O. brumata* at each stage in the life cycle were determined for the years 1950–62. The 'killing power' of the various mortalities, the k-values, were calculated from these life tables as the difference in the log of the population density before and after the action of the mortality factor in each year as described in Varley *et al.* (1973). In this study the key factor that was assumed to cause the changes in abundance from year to year was found to be the mortality responsible for 'winter disappearance', identified by its relationship to the overall generation mortality, K (Fig. 2.35). Winter disappearance occurred during the period from when the females emerged in November–December to lay eggs, right through to the fully-developed larvae in May and thus included most stages of the life cycle. From separate studies, however, it seemed clear that

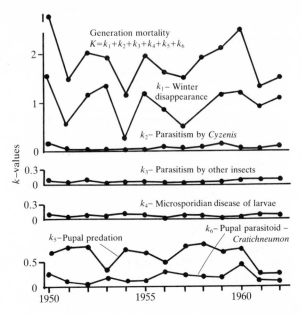

FIG. 2.35. Mortality factors expressed as k-values acting on a population of *Opero-phtera brumata* in Wytham Wood, England (from Varley *et al.* 1973).

mortality of first instar larvae which failed to synchronize with budburst was the real key factor determining the main changes in abundance from year to year (Varley *et al.* 1973). The importance of the synchronization of insects with the appropriate developmental stage of their host plant is discussed further in Chapter 3.

Temporal density-dependence

The k-value for pupal predation (k_5) is positively correlated with the population density of the host (log N) (Fig. 2.36). This mortality, caused by carabid and staphylinid beetles and small mammals is, therefore, density-dependent, since the rate of predation is higher in years when the pupae are more abundant. This kind of intergeneration mortality is usually referred to as temporal density-dependence to distinguish it from spatial density-dependent effects occurring within a single generation.

Although pupal predation of *O. brumata* is clearly directly density dependent there appears to be a time delay in the action of the predators. This is revealed by the anticlockwise spiral formed when the k-values in successive generations are joined up (Fig. 2.36) (Varley *et al.* 1973). This time-lag in response to changes in the density of the prey population is caused by a reproductive delay in the predator population's numerical response. Another cause of delayed density-dependent mortality in insect

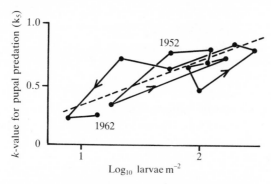

FIG. 2.36. k-values for pupal predation plotted against population density of *Operophtera brumata*. The points for successive years are joined up in a time sequence (see text) (from Varley *et al.* 1973).

populations can be the effect of induced defences in the host tree. After defoliation, for example, the leaves that are produced in the following season can contain higher concentrations of defensive chemicals and this may reduce survival and fecundity of the new generation of herbivores (Chapter 3).

Life table studies of the intergeneration effects of the different components of mortality are essential for an understanding of the factors that influence population change through time. But within each generation, effective predators must seek out their prey which is likely to be distributed unevenly in a spatially complex environment. How efficiently they are able to locate and consume their prey and how they respond to local variations in its density will determine to a large extent their impact on the prey population and, possibly, their value as agents of biological control.

The spatial distribution of attack

In the complex forest environment, prey may be hard to find and individuals are not all equally susceptible to discovery and attack by their natural enemies. Different levels of predation may occur for the same insect species on different kinds of tree or on different parts of the same tree (Eikenbary and Fox 1968). Individuals may hide in bark crevices or feed deep within newly-opened buds where predation pressure may be reduced. The importance of such refuges for the gypsy moth, *Lymantria dispar*, in eastern North America is illustrated by the fact that the number of available sites in the forest for resting, oviposition, and pupation can determine the susceptibility of those stands to outbreaks (Houston and Valentine 1977; Valentine and Houston 1979) (see Chapter 10).

Insects in even more concealed habitats such as those that bore into bark or shoots, mine leaves or form galls may be unavailable to generalist natural enemies and even specialized parasitoids take longer to 'handle' concealed hosts, limiting the number that can be parasitized within the time available. The pine tip moth, *Rhyacionia frustrana*, for example, is less subject to parasitism when feeding on trees with big buds and robust stems than when feeding on small buds (Price *et al.* 1980). Other refuges may include alternative host plants which are not searched by specialized natural enemies and these may be important sources of re-invasion of pest species.

Many predators spend longer searching in areas of high prey density and by exploiting these areas more efficiently, predation may be higher than in low density patches which thus act as a kind of refuge (Rogers and Hubbard 1974; Hassell and May 1974; May 1978; Commins and Hassell 1979). This gives rise to spatial density-dependence, a mechanism which theoretical studies have shown can stabilize the interaction between pre-dator and prey (Hassell 1978; May 1978; but see Kareiva 1987). Two examples of spatial density-dependence from field studies are given in Fig. 2.37.

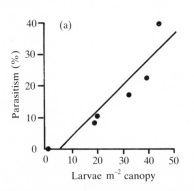 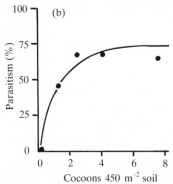

FIG. 2.37. Examples of density-dependent parasitism per patch from field studies (a) parasitism of *Operophtera brumata* on different trees by *Cyzenis albicans*, (b) parasitism of *Neodiprion sertifer* in different plots by *Exenterus abruptorius* (from Hassell 1982).

2.3.4 Natural enemies and biological control

Given the characteristics of different kinds of natural enemies described above and using the insights gained from empirical and theoretical studies, it is possible to make some generalizations about the objectives of biologi-cal control and what attributes natural enemies should have to stand the best chance of success. It is usually assumed that in successful biological control the pest and natural enemy populations exist in a stable low density equilibrium. This suggests that, in general, natural enemies for use in biological control programmes should have a life cycle that is synchronized with that of their specific prey, a well-developed host-finding capacity and an ability to aggregate on dense prey 'patches' and to respond rapidly to increases in their density (Beddington *et al.* 1978). These features are more characteristic of parasitoids and they have certainly been more successfully employed in biological control than predators (Chapter 7). One of the attributes of a 'good' natural enemy, that of spatial density-dependence has been seen as important, even essential, for successful biological control because of its role in establishing a low stable equilibrium density (Beddington *et al.* 1978; Hassell 1980; Heads and Lawton 1983). This view has recently been challenged on the grounds that it has not been identified as an important component in several successful examples of biological control (Murdoch *et al.* 1985; Smith and Maelzer 1986). Reeve and Murdoch (1985), for example, were unable to detect spatial density-dependent parasitism by *Aphytis melinus* on scale insect populations on citrus trees and yet the control achieved seems to be stable and long term. Murdoch *et al.* (1985) suggest that natural enemies that cause local extinctions may be equally effective in biological control and this implies a more significant role for generalist predators which are able to survive local extinctions of one prey species by feeding on alternative ones.

An important consideration in the identification of candidate natural enemies for use in biological control is that their impact on the prey population can vary from place to place. They may, for example, have relatively little impact on prey populations in their native habitat, but may decimate them when both are introduced into a new region. For example, *Cyzenis albicans* does not regulate populations of its host *Operophtera brumata* in Europe (Fig. 2.35) although parasitism levels may sometimes be quite high. In Canada, however, where *O. brumata* is an introduced pest, *C. albicans* causes density-dependent mortality of its host and, together with another introduced parasitoid *Agrypon flaveolatum*, has been extremely successful in halting the spread of *O. brumata* (Embree 1966, 1971; Hassell 1980; see also Chapter 7).

These examples emphasize that, in practice, biological control is essentially an empirical science and the multiplicity of factors that are likely to determine the effectiveness of natural enemies means that it is rarely possible to predict on theoretical grounds alone the outcome of their release in biological control programmes.

2.3.5 Competition

Like the action of some natural enemies, competition can cause density-dependent mortality and so has the potential to regulate insect populations. How often and how intensely insects compete with one another is, therefore, of considerable interest. In order for insects to compete there must be some overlap in their resource requirements, but even then competition is only likely to occur when that resource is in short supply. Since there is a greater overlap in resource requirements between individuals of the same species, *intraspecific* competition is much more frequent than *interspecific* competition, i.e. that between different species of insects.

Competition can occur for a number of different resources such as overwintering or oviposition sites and perhaps even 'enemy-free' space (Lawton 1986) but food is the most common resource for which insects compete. Competition for food is most likely to occur during outbreaks and since they are relatively infrequent events it would seem, superficially at least, that this resource is often not limiting. This line of argument has led some ecologists to conclude that insects must, therefore, be constrained below the carrying capacity of the environment (the maximum theoretical population density it can sustain) by the activities of natural enemies rather than by competition (Hairston *et al*. 1960). As will be seen in the following chapter, it is now widely recognized that although there is often not an absolute shortage of food, there may frequently be a limited time during which food of the right nutritional quality is available, i.e. a relative shortage, and so competition for food may be more frequent than previously supposed. Furthermore, insect feeding may induce both short- and long-term defensive reactions in the host plant so that insects have the potential to interact even though they may not be present on the plant at the same time.

Interspecific competition

Most of the insects that occupy the variety of niches available on trees have little opportunity to compete directly with one another because they are spatially or temporally separated within the habitat. For example, two bark beetle species, *Ips acuminatus* and *Tomicus minor*, that both feed on the inner bark of pine trees in Norway are largely separated along latitudinal and altitudinal gradients. Transects from sea-level in two areas of south-east Norway show that *T. minor*, which has a mainly southerly distribution, occurs from sea-level up to about 400 m whereas *I. acuminatus*, which has a mainly northerly distribution, usually occurs above 200 m (Fig. 2.38). Competition between these two species is thus largely avoided.

There are, nevertheless, some examples of interspecific competition in forest insects and for the two exotic scale insects *Fiorinia externa* and *Tsugaspidiotus tsugae* on hemlock in north-eastern USA, competition may occur even at non-outbreak densities (McClure 1980*b*). Different species of bark beetles and other insects that exploit the bark of weakened trees may compete with one another largely because they are exploiting a discrete resource that is often in short supply and which remains suitable for utilization for only a limited time. In pines, for example, competitive

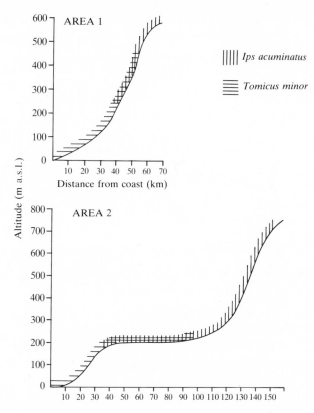

FIG. 2.38. The range of *Tomicus minor* and *Ips acuminatus* in relation to altitude and distance from the coast in south-east Norway (from Bakke 1968).

effects have been reported between the cerambycid, *Monochamus titillator*, and the southern pine beetle, *Dendroctonus frontalis* (Coulson *et al.* 1976), and between *D. frontalis* and the small southern pine engraver, *Ips avulsus* (Payne and Richerson 1985). For some bark beetles, the importance of avoiding interspecific competition is suggested by the fact that some of them respond to the aggregation pheromones of other species and so may avoid trees that have already been colonized by them (Birch and Wood 1975; Byers and Wood 1980; Svihra *et al.* 1980).

Where different species of bark beetle attack the same tree at the same time they usually exploit different parts of the bole and so competitive interactions are minimized. The distribution of attack is determined to some extent by beetle size because it sets an absolute limit to the thickness of bark that can be exploited. An example of this spatial separation for spruce bark beetles in Europe is shown in Fig. 2.39a. Although each species on its own can exploit bark over large areas of the bole, their

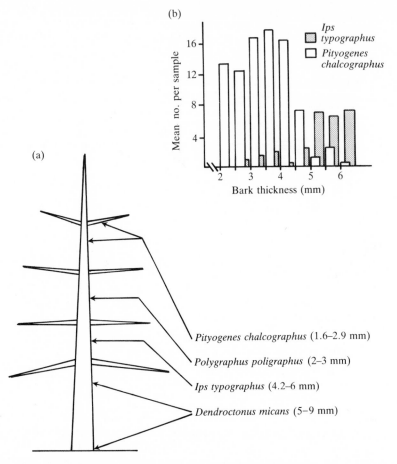

FIG. 2.39. (a) Exploitation of the bark of spruce trees by four bark beetle species in Europe, (b) mean number of *Pityogenes chalcographus* and *Ips typographus* emerging from spruce logs in relation to bark thickness (from Grunwald 1986).

distribution may be more restricted when other species are present, emphasizing the distinction between the potential niche and the actual niche occupied (Price 1984). This difference is illustrated by the emergence pattern of the spruce bark beetles, *Ips typographus* and *Pityogenes chalcographus*, when they colonize the same log (Fig. 2.39b). *Ips typographus* is able to breed in bark down to a thickness of 2.5 mm but loses out in competition with the smaller *P. chalcographus* in bark below 5 mm (Grunwald 1986).

An interesting example of asymmetric competition where only one of the species is adversely affected (Lawton and Hassell 1981) has been reported by West (1985) who demonstrated that early season feeding by leaf-chewing caterpillars caused induced defences in the leaves that reduced the survival of a late-season leafminer species.

Although these and other examples provide clear evidence of inter-specific competition, the question of how widely it occurs and whether it plays a significant role in structuring contemporary communities of herbivorous insects is a subject of considerable debate (Benson 1978; Denno *et al.* 1981; Lawton and Strong 1981; Strong *et al.* 1984; Lawton and Hassell 1984). On balance, present evidence suggests that interspecific competition is too weak or too infrequent to have a significant effect. Certainly, some studies designed specifically to detect it such as that of Bultman and Faeth (1985) on oak leafminers have failed.

In other insect groups, particularly the ants and other social insects as well as some parasitoids, competitive interactions between species are more important (Zwolfer 1971; Lawton and Hassell 1984). One practical consequence of competition between parasitoids that exploit the same host is that potentially it could reduce the efficiency of biological control when multiple introductions are made. This is discussed in Chapter 7 and examples of competitive exclusion of parasitoids are given by Varley *et al.* (1973) and Price (1984).

Intraspecific competition

Intraspecific competition can have a number of effects on insect populations and some results of competition for food among forest Lepidoptera that commonly over-exploit their host plants are given in Table 2.7. During

Table 2.7. *Examples of forest Lepidoptera that regularly over-exploit their food supply, illustrating the effect (+) of an absolute shortage of food caused by the defoliating activities of the larvae*

Insect	Food plant	Starvation	Reduced fecundity	Altered sex-ratio	Increased dispersal
Choristoneura fumiferana	*Abies balsamea*	+	+	−	+
Choristoneura pinus	*Pinus banksiana*	−	+	−	+
Dendrolimus spectabilis	*Pinus thunbergii*	−	−	−	+
Hyphantria cunea	Deciduous trees	−	+	−	−
Lymantria dispar	*Quercus* and others	+	+	+	+
Malacosoma disstria	Deciduous trees	−	+	−	+
Operophtera brumata	*Quercus* and others	+	+	−	+
Orgyia pseudotsugata	*Pseudotsuga menziesii*	+	+	+	+
Phryganidia californica	*Quercus*	+	−	−	+
Zeiraphera diniana	*Larix decidua*	+	+	−	+

From Dempster 1983.

outbreaks, trees may be completely defoliated before development of any of the larvae is complete so that most of them starve to death. Individuals that do survive on a reduced food supply usually form smaller and therefore less fecund adults. An example of this widespread phenomenon is given in Figs 2.40 and 2.41 in which the pine looper moth, *Bupalus piniaria*, reared at high density produces smaller pupae and the resulting

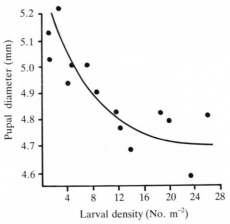

FIG. 2.40. The relationship between larval density and pupal size for female *Bupalus piniaria* (from Klomp 1966).

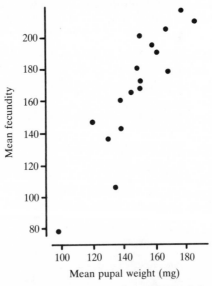

FIG. 2.41. The relationship between pupal weight and fecundity for *Bupalus piniaria* (from Klomp 1968).

moths lay fewer eggs than those developing under less crowded conditions.

Bark beetles also provide some interesting examples of the effects of intraspecific competition and its role in the population dynamics of these highly specialized insects. Many bark beetles that attack living trees must overcome host defensive mechanisms such as resin flow in conifers, a process described more fully in later chapters. A tree is often able to repel attack by small numbers of beetles but when beetles co-operate in a mass-attack, the tree's defences may be overwhelmed. This mass-attack is co-ordinated by the release of an aggregation pheromone by 'pioneer' beetles which are the first to arrive at the tree. Attack by other individuals attracted to the pheromone follows rapidly. However, the initial co-operation can turn to competition as numbers build up on the tree and there is a fine dividing line between these two processes; too few beetles and the attack may fail, too many and there will be insufficient food for all the offspring. This effect can be measured by determining the number of offspring per attacking adult (the productivity) at different attack densities and this is shown for the fir engraver, *Scolytus ventralis*, in Fig. 2.42 (Berryman 1979). The productivity curve which results from the interaction of co-operation and competition initially increases and then declines as attack density increases. The importance of controlling attack density is shown by the fact that some species have evolved anti-aggregation pheromones which are released by colonizing beetles to divert attack onto adjacent trees once the original tree is fully colonized (Fig. 2.43) (Chapter 9).

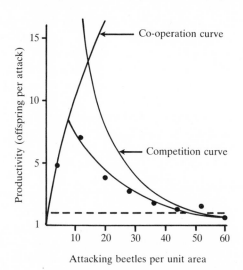

FIG. 2.42. The productivity curve of *Scolytus ventralis* fitted to field data. It results from a combination of the curves for co-operation and competition (from Berryman 1979).

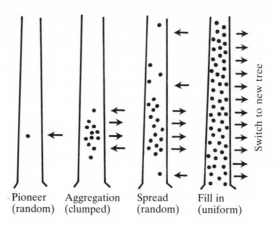

Pioneer   Aggregation   Spread   Fill in
(random)   (clumped)   (random) (uniform)

FIG. 2.43. The distribution of bark beetles on a tree during four stages of mass attack. Incoming arrows represent attraction and outgoing ones repulsion from a particular area as a result of, respectively, aggregation and anti-aggregation pheromones (from Berryman 1982).

The effects of intraspecific competition on both larvae and adults of the spruce bark beetle, *Ips typographus*, have been studied in the laboratory by Anderbrandt *et al.* (1985). Experiments were carried out on spruce logs with densities of 0.5–32 females per 100 cm^2 of bark surface, which covered the range of densities commonly found in the field. About 80 per cent of females eventually re-emerged from the logs but they did so earlier at high densities (Fig. 2.44a), so contributing to the dramatic reduction in the number of offspring produced as density increases (Fig. 2.44b). Offspring which developed at the higher densities were smaller and had less fat which provides energy for flight (Fig. 2.44c), and they were also less fecund. Interestingly, males which emerge from crowded populations had a reduced capacity for pheromone production (Fig. 2.44d) which could affect their ability to initiate a mass-attack on trees. These effects on adult beetle behaviour and on the number and quality of their offspring could significantly affect the population dynamics of this beetle.

Another feature of crowded populations is that individual larvae or adults may disperse to new host plants. Larvae of the gypsy moth, *Lymantria dispar*, are much more likely to disperse, by 'ballooning' on silk threads, from high density populations than those from sparse ones because more frequent contact between individuals disturbs feeding. In addition, adult female moths which develop as larvae in crowded populations lay smaller eggs and the resulting larvae are more active and again more likely to disperse (Leonard 1974). Similarly, in many aphid populations winged individuals (alatae) are formed in response to crowding and this is a regular feature of their ecology (Dixon 1985).

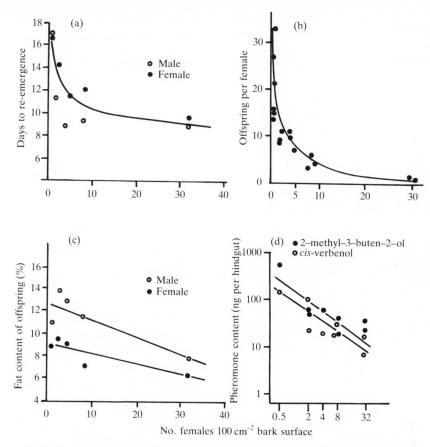

FIG. 2.44. Some effects of intraspecific competition on *Ips typographus* (see text). (a) Time to re-emergence of inoculated male (open circles) and female beetles, (b) number of offspring emerging per female inoculated, (c) percent fat content of male (open circles) and female offspring, (d) the amount of pheromone components *cis*-verbenol (open circles) and 2-methyl-3-buten-2-ol in hindguts of male offspring after exposure to α-pinene and myrcene. Lines in (a) and (c) fitted by eye (data from Anderbrandt *et al.* 1985).

2.3.6 The regulation of insect populations

Although negative feedback or density-dependent mortality factors described in the previous sections are essential for population regulation, their relative importance in natural populations will depend on a number of factors related to the life history of the insects. Since Varley and Gradwell's work on the winter moth, *Operophtera brumata*, a number of insect life tables have been published and summaries showing key or density-dependent factors can be found in Dempster (1983), Price (1984), and Strong *et al.* (1984). Taken as a whole they show that density-dependence, which was most frequently due to the action of natural enemies, was detected in only about half of the populations. Among Lepidoptera, however, a group containing many forest pests, competition for food is probably a more important factor limiting population growth (Table 2.7). Similarly, among bark beetle populations, as we have already emphasized, competition appears to be the most important factor regulating populations.

Given the importance of density-dependence in population dynamics it is somewhat surprising to find that it appears to be absent in many insect populations. In fact this may be a false impression because density-dependence is difficult to detect by conventional life table analysis. In these analyses, populations are usually expressed as numbers per unit area rather than per unit of resource, which may vary from generation to generation, so it is difficult to estimate the impact of intraspecific competition (Dempster 1983). There can also be problems in detecting density-dependence caused by natural enemies especially where time delays are involved (Hassell 1985). Furthermore, the effects of spatial density-dependence, acting within a generation remain undetected in conventional life table analyses which are based on mean host density per generation (Hassell 1985; Murdoch and Reeve 1987; but see Dempster and Pollard 1986). Further studies are needed to clarify these important aspects of insect population dynamics.

Whatever ultimately regulates particular insect populations, it acts against a background of density-independent environmental factors. Such factors may influence the level at which regulation occurs and by altering habitat favourability (e.g. changes in weather patterns or forest management practices) may allow insects to 'escape' from the regulating effects of natural enemies. This may lead to outbreaks which are ultimately controlled by competition or disease. These kinds of interaction have an important influence on the outbreak characteristics of forest pests that were outlined in Chapter 1. But insects interact not only with the biotic and abiotic environment but with the host trees on which they feed and the important role of this interaction in the dynamics of insect populations is being increasingly recognized. This is considered in the following chapter.

3

Trees as a source of food for insects

Because forests cover extensive areas and may be a more or less permanent features of the landscape, trees as a whole are clearly a large and highly predictable resource in time and space. In fact, as emphasized in the previous chapter, trees represent many different kinds of food resource for insects and these different resources may vary in time of appearance (e.g. leaves) or abundance (e.g. flowers and seeds) from year to year or may show seasonal changes in food quality (e.g. leaves and phloem sap) (see also Chapter 4). In addition, many tree tissues contain toxic or repellant secondary compounds which affect their nutritional quality. Thus in common with other insect herbivores, those that feed on trees, are faced with the problem of finding food in sufficient quantity and quality and since the availability of food ultimately affects survival it is an important factor in their population dynamics.

Because different parts of the tree such as bark, wood, leaves, and seeds on which insects feed are of different 'value' to the tree and play different roles in its economy, insects feeding on them will have different effects on tree growth and survival. These aspects are covered in the following chapter on the nature of forest pests.

3.1 NUTRITIONAL REQUIREMENTS OF HERBIVOROUS INSECTS

The nutritional requirements of insects are qualitatively similar to those of other animals and they typically require proteins, carbohydrates, fatty acids, sterols, vitamins, and minerals for normal growth (Beck and Reese 1976; Dadd 1984; Hagen *et al.* 1984). Unlike vertebrates, however, insects are unable to synthesize sterols so these must be obtained from their normal food or from symbiotic micro-organisms. The proportions of the major nutrients that constitute a nutritionally balanced diet, however, depend on the particular adaptations that insects have evolved to utilize their different natural foods which may range from mammalian blood or plant sap to rotting flesh and the leaves of trees.

Feeding on living plants, where the balance of nutrients is very different from that of the insects themselves, has been achieved by relatively few groups of insects and feeding on plant detritus, micro-organisms, or animals is much more common in evolutionary terms. Thus, living plants seem to have represented a 'nutritional hurdle' for insects (Southwood 1973). A number of factors have probably contributed to this but the relatively low concentration of nitrogen (N) in the form of proteins and amino acids in plants has been universally identified as an important limiting factor because it determines many aspects of insect growth and development (Southwood 1973; McNeill and Southwood 1978; Mattson 1980). The influence of N concentration is often most clearly seen in the sap-feeding insects and for the hemlock scale, *Fiorinia externa*, survival, fecundity, and population size are all related to the N content of a number of host species (Fig. 3.1). For some species of chewing insects, however, total N levels may be less important than the form in which the N occurs. Wint (1983), for example, found that growth of larvae of the winter moth, *Operophtera brumata*, on six common host plants was correlated with the amount of protein available which was less than the total amount present because of the protein complexing effects of phenolic compounds in the leaves (see section 3.3).

3.2 NUTRIENT CONTENT OF TREES IN RELATION TO STRUCTURE AND FUNCTION

The different tissues that make up the living tree such as roots and shoots, wood and bark, buds, leaves, flowers, and seeds have characteristic nutrient levels which are largely related to their role in the structure and function of the tree and which also vary in a more or less predictable way during the season. In the spring, reserves are mobilized from sites of storage in the parenchyma tissue of roots, stem, and in conifers also from leaves and transported in xylem and phloem to sites of active growth, especially new leaves and shoots. New leaves eventually become net exporters of photosynthates which are initially used to maintain new growth and later on to restore the main reserves before the end of the growing season. In deciduous trees there is a particularly strong annual cycle of carbohydrate concentration, reserves being considerably depleted during the flush of spring growth followed by a progressive build-up during the growing season. In conifers the older leaves are important storage organs and because photosynthetically active leaves are present in the spring as new shoots expand, seasonal variations in reserves are less marked (Kramer and Kozlowski 1979).

The economy of the tree based on supply and demand is usually described in terms of 'sources' of photosynthate, predominantly the young green leaves, and 'sinks' which utilize it either for growth (e.g. developing buds) or storage (e.g. roots). An important feature of this model of tree physio-

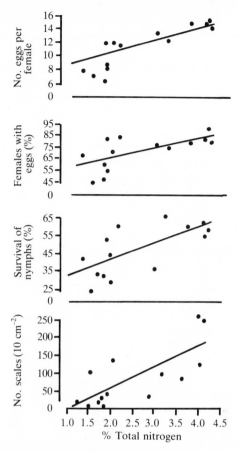

FIG. 3.1. Relationships between the total nitrogen concentration of the young foliage of 14 host species in June during peak colonization by nymphs of *Fiorinia externa* and (from bottom to top) the density of these colonists which survived to maturity, their percent survival, the percentage of females with eggs, and their fecundity (from McClure 1980a).

logy is that it emphasizes that supply and demand are closely linked and levels of photosynthesis will change in relation to the 'strength' of the sink (Wilson 1972; Wareing and Patrick 1975). Thus when trees are partly defoliated during insect outbreaks, the photosynthetic rate of the remaining foliage increases, partly compensating for the loss (Chapter 4).

The limitations of plants as food for insects is nowhere more clearly shown than in the exploitation of trees. Over 90 per cent of the above-ground biomass of forests occurs as wood (Rodin and Basilevic 1967) which is composed largely of cellulose and lignin and contains some of the lowest levels of N of any living material (Mattson 1980). Much of the biomass of the forest, therefore, is inedible to all but a few highly special-ized species many of which have evolved symbiotic associations to enable them to feed on it. The concentration of N in wood is typically around 0.2 per cent dry wt. (Mattson 1980). Variations in its concentration are linked to the ageing processes from its initial production from cambium through sapwood to heartwood as shown semi-diagrammatically in Fig. 3.2 (Cowling and Merrill 1966). The protoplasm of cambial cells is rich in enzymes, peptides, and amino acids but as secondary cell walls develop and lignifica-tion proceeds, most of these cells die and N and other valuable nutrients are redistributed to other parts of the tree.

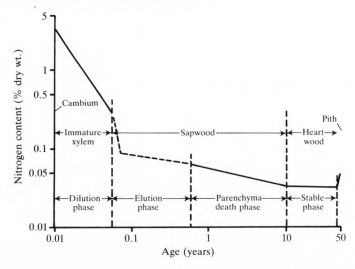

FIG. 3.2. Hypothetical changes in nitrogen content during various stages in the maturation and ageing of xylem tissues in a typical angiosperm or gymnosperm (from Cowling and Merrill 1966).

A significant proportion of the total N content of trees occurs within the leaves. In deciduous broad-leaved trees, concentrations of N at around 2–4 per cent are usually higher than in conifers which have average values of only 1–2 per cent (Mattson 1980). However, there are distinct seasonal changes in N and also water content in both conifers and broad-leaved trees (Fig. 3.3) so that correct timing with leaf phenology is essential if the available N is to be fully exploited by insects (section 3.4.2). In most conifers, leaves of different age classes are present on the tree at any one time and their function and, therefore, their nutrient content, changes as they age. The youngest needles usually contain the highest levels of N and contribute most to photosynthesis whereas older needles are photosyn-

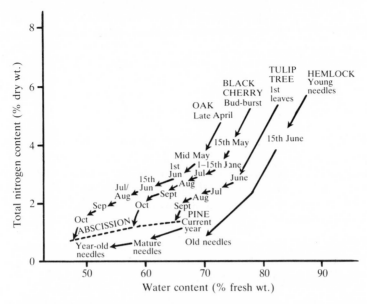

FIG. 3.3. Seasonal trends in leaf water and nitrogen content of some tree species (after Slansky and Scriber 1985).

thetically less active and become increasingly more important as storage organs especially for carbohydrates.

Soluble nutrients are moved around the tree in the xylem and phloem and, naturally, show distinct changes in concentration in relation to the mobilization of reserves and seasonal growth. Thus peaks occur in the spring and, in broad-leaved trees, also in the autumn as nutrients are removed from leaves prior to leaf fall and stored until mobilized in the following spring. In northern latitudes, birch and willow translocate around 14 per cent of their nitrogen from stems and roots into leaves early in summer but by late autumn, 50–60 per cent is removed again (Chapin *et al*. 1980). Xylem sap is important in the transport of inorganic nutrients and water from the roots and is especially low in organic N although carbohydrate content can be quite high. For example, the xylem sap of maples in spring is so sweet (up to 7 per cent sucrose) that it can be tapped and converted to maple syrup (Kramer and Kozlowski 1979). Most of the organic compounds are translocated in phloem sap. Concentrations of organic N are much higher than in xylem sap and sucrose is translocated from sites of storage and from photosynthetically active leaves to growing parts.

Flowers are often consumed by defoliating insects and the pollen they contain is a rich source of N. Seeds may also contain high levels of N; stone pine seeds, for example, contain around 2 per cent and those of horse chestnut around 7 per cent N (dry wt.). Sometimes, protein may be the principal food reserve in seeds, in which case the N content may then exceed 30 per cent (Kramer and Kozlowski 1979).

3.3 FOOD QUALITY AND PLANT DEFENCE

These broad differences in the major nutrient content of tree tissues provide at best only an approximate indication of their nutritional quality for insects. This is because many of the tissues are suffused with chemicals that may be repellent, unpalatable or poisonous. These secondary chemicals (Fraenkel 1959; Ehrlich and Raven 1964) play an important part in defending plants against attack by insects as well as other kinds of herbivore.

3.3.1 Defences against insect feeding

Plants have three main mechanisms of resistance to insect attack: non-preference, antibiosis, and tolerance. These different facets of plant resistance are discussed more fully in Chapter 6. In this section we mainly consider those defence mechanisms that directly affect feeding insects (antibiosis). Such defences are usually preformed within different tissues but some are induced in response to insect attack.

Preformed or constitutive defences

Trees typically contain secondary chemicals such as tannins, terpenes, and lignin within their tissues, which are often present in quite high concentrations. Terpenes, for example, can make up as much as 20 per cent of the dry weight of *Eucalyptus* leaves (Morrow and Fox 1980). Because they occur at high concentration and their effects on feeding insects are dose-dependent, these secondary chemicals are sometimes called 'quantitative' defences. Similarities in their mode of action and their wide distribution among tree species is partly explained by current theories of anti-herbivore defence based on the co-evolutionary interaction between plants and insects and this is discussed in the following section.

Tannins have been particularly well studied in relation to plant defence and these chemicals appear to be effective against many chewing insects through their ability to form complexes with protein and so reduce its availability to insects when ingested with their normal food (Feeny 1968, 1969, 1970). Insects on a diet rich in tannins tend to develop more slowly and are ultimately less fecund than those feeding on tissues low in tannin.

In conifers, terpenes are present in many different tissues such as buds, leaves, bark, and wood and provide an effective defence against a range of different insects. In Douglas fir, for example, terpenes are the most important component of young foliage affecting growth, survival and fecundity of the western spruce budworm, *Choristoneura occidentalis* (Cates *et al.* 1983). Terpenes, which are an important constituent of conifer resin are, however, probably best known for their role in defence against bark beetles. When bark beetles attempt to initiate galleries in the bark of healthy trees, resin flows from severed ducts and can 'pitch-out' attacking beetles and so prevent colonization (Vité and Wood 1961) (Fig. 3.4). As well as providing this kind of physical defence, some of the constituent monoterpenes of resin are also toxic to the beetles. For example, α-pinene is highly toxic to the fir engraver, *Scolytus ventralis*, although it has little effect on the mountain pine beetle, *Dendroctonus ponderosae*. Limonene on the other hand is highly toxic to both species (Table 3.1).

Physical characteristics of tree tissues can also be important in determining how much tissue is eaten by insects, and Coley (1983) found in a study of herbivory among lowland tropical rainforest trees, that leaf toughness appeared to be the single most important factor correlated with damage levels. Tissues which contain large amounts of lignin are difficult to eat and

FIG. 3.4. Resin tube on lodgepole pine formed in response to attack by *Dendroctonus ponderosae*. The beetle has become entrapped in the resin.

Table 3.1. *Toxicity of monoterpenes to adult Scolytus and Dendroctonus bark beetles*

Monoterpene	% Mortality			
	Scolytus		Dendroctonus	
	83 ppm	33 ppm	53 ppm	26 ppm
α-pinene	100	89	10	8
β-pinene	100	67	57	18
δ-3-carene	93	56	63	36
Limonene	100	100	71	40
Myrcene	100	94	—	35

From Raffa and Berryman 1987.

relatively indigestible. The leaf beetle, *Plagiodera versicolora*, for example, feeds at a slower rate on mature, tough leaves of *Salix* spp. where mandibular wear was found to be much higher than when feeding on young leaves (Raupp 1985). Similarly, larvae of the spruce bark beetle, *Dendroctonus micans*, when feeding on bark with a high lignin content (Fig. 3.5) suffer higher mortality, take longer to develop and eventually form smaller adult beetles (Fig. 3.6).

External physical defences such as hairs, trichomes or spines may also deter insects or prevent feeding. The aphid, *Tuberculoides annulatus*, is prevented from feeding on the holm oak, *Quercus ilex*, because movement over the undersurface of the leaves is prevented by dense mats of trichomes and the aphids are unable to hold on to the smooth and shiny upper surface of the leaves (Kennedy 1986) (Fig. 3.7). The leaves of the aphid's normal host *Q. robur* are trichome free.

Co-evolution and tree defences

The quantitative defences of trees, which are largely based on secondary chemicals common to many different tree species, contrast with the 'qualitative' defences of herbaceous plants typically based on low concentrations of highly toxic chemicals such as glycosides and alkaloids, with different herb species usually containing distinct toxins. These different defensive characteristics are assumed to have arisen as a consequence of different probabilities of attack by insects on herbs and trees, related to the obvious differences in spatial distribution, abundance, and longevity (Feeny 1975, 1976; Rhoades and Cates 1976; Rhoades 1979). Thus trees and other perennial plants which are long-lived and tend to occur in association with many other individuals of the same species, are 'apparent' and likely to be encountered relatively frequently by insects. Indeed individual trees may support many generations of insects and so must be well defended if they are to survive and reproduce. By producing chemicals

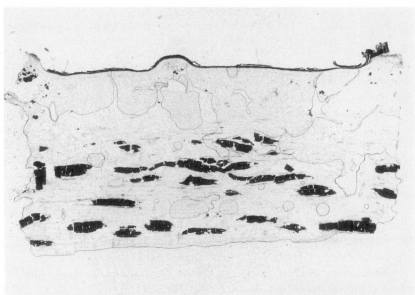

FIG. 3.5. Sections of spruce bark with a low (top) and high (bottom) lignin content. Bark with a high lignin content affects growth and survival of *Dendroctonus micans* larvae.

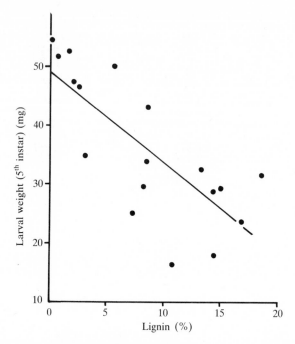

Fɪɢ. 3.6. The weight of larval *Dendroctonus micans* in relation to the lignin content of spruce bark (from Wainhouse and Cross, unpublished).

that affect such basic processes as digestion, the defences of trees should be less readily subject to rapid counter-adaptation and so be effective against both specialist and generalist insects. Ephemeral herbaceous plants on the other hand, must grow quickly and disperse their seeds to allow rapid colonization of new areas and this temporal and spatial unpredictability reduces the likelihood of discovery by many potential insect herbivores. In this situation, 'unique' toxins should be highly effective because, although more readily subject to counter-adaptation by specialized insects, they exert less selection pressure against generalist feeders which in any case could not develop resistance to all the toxins encountered in a range of herbaceous food plants. These two contrasting modes of chemical defence are summarized in Table 3.2.

Although this general theory of anti-herbivore chemistry shows how the broad chemical differences between trees and other kinds of plants might have arisen, it does not explain current levels of attack on different species. Fox and Macauley (1977), for example, found that endemic levels of insect grazing in *Eucalyptus* forests were high, despite a high incidence of tannins and other phenolic compounds. High feeding rates, which may have been a response to the low availability of N in eucalypts, appeared to be respon-

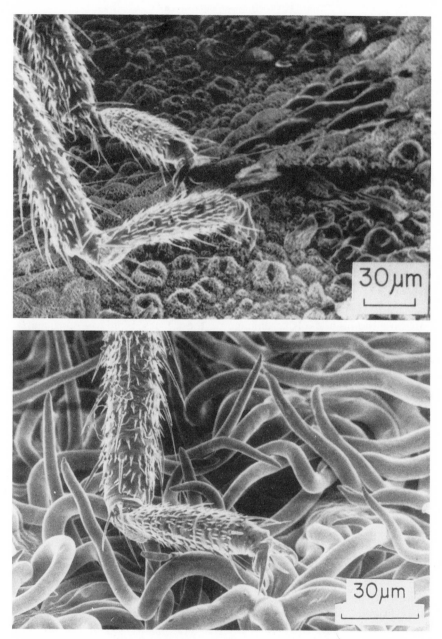

FIG. 3.7. Scanning electron microscope picture of the lower surface of the leaves of two oak species. The trichomes on *Quercus ilex* (bottom) prevent aphid tarsi gripping the surface. Trichomes are absent on *Q. robur* (top) (C. E. J. Kennedy, personal communication).

Table 3.2. *Defensive characteristics of herbaceous and perennial plants based on co-evolutionary theories of anti-herbivore defences*

Plant features	Herbs and ephemeral species	Trees and perennial species
Life history	Short-lived	Persistent
Community	Diverse	Simple
Chance of detection	Low	High
Evolutionary consequences of herbivory:		
Defence	Toxin=qualitative	Digestibility-reducing; dose-dependent=quantitative
Concentration and cost	Low	High
Effective against	Generalists	All species
Counter-adaptation	Easy by specialists	Very difficult, but possible
Examples	Alkaloids, cardiac glycosides, glucosinolates, non-protein amino-acids, terpenes[a]	Silica, tannins, terpenes[a], lignin, toughness

[a] Terpenes appear to have the characteristics of both qualitative and quantitative defences (see text).
After Fox 1981.

sible for the high levels of damage on these trees. Similarly, no negative correlation was found between foliage phenol content of Douglas fir and defoliation caused by the western spruce budworm, *Choristoneura occidentalis* (Cates *et al*. 1983). These results clearly indicate that the quantitative defences of trees are not immune to counter-adaptation and it has been shown experimentally that some insects that feed on other plants are able to digest food normally even though it contains large amounts of tannin (Bernays 1978; Bernays *et al*. 1981).

Since no uniform physical or chemical defences can be considered as immune to counter-adaptation by evolving pests, there is now considerable interest in both the importance of variation between individual plants and in the range of different secondary chemicals in contributing to the long-term stability of defences against herbivory (Schultz 1983).

Variation in tree defences

Because similar kinds of secondary chemicals occur among many different tree species, there would appear, at least superficially, to be an underlying uniformity in tree defences. In fact, considerable quantitative and qualitative variability in secondary chemicals exists both within and between trees. Some differences are related to the 'apparency' of the different tissues (Feeny 1976). The young leaves of deciduous trees, for example, are less well defended than older leaves (section 3.4.2, Figs 3.14 and 3.15). They are less apparent to herbivores because they are present on trees for only a short time and flushing date can vary from tree to tree and from year to year. Young seedling trees appear to be less apparent than mature trees and may also be less well defended (Fowler 1984).

Variability between individual trees has been strikingly demonstrated in two studies of scale insects which have shown that sub-populations can be so adapted to individual host trees that their survival is considerably reduced when they are transferred to nearby individuals of the same host species (Edmunds and Alstad 1978; Wainhouse and Howell 1983). Edmunds and Alstad speculated that monoterpenes, which are known to be under strong genetic control (Hanover 1966, 1967; Sturgeon 1979) were responsible for the differences they observed between individual pine trees. A further example is provided by Douglas fir and the western spruce budworm, *Choristoneura occidentalis*. There is considerable geographic and individual variation in the terpene chemistry of the leaves of Douglas fir and this affects budworm development. Budworms adapted to the average 'pattern' of terpenes are less successful on trees that diverge from this norm (Cates *et al*. 1983).

Induced defences

Induced defences are an important mechanism of plant resistance to attack by pathogenic fungi (Bailey and Mansfield 1982; Kuc 1984) and their role in reducing insect attack is now established in some cases. One of the first and most widely studied induced defensive reactions is that of the dynamic or hypersensitive wound response in the bark of conifers (Reid *et al*. 1967; Berryman 1969; Christiansen and Horntvedt 1983). Bark beetles that are not repelled by primary resin flow, excavate a tunnel in the bark during the first phase of gallery construction. This stimulates a wound reaction in the surrounding bark as the tissues respond to invasion by fungi that are carried by the beetles. Invasion by the symbiotic fungi induces rapid necrosis of cells around the wound and stimulates the local synthesis and deposition of secondary resin (Russell and Berryman 1976; Bordasch and Berryman 1977). Thus a barrier to further fungal infection and beetle feeding is created in the bark (Fig. 3.8).

Defences can also be induced in leaves following attack by defoliators and may affect both nutrient content and the concentration of secondary chemicals. These biochemical changes may occur rapidly, sometimes within hours and affect partially damaged leaves. Longer term changes can also occur, affecting the foliage consumed by the following generation of insects and these defences frequently have relatively long relaxation times.

Rapidly induced defences are stimulated in the leaves of birch trees which have suffered mechanical or insect feeding damage and, in general, affected leaves are less palatable to insects. When larvae of the autumnal moth, *Epirrita autumnata*, feed on damaged leaves, they grow more slowly and take longer to develop than when feeding on undamaged leaves. These

FIG. 3.8. Dynamic wound response in the bark of a conifer. The outer bark around the wound has been removed.

effects appear to result from, among other things, an increase in the phenolic content of the leaves (Niemela *et al.* 1979; Tuomi *et al.* 1984). An interesting feature of rapidly-induced defences is that chemical changes can also occur in adjacent undamaged leaves on the same tree and these may also become less palatable to insects (Edwards and Wratten 1983).

One of the first observations of long-term induced defences was that on larch trees defoliated by the larch budmoth, *Zeiraphera diniana*, in the Engadine valley in Switzerland (Baltensweiler *et al.* 1977). The new needles on previously defoliated trees grow slowly, often to only half their normal length, usually contain more raw fibre and less N and, in addition, buds and needles may be covered with sticky resin. The survival of young budmoth larvae that feed on these needles is reduced and they develop into less fecund adults. Long-term changes are also induced in the leaves of birch trees defoliated by *Epirrita autumnata*. The new leaves of defoliated trees have a lower N content and an increased phenolic content and the effects persist for more than one season (Fig. 3.9) (Tuomi *et al.* 1984). The fecundity of *E. autumnata* feeding on these leaves can be reduced by more than 70 per cent (Haukioja *et al.* 1985*b*).

The ecological significance of the ephemeral rapidly-induced changes in leaves following insect attack has yet to be firmly established, especially as in many cases the effects on the insects themselves appear on the whole to

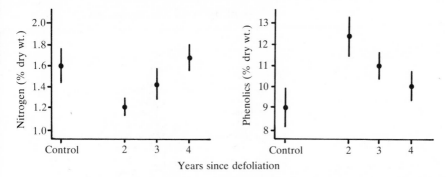

FIG. 3.9. Nitrogen and phenolic content of birch leaves in relation to defoliation history of the trees. Bars denote standard deviations of means (from Tuomi *et al.* 1984).

be fairly small (Fowler and Lawton 1985) and highly variable (Haukioja and Hanhimaki 1985).

Long-term induced defences on the other hand can have a much greater impact on insects and their ecological effects are more clearly established. One of the most interesting is the effect of delayed action (only the new leaves are better defended) in contributing to cyclic changes in the population density of insects such as *Z. diniana* in Switzerland and *E. autumnata* in the Scandinavian mountain chain and northern Finland (Tenow 1972; Baltensweiler *et al.* 1977) (Chapters 1 and 2) (Fig. 3.9). Long-term induced defences are implicated in the periodic outbreaks of *E. autumnata* because they only occur following defoliation of birch provenances from within the outbreak area but not in ones from outside it (Haukioja *et al.* 1981; Haukioja and Hanhimaki 1985). Rapidly-induced defences on the other hand occur in birch provenances from both inside and outside the outbreak area.

3.3.2 Secondary chemicals and feeding specializations

Monophagous or oligophagous insects which feed on one or a few related tree species are able to tolerate the secondary chemicals present in their normal host and indeed for some insects, their presence may be essential for normal development (van Emden 1978). Many species are also able to cue-in on certain secondary chemicals which function as 'token' stimuli in the process of finding and accepting suitable hosts (Chapter 9).

The behavioural effect of some secondary chemicals is shown in Table 3.3 from which it is evident that the same chemical can have different effects on different insects. The study of Tahvanainen *et al.* (1985) on willow leaf beetles is a good example of how secondary chemicals can

Table 3.3. *The behavioural effects of some secondary chemicals*

Chemical	Insect	Effect
α-pinene	*Dendroctonus brevicomis*	Attractant
	Dendroctonus frontalis	Attractant
	Dendroctonus pseudotsugae	Attractant
	Tomicus piniperda	Attractant
	Hylobius pales	Attractant
	Panolis flammea	Oviposition stimulant
	Choristoneura fumiferana	Oviposition stimulant
3-carene	*Dendroctonus brevicomis*	Attractant
	Dendroctonus frontalis	Attractant
	Tomicus piniperda	Repellent
Juglone	*Scolytus multistriatus*	Deterrent
	Scolytus quadrispinosus	Feeding stimulant
Salicortin	*Galerucella lineola*	Deterrent
	Lochmaea capreae	Deterrent
	Phratora vitellinae	Feeding stimulant
	Plagiodera versicolora	Deterrent

See also Tables 9.1 and 9.2. From Gilbert and Norris 1968, Oksanen *et al.* 1970, Payne 1970, Städler 1974, Tahvanainen *et al.* 1985, Leather 1987, Schroeder 1988, and references in Hsiao 1985.

determine feeding preferences. In this study they found that the extent of feeding by four different species was determined mainly by the phenolic glycosides present in different willows. Both the total phenolic glycoside content and the number and relative concentration of different glycosides appeared to be important (Fig. 3.10). In experimental trials, only *Phratora vitellinae* feeds on *Salix nigricans* to any significant extent and is normally found on this species in the field. It has a very high total phenolic glycoside (PG) content, dominated by salicortin which acts as a feeding stimulant for this beetle. *Salix caprea*, on which the other three leaf beetles readily fed, is not an acceptable host for *P. vitellinae* because it has a very low overall concentration of PG, low levels of the feeding stimulant salicortin and also contains unusual PGs such as triandrin and two unidentified compounds not present in the normal host.

Insect feeding patterns within trees can also be influenced by the distribution of secondary chemicals. Like most members of its genus, the pine sawfly, *Neodiprion rugifrons*, eats only old pine foliage. For this insect a single resin acid (13-keto-8(14)-podocarpen-18-oic acid) appears to be responsible for most of the deterrent effect of young needles (Ikeda *et al.* 1977). The concentration of this chemical decreases as the needles mature

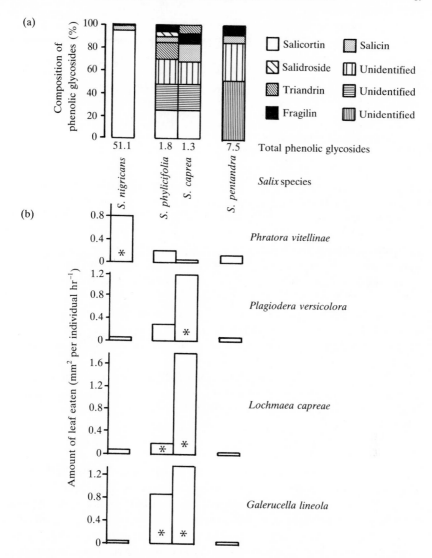

FIG. 3.10. (a) The phenolic glycoside content of the leaves of four species of willow in relation to, (b) the feeding patterns of four species of adult leaf beetle. Both plants and insects are native to eastern Finland. Species of willow on which the beetles are commonly found in the field are indicated with an asterisk (data from Tahvanainen *et al.* 1985).

and they become increasingly acceptable as food. Other examples of secondary chemical variation within trees are discussed in section 3.4.2.

3.4 INSECT LIFE CYCLES IN RELATION TO THE QUANTITY AND QUALITY OF FOOD

3.4.1 Dietary adaptations

Low nutrient levels

In general, insects that feed on tissues of particularly low nutritional quality such as wood tend to have long life cycles and large consumption rates. Xylem-sap feeders such as cicadas have life cycles that can last for up to 17 years as a consequence of feeding on a poor quality diet that is difficult to extract from the tree (White and Strehl 1978). Planthoppers which also feed on xylem sap, have enormous ingestion rates although their digestive efficiencies are similar to those of insects feeding on more nitrogen rich diets (McNeill and Southwood 1978).

The reduction in nutrient content that occurs in some leaves in response to attack (Fig. 3.9) may be an integral part of the plant's defence mechanism, contributing to the reduction in fecundity, increased larval development time, and increased risk of attack by natural enemies (Feeny 1976; Price *et al.* 1980; Moran and Hamilton 1980). However, in the long run, insects may simply eat more of a tissue which is nutritionally inadequate so that the plants suffer more rather than less damage (Fox and Macauley 1977).

The role of symbiotic micro-organisms

Carbohydrate, which forms the main energy source for herbivorous insects, is abundant in plants. However, it occurs largely as the complex polysaccharide cellulose which insects are unable to break down because they lack the necessary cellulolytic enzymes. Many rely instead on associated symbiotic micro-organisms which do have the ability to digest cellulose. Wood-feeding insects usually contain micro-organisms within their gut although some carry specific symbiotic fungi which infect and decay the wood around the galleries. Woodwasps such as *Sirex noctilio*, for example, introduce an *Amylostereum* fungus during oviposition which decays the wood and provides nutrients for the developing larvae. Some insects which inhabit wood have come to depend solely on fungus as a source of food, as in the case of ambrosia beetles (Chapter 4). Termites, which are perhaps the most voracious of wood feeders, are associated with a complex of external and internal symbiotic micro-organisms including fungi, bacteria, and protozoa (Batra and Batra 1979).

Micro-organisms may also be important in increasing the availability of N for insects. *Azotobacter*, which is a common gut symbiont occurring in many aphid species and in *Sirex* may be able to provide additional N by fixing it from the atmosphere (McNeill and Southwood 1978).

3.4.2 Temporal variations in the quantity and quality of food

Temporal variation in the quantity and quality of food available are an important cause of fluctuations in forest insect populations. Seed-feeding insects face a particularly acute problem because seeds, which are usually only present on older trees, vary considerably in abundance from year to year (Fig. 3.11) and in some years may be completely absent. Insects that feed on seeds, therefore, often have an extended diapause that enables them to survive periods of low seed incidence and development is resumed in those conditions that are likely to favour seed production (see Chapters 2 and 4).

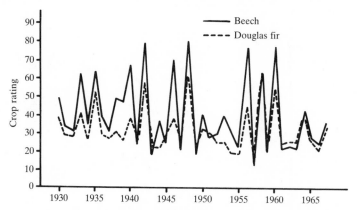

FIG. 3.11. Cone crop ratings of Douglas fir and beech in The Netherlands over a 37-year period (from la Bastide and van Vredenburch 1970).

Insects that feed on young leaves of deciduous trees also exploit an unpredictable resource, not because of large variations in abundance from year to year but because of variation in the precise time of budburst and the subsequent rapid decline in nutritional quality. There are large differences in the median time of budburst for broad-leaved trees (Fig. 3.12) so that insect emergence needs to be synchronized with specific hosts. There can also be considerable intraspecific variation in budburst, with early or late flushing individuals occurring in the same population (Fig. 3.13). Seasonal factors also influence the time of budburst each year and this can lead to asynchrony because insect and host may respond differently to changes in environmental conditions (Fig. 2.29).

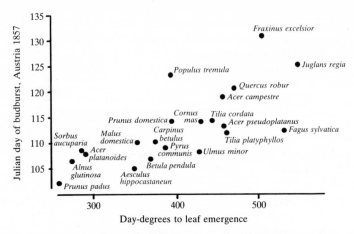

FIG. 3.12. Median day of budburst for trees in central Europe. Species from the lower left to the upper right flush progressively later (from Lechowicz 1984).

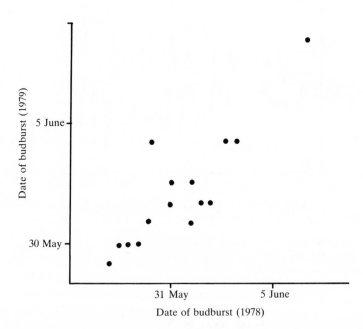

FIG. 3.13. Time of budburst of individual birches in consecutive years at Jesnal-vaara in Finland (from Haukioja *et al.* 1985*a*).

The decline in nutritional quality of birch and oak leaves following budburst is shown in Figs 3.14 and 3.15. In both species, N and water content are high in young leaves but decline during the season, while tannin and phenol content both increase with leaf age. For species such as the winter moth, *Operophtera brumata*, which feed on oak, timing of emergence of young larvae with the appearance of the young nutritious leaves is critical. The consequences of asynchrony are shown diagrammatically in Fig. 3.16. Larvae which emerge late must feed on the older tougher leaves of poor nutritional quality and, consequently, small larvae suffer a high mortality. When egg hatch occurs too early, many larvae die of starvation before the buds have opened.

The young needles of pines are also relatively rich in N, but unlike oak

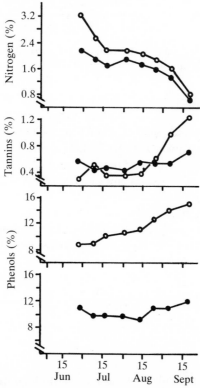

● Low altitude (100 m a.s.l.)
○ High altitude (230 m a.s.l.)

FIG. 3.14. Seasonal trends in the concentration of nitrogen, phenols and tannins in birch leaves. Lines connecting points are means from sample trees (after Haukioja *et al.* 1978).

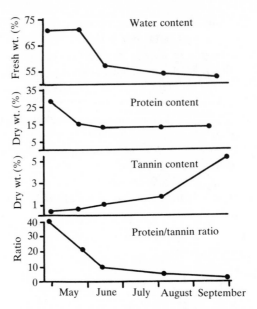

FIG. 3.15. Seasonal variation of water content, protein content, tannin content and
protein/tannin ratio of oak leaves (from Feeny 1970).

leaves are well-defended because they contain large amounts of resin. In a
study of the insects feeding on mature Scots pine, Larsson and Tenow
(1980) found that most species fed on 1-year-old needles which were of
intermediate nutritive quality (Table 3.4). This suggests that in pine-feeding
insects at least, there is a trade-off between the exploitation of the nutritious
but well-defended young leaves and older leaves which are less nutritious
but also less well-defended.

Some insects may respond to temporal and spatial changes in nutrient
levels within trees by switching to different feeding sites. Defoliators, for
example, will often feed on the more nutritious flowers when they appear.
Similarly, the pine aphid, *Cinara pini*, moves from feeding on the bark of
young internodes in the top of the tree in early summer to the older
internodes lower down later on in the summer in response to soluble N
levels in the phloem (Fig. 3.17). During the autumn, many aphids appear
on the younger internodes prior to egg laying on the needles (Larsson
1985).

3.4.3 Reproduction and dispersal in relation to food quality

The effects of food quality on reproduction and dispersal have been particularly well studied in aphids which have a short generation time and can

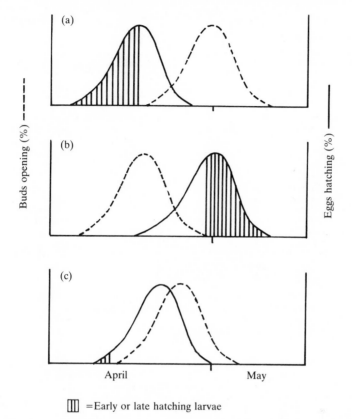

[[[=Early or late hatching larvae

FIG. 3.16. Three theoretical effects of variation in the time of budburst of oaks in relation to egg hatch on mortality of *Operophtera brumata*. Early or late hatching larvae starve or disperse (from Feeny 1976).

respond rapidly to seasonal changes in the host plant. The reproductive rate of the sycamore aphid, *Drepanosiphum platanoidis*, has two distinct seasonal peaks in relation to the amino-N content of the phloem sap (Dixon, 1970). Soluble N content is high during the spring flush as nutrients are translocated in the phloem to the growing leaves (Fig. 3.18). The aphids complete development early in the year and begin to reproduce during this period of high N availability. Reproduction reaches a peak and then declines as the leaves mature. Amino-N levels are high during the autumn as nutrients are removed from senescing leaves and reproduction again increases to a peak and then declines as the leaves dry out.

In conifers where the leaves are retained for several years, different seasonal patterns of amino acid concentration are observed. In spruce needles, amino acid concentrations are high during winter and spring and

Table 3.4. *Needle age preferences of insect larvae feeding on Scots pine, Pinus sylvestris*

Insect species	Needle age class			
	C	C+	C+1	C+2
Lepidoptera				
Bupalus piniaria	x	x	x	—
Cedestis spp.	—	x	—	—
Cidaria firmata	—	x	x	x
Dendrolimus pini	x	x	x	—
Ellopia fasciaria	—	x	—	—
Hyloicus pinastri	—	x	—	—
Panolis flammea	x	x	x	—
Semiothisa liturata	—	x	—	—
Hymenoptera				
Diprion pini	x	x	x	—
Diprion simile	—	x	—	—
Gilpinia frutetorum	—	x	x	—
Microdiprion pallipes	x	x	x	x
Neodiprion sertifer	—	x	x	x

C = Current-year needles; C+ = needles older than current; C+1 = 1-year-old needles; C+2 = 2-year-old needles; — = no information available.
From Larsson and Tenow 1980.

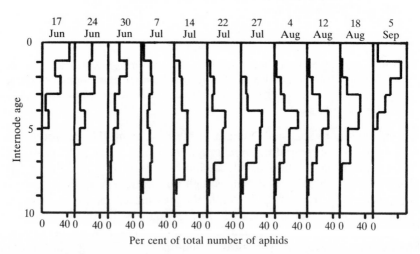

FIG. 3.17. Distribution of *Cinara pini* on internodes of different ages (internode 1 = internode of current years growth) at different times of year (from Larsson 1985).

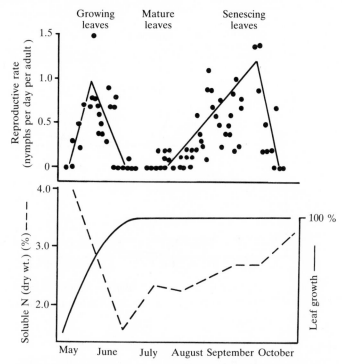

FIG. 3.18. Reproduction of *Drepanosiphum platanoidis* in relation to the growth, maturation and senescence of sycamore leaves (from Dixon 1970).

the green spruce aphid, *Elatobium abietinum*, reproduces during this period. Production of winged aphids (alatae), which is controlled by day-length (Fig. 2.11) coincides with a sharp decline in the amino acid concentration in needles during late spring and early summer and the aphids disperse to new host trees during this period (Fig. 3.19).

3.4.4 Increases in nutritional quality induced by insects

Although insects can induce defensive reactions during feeding on tree tissues, gall-forming insects and those that form local aggregations on plants initiate physiological changes in their hosts that may, at least temporarily, increase nutritional quality. Many different kinds of galls are formed on the leaves of trees, especially oaks and willows. As well as providing protection, the gall tissues may also be more nutritive (McNeill and Southwood 1978). The beech scale, *Cryptococcus fagisuga*, which feeds on bark parenchyma causes the formation of local cell complexes ('galls') around the tip of the mouthparts which are assumed to enhance the nutritive value of the tissues (Kunkel 1968; Lonsdale 1983).

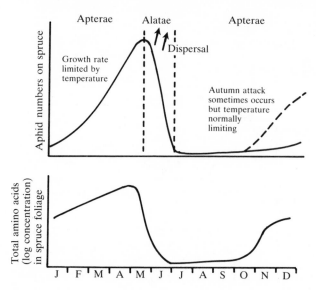

FIG. 3.19. Numbers of *Elatobium abietinum* in relation to total leaf amino acid levels (from McNeill and Southwood 1978, after Carter unpublished).

An interesting interspecific effect of improved host nutritional quality has been reported by Kidd *et al.* (1985). The pine aphids, *Schizolachnus pineti* and *Eulachnus agilis*, are significantly associated on shoots and needles in the field. *Eulachnus agilis* benefits from the association through increased survival and growth rate, presumably as a result of the improved nutritional quality of needles on which *S. pineti* is feeding.

3.5 HOST STRESS AND FOOD QUALITY

Broadly speaking, *stress* can be defined as any factor that affects a plant's normal function and which produces a potentially injurious *strain* manifest by a metabolic or physical change in the plant (Levitt 1972, 1980). Stress, which may be short-lived or a more or less permanent feature of the environment, is an important concept in both forestry and forest entomology because it affects not only the growth and productivity of forests but also the susceptibility of trees to pests and diseases (Schoeneweiss 1975; Mattson and Haack 1987) (see also Chapter 5). Stress has been attributed to many different kinds of environmental factor, two or more of which may sometimes be present together. Long-term stress, for example, may be induced by low nutrients, low light levels, and low or high soil pH and short-term stress by drought or flooding and by high or low temperatures.

The severity of stress is an important factor determining its effect on trees but even low to moderate levels can initiate a complex series of physiological and biochemical changes. During extreme stress, all physiological activities may be adversely affected and ultimately the tree may die. The effect of a given level of stress on trees will depend on the species concerned, its adaptations to conditions in its natural habitat, the nature of the stress and whether it is short- or long-term (Speight 1986). As far as insects are concerned, the most important changes are those affecting the availability of nutrients and the concentration of defensive secondary chemicals. Not enough is known about the stress physiology of trees to predict how different kinds of stress will modify a particular insect/host interaction. The issue is further complicated by the fact that the response to different levels of stress in terms of changes in food availability or secondary chemicals is not necessarily linear, so that the effects on insects may change in relation to the severity of stress. Despite these complications, a number of empirical relationships have been established (see Table 3.6 and Chapter 5 and 10) and there are a number of broad generalizations that can be made about the nature of tree responses to adverse conditions and their effects on forest insects.

3.5.1 Stress and defence against insect herbivores

The defences of trees against insects are often assumed to be compromised during periods of stress, largely because of the well established relationship between stress and outbreaks of certain forest insects (section 3.6.2). However, a number of studies have shown that production of defensive chemicals may actually increase during periods of stress, largely as a result of a re-allocation of resources within the tree (Gershenzon 1984; Sharpe *et al.* 1985) and this is also the theoretical prediction of optimal defence models (Fagerström *et al.* 1987).

During normal growth, carbohydrate resources are allocated according to a system of priorities such as that proposed for lodgepole pine in Fig. 3.20. The highest priority is given to the development of new foliage and buds followed by new root growth and then storage in various parts of the tree. A lower priority is accorded to stem growth and the production of defensive chemicals. Stress, however, can modify this pattern, partly by affecting the balance between sources (photosynthesis) and sinks (e.g. growth) within the tree.

The generalized inter-relationship between stress, tree physiology and insect herbivores is shown in terms of feedback loops in Fig. 3.21. Stress usually has negative effects on growth and the photosynthetic capacity of trees but the relative impact on these two processes will depend, among other things, on the nature of the stress (Sharpe and Wu 1985). When

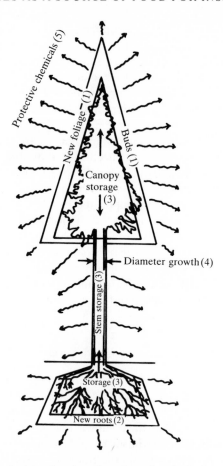

FIG. 3.20. Likely priorities for the allocation of carbohydrate in lodgepole pine. Priorities are numbered from 1 (highest) to 5 (lowest). (from Waring and Pitman 1985).

growth is affected more than photosynthesis, the carbohydrate pool increases and carbohydrates may be diverted to the synthesis of defensive secondary chemicals so that trees become more, rather than less, well defended. In boreal forests, for example, tree growth is often limited by nutrient availability. Light is not limiting during the northern summer and excess carbohydrate is diverted from growth to synthesis of carbon-based defensive compounds (phenolics and terpenoids) which protects them from vertebrate (and presumably insect) herbivores (Bryant *et al.* 1983). Trees adapted to more favourable growing conditions appear to respond in a similar way to nutrient limitation, and experimental evidence for this is provided by Waring *et al.* (1985). They analysed the composition of willow

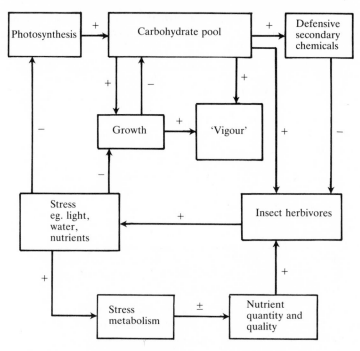

FIG. 3.21. The inter-relationships between stress, vigour and susceptibility of trees to insect herbivores.

leaves from young trees grown under different nutrient and light conditions (Table 3.5). Trees supplied with abundant mineral nutrients had a high N concentration in the leaves. Total N levels were much lower, however, in trees with a restricted nutrient supply but the carbohydrate and tannin contents were significantly increased. There is thus evidence that trees affected by both long-term and short-term nutrient stress may become more rather than less well defended against insect herbivores at least for moderate levels of stress.

During moderate levels of drought stress, both growth and photosynthesis are reduced but because growth is affected more quickly carbohydrates continue to be available for synthesis of secondary chemicals (Kramer 1983; Sharpe *et al.* 1985; Lorio 1986). Higher levels of drought stress, however, have more profound effects on tree physiology and, under these circumstances, the production of secondary chemicals may be reduced (Gershenzon 1984). Thus there appears to be a dome-shaped relationship between the production of secondary chemicals and increasing drought stress (Mattson and Haack 1987). During even moderate levels of drought stress, however, existing defences may be compromised and in conifers this

Table 3.5. *Chemical composition of willow leaves, Salix aquatica, grown under specified environments at stable growth rates and stable mineral nutrition*

Compound	High light, high nutrients	Low light, high nutrients	High light, moderate nutrients
Total N, (% dry wt.)	5.04[a]	5.11[a]	1.91[b]
Total N, (mg N dm^{-2} leaf)	21.5[a]	13.4[b]	14.0[b]
Amino acids, (mg N dm^{-2} leaf)	2.4[a]	2.3[a]	0.9[b]
Starch, (% dry wt.)	5.1[a]	5.3[a]	20.7[b]
Tannins, relative units	0.65[a]	0.64[a]	1.00[b]

Note—values with different superscripts within a row differ significantly at $P=0.05$.
From Waring *et al.* 1985.

results in a reduction in oleoresin exudation pressure, flow rate, and rate of crystallization as well as changes in composition of the resin (Vité 1961; Hodges and Lorio 1975). This reduction in the efficacy of existing defences appears to be the main cause of the increased susceptibility of conifers to bark beetles during periods of drought (Chapter 4).

As well as contributing to the production of preformed defences, carbohydrates that accumulate during stress may also be utilized in local induced defensive reactions such as the synthesis of secondary resin in the dynamic wound response (Hodges and Lorio 1969; Miller and Berryman 1985; Christiansen and Ericsson 1986) (section 3.3.1).

3.5.2 Stress and the nutritional value of trees

As well as indirectly affecting the concentration of defensive chemicals in trees, carbohydrates can also improve directly the nutritional quality of tree tissues during stress. Carbohydrates in conifer bark, for example, may benefit both bark beetles and the fungi which they carry into their galleries (Barras and Hodges 1969). However, during stress, other more complex biochemical changes occur (stress metabolism) that can alter the tree's nutritional quality (Fig. 3.21).

The biochemical changes that occur during drought stress, for example, are an important part of the mechanism of osmotic adjustment, aimed at minimizing the loss of water (White 1969; Kramer 1983; Mattson and Haack 1987). During moderate levels of stress there is an increase in the concentration of sugars and the conversion of existing protein to soluble form (amino acids) and these changes in the quantity, distribution and quality of N can affect the growth and survival of insects.

The relative importance of changes in the defensive and nutritive characteristics of trees in determining the impact on insect populations will depend on the feeding strategies of particular insects. Sap-feeding insects in particular, respond to the elevated levels of amino acids in phloem sap, especially as they are able to avoid ingesting secondary chemicals that are present largely in the cells of the non-vascular tissue.

3.5.3 Stress and vigour

Vigour is usually relatively loosely defined as an integration of all the factors affecting the health and growth of trees and 'vigorous' forest crops are widely assumed to be more 'resistant' to pests and diseases (Chapter 5). Vigour and stress are clearly inter-related (Fig. 3.21) and sometimes the terms have been used more or less interchangeably and indeed have been measured by the same parameters. For example, the amount of stemwood produced per unit leaf area of a tree (stem-growth efficiency), has been related to the leaf area index (canopy density) of the forest as a measure of light stress (competition for light), and also as an estimate of tree vigour in relation to the size of the bark beetle infestation required to kill trees (Waring 1982, 1983; Waring and Pitman 1985).

However, indices of stress or vigour do not necessarily reflect the underlying physiological condition of the tree and so may not accurately reflect the level of susceptibility to insect attack. For example, trees with few energy reserves and poor growth (i.e. of low vigour) are likely to be inadequately defended against insect attack. However, stress can also result in poor growth but as discussed above, this may actually increase the carbohydrate pool and allow greater allocation to defence. Clearly, the relationship between estimates of stress or vigour and susceptibility of trees to particular forest pests needs to be established empirically before it can be used in a predictive way.

Some examples of the use of vigour indices to predict susceptibility of mature conifers to bark beetle attack are discussed in Chapter 10. The assumption behind the use of these indices is that as trees grow larger and increase in biomass the ratio of photosynthetic to non-photosynthetic tissue changes, resulting in a higher demand for carbohydrates for maintenance. The canopy may be increasingly unable to meet this demand, especially in dense stands where there is competition for light. Since carbohydrate allocation to wood production and secondary chemicals is low on the list of priorities (Fig. 3.20) growth can be used to indicate the level of carbohydrate stress and to reflect the defensive status of the tree (Waring 1983).

3.6 TREES AND INSECT POPULATION DYNAMICS

3.6.1 Interactions between trees, herbivores and natural enemies

As well as affecting the insects that feed on them, trees may also influence the activities of natural enemies both directly and indirectly. Indeed Price *et al.* (1980) have suggested that natural enemies should be considered as part of a plant's complement of defences against herbivores (see also Lawton and McNeill 1979).

Food in the form of nectar and pollen (and even aphid honeydew) may enhance survival of natural enemies and by responding to specific secondary chemicals they can locate the trees on which their prey normally feeds (Hagan 1986; Price 1986). Efficient location of host trees by natural enemies can have a significant influence on the intensity of attack on their prey.

An important effect of secondary chemicals, especially the quantitative defences of trees, is that they cause a reduction in the growth rate of insect herbivores. This can benefit natural enemies because the extended development period increases the chance of detection (Feeny 1976; Price 1986; van Emden 1986). There is also some evidence that insects on a poor diet may succumb more readily to parasitoids because the encapsulation reaction against internal parasitoids is weaker and resistance to pathogens may also be reduced (Cheng 1970; Rhoades 1983).

However, plant toxins can be used to advantage by some insect herbivores that are able to sequester them for defence against their natural enemies. Sawfly larvae in the family Diprionidae, for example, sequester host terpenoids and regurgitate them when disturbed (see Chapter 4). There is also evidence that pathogenic micro-organisms are inhibited by secondary chemicals in leaves (Smirnoff and Hutchison 1965).

3.6.2 Stress and insect outbreaks

There are many examples where outbreaks of forest insects appear to be associated with stress or reduced host vigour. Outbreaks of bark beetles are often mentioned in this context but other insects are also affected, with drought and poor site conditions being two of the most commonly observed predisposing factors (Table 3.6). Attack by insects themselves is an important cause of stress (Fig. 3.21) which can increase susceptibility of trees to secondary pests (Chapter 4). Other organisms such as fungal pathogens can also predispose trees to bark beetle attack. For example, the shoot disease caused by *Brunchorstia pinea* can weaken pines sufficiently to allow successful attack by the pine shoot beetle, *Tomicus piniperda*.

Table 3.6. *Factors that predispose trees to outbreaks of herbivorous insects*

Insect	Predisposing factor
Sap feeders	
Pulvinaria regalis	Sites surrounded by impermeable surfaces, close to buildings
Defoliators	
Neodiprion sertifer	Drought and low soil nutrients
Orgyia pseudotsugata	Dry sites
Lymantria dispar	Several factors, e.g. poor, shallow soils, dry sites, and other meteorological extremes
Coleotechnites milleri	Nutrient-poor, low-water-capacity soils
Panolis flammea	Deep, unflushed peat soils
Bupalus piniaria	Sandy sites of low–moderate rainfall
Choristoneura fumiferana	Several warm, dry summers, over-mature trees
Shoot borers	
Rhyacionia buoliana	Excessively wet or dry soils, low nutrients
Bark borers	
Dendroctonus frontalis	Lightning-struck trees, drought
Dendroctonus ponderosae	Stands of low vigour, drought
Ips typographus	Over-mature trees, drought

From Thatcher 1960, Bakke 1982*a*, Coulson *et al.* 1983, Waring and Pitman 1983, Worrell 1983, Thomson and Shrimpton 1984, Speight 1986, Leather and Barbour 1987, Barbour 1988, and references in Rhoades 1983.

Host stress plays a significant role in the population dynamics of the psyllid, *Cardiaspina densitexta*, on *Eucalyptus fasciculosa* (White 1969). In Australia, the soils on which the trees grow are subject to acute water shortages in summer and waterlogging in winter so that the trees undergo prolonged water stress in some years. White calculated a 'stress index' based on deviation from normal summer and winter rainfall (Fig. 3.22a). A high positive index, which resulted when winters were much wetter than summers, was associated with outbreaks of this insect (Fig. 3.22b).

From the previous discussion of the effects of stress on trees, it seems likely that changes in both the defensive and nutritional characteristics of the trees contribute to stress-induced outbreaks of forest insects. White (1974), however, has emphasized the importance of nutritional changes and argues that low N levels in plants reduce survival of very young insects and that the main effect of stress, is to cause a sudden area-wide increase in plant nutritive status. This is assumed to increase dramatically early instar survival and so precipitate an outbreak. This may well be the main effect of drought stress, but more research is needed to determine whether this applies to other kinds of stress.

A descriptive model of the possible effects of short-term stress on insect population dynamics, incorporating changes in nutritive status, induced defences and natural enemies is shown in Fig. 3.23 (Rhoades 1983). Following a stressful event, the overall nutritional quality of the host

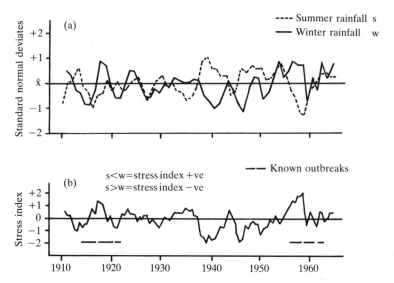

FIG. 3.22. Stress index for Keith, South Australia, and outbreaks of *Cardiaspina densitexta* on *Eucalyptus fasciculosa*. (a) dotted line shows summer rainfall(s), and solid line shows winter rainfall (w), both plotted in units of the normal deviate about its 3-year running mean. (b) Stress index, calculated as w minus s in (a). The stress index is positive when s is less than w, i.e. when summers were dry relative to the preceding winters (from White 1969).

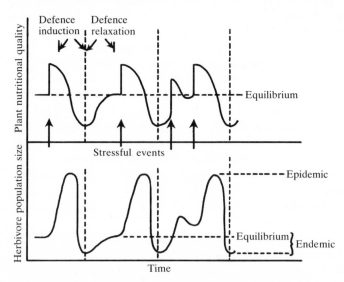

FIG. 3.23. Model of insect herbivore population fluctuations based on changes in food plant nutritive quality caused by stress and attack-induced defensive responses in the plants (from Rhoades 1983).

increases, reducing mortality, increasing fecundity and leading to an increase in population size. Changes in the host plant during stress may also affect natural enemies as discussed above. Assuming that the stress eventually relaxes, defences induced by high levels of insect feeding cause a reduction in food quality and this together with the effects of natural enemies results in a collapse of the insect population. At low population density the equilibrium nutritional quality is re-established as the induced defences are relaxed. During this period of transition, outbreaks are less likely should stress re-occur. Depending on the relaxation time and the frequency of stressful events, such factors could contribute to cyclic population change.

3.7 IMPLICATIONS OF INSECT–TREE INTERACTIONS FOR FOREST MANAGEMENT

The way in which forests are managed can have an important bearing on the occurrence of stress in trees. In dense stands there may be competition between trees for light and other resources. Thinning may relieve light stress but other complex environmental changes involving water, insolation, and nutrient status of the site can occur (Chapter 2). During the establishment of plantations, the selection of appropriate species for available sites is an important way of minimizing the likelihood of stress-induced outbreaks and this important aspect of forest management is discussed in Chapter 5.

3.7.1 Soil nutrients and fertilization

Where plantations are established on poor soils, tree growth may be limited by soil nutrient availability and the addition of fertilizers is an increasingly important, direct way of improving tree growth in young plantations. There have been relatively few studies to determine what actually happens to a tree in terms of the quality and quantity of food for insects when forests are thinned or fertilized or when trees are planted on sub-optimum sites. By improving the growth and 'vigour' of trees, fertilization might increase resistance to insect pests. But it could increase the nutritive value of tree tissues (e.g. by supplying N) and by stimulating growth, may limit resources available for synthesis of defensive secondary chemicals so that overall, susceptibility may increase. From early studies, Stark (1965) suggested that fertilization of trees tended to increase populations of sap-feeding insects and decrease those of chewing ones but subsequent studies have revealed a much more complex situation.

Many studies have, in fact, demonstrated effects of fertilization on insect

Table 3.7. *The effects of tree fertilization on survival and/or abundance of insects*

Insect	Host	Feeding on	Fertilizer	Element	Effect	Reference
Adelges piceae	Grand fir	Parenchyma	Urea	N	+	Carrow and Betts (1973)
Aradus cinnamomeus	Pine	Parenchyma	Ammonium nitrate	N	−	Heliovaara et al. (1983)
			Ammonium nitrate	NPK	+	
Toumeyella numismaticum	Jack pine	Parenchyma in needles and bark	Urea	N	+	Smirnoff and Valero (1975)
			Potassium	K	−	
Chewing insects	Black locust	Leaves		NPK	+ then −	Hargrove et al. (1984)
Neodiprion sertifer	Scots pine	Needles	Urea	N	−	Larsson and Tenow (1984)
Neodiprion swainei	Jack pine	Needles	Urea	N	−	Smirnoff and Bernier (1973)
Cydia strobilella	Norway spruce	Cones	Urea + superphosphate	NK	+	Bakke (1969)
Hylobius rhizophagus	Jack pine	Root bark	Ammonium nitrate + superphosphate	N+P	−	Goyer and Benjamin (1972)

Examples have been selected to show effects on insects attacking different parts of trees.

abundance but both positive and negative effects have been reported on insects feeding on the different parts of a tree (Table 3.7). Fertilization of pine trees with urea adversely affected larvae of the jack pine sawfly, *Neodiprion swainei*, and mortality rose to 36 per cent after 30 days and was twice that recorded on unfertilized trees which therefore suffered considerably more feeding damage (Fig. 3.24). In contrast, both positive and negative effects were observed on the balsam woolly aphid, *Adelges piceae*,

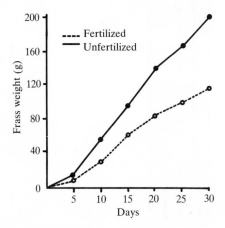

FIG. 3.24. Feeding damage estimated by the cumulative frass weight of third instar larvae of *Neodiprion swainei* on jack pine. Fertilized trees were treated with urea in two consecutive years (from Smirnoff and Bernier 1973).

on grand fir, depending on the form in which the N was applied (Carrow and Betts 1973). On trees fertilized with urea, population increase over five generations was about three times higher than that on unfertilized ones. However, when the trees were fertilized with ammonium nitrate, populations decreased relative to control trees. In this study an important effect of fertilization was to alter the relative concentration of different amino acids in the bark (Fig. 3.25). On trees fertilized with ammonium nitrate, the arginine concentration of bark increased considerably whilst phenylalanine and asparagine (not shown) virtually disappeared. Since the proportions of different amino acids in the diet is important for normal development of some sap-feeding insects (van Emden *et al.* 1969; van Emden and Bashford 1971) this may explain the differential effects of fertilization on *A. piceae*.

Hargrove *et al.* (1984), in a study of insect feeding on black locust, observed first an increase then a decrease in feeding following fertilization with NPK. The results were explained by proposing a two-stage response in which an initial increase in nutrient content of leaves increased insect feeding, followed by an active defence response which reduced it, even though nutrient levels were still higher than control trees.

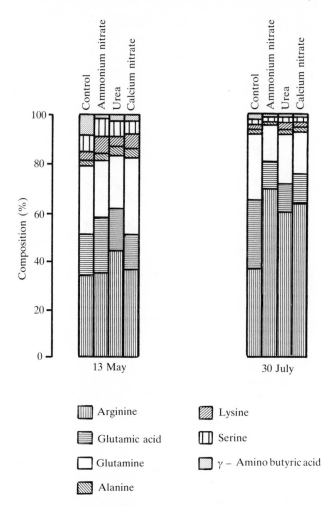

FIG. 3.25. Changes in the proportions of major free amino acids from spring to summer in bark tissues of 3-year-old grand fir treated with foliar applications of fertilizer (from Carrow and Betts 1973).

Clearly, the effects of fertilization on tree physiology are complex and may include an increase in the photosynthetic capacity of leaves, alteration in the balance of minerals or the ratios of important amino acids (Brix 1971; Smirnoff and Bernier 1973; Carrow and Betts 1973; Kellomaki *et al.* 1982). Different tree species may also respond to fertilization in different ways. The Alaska paper birch responds strongly to fertilization (N and P) with an increase in growth and reduction in concentration of secondary chemicals. Green alder on the other hand shows only a small growth response and secondary chemical concentrations are relatively little affected (Bryant *et al.* 1987).

Until the effects of fertilization in relation to insect nutrition and plant defence are more clearly understood for particular insect/plant interactions we are unlikely to be able to predict the outcome of fertilization on damage levels in particular forest crops.

4

The nature of forest insect pests

In Chapters 2 and 3 we emphasized the great variety of niches on individual trees that can be occupied by insects and the different food resources that they exploit. The particular part of the tree on which insects feed and the adaptations necessary to exploit it are important factors determining the nature of forest pest problems. But as well as determining the impact of insect feeding on the tree these life-history characteristics also influence the way in which insects can be controlled. In the first part of this chapter we give some examples of forest pests before going on to consider the impact that insects have both on trees and the forest ecosystem as a whole. The ways in which forest insect pests can be controlled are discussed in detail in subsequent chapters.

4.1 PEST PROBLEMS IN RELATION TO THE GROWING FOREST

The growth curve of an even-aged plantation (Chapter 1, Fig. 1.1) has been related to its changing susceptibility to pest attack as the current annual increment peaks and then declines. On this model, trees are regarded as vulnerable during the early stages of growth and again increasingly so as their growth rate slows with age (Way and Bevan 1977). While in general terms this is a useful guide to the vulnerability of even-aged stands to pest attack at different times, it obscures that fact that the nature of the resource changes during this period. Thus newly-planted trees are small and exposed to the elements and initially have little impact on each other even though density is high. As they grow they become structurally more complex and begin to shade the ground vegetation and compete with each other. After canopy closure the environmental conditions within the forest are modified (Chapter 2) and competition for light and nutrients results in notable size differences between individual trees. Tree density may be reduced by thinning during this period and as the trees approach maturity, variation in size will be reduced as the final crop trees are selected. As tree density declines the forest becomes more open allowing the development of a ground flora.

Certain kinds of insect pests characterize these different growth stages.

Thus plantation forests, and to a large extent natural forests too, are attacked by a sequence of different kinds of pests as the young forest develops to maturity (Crooke 1979). The examples discussed in this chapter are selected largely to illustrate the variety of feeding habits among some of the important pests that attack the trees at each stage of growth. More detailed treatment of the identification and biology of these and other insect pests can be found in Dajoz (1980), Coulson and Witter (1984), Berryman (1986), Szujecki (1987), Bevan (1987), and various national forest service handbooks.

4.1.1 Forest nurseries

Forest nurseries occupy very small areas in comparison to the forests themselves and resemble agricultural crops in so far as the seedling trees are planted at high density in uniform cultivated areas under intensive management. Seedling trees are obviously much smaller in relation to insect size than established trees in the forest so that attack by relatively few insects can be very damaging and indeed several plants may be destroyed by a single insect. Seedling trees with their immature root systems and small energy reserves may be unable to recover from insect attack, and sublethal effects such as distortion through multiple leadering can render them useless for forest establishment.

Insects that attack seedling trees in forest nurseries are represented among several orders of insects, some examples of which are given in Table 4.1. Many of them are polyphagous on both broad-leaved and coniferous trees and several important pests are soil dwelling, feeding on the roots or lower stem. Root feeding insects such as cockchafers (*Melolontha* spp.), whose larvae feed over two or three seasons, and cutworm larvae (*Agrotis* spp.), feed on many seedlings during development. Cutworms emerge from the soil at night to feed at the root collar level and older larvae may sever the plants and pull them down into the soil. Another polyphagous soil-dwelling pest, the collembolan *Bourletiella hortensis* (taxonomically no longer an insect), may kill conifer seedlings immediately after germination but, more commonly, attacked seedling trees survive although they are often deformed and unusable.

The aerial parts of seedling trees are also vulnerable to attack by a range of insects, many of which are more host-specific than those that feed on the roots. On young beech trees, the woolly aphid, *Phyllaphis fagi*, feeds on the underside of leaves and at high population densities the leaves may become distorted and the excreted honeydew drops onto the leaves below which then become covered with sooty mould. The green spruce aphid, *Elatobium abietinum*, causes yellowing and loss of needles on seedlings and is one of the few nursery pests that also damages forest trees.

Table 4.1. *Examples of insect pests in European forest nurseries*

Insect species	Order	Main host(s)	Part attacked	Damage
Bourletiella hortensis	Collembola	Conifers/broad-leaves	Cotyledon and hypocotyl	Seedlings distorted; multiple-leaders may develop
Elatobium abietinum	Hemiptera	Spruce	Needles	Yellowing of needles; needle fall in heavy infestations
Phyllaphis fagi	Hemiptera	Beech	Leaves	Young leaves distorted; wax, honeydew and sooty mould contamination
Agrotis segetum	Lepidoptera	Conifers/broad-leaves	Root collar	Seedlings girdled or severed by larvae in the soil
Melolontha melolontha	Coleoptera	Conifers/broad-leaves	Roots	Young larvae prune roots; older larvae may sever plant; larvae feed for more than one year
Otiorhynchus singularis	Coleoptera	Conifers/broad-leaves	Bark and leaves	Seedlings girdled by bark-feeding adults

Selected references: Browne (1968), Jones and Jones (1974), Hobart (1977), Bevan (1987).

The aim of forest nurseries is to produce plants of high quality that are free from pests and diseases so that they have the best chance of establishment in the forest. In many nurseries, the regular cultivation of the soil, weed control and in some cases routine soil sterilization minimizes the risk from soil pests. The use of insecticides is an important and usually appropriate control method for many nursery pests because accurate timing and placement with minimum environmental contamination is possible within these discrete areas.

The location of nurseries in relation to elevation, rainfall, exposure, and soil type may affect the susceptibility of the trees to pest attack and so is an important consideration in nursery establishment.

4.1.2 Establishment of the forest to canopy closure

Newly-established plantations, especially those remote from other forested areas, may be relatively free from pest attack during the vulnerable early establishment phase. Not only does 'isolation' reduce the chances of location by dispersing insects but some important pests of young conifers such as the pine weevil, *Hylobius abietis*, (Fig. 4.1) breed only in the stumps of dying or clearfelled trees and since they cannot breed in young plantations they must re-invade them every year from established forests. Following

FIG. 4.1. (a) *Hylobius abietis* adult; (b) Damage to the stem of young spruce by adult *H. abietis*.

the felling and replanting of conifer forests, however, the stumps of the previous crop and the young transplants are in close proximity (Fig. 5.11). The females lay eggs in the bark of stumps just below ground level or sometimes where logs are in contact with the soil. Larvae feed within the bark and usually overwinter in the final instar, the young weevils emerging in the following spring. In northern parts of Europe, however, the life cycle may take two years. After emergence the adult weevils feed on the bark of the young transplants at or above soil level and several trees may be damaged or killed by one insect. Attacks by *H. abietis* can continue over several years because the tree stumps may be utilized for more than one season and the adult weevils themselves often live for over a year.

Black pine beetles, *Hylastes* spp., also breed in conifer stumps and damage young plants as adults. These small scolytids often breed in the smaller diameter roots of the stumps and so can avoid competition with *H. abietis* (Scott and King 1974). The adults may continue to feed within the bark of stumps in which they develop, especially when the bark is still fresh. However, they will also attack transplants, feeding in the bark from the root collar down to the fine roots.

Insecticides are used prophylactically in many countries to protect young transplants but once the stumps have become unsuitable for breeding, the populations of beetles decline and these pests are no longer a threat to the young trees. During this early period of forest establishment, it is usually standard practice to replace trees that die during the first two or three years.

Trees damaged or killed after this initial establishment period cannot be replaced, largely because the small transplants would be unable to compete with surrounding established trees. A number of important pests attack trees from this stage of growth up to the time of canopy closure and sometimes beyond. Although trees killed or damaged by insect attack are lost at this stage the density of trees in the forest is still relatively high and therefore some mortality is acceptable, provided that damage is distributed throughout the forest rather than concentrated in small areas of high mortality.

The pine shoot moth, *Rhyacionia buoliana*, is a typical native pest of young plantations in Europe and an introduced one in North America. The young larvae mine in buds in the summer and autumn and attack may be evident from the presence of frass, resin and silken webbing on the buds (Fig. 4.2a). Older larvae tunnel in shoots in the following spring and, where leading shoots are killed, forked trees or trees with multiple leaders can develop. Occasionally, attacked leaders may survive but the weakened shoots bend over before resuming upward growth so that a 'posthorn' deformation results (Fig. 4.2b). Clearly, relatively few attacks on trees can cause considerable damage especially when leaders are affected so this

Fig. 4.2. (a) *Rhyacionia buoliana* larva on pine shoot tip, showing the resin exudation from the entrance to the larval tunnel. The larva has been removed from the broken shoot for inspection; (b) Damage to lodgepole pine leader by *R. buoliana*, showing the 'posthorn' effect.

insect can be a pest at a relatively low population density. In many cases, however, damaged trees can be removed during later thinning operations so that ultimately, economic losses may be small, and after canopy closure attacks by shoot moths are usually regarded as unimportant. In special crops such as seed orchards, however, where high value trees are planted at low density, the impact of this pest can be considerable and direct control by insecticides may be required. Because the larvae are exposed on the surface of the plant for a relatively short time insecticide applications need to be carefully timed (Chapter 8). As an alternative control method, the female sex pheromone may be used to disrupt mating in low density populations and this is discussed in Chapter 9.

Some forest insects are pests of both young and old trees so that when outbreaks occur early in the rotation they have the potential to cause repeated damage to the trees. Two defoliators of pine, the pine beauty moth, *Panolis flammea*, and the European pine sawfly, *Neodiprion sertifer*, (Table 4.2a, b) damage young plantations in Britain but attack older trees in other parts of Europe (Figs 4.3, 4.4). In central Europe, *P. flammea* is an important pest of its native host, Scots pine, and a number of outbreaks have been recorded since the early nineteenth century (Watt and Leather 1988). Its host range now embraces the introduced lodgepole pine which is widely planted in Scotland and serious outbreaks on this species first occurred on 10–19-year-old trees in Sutherland in 1976. Eggs are laid during the spring and the young larvae feed on the developing shoots but later, in the third and fourth instar, they feed on the older needles (Fig. 4.3). During outbreaks, defoliation usually occurs by about mid-July and the trees are unable to survive the long dormant period in these northern areas. The initial outbreaks were controlled by insecticides and less than 10 years later, many of these original outbreak areas have become severely reinfested necessitating further spraying operations (Chapter 8) (Stoakley 1977).

Young pines defoliated by *N. sertifer* usually survive attack because only the old needles are eaten by the larvae and the current year's needles usually remain unattacked. Trees are thus able to survive several years of successive defoliations although accumulated increment loss may be considerable. The female sawflies oviposit into current needles (Fig. 4.4a) in autumn and in the following year the larvae emerge to feed on both these and older needles (Fig. 4.4b, c). Occasionally, this sawfly may be present in lodgepole pine stands affected by *P. flammea* so that even though both insects may be present at sub-outbreak densities, the trees may suffer extensive defoliation of both young and old foliage.

The pine processionary moth, *Thaumetopoea pityocampa*, (Table 4.2a) is an important defoliator of young pines in southern Europe and North Africa (Fig. 4.5). Monocultures of Corsican pine planted outside its natural

Table 4.2.(a) *Feeding strategies of important European forest defoliators (Lepidoptera)*

Insect species	Main host(s)	Larval behaviour	Larval feeding		Winter stage	Biological notes
			Early instars	Late instars		
Bupalus piniaria	Pine	Solitary	Epidermis on older needles	Whole or part needle removed	Pupa	
Coleophora laricella	Larch	Solitary	Needles mined	Externally on buds and young needles	Larva	
Lymantria dispar	Oak and other broad-leaves	Solitary	Epidermis of new leaves	Leaf margins/entire leaves	Egg	Early instars disperse on silk
Panolis flammea	Pine	Solitary	Opening buds, young needles	Older needles	Pupa	
Thaumetopoea pityocampa	Pine	Colonial	Older needles	Older needles	Larva	Larvae shelter in communal silk tents, extended summer diapause as pupae
Tortrix viridana	Oak	Solitary	Unopened leaves	Expanded leaves rolled and held together by silk	Egg	
Zeiraphera diniana	Larch, pine spruce	Solitary	Buds mined	Older needles spun together	Egg	

Selected references: see Table 4.2.(b).

Table 4.2.(b) *Feeding strategies of important European forest defoliators (Hymenoptera)*

| Insect species | Main host(s) | Larval behaviour | Larval feeding | | Winter stage | Biological notes |
			Early instars	Late instars		
Diprion pini	Pine	Solitary	Needle margins	Whole needles, bark of shoots	Prepupa	Extended diapause
Gilpinia hercyniae	Spruce	Solitary	Older needles	Older needles	Prepupa	Extended diapause
Neodiprion sertifer	Pine	Colonial	Older needles	Older needles	Egg	
Pristiphora erichsonii	Larch	Colonial	Single needles	Needle tufts	Prepupa	Extended diapause

Selected references: Browne 1968, Leonard 1974, Baltensweiler *et al.* 1977, Hobart 1977, Doane and McManus 1981, Coulson and Witter 1984, Bevan 1987, Berryman 1988.

FIG. 4.3. *Panolis flammea* larva on pine.

range seem to be most susceptible to outbreaks but exotic pines are also attacked (Buxton 1983). The adult moths emerge in summer and oviposit on the needles, especially on trees standing out in silhouette such as edge trees and those in young open stands. Most of the eggs are laid in one spot and the larvae remain together constructing a series of large nests of silk where they spend the day, emerging to feed on the surrounding foliage at night. Later on, special overwintering nests are constructed which are positioned for maximum sun exposure. Winter sun can warm the nests to several degrees above ambient, protecting the larvae against low temperatures and allowing them to feed on some winter days (Huchon and Demolin 1971, Chapters 2 and 10). The need for good sun exposure in the autumn and winter feeding periods partly explains the susceptibility of young crops prior to canopy closure. During the spring the larvae form their characteristic head to tail processions as they leave the winter nest and enter the soil prior to pupation. Because of geographical variation in development rates and the occurrence of extended diapause in populations, monitoring is an important aspect of the integrated control of this pest.

4.1.3 Pole stage and maturation

By this stage in the development of the forest, trees may differ considerably in size through genetic differences in growth rate and as a result of

FIG. 4.4. (a) *Neodiprion sertifer* egg niches in pine needles; (b) *N. sertifer* larvae aggregating on lodgepole pine foliage; (c) Lodgepole pine defoliated by larvae of *N sertifer*. Note that the current years needles are untouched by the larvae.

FIG. 4.5. Tents of *Thaumetopoea pityocampa* in pine.

competition for light and nutrients. Large dominant trees occur together with subdominant and suppressed ones and these differences in size and vigour can result in differences in susceptibility to insect attack. However, in managed forests this stage in forest development is characterized by a sequence of thinning operations in which inferior trees and those damaged by insects at an earlier stage can be removed.

Defoliators (chewers and miners)

Several defoliators of well-established crops are among the most damaging forest insects, causing outbreaks that may extend over thousands of hectares and last for several years. Most defoliators belong to the orders Lepidoptera and Hymenoptera and their larvae display a bewildering variety of form and feeding strategy that allows them to exploit the host and avoid natural enemies (Table 4.2a, b). Many are cryptically coloured, resembling twigs or leaves, others are brightly coloured or hairy and often poisonous. Many feed singly on the leaves but some important pests are colonial, feeding together in a close group and adopting common defensive postures when disturbed by natural enemies and may even regurgitate defensive chemicals sequestered from the tree (Fig. 4.6). Colonial larvae often use silk to

FIG. 4.6. Anti-predator defence posture of *Neodiprion sertifer* larvae.

spin leaves and sometimes whole branches together while feeding and others construct discrete nests from which they emerge to feed. Trails of silk may also be used by some larvae to aid dispersal.

One of the most widespread forest pests is the gypsy moth, *Lymantria dispar*, which has the dubious distinction of having been deliberately introduced into North America where it is now one of its most serious pests, defoliating tens of thousands of hectares of forest in some years (Doane and McManus 1981). *Lymantria dispar* is polyphagous on broad-leaved trees though conifers may also be attacked and in the Old World it feeds on a range of trees from cork oak in southern Europe and North Africa (Fraval 1986), to larch and birch in Japan (Furuta 1982). The effects of defoliation include reduced increment, reduced acorn set in oaks and, in the cork oak, defoliation can reduce the thickness and density of cork. Trees may die following successive defoliations and in mixed natural forests it can change the species composition.

The flightless females usually lay their eggs in a single mass on tree trunks but inanimate objects are also used as oviposition sites and egg masses have been transported long distances on vehicles to initiate new outbreaks (Doane and McManus 1981). In the spring young larvae feed initially on buds but later turn their attention to flowers and the young leaves. Because the females are flightless, the young larvae are the main dispersive stage and 'balloon' on silken threads (Chapter 2). Aerial sprays have been used extensively to control this pest, especially in the USA, but alternative control methods have been tried including biological control, and the potent sex pheromone has been used in trials of mating disruption (Chapter 9).

The pine looper moth, *Bupalus piniaria*, (Fig. 4.7a), is an important pest of pine particularly in central Europe. There have been a number of damaging outbreaks, the largest of which occurred in Bavaria at the end of the last century when some 40 000 ha was defoliated in a 5-year period (Escherich 1931). The population dynamics of this insect which may be cyclic in some forests is briefly discussed in Chapters 1 and 2. Outbreaks in British plantations have been tiny in comparison to those in mainland Europe, beginning with the defoliation of 40 ha of Scots pine in the early 1950s. But further outbreaks of this pest have occurred and damage over much more extensive areas has only been prevented by aerial application of insecticides. The adults are active in the summer during which the females oviposit on the pine needles. The larval feeding period extends from June to the late autumn so that during outbreaks when trees are completely defoliated, they are unable to reflush until the following spring (Fig. 4.7b). These weakened trees have a high probability of being attacked by the pine shoot beetle, *Tomicus piniperda*, which acts as a secondary pest (see section 4.3).

The larch casebearer, *Coleophora laricella*, is another European pest that has been accidentally introduced into North America. The main damage occurs in the spring when the later instars feed on the young needles (Fig. 4.8). Eggs are laid during the summer and the early instars mine within the needles. Third instar larvae, however, construct a case of mined needles which they enlarge as they grow. These casebearing larvae overwinter and in the spring continue feeding on the young needles by mining into them from the outside. Because larch is deciduous, the trees are able to reflush in the same season following an early defoliation and can thus survive several successive years of attack without mortality although growth losses can be significant. Other species which defoliate larch such as the budmoth, *Zeiraphera diniana*, and the sawfly, *Cephalcia lariciphila*, also rarely kill their host and indeed defoliated trees may be more resistant to subsequent attack because the reflushed foliage may be less palatable to larvae (Chapter 3).

Sap and parenchyma feeders

In general, aphids and other sap-feeding insects are relatively less important as pests of forests in comparison to those that attack agricultural crops

FIG. 4.7. (a) *Bupalus piniaria* larvae on pine foliage. (b) Pine trees defoliated by *B. piniaria*.

and, in particular, the transmission of virus diseases is much less important. The one notable exception is the transmission of the elm phloem necrosis virus by the elm leafhopper, *Scaphoides luteolus*, in the eastern USA (Baker 1948, 1949). Some examples of sap-feeding insects are given in Table 4.3.

FIG. 4.8. *Coleophora laricella* defoliation of larch needle rosettes.

Aphids feeding on the phloem sap in leaves usually have a less dramatic visual effect on the trees than insects which consume whole leaves but, nevertheless, they can still cause significant reductions in annual increment. The green spruce aphid, *Elatobium abietinum* (Fig. 4.9a), feeds on both native and introduced spruce species in Europe and it frequently occurs in forest nurseries. In central Europe where there are sexual and asexual generations, overwintering occurs in the egg stage but in Britain, the sexual stage is absent so that the parthenogenetic females remain on the needles throughout the winter. The factors that affect the appearance of alatae which disperse to new hosts during the summer are discussed in Chapter 2. The nymphs and adults feed on the undersides of the older needles and can completely defoliate trees (Fig. 4.9b). Later in the year, the current year's needles may also be attacked. The anholocyclic life cycle in Britain contributes to its pest status because the aphids continue to feed during mild winters and contribute to a rapid build-up in populations during the spring. The considerable differences in susceptibility between North American and Eurasian spruces are discussed in Chapter 6.

The balsam woolly aphid, *Adelges piceae*, is a parenchyma-feeding species found on the bark of fir trees. In infested forests in Europe many trees have some insects on them but only a few become heavily infested. Populations on heavily infested trees often decline after 2 or 3 years partly as a result of host reaction to attack, which results in the growth of new outer bark tissues, and partly to the effect of predators (Franz 1958). In North America where *A. piceae* is an introduced species it has become a

Table 4.3. *Examples of sap-feeding insects attacking forest trees in Europe*

Insect species	Order	Main host(s)	Part attacked	Food source	Damage
Adelges abietis	Hemiptera	Spruce	Newly developing needles	Parenchyma in needle	Conspicuous galling of new shoots; kinking and discoloration of needles
Adelges piceae	Hemiptera	Firs	Trunk, twigs branches	Parenchyma in bark	Abnormal xylem known as 'rotholz' on trunk; gouting of twigs and buds in crown
Cryptococcus fagisuga	Hemiptera	Beech	Trunk, branches	Parenchyma in bark	Tissue necrosis associated with pathogenic fungus
Elatobium abietinum	Hemiptera	Spruce	Needles	Phloem sap	Yellowing and loss of older needles, especially serious in Christmas trees
Matsucoccus feytaudi	Hemiptera	Pine	Trunk, branches	Parenchyma in bark	Resin exudation; fissuring and death of bark; yellowing and loss of needles; flagging of twigs

References: Carter 1971, Dajoz 1980, Bevan 1987, Wainhouse and Gate 1988.

(b)

FIG. 4.9. (a) *Elatobium abietinum* on spruce needles; (b) Spruce tree defoliated by heavy attacks of *Elatobium abietinum*. Current year leader length has been considerably reduced by the attack (see also Fig. 4.31).

serious pest of Frazer fir, subalpine fir and balsam fir (Coulson and Witter 1984). These highly susceptible species do not appear to have the effective defence mechanism present in the native European hosts. They react to secretions injected into the bark during feeding by forming abnormal xylem which becomes characteristically red in colour (redwood or 'rotholz') and non-conducting so that heavily attacked trees may die in 3–4 years (Steffan 1972; Bryant 1974). Although predators can be important in population decline, this insect has no known parasitoids. The planting of resistant firs would seem to be the most effective means of combating this pest.

The beech scale, *Cryptococcus fagisuga*, is another bark parenchyma-feeding insect that occurs widely in Europe and as an introduced species in North America. Infestations are usually confined to the main trunk which can appear white from the accumulated woolly wax secreted by this insect (Fig. 4.10). Although heavily infested trees have very low growth rates, the main importance of this pest arises from its association with a *Nectria* fungus, which colonizes the bark, usually resulting in the death of trees (Lonsdale and Wainhouse 1987, section 4.3).

Host resistance is an important factor limiting the impact of this insect in

FIG. 4.10. Beech trunk infested with *Cryptococcus fagisuga*.

European beech forests so that although many trees support some insects, relatively few become heavily infested. The American beech, however, has little natural resistance and in outbreaks most trees are extensively colonized and they die following fungal infection. As for *A. piceae*, chemical control of this insect is impractical and uneconomic on a forest scale. Silvicultural methods presently form the basis of control of this insect and its associated fungus.

Flower, fruit, and seed feeding

The reproductive organs usually only appear on well-established trees but even in trees of reproductive age, seeds are not always produced every year (Chapter 3). Thus insects that specialize on seeds and cones need adaptations such as prolonged diapause to survive years when seed set is low (Chapter 2).

Some insects that feed on the reproductive organs of trees have complex life cycles. The knopper gall wasp, *Andricus quercuscalicis*, which forms a gall on acorns of the pedunculate oak, *Quercus robur*, appears to have been introduced to Britain from mainland Europe. The large convoluted 'knopper' gall supports development of a single larva which will form the asexual generation of the wasp. The galls fall to the ground with the normal acorns in the autumn and those individuals not in extended diapause emerge in the following spring and the females lay eggs in the male flowers of the Turkey oak, *Q. cerris*. Males and females of the sexual generation develop quickly in tiny galls in these flowers and emerge later in the year when the females fly to pedunculate oaks, oviposit in the developing acorns, and so complete the life cycle.

In plantations established for wood production, insects that eat seeds and cones have little economic impact even though over half the seed crop can be lost to these insects. Even in natural forests, seed pests are relatively unimportant and in the long run probably do not affect natural regeneration. Indeed heavy and frequent seed production is an undesirable characteristic in plantation trees since it can divert resources away from wood production and so reduce stand productivity. In these circumstances, destruction of cones and seeds by insects could actually be beneficial (Mattson 1978). But in seed orchards and other specialized crops such as the stone pine, *Pinus pinea*, and sweet chestnut, *Castanea sativa*, which produce edible seeds, insects that attack the reproductive organs of trees can be important pests, some of which are discussed in section 4.2.

Many defoliators indirectly affect seed production by feeding on flowers as well as leaves during their development. Even moderate defoliation of the holm oak by the oak leaf roller moth, *Tortrix viridana*, for example, considerably reduces the number of acorns set. Where pannage is an important part of the rural economy as in some areas of Spain, insecticide spraying of forests is aimed at increasing acorn production (Torrent 1955; Robredo, personal communication).

Bark feeders and wood borers

Scolytid beetles are the most important group of insects that consume bark wherein they produce species-characteristic gallery systems (Fig. 4.11). Many species feed only on dead or dying bark and so are not pests but some can, under certain circumstances, attack living trees and they are among the most destructive forest pests. Many bark beetles have evolved specific associations with symbiotic blue-stain fungi. The role played by these fungi varies from species to species but they are often important in the initial colonization of trees and they appear to 'condition' the phloem for the feeding larvae, increasing its nutritive value or in some cases providing the sole food. Thus, successful attacks by bark beetles on still living trees often depend on a complex interaction between the host trees, beetles, and the symbiotic fungi associated with them. The co-evolution of bark beetles and fungi is discussed by Beaver (1989) and Berryman (1989).

The feeding strategies of some bark beetles are shown in Table 4.4. At endemic population densities even pest species like the spruce bark beetle, *Ips typographus*, utilize only dying or recently dead host material such as the bark of broken branches or dying trees and also, in managed forests, recently cut logs. Trees in normal health are not successfully attacked when beetle population density is low because they are well defended by resin which 'pitches out' attacking beetles (Fig. 3.4), and by defensive responses induced in the damaged tissue (Fig. 3.8). Natural disasters such as storms which blow over, snap, or partially uproot trees, can provide beetles with abundant breeding material and so may trigger outbreaks. Similarly, extreme environmental conditions such as prolonged drought may impair defensive responses of standing trees, dramatically increasing breeding success, especially in over-mature stands (Rudinsky 1962; Stark 1965; Coulson 1979). Once beetle population density is high, trees in apparently normal health may also be attacked.

During outbreaks, the simultaneous attack of individual trees by a large number of beetles (mass-attack) is co-ordinated by the release of aggregation pheromones, a process described in more detail in Chapter 9. Attacked trees succumb because the local resin flow and induced defensive response is reduced when many beetles attack within a short period. For many bark beetle species the role of the fungus in mass-attack is crucial because once attack density is sufficiently high, it rapidly colonizes the bark and sapwood, disrupting the transport system and further weakening the tree's defensive response (Fig. 4.12) (Horntvedt *et al.* 1983; Raffa and Berryman 1983). The relationship between the number of attacks by *I. typographus*

FIG. 4.11. (a) Galleries in elm produced by *Scolytus scolytus*; (b) Galleries in spruce produced by *Ips typographus*.

Table 4.4. *Examples of feeding strategies of European bark beetles*

Insect species	Main host	Adult pre-oviposition (maturation) feeding	Larval feeding strategy	Larval food	Main associated fungus
Dendroctonus micans	Spruce	Extension of larval gallery	Aggregative	Fresh phloem	None
Ips cembrae	Larch	Mine centre of young larch shoots or extension of larval gallery	Solitary	Fresh and fungus-infected phloem	*Ceratocystis laricicola*
Ips typographus	Spruce	Extension of larval gallery	Solitary	Fresh and fungus-infected phloem	*Ophiostoma polonica*
Scolytus scolytus	Elm	Twig crotches of healthy elms	Solitary	Mainly fresh phloem	*Ophiostoma ulmi*
Tomicus minor	Pine	Tunnel up centre of young pine shoots	Solitary	Mainly fungus	*Trichosporium tingens*
Tomicus piniperda	Pine	Tunnel up centre of young pine shoots	Solitary	Fresh phloem	None

Selected references: Browne 1968, Coulson 1979, Långström 1983, Redfern *et al.* 1987, Webber and Gibbs 1989, and Grégoire 1988.

FIG. 4.12. Colonization of the sapwood of spruce by the blue-staining fungus *Ophiostoma (Ceratocystis) polonica* which is carried by *Ips typographus*.

on spruce and fungal colonization of sapwood is shown in Fig. 4.13. Symbiotic fungi may be carried in special structures called mycangia which can range from simple pits on the body surface to complex cavities associated with the mouthparts that secrete a special fluid promoting both survival and germination of the symbiotic fungus (Beaver 1989). In some species, however, the spores simply adhere to the body surface.

The 'aggressiveness' of bark beetles is usually judged by the degree of host stress required for successful mass-attack and reflects their relative importance as forest pests. Bark beetles of the genus *Dendroctonus* are usually regarded as the most aggressive and outbreaks of the mountain pine beetle, *D. ponderosae*, for example, can be more or less self-sustaining once beetle populations are sufficiently high (Berryman 1978; Chapter 1). Species in the genus *Ips* on the other hand, although containing some notable pests such as *I. typographus*, usually require a greater degree of host stress for initial attacks to be successful (Fig. 4.14). The relationship between attack density of *I. typographus*, host vigour, and tree death is shown in Fig. 4.15 and the subject is discussed further in Chapter 10 in relation to risk-rating of stands.

Ips typographus has an annual life cycle in northern Europe and adults

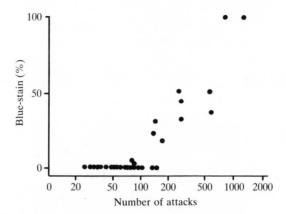

FIG. 4.13. The extent of blue-staining fungus colonization of the sapwood of Norway spruce in relation to the number of attacks by *Ips typographus*. Percent blue-stain indicates the portion of sapwood periphery which is discoloured (from Christiansen 1985).

overwinter under bark or in the soil. The spring flight is temperature dependent and males are the first to attack the host material and release the aggregation pheromone. They are polygamous and each of the two or three females bores a longitudinal egg gallery from the central nuptial chamber excavated in the phloem. Eggs are deposited in niches along the gallery and the larvae excavate individual feeding tunnels (Fig. 4.11b). After establishing a first brood, some parent beetles may re-emerge to attack other trees and establish sister broods and this is usually more common during epidemics (Bakke *et al.* 1977*a*).

The pine shoot beetle, *Tomicus piniperda*, is monogamous and a single longitudinal gallery is constructed in the phloem during the spring by adults that have overwintered. This bark beetle is a non-aggressive species that usually breeds in fallen trees and logs left in the forest and only attacks standing trees when highly-stressed (see section 4.3). After breeding, these adults may re-emerge to feed in the pith of young pine shoots (regeneration feeding) and are joined later in the year by the new generation of young adults which feed until sexually mature (maturation feeding) (Fig. 4.16). Although some beetles may overwinter in the shoots, most leave by the late autumn to overwinter in bark at the base of pine trees. The main damage caused by this bark beetle results from the shoot feeding (Fig. 4.17) which is particularly damaging because it destroys both the current shoots and the buds that would form shoots in the following year. The effects on tree growth may last for several years and total increment loss may be as much as 20–40 per cent after severe attacks (Fagerström *et al.* 1978).

FIG. 4.14. Gale damage to pines showing windblown and snapped trees, which are highly susceptible to *Ips typographus* attack.

The spruce bark beetle, *Dendroctonus micans*, which is widely distributed in Europe has an 'atypical' life cycle because it is able to exploit living trees in the absence of symbiotic fungi and without pheromone mediated mass-attack. Female *D. micans* which mate before leaving the larval gallery may re-attack the original host tree or disperse to establish broods on surrounding trees. The bark of the trunk or main roots can be attacked and eggs are laid in a single mass within an oval egg gallery in the phloem. Although the adults are solitary and do not communicate via aggregation pheromones, the larvae have an aggregation pheromone which mediates their communal feeding behaviour within a large continuous gallery (Grégoire 1988) (Fig. 4.18). The life cycle usually takes more than one season in most parts of Europe and the different developmental stages can be found at most times of the year.

Bark beetles that attack standing trees are not readily susceptible to control by insecticides and only rarely has this been attempted (Chapter 8). Since the food supply is the main determinant of population size, silvicultural methods which maintain vigorous tree growth and minimize the amount of moribund breeding material are the main means of controlling these

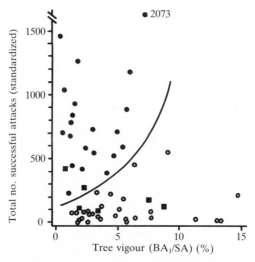

FIG. 4.15. Relationship between attack density of *Ips typographus* and the vigour of the host, Norway spruce. Vigour was estimated from relative sapwood growth. Solid circles = dying trees, circles with white centre = surviving trees, solid squares = death of strips of bark. BA_1 = basal area of the most recent complete annual ring. SA = sapwood cross-sectional area. The line, fitted by eye, represents threshold for successful attack (from Mulock and Christiansen 1986).

FIG. 4.16. Pine shoot bored out by *Tomicus piniperda* during maturation feeding.

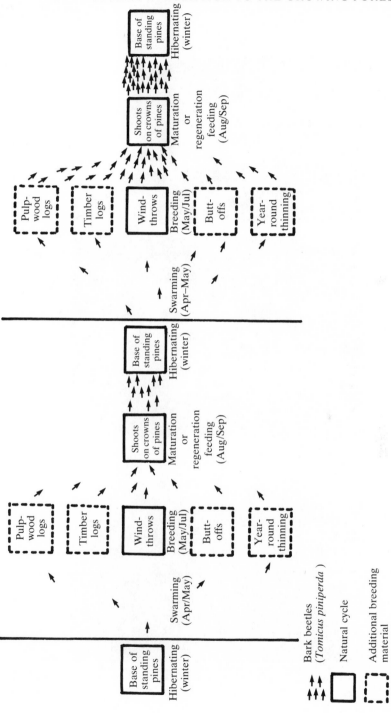

FIG. 4.17. The life cycle of *Tomicus piniperda*. Populations increase when breeding material is abundant, and the main economic damage occurs when adults feed in the shoots of healthy pine trees (after Nilsson 1976).

FIG. 4.18. (a) *Dendroctonus micans* adult; (b) *D. micans* larvae in colonial group under spruce bark; (c) Spruce trees killed by *D. micans*.

insects (Chapter 5). Natural enemies are relatively unimportant in most bark beetle populations but *D. micans* with its atypical life cycle is an exception. A specific predatory beetle, *Rhizophagus grandis* which locates its host through a kairomone response to frass produced by the bark beetle larvae has been released in a number of countries in attempts to control outbreaks of this pest (Chapter 7).

With one or two exceptions, insects that feed on wood in temperate regions are less important pests than those that feed on bark. In tropical forests, on the other hand, wood-boring insects such as longhorn beetles (family Cerambycidae) may cause economic damage to living trees. Wood-boring insects cause a technical degrading of the timber and also introduce wood-rotting fungi into the tree.

In Europe the larch longhorn, *Tetropium gabrieli*, will attack dying or severely-stressed standing trees such as those affected by the root rot fungi *Armillaria* spp. or *Fomes* spp. Eggs are laid in the bark during the summer and the larvae (Fig. 4.19) initially tunnel beneath the bark but penetrate into the wood later in the year. The adults emerge during May and June.

The European woodwasps, *Sirex noctilio* and *Urocerus gigas* (Fig. 4.20), are pests of pines although other conifers may be attacked. In Europe, they are relatively unimportant forest insects, attacking mainly moribund or fallen trees and logs. In New Zealand, Tasmania, and Australia, however, where the former species has been introduced, it is a serious pest of radiata pine plantations. The females usually attack trees affected by drought, suppression or other stress factors and, during oviposition, a phytotoxic mucus and spores of the pathogenic fungus, *Amylostereum areolatum*, are injected into the wood. The mucus is rapidly translocated around the tree

FIG. 4.19. Cerambycid larva.

FIG. 4.20. *Urocerus gigas* adult.

and its phytotoxic effects amplify the tree's stressed condition (Coutts 1970). The fungus, which is carried by the females in mycangia located at the base of the ovipositor, conditions the wood for the larvae by reducing its moisture content, causing decay, and providing nutrients for the larvae (Neumann and Minko 1981). Trees die through the joint action of the mucus and fungus and not through the activities of the woodwasp larvae. The biological control of this pest with a parasitic nematode is described in Chapter 7.

Hardwood trees may also be attacked by wood-boring insects. The leopard moth, *Zeuzera pyrina*, attacks a number of hardwood species, laying eggs during the summer in bark crevices on branches or the upper stem. As in cerambycids, the larvae initially burrow beneath the bark before entering the wood, destroying small branches and damaging the main stem. The life cycle takes 2–3 years to complete. A relative of this species, the goat moth, *Cossus cossus*, often attacks the base of trees, the larvae boring into the heartwood and occasionally killing them. As with other wood-boring insects the life cycle is prolonged and may take 2–4 years.

The longhorn beetle, *Phoracantha semipunctata*, is a serious pest of *Eucalyptus* plantations in the coastal zone of North Africa and the western Mediterranean. In Australia, this insect only attacks fallen or highly-stressed standing trees but in areas where it has been introduced, it is able to attack trees that are only moderately stressed or of generally low vigour and at high density may even kill more vigorous trees.

Timber infested by wood-boring insects is not always easy to detect during in quarantine inspection and a number of wood-boring insects have become widely distributed through the movement of infested timber.

4.1.4 Felling and post-harvest

Many of the bark beetles described in the previous section attack forest produce during thinning and felling operations, and this can lead to a build-up in population density. The importance of forest products in the life cycle of *Tomicus piniperda* is illustrated in Fig. 4.17. The role of forest hygiene in minimizing the build-up of such pests is discussed further in Chapter 5.

Ambrosia beetles or pinhole borers can cause considerable damage to the wood of both conifer and hardwood species after felling (Fig. 4.21). Adults bore through the bark and straight into the wood producing the characteristic 'pinhole' galleries which are usually surrounded by a dark area of fungal stain. The striped ambrosia beetle, *Trypodendron lineatum*, is widely distributed in the Old and the New World where it attacks a range of coniferous species. Its extensive host range is due, in part, to the fact that its specialized food requirements are met by the fungi on which it feeds rather than the host tissue itself. Its natural breeding material is in wind-blown trees, branch material, or trees dying or dead from other causes. But during forest operations, logs both in the forest and timber processing areas are vulnerable to attack and this is the main source of economic damage. The adults overwinter in the litter and duff on the forest floor and in the spring attack logs cut in the previous year. The ambrosial fungus is

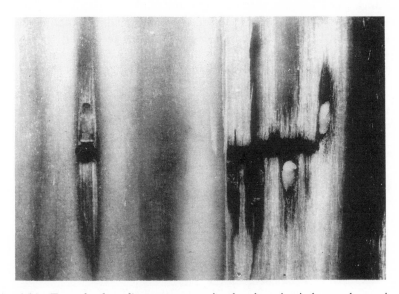

Fig. 4.21. *Trypodendron lineatum* pupae in chambers in timber and associated staining of the sapwood.

carried in special mycangia by the adults which introduce it into the wood during gallery construction.

Logs may be effectively protected from bark and ambrosia beetles by insecticides but in large felling operations and in timber yards this is usually impractical and expensive. Mass-trapping of ambrosia beetles using pheromone baited traps has been successfully used in timber processing areas in Canada (Chapter 9).

4.2 SPECIAL PLANTATIONS AND URBAN PEST PROBLEMS

Seed orchards, Christmas trees and high productivity 'biomass' plantations are all specialized forest crops that differ from ordinary plantations in their vulnerability to insect attack because they have a much higher value per unit area. Town trees on the other hand, have considerable amenity value which can be reduced by insect infestations.

4.2.1 Seed orchards

Within the forest, insects that attack seeds and cones are relatively unimportant (section 4.1.3) but in seed orchards, these insects are important pests and losses can be considerable (Table 4.5). With increasing interest in breeding trees for improved growth and pest resistance involving the establishment of seed orchards for controlled breeding experiments, the damage caused by such pests is likely to become more important in the future. Defoliators and shoot moths that do not directly damage seeds and cones can, nevertheless, reduce seed production, but those insects that

Table 4.5. *Cone and seed losses caused by insect attack recorded in some European seed orchards*

Tree	Insect species	Structure attacked	Percent damaged
Scots pine	*Pissodes validirostris*	Cones	10–75
Lodgepole pine	*Pissodes validirostris*	Cones	70–90
Norway spruce	*Zeiraphera ratzburgiana* *Dioryctria schuetzeella*	Strobili	20
	Cydia strobilella *Dioryctria abietella*	Cones	50
Larch	*Eurytoma* spp. *Megastigmus* spp.	Seeds	60
Douglas fir	*Megastigmus spermotrophus*	Seeds	up to 100

From Annila 1976.

attack the reproductive organs directly are the most damaging pests of seed orchard trees.

The abundance of insects that specialize on reproductive structures is largely determined by the availability of that resource. From the practical point of view this means that damage to cone crops is usually less in years following a small cone crop and larger when cones were abundant in previous years (Hedlin 1964; Mattson 1971). However, seed orchards are likely to be sited in areas favourable for flowering, planted with good-flowering clones and perhaps treated with fertilizers which are known to increase flower initiation and this will increase the amount and predictability of the food supply and increase the damage caused by seed-feeding insects (Sweet 1975).

In contrast to defoliators, important seed and cone insects are represented among several different insect orders (Table 4.6). The Douglas fir seed wasp, *Megastigmus spermotrophus*, is an introduced species in Europe and is the most important of a number of *Megastigmus* spp. that attack other conifers such as larch, spruce or firs. Female *M. spermatrophus* oviposit directly into the endosperm of young seeds within the developing cone. A single seed supports full development of an individual larva and during feeding there are no external signs of damage until the adults emerge through a hole made in the seed. This concealed feeding behaviour has been a factor in the transport of this insect in infested seed to many parts of the world. X-ray photography has been successfully used to examine seeds for the presence of larvae.

The spruce seed moth, *Cydia strobilella*, oviposits between the scales of spruce flowers. Larvae feed initially on the cone rachis but later the developing seeds are attacked, each larva consuming several seeds during development. Fourth instar larvae overwinter in the rachis and some then remain in extended diapause for two or more winters (see Fig. 2.10).

The pine cone weevil, *Pissodes validirostris*, is not an important pest in Britain but in southern Europe this insect can cause extensive damage to the stone pine, *Pinus pinea*, which is often cultivated for its edible seeds. Adult females oviposit in the scales of pine cones which are in the final year of development and the larvae form galleries which can completely destroy the cone and cone rachis. The adults can cause damage in the crown of the tree by feeding on the bark of small branches.

Insecticidal control of specialized seed-feeding insects is possible but careful timing is essential because much of the life cycle is spent within the host. The tendency of many species to overwinter as larvae on the trees (Table 4.6) suggests that the complete removal of cones in infested orchards can be an effective means of control especially for isolated seed orchards where the likelihood of reinvasion from forested areas is small.

Table 4.6. *Examples of insects that damage the reproductive parts of trees in Europe*

Insect species	Order	Main host(s)	Part attacked	Damage	Overwinter stage
Cydia strobilella	Lepidoptera	Spruce	Seeds	Larvae feed on seeds inside cones	Larvae in cones
Dioryctria abietella	Lepidoptera	Spruce	Cones/shoots	Larvae feed extensively within cones	Larvae in hibernaculae on cone surface
Tortrix viridana	Lepidoptera	Oak	Flowers/foliage	Young larvae feed on flowers when present	Egg
Andricus quercuscalicis	Hymenoptera	Oak	Flowers on turkey oak/acorns on pedunculate oak	Acorn knopper galls prevent germination	Larvae or adults in extended diapause in galls in litter
Megastigmus spermotrophus	Hymenoptera	Douglas fir	Seeds	Each larva develops within a single seed in cone	Fully grown larvae in seeds in litter
Lasiomma melania	Diptera	Larch	Cones	Larvae feed extensively within cones	Pupae in litter
Pissodes validirostris	Coleoptera	Pine	Cones/shoots	Larvae feed in cones adults on twig bark	Adults under bark flaps or in soil

Selected references: Bakke 1963, Hedlin *et al.* 1981, and Roques 1983.

4.2.2 Christmas tree plantations

Norway spruce is the traditional Christmas tree in many parts of Europe and plantations may be attacked by a number of spruce pests. Because the visual appearance of the tree is so important in determining its value, trees may be damaged at relatively low insect population densities. Insects that are unimportant in the forest, therefore, can be pests of Christmas tree plantations. An example is provided by the woolly aphid, *Adelges abietis*, (Fig. 4.22a). Unlike most adelgids, this species has no alternate host, feeding only on spruce. Nymphs from the overwintering generation feed at the bases of needles in the spring, causing the development of a characteristic 'pineapple' gall. The galls mature in the late summer when they open to release the alate generation. Shoots may be distorted by the galls which later became dry and brown, so disfiguring the tree that it may be unsaleable. *Adelges cooleyi* also forms galls on spruce but unlike *A. abietis* has an alternate host, Douglas fir. On this host, the feeding stages, which produce a white 'wool', can cause a characteristic distortion of the needles (Fig. 4.22b).

The stem-feeding aphid, *Cinara pilicornis*, overwinters in the egg stage and a succession of generations of viviparous females in spring and summer can lead to a rapid build-up of aphids on the young spruce trees. Copious quantities of honeydew are secreted by this insect so that trees become sticky and covered with sooty mould. The green spruce aphid, *Elatobium abietinum*, which occurs on spruce at all stages of growth can also be a pest in Christmas tree plantations causing yellowing and even loss of needles in heavy infestations.

Insecticides are commonly used to achieve the levels of 'cosmetic' control required within these specialised plantations.

4.2.3 Biomass forestry

Biomass or energy plantations usually consist of coppiced broad-leaved species such as willow and poplars and are cultivated to achieve maximum fibre and fuelwood production (Cannell and Smith 1980) (Chapter 1). Because the trees are at high density and intensively cultivated, resembling agricultural crops in this respect, they would appear to be vulnerable to pest outbreaks (Wilson 1976). However, although there are a number of potential pests of these trees such as the tortricid, *Gypsonoma aceriana*, the satin moth, *Leucoma salicis*, and the chrysomelid beetle, *Galerucella lineola*, no outstanding problems have developed on the relatively small areas so far established in Europe.

Several studies have shown that coppiced plants have a considerable

FIG. 4.22. (a) *Adelges abietis* 'pineapple' gall on spruce; (b) *Adelges cooleyi* 'wool' and needle kinking on Douglas fir.

capacity to recover from moderate levels of insect attack (Bassman *et al.* 1982; Larsson 1983).

4.2.4 Urban pest problems

Trees in towns, especially those along roadsides, are often growing in less than ideal conditions. The local concentration of pollutants from car exhausts may be quite high, roots may be covered by tarmac or pavement or otherwise damaged during repair or construction work and the aerial parts of trees may sustain physical damage. Many insect infestations, particularly those of aphids and scale insects, are often regarded as a symptom of this kind of damage rather than a cause of ill health in urban trees. The urban environment can, of course, also affect insect populations as graphically illustrated by examples of industrial melanism.

As well as directly affecting urban trees, insect infestations can disfigure them (defoliation, silk webbing, waxy secretions), and aphid honeydew can result in the development of sooty mould on leaves and on parked cars and other objects underneath infested trees.

Some insect infestations such as those of the horse chestnut scale, *Pulvinaria regalis*, seem to be largely confined to urban trees and are rare or absent from hosts in rural areas or in forests (Fig. 4.23). This insect spends the summer feeding as an inconspicuous nymph on the underside of leaves and can attack a range of broad-leaved trees. Prior to leaf-fall they move onto twigs to overwinter and in the following spring move down on to the main trunk to lay eggs which are surrounded by a conspicuous woolly wax. This introduced insect first appeared in London in the early 1960s and, interestingly, appeared to spread along certain bus routes as the mobile nymphs in the crown were swept from tree to tree in the wake of double-decker buses (Harris 1970)!

Some insects that feed on town trees may also affect people. Larvae of the pine processionary moth, *Thaumetopoea pityocampa*, and the brown-

FIG. 4.23. *Pulvinaria regalis* adults with egg masses on horse chestnut.

tail moth, *Euproctis chrysorrhoea*, for example, have urticating hairs which can cause skin rashes and eye irritation upon contact and this can be severe for some people. Direct control of such pests is often necessary and is aimed at protecting people rather than trees.

The control of urban pests in general is influenced by the need to avoid the use of toxic insecticides in public places. New techniques for the injection and implantation of systemic insecticides directly into trees can minimize such hazards (Chapter 8). Microbial insecticides and biological control are possible alternatives to the use of chemical insecticides (Chapter 7).

4.3 INTERACTION WITH OTHER INSECTS AND DISEASE ORGANISMS

Insect pests may interact in a number of different ways and the net result is usually an increase in the damage done to trees. For example, two pests may attack the same tree simultaneously, one example being the pine sawfly, *Neodiprion sertifer*, and the pine beauty moth, *Panolis flammea*, on lodgepole pine discussed in section 4.1.2. These defoliators derive no mutual benefit from the association and may even compete when food is limited. Other species, however, may only attack trees after they have been weakened by the attack of a so-called 'primary' pest. These 'secondary' pests are almost always bark beetles because many of them require a stressed host for successful attack although during outbreaks, aggressive bark beetles can behave as primary pests (section 4.1.3). For example, pines defoliated by the pine looper moth, *Bupalus piniaria*, which is a primary pest, are often attacked and killed by the secondary bark beetle, *Tomicus piniperda* (Bevan 1974). Similarly *T. destruens* or the weevil, *Pissodes notatus*, attack maritime pine affected by the scale insect, *Matsucoccus feytaudi*, in southern Europe.

In the USA, firs defoliated by the Douglas fir tussock moth, *Orgyia pseudotsugata*, are susceptible to attack by the fir engraver, *Scolytus ventralis*, and the Douglas fir beetle, *Dendroctonus pseudotsugae*. In forests defoliated by *O. pseudotsugata*, beetle populations increased for 2 or 3 years, but as trees regained their normal vigour following refoliation the bark beetle populations crashed to very low levels (Fig. 4.24a, b).

Fungi may act as primary pathogens of trees in some instances or as secondary pathogens following attack by primary insect pests. In beech bark disease, trees extensively colonized by the scale insect, *Cryptococcus fagisuga*, are susceptible to attack by the fungus, *Nectria coccinea*, which can kill the tree. This weakly pathogenic fungus is able to invade bark debilitated by scale-feeding although, as with many secondary pests and

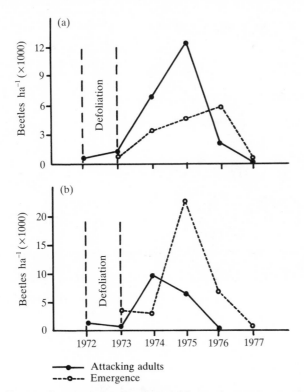

FIG. 4.24. Changes in population density of (a) *Dendroctonus pseudotsugae*, and (b) *Scolytus ventralis*, following defoliation of grand and Douglas fir by *Orgyia pseudotsugata* (after Wright *et al.* 1984).

diseases, *N. coccinea* is also able to attack hosts stressed by abiotic factors such as drought (Lonsdale 1980). Diseased trees are often attacked by ambrosia beetles whose galleries in the xylem can become colonized by white-rot fungi. Stems weakened by decay often snap in strong winds (Fig. 4.25).

Another important interaction occurs when insects transmit tree diseases. Transmission of the elm phloem necrosis virus by *Scaphoides luteolus* has already been mentioned but a particularly well-known example is that of Dutch elm disease, the aggressive strain of which has decimated elm populations in North America and Eurasia (Fig. 4.26) (Gibbs 1978). Dutch elm disease is caused by the pathogenic fungus, *Ophiostoma (Ceratocystis) ulmi*, and transmitted by the elm bark beetles, *Scolytus scolytus* and *S. multistriatus* in Europe and *Hylurgopinus rufipes* and the introduced *S. multistriatus* in North America. The beetles transmit the fungus to elm trees during maturation feeding on twigs in the crown and the fungal spores enter xylem vessels causing severe wilting and death of the trees. The inner

FIG. 4.25. Beech tree blown over by high winds showing ambrosia beetle tunnels in the timber at point of snap.

FIG. 4.26. Dutch elm diseased trees in a hedgerow.

bark of these dead or dying trees forms a suitable breeding substrate for the beetles. As the larvae develop, the bark becomes colonized by *O. ulmi* which begins to sporulate so that, following pupation, the emerging adults carry the spores with them to the crowns of healthy elm trees.

In Japan the pine sawyer beetle, *Monochamus alternatus*, transmits the pathogenic nematode, *Bursaphelenchus xylophilus*, which causes pine wilt disease. The nematode was probably introduced into Japan from North America where it does little damage to the native pines (Wingfield *et al.* 1984). In Japan, however, it has had a tremendous impact on the local pines and in 1981 alone it was estimated that 10 million trees died with 25 per cent of the nation's pine forests affected (Mamiya 1983).

The adult longhorn beetles emerge from dead pines in the early summer and fly to the crowns of healthy pines where they feed on the bark of young twigs. Nematode larvae emerge from their spiracles and drop onto the twigs, penetrating the woody tissue through the feeding wounds. Trees begin to decline after about 3 weeks and such trees are attractive to adult beetles which oviposit in the bark. The larvae initially tunnel under the bark but later enter the sapwood and eventually pupate there. The nematodes, which aggregate around the pupal chamber, enter the spiracles of the callow adults to complete the cycle (Kobayashi *et al.* 1984).

The tremendous impact of these two diseases arises largely from the fact that new associations have occurred when one of the organisms was introduced into a new region and again emphasizes the need for the stringent plant health regulations outlined in Chapter 5 as a component of effective integrated pest management.

4.4 THE IMPACT OF INSECTS ON FORESTS AND FOREST TREES

By affecting the growth and survival of individual trees, insects directly reduce the productivity of forests and this is the most important practical result of insect outbreaks. But insects also have indirect effects on the forest ecosystem that in the long term may also affect tree growth.

4.4.1 Endemic levels of herbivory in forests

The 'background' level of herbivory owing to endemic populations of forest insects has been estimated in several studies which suggest that typically 5–15 per cent of the foliage is removed each year. However, the estimates from different kinds of forest vary widely. In a mature pine forest in Sweden, for example, 0.7 per cent of the total needle biomass was eaten by insects in one year (Larsson and Tenow 1980), whereas in Australian rainforests herbivory may exceed 20 per cent if partially eaten leaves are included (Loman 1984). Background levels of herbivory probably have little impact on wood production because trees, like other plants, can compensate for some loss of tissue (Crawley 1983; Belsky 1986). Seed production, however, might suffer even after relatively low levels of insect attack. In pedunculate oaks, for example, acorn production can be reduced by a factor of 2–4 by endemic levels of feeding (Crawley 1985), suggesting that such levels of herbivory could have a significant effect on yields from seed orchards and might have long-term effects in natural forests as a result of reduced recruitment.

Most damage to forests undoubtedly occurs during outbreaks which can vary in extent and frequency and which often have dramatic effects on the forest ecosystem.

4.4.2 The scale of pest outbreaks

Most outbreaks of forest insects are usually of only local significance but some pests may have regular and, occasionally, very extensive outbreaks affecting whole regions and sometimes assuming national proportions in which the economic and environmental consequences may be impossible to estimate. Some examples of extensive outbreaks of forest insects are given in Table 4.7.

Outbreaks of the nun moth, *Lymantria monacha*, have occurred in many European countries over the past 100 years (Fig. 4.27). One of the most recent occurred in Poland in the early 1980s and it affected 25 per cent of the country's forest. Chemical control was required on an area of over 6

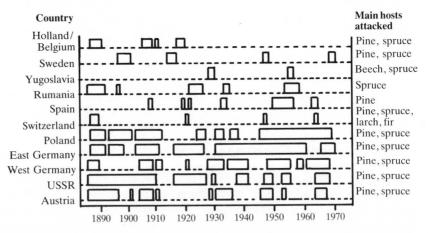

FIG. 4.27. Outbreaks of *Lymantria monacha* on different host species in Europe (from Schmutzenhofer 1975).

Table 4.7. *Examples of forest insect outbreaks*

Insect species	Main host(s)	Outbreak region and dates	Volume lost, area attacked (1), area treated (2)	Reference
Choristoneura fumiferana	Fir/spruce	Eastern Canada	1909–20 1937–58 1967–present	300 000 km² (1) 1 100 000 km² (1) 900 000 km² (1)	Martineau (1984)
Dendroctonus micans	Spruce	Turkey	1966–84	55 000 ha (1)	Benz (1985)
Dendrolimus superans sibiricus	Pine	USSR	1953–7	4 500 000 ha (1)	Kolomiets (1980)
Ips typographus	Spruce	Norway Sweden	1970–82 1970–9	5 000 000 m³ 2 000 000 m³	Bakke (pers. comm.) Bakke and Riege (1982)
Lymantria dispar	Oak and other broad-leaves	USA	1971	800 000 ha (1)	Doane and McManus (1981)
Lymantria monacha	Spruce/pine	Poland	1978–84	6 450 000 ha (2)	Schönherr (1985)
Panolis flammea	Pine	Scotland	1977–80 1984–7	10 000 ha (1) 10 000 ha (1)	Stoakley (pers. comm.)

million ha and this outbreak can only be described as a national disaster. Other pests such as the pine weevil, *Hylobius abietis*, attacking young transplanted trees may have a less dramatic impact, but year-in and year-out losses make it an extremely important pest in countries with significant replanting programmes. In southern and central Sweden and in Denmark conifer seedlings in areas of reafforestation that are not protected by prophylactic insecticide treatment can suffer 30 per cent mortality. These losses and the delay in replanting, cost the Swedish forestry industry millions of pounds annually.

In North America, the gypsy moth, *Lymantria dispar*, and the spruce budworm, *Choristoneura fumiferana*, are major defoliators of forest trees. In the 1950s and 60s, tens of thousands of hectares were sprayed with DDT to control spruce budworm, a practice which probably perpetuated outbreaks by keeping alive highly susceptible trees (Chapter 8).

4.4.3 Indirect effects of insect outbreaks

As well as affecting the growth and survival of forest trees, outbreaks of forest insects can have more wide-ranging effects on the environment and may even change its perceived amenity 'value'. Among the most important effects on the forest ecosystem are those on the water and nutrient relations of the site but there may also be long-term effects on succession in natural forests.

Microclimate and water relations

Defoliation of trees can have a temporary but dramatic effect on the microclimate within the forest by increasing windspeed and the penetration of sunlight and rainfall as discussed in Chapter 2. When trees are killed, however, the changes within and sometimes outside the affected area persist until the forest is re-established. This was dramatically illustrated following an outbreak of the spruce beetle, *Dendroctonus rufipennis*, during the 1940s which killed spruce and pine in 585 km^2 of forest in an important watershed area in Colorado USA. Rainfall, which was normally intercepted and evaporated from the canopy, penetrated to the forest floor and transpiration losses were also considerably reduced. The effect of this was to increase significantly stream flow in the area for at least 25 years (Love 1955; Bethlahmy 1975).

Nutrient cycles

When streamflow through forests is increased more nutrients may be exported from the site and so indirectly affect tree growth in the long term. But insect feeding itself can also affect nutrient availability because defoliators increase litter fall and by damaging leaves may also enhance nutrient leaching (Mattson and Addy 1975; Schowalter 1981). Dead insects, cast cuticles, and frass in litter fall are a source of readily available easily mineralized nutrients in high concentration. It is not clear how important these insect-mediated effects on nutrient cycling are at the ecosystem level but, in general, growth responses of trees to the addition of nutrients will only occur when growth at that site is nutrient limited. However, it has been shown that nutrients from frass can be taken up rapidly by individual trees and can affect their physiology (Haukioja *et al.* 1985*b*). The effects of fertilization of forest trees on insect–plant interactions is discussed in Chapter 3.

In a study of N and P flow in litter fall following defoliation of two oak species by the California oak moth, *Phryganidia californica*, Hollinger (1986) found that 40–70 per cent of the N and P flow to the ground was via frass and insect remains (Fig. 4.28). Where regular outbreaks occurred, this insect had a significant impact on nutrient flow, although the seasonal nature of the rainfall in this area resulted in a net loss of N and P from this particular system. In boreal forests increased leaf-fall during outbreaks of defoliators will not provide an immediate boost of nutrients because of the slow rates of decomposition.

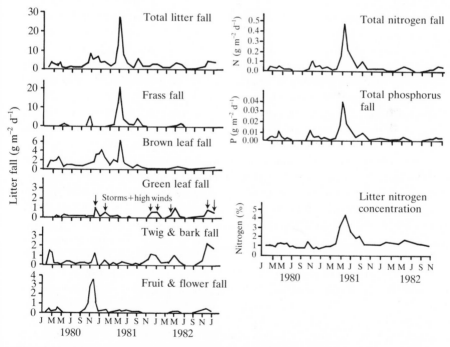

FIG. 4.28. Litter and nutrient fall from *Quercus agrifolia* defoliated by *Phryganidia californica* in 1981 (from Hollinger 1986).

Forest succession

Selective herbivory can alter the competitive interactions between trees and may in some cases accelerate the rate of successional change (Connell and Slatyer 1977). Where climax species are killed, gaps in the canopy may allow the establishment of early successional species whereas widespread mortality can return the whole forest to an earlier successional stage. The spruce budworm, *Choristoneura fumiferana*, which kills mature balsam fir in eastern North America is part of a co-evolved system in which budworm outbreaks renew the successional cycle by destroying forests dominated by the climax balsam fir. Alternatively, forest insects may delay natural succession. For example, outbreaks of the larch budmoth, *Zeiraphera diniana*, in the Engadine valley in Switzerland cause considerable mortality of young cembran pine trees in the undergrowth of larch stands. This favours larch and delays the natural succession from pure larch stands to larch–cembran pine climax forest (Baltensweiler 1975). The effects of other insects on forest ecosystems are discussed by Schowalter *et al.* (1986).

4.4.4 Direct effects of insect outbreaks

Insects have their most obvious effect on timber production when trees are killed during outbreaks. Under these circumstances estimation of the loss of current and projected timber yield is relatively straightforward. More commonly, however, trees survive attack but their reduced height growth or stem diameter increment results in loss of wood volume and timber quality may also be reduced, especially in the more valuable hardwood species. Quantifying these sublethal effects on trees is more complicated not least because trees are often able to increase their growth following attack (Crawley 1983). The ability to compensate for insect damage can occur at both the individual and population level. Differential attack on trees in a mixed forest or in a monoculture where trees have different susceptibilities reduces competition and can allow unattacked individuals to increase their growth at the expense of their attacked neighbours. When individual trees are killed following attack, the effect in young dense stands would be similar to that of a silvicultural thinning. But insect attack is rarely evenly distributed within the forest and clearly where large gaps are formed in the stand loss of productivity is inevitable (e.g. Fig. 5.14).

The ability of individual trees to compensate for insect damage depends on a number of factors including the tissue affected and the timing and severity of attack. Insect attack, like that of stress discussed in Chapter 3, can affect the balance between sources and sinks, and the consequent reallocation of resources within the tree allows for a range of different outcomes as discussed below.

Although it is usually assumed that the effects of insect attack will be reflected in the growth of the aerial parts of the tree, root growth may also be affected especially in young trees. For example, roots of lime saplings attacked by the aphid, *Eucallipterus tiliae*, do not increase in size although above ground parts of the plant appear to grow normally (Dixon 1971).

Defoliation is perhaps the commonest form of insect damage to trees and most studies have shown that growth loss is proportional to the intensity of defoliation (Kulman 1971). However, the timing of defoliation and, in conifers, the age of the needles removed determine the impact on the tree, both in the year of attack and in subsequent years. An example of the effects of artificial defoliation of young Scots pine in Sweden is shown in Fig. 4.29 (Ericsson *et al.* 1980). When both 1- and 2-year-old needles were removed in early summer (mid-June), ring growth was slightly reduced but shoot growth was unaffected, demonstrating the capacity of trees to compensate during the season for the loss of needles. Effects on both ring and shoot growth were, however, observed in the two following years, with ring growth affected more than shoot growth (see Chapter 3 and Fig. 3.20).

Needles removed in 1976	Ring width			Shoot length (mean of leaders and laterals)		
	1976	1977	1978	1976	1977	1978
1yr old in mid-June	○	○	○	○	○	○
1+2yr old in mid-June	●	●●	●●	○	●	●
Current in mid-August	○	○	●	○	●	●
Current + 1yr old in mid-August	○	●●	●●●	○	●●	●●●

FIG. 4.29. The effects of different artificial defoliation treatments on growth of 15–20-year-old Scots pine. Open circles denote no effects, and closed circles increasing growth reduction (from Ericsson *et al.* 1980).

When the trees were heavily defoliated in the late summer (mid-August), they started the new season without the highly productive current and 1-year-old needles and this had a big effect on both radial growth and shoot growth for at least two seasons. The extent of growth reduction following insect attack also depends on factors such as the tree's age and vigour, competitive position in the canopy and the site on which it is growing. Previous history of outbreaks is also important since attacks in successive years are likely to have much greater impact on tree growth than a single attack. Studies on the spruce budworm, *Choristoneura fumiferana,* have shown that the percentage loss in radial increment after defoliation of balsam fir was less in slow than in fast growing trees although mortality was lower among the faster growing ones (Miller 1977; MacLean 1981). Site factors including variables such as rainfall and insolation may determine the rate of recovery of trees following attack. For example, increment losses in larch defoliated by the sawfly, *Cephalcia alpina*, in Holland were lower on loamy than on sandy soils (Luitjes 1958).

Estimation of growth losses caused by forest pests

Methods for using annual rings to measure tree growth were developed by Duff and Nolan (1953) but care needs to be taken in interpreting these measurements. An important fact that emerged from their detailed studies, was that there were species-specific patterns of radial growth in relation to height up the tree so that single measurements, for example at breast height (1.3 m), may give a misleading picture of the growth of the tree as a whole. Also, defoliation itself can have different effects on radial increment at different heights up the tree, the biggest effect usually being in the crown as shown for the eastern spruce budworm, *C. fumiferana* (Mott *et al*. 1957; Williams 1967; Piene 1980). However, no large differences in ring width at different heights were detected when Douglas fir was defoliated by the western spruce budworm, *C. occidentalis*, and so there are exceptions to this general rule. In some cases, annual rings may be completely missing following defoliation and this can complicate estimates of growth loss in some tree species (O'Neil 1963).

In trying to attribute variation in annual ring growth to current insect attack, account must be taken of the between-year variation in growth rate due, for example, to weather factors, stand management or even previous insect attack. When trees are subject to frequent or sustained attack, they may not reach their potential growth on that site so that overall impact on growth may be difficult to establish (Morrow and LaMarche 1978).

In natural infestations, estimates of growth loss from annual ring measurements can be made in two main ways; by comparing attacked with unattacked trees from the same or nearby stands or by comparing growth during attack with pre- and post-attack levels assuming these represent 'normal' growth on the site. Errors can arise from using naturally unattacked trees as controls because they may have avoided attack for a variety of reasons that may not be independent of the growth rate, e.g. differences in vigour or flushing time (Kulman 1971).

The most accurate estimates of growth loss caused by insects are obtained from experiments in which comparisons are made between plots of trees with different degrees of infestation and control plots protected from attack with insecticide.

Some examples of growth losses in forest trees

The effects of some Lepidoptera and sawfly defoliators on tree growth are summarized in Table 4.8. Growth loss is usually proportional to defoliation

Table 4.8. *Effects of some defoliating insects on trees in Europe*

Defoliator	Tree	Defoliation	Reduction in stem growth (%)	Country
Hymenoptera				
Neodiprion sertifer	Scots pine	heavy for 1–2 years	39–52	Sweden
Neodiprion sertifer	Scots pine	light/heavy	10–45	Hungary
Diprion pini	Scots pine	20–85%	21–57	Holland
Lygaeonematus abietinus	Norway spruce	light/very heavy	24–32	Denmark
Cephalcia alpina	Japanese larch	20–85%	10–50	Holland
Lepidoptera				
Zeiraphera diniana	Spruce	Complete	16	Germany
Coleophora laricella	European larch	40%	33–45	Germany
Lymantria monacha	Spruce	heavy	50–80	Romania
Dasychira pudibunda	Beech	90% for 1–2 years	7–13	Germany
Pygaera anastomosis	Poplar	1–2 defoliations in same year	12–30	Italy

From Kulman 1971.

although different tree species are affected to varying degrees by a given level of defoliation. Some specific examples show how such growth losses can be estimated.

The western spruce budworm, *Choristoneura occidentalis.*   Several studies have been made of the impact of defoliation by *Choristoneura occidentalis* on the growth of Douglas fir in western North America (Alfaro *et al.* 1982, 1985; Van Sickle *et al.* 1983). Severe defoliation causes loss of both radial and height increment and leaders may be killed as a result of defoliation and pre-outbreak internodes may also die back. This results in misshapen trees which can limit the length of merchantable timber.

Growth losses occur during two distinct phases, with growth declining during the main period of budworm feeding and remaining below normal during the period of recovery after population collapse (Fig. 4.30a). Loss of radial increment was estimated on individual trees by comparing growth during the outbreak with that in non-outbreak periods, ignoring the period of rapidly increasing radial growth early in the tree's life (see Thomson and Van Sickle 1980; Alfaro *et al.* 1985 for details).

Height increment depression occurs suddenly and it remains depressed for longer than radial growth. Potential height growth during outbreak and recovery periods, like that for radial growth, was estimated from a regression of the height increase data for non-outbreak periods, again omitting data from the juvenile phase (Fig. 4.30a).

Volume losses, estimated from a series of bole segments up the tree (Thomson and Van Sickle 1980) amounted to around 44 per cent of potential in trees which had been defoliated four times since the 1920s. Actual and potential height growth during a similar period is shown in Fig.

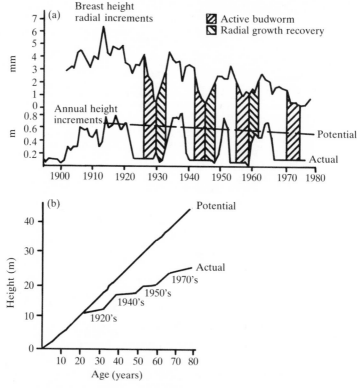

FIG. 4.30. The effect of defoliation of Douglas fir by *Choristoneura occidentalis*, (a) effect of successive outbreaks on mean annual radial growth and height increment, (b) actual and potential height growth of attacked trees (from van Sickle *et al.* 1983).

4.30b, trees losing about 32 per cent of potential height increment. Mortality of trees and reduction in wood quality were important additional losses (Alfaro *et al.* 1985).

In this example, estimates of growth based on comparison of attacked and unattacked periods was chosen because most trees in the stands were attacked, and unattacked trees at other sites may have differed in important respects from those under study. The method assumes, however, that normal growth is resumed between outbreaks but this may not be true, especially if some trees in the stands have been killed during outbreaks, reducing competition between trees (thinning effect) and increasing the growth rate of surviving ones (Alfaro *et al.* 1985).

The green spruce aphid, *Elatobium abietinum.* In young spruce plantations, defoliation by *Elatobium abietinum* has been shown to reduce both diameter and height growth. Following a natural infestation in which some

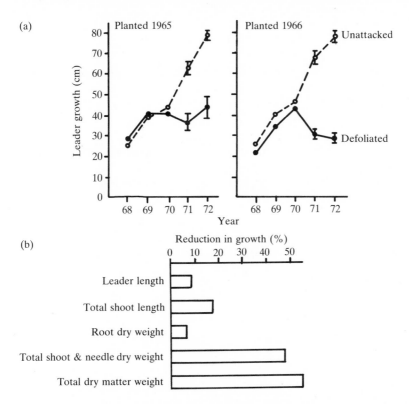

FIG. 4.31. The impact of *Elatobium abietinum* on growth of Sitka spruce, (a) effect of a complete defoliation in 1971 on leader growth of forest trees (bars = ±1 standard error), (b) effect on growth of 2-year-old potted trees artificially infested with the aphid compared with uninfested controls (from Carter 1977).

5–6-year old Sitka spruce trees were completely defoliated, leader lengths were reduced for at least two years compared to unattacked trees (Fig. 4.31a). Although naturally unattacked trees are not the best controls, in this example growth prior to defoliation was similar in both attacked and control trees.

This aphid commonly infests very young trees as in forest nurseries for example and so it is possible to study in detail the effects of attack on those aspects of growth that would be impossible to study in larger forest trees. When young potted trees were artificially infested with aphids, root as well as shoot growth was affected and total dry matter production was reduced by over 50 per cent compared to uninfested controls (Fig. 4.31b) (Carter 1977).

The spruce bell moth, *Epinotia nanana.* Outbreaks of this needle miner are relatively rare but it has occasionally caused extensive defoliation of trees in Germany and Scandinavia. The related *Epinotia tedella* occasionally causes damage to Christmas trees in Britain, the brown mined needles significantly reducing 'quality' of the trees. In Norway, Austarå (1984) made diameter measurements on naturally attacked trees and on unattacked ones 35 km away. This study uses naturally uninfested controls some distance away from the infested stands, and attacked and control trees were clearly growing at different rates prior to attack (Fig. 4.32). Maximum defoliation of about 80 per cent occurred in two consecutive years but there was significant defoliation of trees over a period of about 4–5 years. Diameter growth was reduced during the main period of defoliation followed by a recovery phase during which the effects of defoliation were still evident (Fig. 4.32).

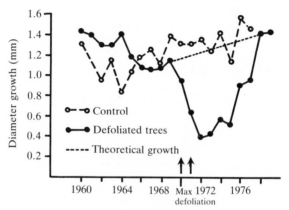

FIG. 4.32. Effect of defoliation of Norway spruce by *Epinotia nanana*. Maximum defoliation occurred in 1970 and 1971, as indicated by arrows (from Austarå 1984).

The spruce bark beetle, *Dendroctonus micans.* Larvae of *Dendroctonus micans* excavate large contiguous galleries in the bark of spruce trees, destroying the cambium in discrete patches on attacked stems. When several broods are established on the tree or when attacks occur in successive years the tree may be killed. Those that survive attack often sustain wounds on the lower most valuable part of the tree, reducing both volume and quality of the timber (Fig. 4.33).

FIG. 4.33. Section of Norway spruce tree attacked by *Dendroctonus micans* in 1973.

5

Management 1: forest practices

In considering the management of forest insects, it seems appropriate to start with the forest itself and how the planning and establishment of plantations and the management and ultimate harvest of both natural and plantation forests can affect insect populations. Such forest practices can play a significant role in the direct control of forest insects by felling or thinning infested trees, for example, but damage by forest insects may be linked to certain cultural conditions such as the 'site' on which the trees are grown, the stage or rate of growth, and the density of trees (Chapters 3 and 4). Forest practices can also play an important role here, indirectly affecting insect populations through manipulation of the forest itself and they are especially useful in plantations which are more or less intensively managed.

In general, traditional silvicultural practices of planting the right species in the right environment and managing the forest for vigorous growth followed by timely harvest has been an important factor in minimizing the risk of insect outbreaks triggered by site or other cultural factors. But the increasingly widespread practice of planting exotic tree species in new ecological settings, not only in Europe and other developed countries but also in tropical regions (Evans 1982; Savill and Evans 1986; Chapter 1) places greater emphasis on the role that forest practices can play in insect control. The novel interaction between insects, trees, and site that can result when exotic trees are widely planted can make it difficult to predict their vulnerability to insect attack over a complete rotation and this emphasizes the empirical nature of some aspects of plantation silviculture. However, one obvious risk to exotic trees and of course native ones as well, comes from the accidental introduction of exotic pests as a result of the increasing international trade in timber and we will first consider how these risks can be minimized.

5.1 ACCIDENTAL INTRODUCTION OF PESTS

The gypsy moth, *Lymantria dispar*, is one of the most destructive forest pests in the USA and has the unique distinction of being a deliberate introduction that went wrong. This insect was originally introduced for hybridization experiments with the domestic silkworm, *Bombyx mori*, but it escaped to cause widespread destruction to eastern broad-leaved forests (Doane and McManus 1981). Of course, most introductions are accidental and the process has been going on for over a century and, as the examples in Table 5.1 make clear, many of the insects now established in different parts of the world originated from Europe. Some of the early introductions into the New World, in the late nineteenth and early twentieth centuries, occurred as a result of the demand for familiar European trees by the large immigrant population and some of these insects have become serious pests of the native forests (Gibbs and Wainhouse 1986). Nevertheless, forest pests are still relatively localized when compared with agricultural pests and some measure of this is given by their predominance on lists of pests excluded from various countries. For example, the European and Mediter-

Table 5.1. *Examples of forest insects introduced into new countries where they have become serious pests*

Insect species	Common name	Native to	Introduced to	Approximate date of introduction or discovery
Adelges piceae	Balsam woolly aphid	Europe	USA	1900
Cryptococcus fagisuga	Beech scale	Europe	Canada	1890
Pulvinaria regalis	Horse chestnut scale	Asia (?)	UK	1960s
Coleophora laricella	Larch case bearer moth	Europe	USA	1886
Fenusa pusilla	Birch leafminer	Europe	USA	1923
Hyphantria cunea	Fall webworm	N. America	E. Europe	1940
Lymantria dispar	Gypsy moth	Europe	USA	1869
Operophtera brumata	Winter moth	Europe	Canada	1930
Rhyacionia buoliana	European pine shoot moth	Europe	USA	1914
Diprion similis	Pine sawfly	Europe	USA	1914
Gilpinia hercyniae	European spruce sawfly	Europe	Canada	1922
Neodiprion sertifer	European pine sawfly	Europe	USA	1925
Sirex noctilio	Woodwasp	Europe	New Zealand Australia	1900 1950
Dendroctonus micans	Great spruce bark beetle	Continental Europe	UK	1970
Phoracantha semipunctata	*Eucalyptus* longhorn	Australia	S. W. Europe	1970s
Scolytus multistriatus	Lesser elm bark beetle	Europe	USA	1909
Ips grandicollis	Five-spined bark beetle	N. America	Australia	1943

From Bevan and King 1983, Coulson and Witter 1984, Anon. 1985, Gibbs and Wainhouse 1986, Eldridge and Simpson 1987, and Speight unpublished.

ranean Plant Protection Organization (EPPO) produces a list of exotic pests and diseases of all crops that are still absent from the 35 member countries and 40 per cent of them are pests of forest trees (Smith 1979). Thus, preventing the introduction of exotic pests is an important way of protecting forests.

5.1.1 Import restrictions

Countries with extensive areas of non-indigenous trees and which import large volumes of timber from within the tree's natural range are particularly vulnerable to the importation of exotic pests. An important way of minimizing this risk is the formulation and implementation of a quarantine policy aimed at identifying potential pests and, if possible, preventing their introduction. Within Europe, EPPO formulates plant health guidelines for the member countries on which legislation can be based. The aim of such legislation is to provide an acceptable level of protection without unacceptable barriers to trade (Phillips 1978; Rohwer 1979).

In formulating and implementing plant health legislation it is, of course, essential that potential forest pests can be identified and that imported timber can be adequately inspected but this is not always straightforward. For example, insects which are important pests in their native regions can be clearly identified and added to the list of excluded insects, but others may be harmless within their host's natural range and yet still have the potential to cause serious damage when introduced into a new habitat. Such insects are not covered by present quarantine regulations (Gibbs and Wainhouse 1986). The principal risks in Europe arise from the importation of bark beetles in bark still attached to timber, or in bark products (Fig. 5.1). The risk from new defoliators is much smaller because tree foliage is not generally imported. Within the European Economic Community, present legislation seeks to exclude North American bark beetles of pine, spruce and Douglas fir and the UK also excludes the major bark beetle pests of spruce from mainland Europe (Phillips 1978). This legislation is implemented through the issue of phytosanitary certificates which are legal documents of declaration completed in the country of origin and which must accompany the import of most forest products. This system relies heavily on the thoroughness of inspectors in the exporting country although checking of the imported material on arrival provides an additional safeguard. Inspectors have legally enforceable authority to examine and sample imported material and, where necessary, order the treatment, reshipment, or destruction of infested loads.

In practice, of course, it is not possible to check all imported material, bearing in mind that the UK for example imports around 85 per cent of its timber annually. Bain (1977) reports the experience of the New Zealand

FIG. 5.1. Softwood planks imported from North America into Europe, a potential source of exotic forest pests.

Forest Service which intercepted 180 species of insects in 19 families arriving in the country over a 3-year period. The major families included Cerambycidae, Scolytidae, Bostrychidae, Lyctidae and Siricidae, all potential pests of forests or timber and they were found in materials as diverse as sawn timber, cricket bats and chopsticks! (see also Wylie and Peters 1987). Plant health legislation, therefore, cannot provide absolute barriers to pests and some will inevitably become established in the long run (Southey 1979). If and when they become established it may be possible to restrict their spread by internal quarantine measures and so minimize or delay their impact on the forest.

5.1.2 Internal quarantine

The establishment of effective quarantine areas depends on the early detection and identification of introduced pests and so emphasizes the importance of trained field staff, public awareness and good taxonomic services. For most introduced pests, eradication is not a practical objective although it may be possible for some species which have a low reproductive potential and limited powers of dispersal. For example, the European house borer, *Hylotrupes bajulus*, which attacks seasoned softwood timber and is potentially a pest of great economic importance, has been eradicated from southern Australia following its introduction in the early 1950s

(Eldridge and Simpson 1987). Restriction of the infested area is usually the main goal of internal quarantine and is most likely to be effective for pests which attack bark or wood because they often form discrete infestations and the movement of timber following thinning or felling operations in the infested area can be effectively controlled. Felling and destruction of infested material on site directly reduces pest density and restrictions on the movement of host material should limit the rate of spread, at least for pests with limited powers of dispersal.

In the Australian state of Victoria, where the woodwasp, *Sirex noctilio*, is an introduced species, frequent inspection of softwood mills and the insecticidal treatment, processing or drying of timber before transport to unaffected areas helps to restrict the spread of this insect (Neumann 1979). It has, nevertheless, spread into New South Wales where it was discovered in 1981 and despite biological control (see Chapter 7) and other measures it continues to spread at a rate of about 30 km year^{-1} (Eldridge and Simpson 1987). In the UK, quarantine measures have been applied against two bark beetles, *Scolytus* spp., vectors of Dutch elm disease and the spruce bark beetle, *Dendroctonus micans*; the controlled areas are shown in Fig. 5.2. The *Scolytus* bark beetles are native insects but they are vectors of the aggressive strain of the pathogenic fungus, *Ophiostoma (Ceratocystis) ulmi*, which was introduced from North America (Gibbs 1978). Although it was not possible to prevent the rapid spread of the disease throughout southern England, it has proved possible within Brighton, Hove, and parts of East Sussex, to reduce the mortality rate from disease and so preserve many of the mature elms. This was achieved by an intensive campaign of routine inspection followed by felling and destruction of diseased trees and by restrictions on the movement of elm wood (Greig and Gibbs 1983). The annual cost of the sanitation programme was estimated to be around £20 000 and compares favourably with the estimated cost of £1.5 million to remove dead and dying elms which would have been present in the absence of control.

Dendroctonus micans was introduced into the UK in about 1970 and had become well-established by the time it was discovered in 1982 (Bevan and King 1983). Nevertheless, the infested area could be delimited and strict quarantine was enforced within this Scheduled Area (Forestry Commission 1984) to prevent spread of the beetle to the more extensive spruce growing areas in northern England and southern Scotland. Survey, sanitation felling, bark removal from logs, and monitoring the movement of spruce timber (Fig. 5.3) together with a programme of biological control (Chapter 7) has so far contained this insect to a relatively small proportion of its host's range (see also Chapter 10).

FIG. 5.2. The scheduled area of *Dendroctonus micans* in the UK, and (inset) the East Sussex Dutch elm disease control area. SY = Surrey, WS = West Sussex (from Greig and Gibbs 1983; Wainhouse 1987).

FIG. 5.3. Spruce logs with bark removed being taken for processing from sites infested by *Dendroctonus micans*.

5.2 PLANNING OF FOREST PLANTATIONS

The factors that need to be considered in the planning and establishment of plantations are shown in Fig. 5.4. The choice of tree species will be influenced by its silvicultural characteristics in relation to the objective of planting and the environmental qualities of the planting site. Thus the broad ecological requirements of the species can be compared with the characteristics of a site, for example, the soil type (pH, drainage, rooting, and nutrient qualities), ground vegetation, and local terrain (Savill and Evans 1986). Species selection should also be influenced by the risk of attack by pests and diseases taking into account not only the tree's inherent susceptibility but also susceptibility that may be associated with growth on specific sites.

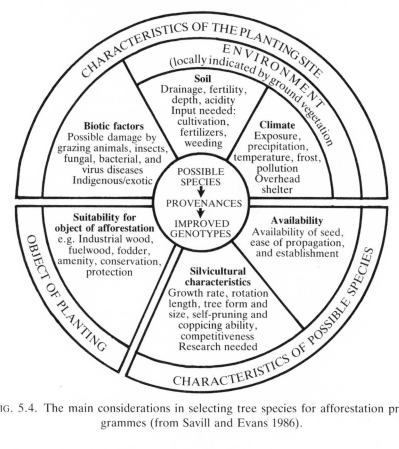

FIG. 5.4. The main considerations in selecting tree species for afforestation programmes (from Savill and Evans 1986).

5.2.1 The influence of site and choice of tree species on future pest problems

Trees that are known to be highly susceptible to insect attack are unlikely
to be suitable for large scale planting and can be rejected at the planning
stage. For example, the European silver fir is a silviculturally desirable
species, but in the UK, it is not widely planted because of its extreme
susceptibility to the introduced silver fir adelgid, *Adelges nordmannianae*
(Varty 1956; Lines 1960; Crooke 1979).

Many exotic tree species suitable for establishment in plantations have a
wide geographical range and like many plants, they commonly evolve
locally-adapted ecotypes or provenances and this variation must be taken
into account when selecting species for planting. Sitka spruce, for example,
occurs over 20° of latitude along the western seaboard of North America
(Fig. 5.5) and when different provenances are planted outside their natural
range they retain many of the characteristics that adapt them to their

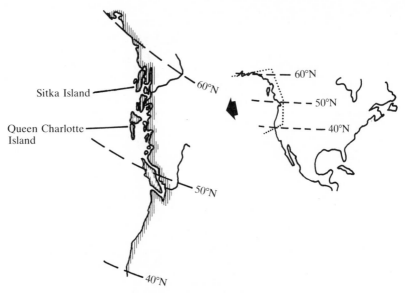

FIG. 5.5. The natural distribution of Sitka spruce along the west coast of North America. The species is named after Sitka Island, but the main source of seed for trees planted in Britain is Queen Charlotte Island (from Cannell 1984).

normal habitat. The height growth of four Sitka spruce provenances planted in Britain is shown in Fig. 5.6. Provenances from Alaska stop growing much earlier than more southerly provenances, reflecting the short growing season in the northern part of the range. Northerly provenances are more susceptible to the green spruce aphid, *Elatobium abietinum*, because populations can build up during the long dormant period (Carter and Nichols 1988; Chapter 3). More southerly provenances have a longer growing season and so are more productive but are vulnerable to frost damage when planted in northern areas of Britain. Queen Charlotte Island is the major source of seed for Sitka spruce in Britain and although a somewhat fortuitous choice (Cannell 1984), it has proved very well suited to conditions in western upland Britain (Fig. 5.7).

The importance of the process of species selection in relation to the planting site is shown by the many examples of outbreaks of forest insects related to the 'site' on which the trees are growing as discussed in Chapter 3 (see also Bevan and Stoakley 1985). In many cases, such outbreaks occur as a result of stress-induced changes in the trees and this is more likely to occur when they are planted on inappropriate or inhospitable sites. Speight (1986) proposed a general relationship between increasing levels of stress and attack by different kinds of forest insects (Fig. 5.8). It is worth emphasizing, however, that local environmental factors can affect insect survival

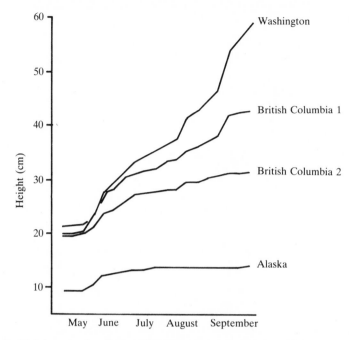

FIG. 5.6. Height growth of some Sitka spruce provenances which were grown in northern England. The Alaskan provenance has a very short growing period (from Lines and Mitchell 1965).

and reproduction directly as discussed in Chapter 2 and the activities of the insects themselves may affect some site qualities (Chapter 4) (Fig. 5.9). The establishment of pine plantations in the Philippines provides an extreme example of the effect of site factors on the susceptibility of trees to insect attack. The pines have been planted on infertile soils with poor water retention capacity, previously occupied by tropical rainforest. The indigenous forest trees are adapted to these conditions because they are able rapidly to recycle the scarce minerals through leaching from leaves and the rapid breakdown of dead trees. The pines, however, do not grow well on these soils and are subject to repeated attacks by forest pests (Speight and Speechly 1982). In northern Scotland, areas of open moorland have been planted with lodgepole pine. Although this tree grows well relative to other species on poor quality exposed sites, it has proved vulnerable to outbreaks of the pine beauty moth, *Panolis flammea*, particularly on deep unflushed peat soils (Leather and Barbour 1987). *Panolis flammea* is not a pest on native Scots pine in Britain and susceptibility of lodgepole pine on these sites could not have been predicted in advance.

Some specialized forms of silviculture such as planting on derelict land

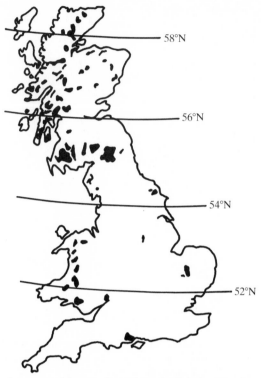

FIG. 5.7. The main areas of forest plantations in Britain. The large plantations in the uplands of south and west Scotland, northern England, and Wales have a high percentage of Sitka spruce. Pines are planted mainly in the drier eastern part of the country (from Cannell 1984).

have also been associated with increased risk of insect damage. In south Wales, young lodgepole pines planted on infertile, hard-pan soils produced after open-cast colliery landscaping work suffer heavy attacks by the pine shoot moth, *Rhyacionia buoliana* (Fig. 5.10).

5.2.2 Planting regime

Plantations are usually even-aged and composed of a single tree species planted in rows with silvicultural and economic considerations usually determining the planting density. The density of trees can influence the likelihood of attack by some insects. For example, pines are most susceptible to *R. buoliana* up to the stage of canopy closure. The initial density of trees influences how quickly this less susceptible stage is reached. Open stands are also more susceptible to pine processionary moth, *Thaumetopoea pityocampa*.

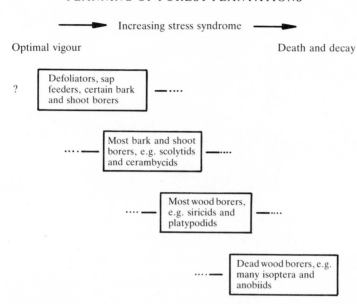

FIG. 5.8. Hypothetical relationship between environmentally induced stress in trees and their susceptibility to attack by successive groups of insects (from Speight 1986).

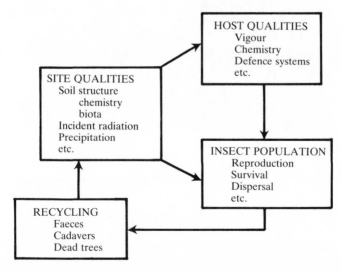

FIG. 5.9. Direct and indirect interactions between characteristics of the planting site and insect populations (after Berryman 1981).

FIG. 5.10. (a) Young lodgepole pine trees planted on sites reclaimed from open cast coal mining in south Wales; (b) Severe shoot damage to the trees in (a) by *Rhyacionia buoliana*. Note the bent shoots and stunted growth.

There are sometimes silvicultural advantages to establishing more than one species in a plantation. For example, an additional species may be planted to 'nurse' the main one through an early vulnerable stage by providing protection against frost and exposure. In the UK, larch or more frequently Norway spruce is mixed with oak and when removed during thinning, the conifer species has the additional benefit of providing interim revenue. Other advantages of planting mixtures include greater market flexibility, improved growth rate of the trees, and enhanced amenity value (Savill and Evans 1986) and, sometimes, reduced risk of insect damage.

In Lower Saxony, spruce in plantations on unsuitable soils, such as pseudogley, only roots superficially because of poor soil aeration. Such stands are prone to windthrow and when this happens the inner trees are suddenly exposed to sunshine and the rise in cambial temperature (see Chapter 2) weakens the trees and predisposes them to the spruce bark beetle *Ips typographus*. When planted in mixture with beech, however, the roots of spruce are able to penetrate the soil more deeply, following those of the beech and the stands are thus more stable and less vulnerable to bark beetle attack (Otto 1985). The question of whether mixed stands in general are less susceptible to insect attack is discussed in section 5.4 (see also Chapter 1).

At present, most tree species grown in plantations are genetically unre-fined by selective breeding to improve productivity. But the use of clonal material through vegetative propagation, which can significantly increase productivity (Savill and Evans 1986), may significantly increase the risk of destructive pest outbreaks as has occurred with plant pathogens on geneti-cally uniform agricultural crops (Gibson *et al.* 1980).

5.3 THE POST-PLANNING STAGE; SILVICULTURAL TECHNIQUES FOR PEST MANAGEMENT

Once the important decisions concerning site, tree species, and planting regime have been made and the plantations established, silvicultural prac-tices can be important in minimizing pest damage but, as with other direct control measures, economic factors may determine their role in any parti-cular pest outbreak.

The use of hazard- or risk-ratings to assess the vulnerability of certain forests to insect attack can aid in the planning and implementation of silvicultural control measures but discussion of this topic is deferred to Chapter 10.

5.3.1 The nursery and post-planting stages

Cultural conditions in the nursery resemble those of an agricultural crop, with high plant density, intensive management and a relatively rapid turn-over of plants. Nursery plants can be particularly vulnerable to insect attacks although they can often be controlled with insecticides. The loca-tion of the nurseries can be important in determining the likelihood of attack; surrounding forest areas, for example, may be reservoirs of pests that may infest young trees, but also, agricultural areas can harbour polyphagous pests. In parts of the USA, Douglas fir nursery stock is attacked by larvae of a pyralid moth that is a pest of grasses. Where there are grasslands around the nurseries, they should be included in any insecticide treatment programme to control this pest (Kamm *et al.* 1983).

When seedling trees are planted out in the forest they are particularly vulnerable to attack by insect pests and to competition with ground vegetation. The quality of plants from the nursery can affect the vigour of the transplanted trees and thus the likelihood of successful establishment. Careful nursery management producing healthy transplants, followed by rapid transport to the forest and planting of the young trees as quickly as possible, maximizes survival during the first year.

An important factor in plantation establishment is that site conditions can be modified through drainage, fertilization, and other cultural practices to improve early growth of the trees (Savill and Evans 1986). Fertilizers are commonly used during the establishment of plantations on infertile soils (Everard 1974) and their effects on trees are most significant prior to canopy closure. By increasing the growth and vigour of young trees, fertilization may be of value in minimizing the impact of some pests although it cannot yet be considered as a method of silvicultural pest control. Some effects of fertilization of trees on forest insects are discussed in Chapter 3.

In Europe, the main problem affecting young conifers in replanted areas is caused by the pine weevil, *Hylobius abietis*, which breeds under the bark of stumps left after felling (Fig. 5.11) and adults feed on the bark of the young transplants (Chapter 4). The impact of this pest can be reduced, but not eliminated, by a number of silvicultural measures and insecticides are still widely used to control this insect (Chapter 8). A fallow period of 1–3 years can reduce damage significantly but as well as delaying the next crop, this cultural practice allows the site to be colonized by weeds, making subsequent establishment more difficult (Doom and Frenken 1980). The adoption of whole-tree harvesting systems that utilize stumps and roots would remove a large proportion of the breeding substrate and such methods could reduce weevil populations by 50 to 70 per cent, but this would be impractical in mountainous areas, and in the long run such practices would increase the nutrient drain and may reduce site fertility (Carey and O'Brien 1979; Miller 1979).

Damage by *H. abietis* is usually more severe when the young trees are surrounded by other vegetation. Transplants in bare soil may be less subject to attack because the adults usually avoid exposed positions during feeding (Christiansen and Bakke 1971) so that by scarifying the soil around transplants damage can be reduced by up to 50 per cent (Eidmann 1979).

FIG. 5.11. Clear-felled site replanted with young conifers, showing old stumps and other debris which form breeding sites for *Hylobius abietis*.

However, the size of the weevil population and the availability of alternative food sources such as woody and semi-woody plants (e.g. bramble) are likely to be important factors in determining the success of this technique.

Similar methods have been used against the pine root collar weevil, *Hylobius radicis*, in the USA. This species attacks larger trees than its European relative but it is the larvae rather than the adults which damage the young trees by feeding below ground in the bark tissues of the root collar and roots. Damage is most severe close to infested plantations but those about 1 km or more away are usually only lightly infested. Pruning low branches, litter removal and soil scraping creates conditions close to the root collar that are unsuitable for ovipositing beetles. When combined, these treatments reduce larval density below the mortality threshold of two larvae per tree (Fig. 5.12) and the cost of this method of control compares favourably with that of chemical control (Wilson and Millers 1983). Other pests such as shoot moths in the genus *Rhyacionia* also appear to be deterred by this method. Wilson and Millers have incorporated these methods into a risk-rating and decision-making system (see also Chapter 10) for *H. radicis* management and it provides a good example of the integration of silvicultural techniques into a pest management programme (Fig. 5.13). In this system, developed for use in Michigan, summer and

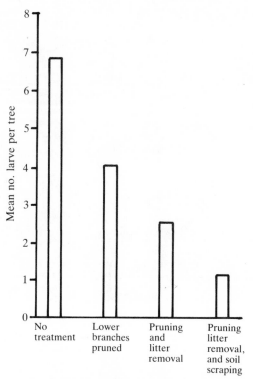

FIG. 5.12. Mean number of *Hylobius radicis* larvae per pine tree following removal of lower branches and litter, and scraping the soil surrounding young trees (from Wilson and Millers 1983).

winter temperatures, distance from the source of infestation, and host susceptibility are important factors determining risk.

Physical methods of protecting transplants have met with mixed success. In Sweden, where 30 per cent mortality from *H. abietis* is expected after the first two years (Eidmann 1981), protective plastic collars around the base of transplants appear to be economically viable, reducing losses from 60 per cent in non-collared transplants to 20 per cent in those protected by collars (Hellqvist and Lindström 1982; Lindström 1983).

5.3.2 Stand management and forest hygiene

Thinning of stands is an integral part of forest management (Savill and Evans 1986). It can also be a powerful technique for the manipulation of insect populations. Removal of infested trees affects insects directly, but by reducing competition and increasing growth and vigour of the remaining trees, thinning can also affect insects indirectly.

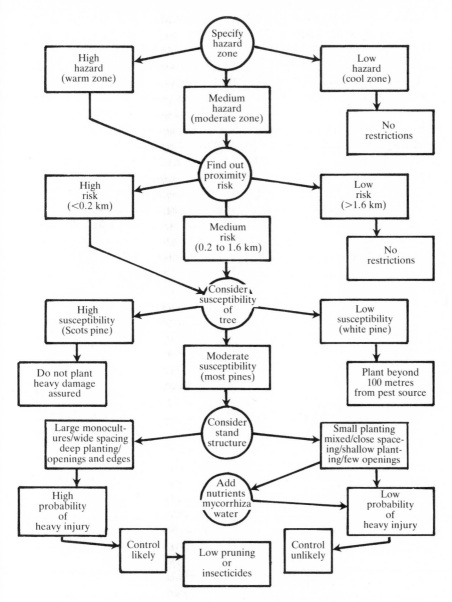

FIG. 5.13. Decision-making guidelines and the probable consequences of management of *Hylobius radicis* (from Wilson and Millers 1983).

In Australia, the woodwasp, *Sirex noctilio*, is particularly damaging in young dense pine stands (1770–2400 trees ha^{-1}) (Neumann and Minko 1981). Trees that are suppressed, drought-stressed or damaged in some other way are particularly susceptible. Unthinned stands suffer considerable mortality and surviving trees are usually unevenly distributed so that further thinning is often necessary to ensure good growth of remaining trees (Fig. 5.14). Early thinning of stands is clearly a priority where large areas of overstocked plantations are grown but this is affected by market and other economic factors (Neumann and Minko 1981).

Thinning is also an effective technique for reducing the susceptibility of stands to bark beetles. The effect of thinning stands of ponderosa pine on mortality caused by the mountain pine beetle, *Dendroctonus ponderosae*, is shown in Table 5.2. Within such stands, large slowly growing trees with thick bark are most at risk and should be selectively taken out during thinning, and where stands are dominated by such trees they should be the first to be removed during felling operations (Amman *et al.* 1977).

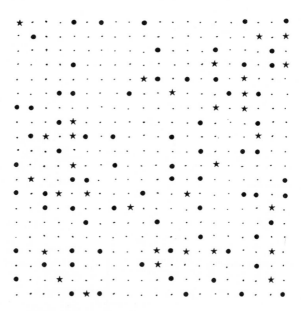

- ● healthy tree (final crop)
- ★ healthy tree (to be felled)
- · *Sirex*-killed tree

FIG. 5.14. The distribution of healthy and *Sirex noctilio*-killed trees in a 0.25 ha plot of an unthinned 17-year-old *Pinus radiata* plantation in Victoria, Australia (from Neumann and Minko 1981).

Table 5.2. *Cumulative mortality of ponderosa pine following attack by Dendroctonus ponderosae after various thinning treatments*

Thinning to	Mortality causes[a]		
spacing of	Beetle	Other	Total
Unthinned	2.70	2.19	4.89
3.5 by 3.5 m	0.75	0.63	1.38
4.5 by 4.5 m	0.06	0.06	0.12
5.5 by 5.5 m	0.00	0.17	0.17
6.5 by 6.5 m	0.00	0.17	0.17

[a] Mortality measured as loss in stem basal area (m^2 ha^{-1}) and determined in the five years after thinning (from Sartwell and Dolph 1976).

One of the earliest links established between forest practices and insect damage was the recognition in Europe in the late 1700s of the importance of felled timber, residual felling waste and branches remaining in the forest in contributing to the build-up of bark beetle populations which may then attack standing trees. This established the principle of forest hygiene which was incorporated into contemporary silvicultural practices (Schwerdtfeger 1973). Removal of breeding material from the forest is a simple but effective way of maintaining some bark beetle pests at low endemic levels, and when neglected for economic or other reasons the result can be an increase in insect damage. For example, the pine shoot beetle, *Tomicus piniperda*, which feeds within the shoots of standing trees during the period of egg maturation, can cause 20 per cent loss of lateral and leading shoots when populations build-up following neglect of forest hygiene (Doom and Luitjes 1971) (Fig. 5.15).

The seasonal timing of thinning or felling operations in relation to bark beetle flight periods can determine the extent of attack on logs. Summer and autumn thinning of spruce stands in the Netherlands, for example, resulted in significantly lower attack by the bark beetle, *Pityogenes chalcographus*, than when thinning was done at other times of the year (Grijpma and Schuring 1984). Similarly, thinning pine during July and August reduces attack by *T. piniperda* (Doom and Luitjes 1971). In the UK, if pine logs are present in the forest during March–June they should be treated with insecticide or removed from the forest within about six weeks, i.e. the average period from attack by *T. piniperda* to emergence of the next generation (Fig. 5.16) (Bevan 1974). Obviously, economic and logistic considerations may determine how rigorously these simple rules are adhered to.

FIG. 5.15. Stacks of pine logs in a forest; potential breeding sites for *Tomicus piniperda*, and a subsequent source of beetles that attack the shoots of standing trees.

5.3.3 Salvage and sanitation thinning and the use of trap trees

Salvage and sanitation thinning operations may be incorporated into normal thinning programmes but can also be used as a quite separate management technique. Salvage thinning is usually undertaken to remove dying or recently dead trees before their commercial value is reduced by further insect (or fungal) attack. In sanitation thinning on the other hand, the objective is to reduce the pest population by removing infested material and perhaps decrease the rate of spread through the forest. In severe outbreaks on the other hand, whole forest blocks may need to be felled.

Sanitation felling is usually an important part of internal quarantine measures. In the Dutch elm disease control area (section 5.1.2), most of the diseased trees in which the *Scolytus* bark beetle vectors could breed were removed during the sanitation felling programme and this significantly reduced mortality from the disease. Although all mature elms have been killed in the countryside around the controlled area, within it, 50–80 per cent of the mature elms are free from disease (Greig and Gibbs 1983). Similar but much larger scale removal of infested trees was used during the initial outbreaks of the spruce bark beetle, *Dendroctonus micans*, in the UK (Fig. 5.17).

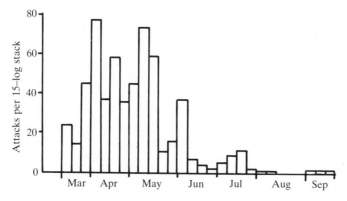

FIG. 5.16. The number of attacks by *Tomicus piniperda* on pine logs in the forest during spring and summer (from Bevan 1974).

FIG. 5.17. Spruce stand in Shropshire, UK, clear-felled after an outbreak of *Dendroctonus micans*.

Like the notion of forest hygiene, the idea of using 'trap' trees to concentrate attacks by bark beetles and weevils onto a few trees which can then be removed from the forest was one of the earliest forest practices developed for insect control. Originally, trees were made attractive to bark beetles by felling or girdling standing trees (Escherich 1923) but herbicide poisoning has also been tried. Although trap trees have been widely used in bark beetle management it is not clear to what extent their population density and attacks on other trees in the forest are reduced by this practice (cf. mass-trapping, Chapter 9). The method is also time-consuming and expensive because trees need to be distributed throughout the affected forest area and removed promptly following colonization by the insects.

In an experimental trial of a trap tree technique against the woodwasp, *Sirex noctilio*, in Australia, groups of radiata pine throughout susceptible (densely stocked) stands were injected with herbicides. These trees were preferentially attacked by *S. noctilio* and, in a most elegant procedure, the trees were then injected with insect parasitic nematodes which infest but do not kill the larvae. Emerging female woodwasps are sterile but disperse and can transmit the nematodes to other *Sirex*-infested trees during oviposition (Neumann and Minko 1981, see also Chapter 7). This control method could reduce the need for precommercial thinning of susceptible stands.

5.3.4 Felling and post-harvest protection

The time of felling, which in a plantation is usually around the culmination of mean annual increment (Chapter 1) may be brought forward in forest stands which prove vulnerable to pests late in the rotation. In Denmark, Sitka spruce stands on soils susceptible to drought are attacked by the spruce bark beetle, *Dendroctonus micans*. Sitka spruce is, nevertheless, more productive than other spruces on these sites and the best solution appears to be to continue to grow Sitka spruce but on a shorter rotation (Bejer-Petersen 1976).

Once removed from the forest, timber stored prior to processing can still provide important breeding sites for a variety of insect pests that not only degrade the timber but can also damage growing trees (Loyttyniemi and Uusvaara 1977). Most, if not all, damage to logs can be prevented by debarking, at least in temperate regions, but this is often not practicable when large volumes of timber are handled. However, some protection is afforded by debarking only those logs that form the outer layers of large stacks as shown for the spruce bark beetle, *Ips typographus* (Table 5.3).

An alternative method of deterring both insect and fungal attack is to store logs in wet conditions so that their moisture content remains high and

Table 5.3. *Incidence of the bark beetle Ips typographus in 1000 m³ stacks of spruce logs in Sweden*

Treatment	No. beetles	No. beetles emerging in next generation
Control (no. debarked logs)	130 100	507 700
Top logs debarked	10 660	3 200

The treated stacks were covered with a layer of debarked logs, 3 to 5 logs thick (from Regnander 1977).

the surrounding air is at 100 per cent relative humidity. This can best be done with sprinkler systems but storage in lakes and ponds can also be effective. This method of storage is particularly useful when natural disasters dramatically increase timber supply and disrupt normal processing and marketing schedules. Large volumes of timber can be stored for several years by this method so avoiding problems of market saturation and consequently depressed timber values. Wet storage was widely used in Germany following the extensive windblow of 1972 in which 200 km h^{-1} winds flattened 100 000 ha of pine and other species representing 10 per cent of the forest area of the affected region (Liese 1984). Clearing and reafforestation involved the removal of 16 million m^3 of merchantable timber of which about 10 per cent was held in wet storage. On this occasion, storage in lakes although moderately effective in protecting logs was found to have a number of disadvantages including the limited area available, logistic problems of getting logs in and out of the water, and possible pollution of the water by leachates from the logs. Sprinkler systems (Fig. 5.18) were much more effective, adequate water coverage preventing attack by such insects as the weevils, *Pissodes pini* and *Hylobius abietis*, the pine shoot beetle, *Tomicus piniperda*, and the ambrosia beetle, *Trypodendron lineatum* (Peek and Liese 1974; Regnander 1976). This system probably kills a high proportion of insects already in the bark and prevents invasion by blue-stain and wood decay fungi during several years

FIG. 5.18. Water sprinkling of log stacks to prevent insect attack.

storage. Wet storage of logs is now a part of normal post-felling operations in many parts of Europe.

An economic appraisal of water sprinkling to protect logs from ambrosia beetles in Canada showed that water spraying costs estimated at $2 per cubic foot per annum were considerably lower than the losses of $15 per cubic foot per annum which resulted following attack by ambrosia beetles (Richmond and Nijholt 1972).

5.4 FOREST DIVERSITY AND PEST OUTBREAKS

The absence of extensive insect outbreaks in tropical forest areas is often cited as supporting evidence for the importance of diversity in stabilizing communities (but see Gray 1972). This situation is usually contrasted with the uniform monoculture conditions in many forest plantations which are assumed to be more susceptible to outbreaks of forest pests (but see Chapter 1). This assumption has led to the recommendation that establishing mixed forests would increase regulation of forest pests (Atkinson 1953; Schwerdtfeger 1954; Voûte 1964; Gibson and Jones 1977).

It is in fact difficult to test experimentally the link between diversity and stability, separating out the effect of diversity *per se* from the influence of climate and also the co-evolved relationships between organisms within the community. On balance there seems to be little evidence that plantation monocultures as a whole are more susceptible to outbreaks than 'natural' forests and indeed several pests such as the nun moth, *Lymantria monacha*, the balsam woolly aphid, *Adelges piceae*, the pine sawfly, *Diprion pini*, and the gypsy moth, *L. dispar*, are serious pests of both kinds of forest (Gibson and Jones 1977). There are, however, examples where some particular aspect of diversity appears to influence the likelihood of pest outbreaks and, as in agricultural systems, the 'quality' rather than the 'quantity' of diversity seems to be important in affecting pest outbreaks (Way 1966). For some forest insects, 'too much' diversity in the form of alternative hosts may contribute to pest population build-up. The Douglas fir woolly aphid, *Adelges cooleyi*, has two main hosts and both are required for the full life cycle incorporating both sexual and asexual forms. Galls are formed on spruce and the secondary host is often Douglas fir. In western Canada mixtures of these two species can lead to outbreaks (Savill and Evans 1986) and clearly, a reduction in diversity in this instance would be beneficial. In contrast, increasing diversity in forests susceptible to the gypsy moth, *L. dispar*, by adding appropriate species to the herb layer may help to stabilize their populations because many secondary hosts of parasitoids that attack *L. dispar* feed on forest undergrowth (Györfi 1951).

Outbreaks of the spruce budworm, *Choristoneura fumiferana*, in North

America are associated with reduced diversity of the natural forest but the relationship is a complex one. This insect has a long history of outbreaks in eastern Canada that have become increasingly more frequent and severe (Fig. 5.19). Outbreaks are more likely in stands with a high proportion of mature balsam fir and once started, usually continue until most of the fir trees are killed (Fig. 5.20). Commercial exploitation of forests together with fire control has favoured the regeneration of fir and allowed forests to proceed to the susceptible fir/spruce climax. So in this example the simplifi-

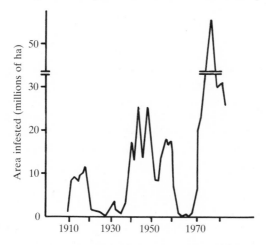

FIG. 5.19. The area of eastern Canada moderately or severely infested by *Choristoneura fumiferana*, from 1909 to 1979 (from Blais 1983).

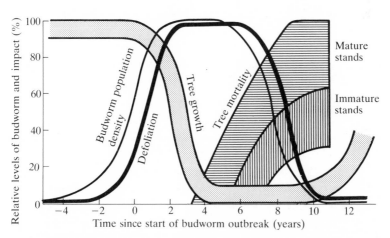

FIG. 5.20. Generalized pattern of outbreaks of *Choristoneura fumiferana*, and their impact on tree growth and mortality (from MacLean 1981).

cation of the forest that has occurred during development of a 'natural' climax has contributed to the development of outbreaks. Rather than providing evidence for the dangers of simplifying forests, outbreaks of this pest are perhaps best considered as part of a co-evolved forest system in which budworm outbreaks renew the successional cycle by killing mature and over-mature fir, returning the forest to an earlier, more productive successional stage (Blais 1983; Sanders *et al.* 1985).

5.5 FOREST PRACTICES AND INTEGRATED PEST MANAGEMENT

Successful implementation of forest practices for the control of insect pests depends on efficient organization at the local and regional levels and may require government support and legislation. This can be seen in the integration of government plant health and import directives with the planning and management of new or established forests. The ways in which forests are managed depends largely on the nature of the resource they provide as discussed in Chapter 1. But in general, plantations will be more amenable to silvicultural manipulation than extensive and inaccessible natural forest areas. We should emphasize, however, that silvicultural methods alone are often not sufficient to give the required level of control against particular pests and their contribution should be seen in the context of an integrated approach to pest management discussed in Chapter 10.

6
Management 2: plant resistance

The conditions under which trees are grown have an important influence on their resistance to insect pests as discussed in the previous chapter. But some trees are inherently more resistant to insect attack than others, and this genetic variation could potentially be exploited in breeding programmes aimed at increasing levels of pest resistance. However, there are a number of practical and economic constraints on the identification and exploitation of insect resistance in trees, some of which are discussed in this chapter. Although we only consider resistance to insects, some important pests are associated with pathogenic organisms such as fungi (Chapter 4), so that resistance to these organisms, as well as to the insects themselves, will be an important factor in the successful exploitation of the tree.

The basis for any programme aimed at exploiting resistance for insect control is the existence of natural variation in susceptibility in the tree population. This provides the raw material on which breeding programmes aimed at increasing host resistance can be built.

6.1 VARIATION IN TREES AND INSECTS

Most tree species are in fact highly genetically variable (Perry 1979; Forrest 1980; Hamrick *et al.* 1981), so there is considerable scope for differences in the degree of resistance both between and within species (see also Chapter 3).

Intraspecific variation may be apparent between trees growing in different geographic regions, among different forest stands within a region and also between individual trees within a stand. But insect populations also vary and differences within and between host tree populations may be associated with corresponding variations within the insect populations themselves. The diprionid sawflies, for example, are a particularly variable group and exist as distinct races or physiological strains adapted to specific host plants (Knerer and Atwood 1973). Among bark beetles, electrophoretic studies of isoenzyme variation have shown that genetic differences occur both within and between populations. For example in a study of the southern pine beetle, *Dendroctonus frontalis*, in the southern USA and Mexico, eastern and western populations show significant differences at two enzyme loci, one of which is shown in Fig. 6.1. Similarly in north-western North America, mountain pine beetle, *D. ponderosae*, popula-tions on lodgepole pine trees from the Sierras and western Oregon (var. *murrayana*) were genetically different from those feeding on trees with a more easterly distribution (var. *latifolia*) (Stock *et al.* 1978).

6.2 DEFINING RESISTANCE

There are many different definitions of resistance (see Harris and Frederiksen 1984). Beck (1965) defines it as the collective heritable characteristics by which a plant species, race, clone, or individual may reduce the probability that an insect species, race, biotype, or individual may use it as a host. This strict definition, which has been widely used, specifically excludes toler-ance which should really be included in any broad definition of resistance, especially since it can be of considerable practical significance. Also excluded are factors that allow trees to avoid insect attack through, for example, differences in phenology or as a result of transitory environmental changes, such as in nutrient availability that may affect plant suitability as food. Such phenomena are usually described as pseudoresistance (Painter 1951)

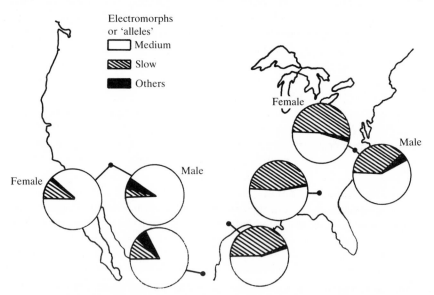

FIG. 6.1. Percentage frequencies of electromorphs or 'alleles' at the phosphoglu-coisomerase locus in 5 populations of *Dendroctonus frontalis* in the USA. Popula-tions were sampled from Virginia, Georgia, Texas, Arizona and Mexico. Differ-ences were evident between males and females from Arizona and Virginia, for which frequencies are shown separately (from Anderson *et al.* 1979).

and are referred to in Chapters 3 and 5. The term immunity which is implicit in some definitions of resistance is best avoided because a tree species that is never attacked by a particular insect species, i.e. is immune, cannot be considered as part of its host range (Horber 1980). Whatever definition of resistance is used, it is clear that it is a relative term that must be defined in relation to both the tree and insect populations and the level of resistance determined by comparison with susceptible individuals, varieties, or species.

The genetic control of resistance, originally described by van der Plank (1968), has been widely explored in the literature on plant diseases. The concepts of 'vertical' and 'horizontal' resistance which he introduced can be extended to cover resistance to insects as well (Gallun and Khush 1980). Vertical or biotype-specific resistance is controlled by one or a few major genes and is only effective against some fungal or insect biotypes. Thus, for fungal pathogens at least, there is a direct relationship between genes for resistance in the host and genes for virulence in the disease organism. Although vertical resistance can be highly effective it is ultimately unstable, because the intensive selection pressure that is exerted on the pathogen population can lead to rapid counter-adaptation, and indeed, there are a number of examples where this has occurred in rust fungi on agricultural crops (Johnson 1987). Horizontal or general resistance on the other hand is effective against a range of fungal or insect biotypes and is usually polygenically controlled and, so, much less vulnerable to rapid counter-adaptation. It is therefore much more appropriate for long-lived trees where durability of resistance in the forest is an important consideration. The classification of resistance into these two distinct types may in fact be somewhat artificial, and in reality there probably exists a continuum between vertical and horizontal resistance (Nelson 1982).

6.3 RESISTANCE MECHANISMS

An understanding of the mechanisms of resistance, although not essential for the identification of resistant trees, can provide important clues to the level of resistance likely to occur and how best to develop and use it for insect control.

Plants have three main mechanisms of resistance which were originally described by Painter (1951, 1958), all of which may contribute to a greater or lesser extent to the total resistance of a plant. These are referred to as non-preference, antibiosis, and tolerance. The mechanism of non-preference works by affecting insect behaviour so that plants are largely avoided for feeding or oviposition. Non-preferred plants may lack certain token stimuli and so insects are not attracted to them or alternatively, they may contain repellent chemicals that are avoided by insects. Some examples of secondary chemicals that act as attractants, repellents, and oviposition stimulants are given in Tables 3.3, 9.1, and 9.2. Non-preferred plants may nevertheless be able to support insect development and so are vulnerable to damage especially during outbreaks of polyphagous pests. The development of insects on non-preferred hosts can lead to the establishment of new host associations; an example is given in Chapter 2 of the winter moth, *Operophtera brumata*, a polyphagous pest of broad-leaved trees, developing on Sitka spruce.

In many cases, chemicals that affect insect behaviour may actually be toxic and so are important in antibiosis. Antibiosis includes all the factors that adversely affect the survival, development, and reproduction of insects when they actually begin feeding on the plant. The kinds of chemical and physical defences that adversely affect insects are discussed in relation to their nutrition in Chapter 3. Both preformed (constitutive) and induced defences can contribute to antibiosis and their relative importance will depend to a large extent on the nature of the insect/tree interaction. Induced defences have been studied particularly in relation to defoliators and have been found in a number of different tree species (Wagner 1988). In birch, both rapidly-induced and long-term induced defences occur, but these differ in importance between different provenances as discussed in Chapter 3. Induced defences are also important in resistance against fungal attack (Horsfall and Cowling 1980).

Tolerance, in contrast to antibiosis, has no direct effect on insects, but relates to the ability of plants to survive and recover from attack. There is thus no strong selection pressure on the insect population so this resistance mechanism is potentially very stable (Gould 1983). Tolerant plants may, for example, be insensitive to toxins injected during feeding by such insects as aphids or mirid bugs, or they may have rapid wound repair mechanisms following mechanical damage. Tolerance can be an important defence mechanism in perennial plants especially as in some cases they may be able to compensate in part for lost biomass following insect attack (Chapter 4). This ability, however, varies from species to species and will depend, among other things, on the habitat in which the trees grow. Those on nutrient poor soils, in boreal forests for example, have little opportunity to compensate for insect attack and so tend to be well defended by secondary chemicals (Mattson *et al.* 1988).

6.4 DETECTING GENETICALLY DETERMINED RESISTANCE IN TREES

Differences in the degree of attack on forest trees are often seen at endemic population densities and, even during outbreaks, some trees may remain

unattacked. But these phenotypic effects may or may not indicate underlying genetic differences in resistance. For example, trees may simply have
escaped attack, especially in lightly or moderately infested stands; site or
microsite effects may have affected their vigour (Chapters 3 and 5); or
there may be differences in phenology, age, or developmental factors that
have affected the likelihood of attack (DeHayes 1983).

A genetic basis to resistance is suggested where, for example, striking
differences in attack occur between adjacent compartments planted at the
same time on apparently uniform sites (Fig. 6.2) or where there are
consistent differences in attack between individual trees growing in close
proximity (Fig. 6.3). But, although field observations of natural attack
patterns can point to possible genetic differences in resistance both within
and between species, the presence and extent of genetic variation in
resistance can only be properly investigated using carefully designed progeny trials. A procedure for demonstrating resistance of trees to insects
which combines field observations with experimental testing is outlined in
Figure 6.4.

Differences in resistance of trees at the species, varietal, and individual
level, which are apparently gentically based, have been reported for a
number of insect/tree associations (Table 6.1). Sitka spruce, *Picea sitch-
ensis*, which is widely planted in Britain, is highly susceptible to the green
spruce aphid, *Elatobium abietinum*, but other spruce species are more
resistant. Nichols (1987) determined the degree of natural infestation on
several spruce species grown in an arboretum by taking branch samples

FIG. 6.2. Differences in defoliation of lodgepole pine by *Panolis flammea* in
adjacent compartments.

FIG. 6.3. Beech trees heavily infested by *Cryptococcus fagisuga* surrounded by other beech which are unattacked.

from mature trees in May and June. Aphid performance estimated by the mean relative growth rate (van Emden 1969) was subsequently determined on potted trees of some of these species (Table 6.2). This study revealed that in general the American spruces, including Sitka spruce, were most susceptible, supporting rapid growth of aphids and high natural infestations. The Eurasian species on the other hand, with the exception of Norway spruce, *P. abies*, were less suitable hosts and tended to remain uninfested even when growing among aphid infested trees. Although Norway spruce is the most susceptible species, it is also the most silviculturally desirable, so there appears to be little opportunity to exploit natural variation in resistance within the genus in this case.

An example of varietal differences in susceptibility is provided by Scots pine, *Pinus sylvestris*, which, as well as having an enormous natural range in Eurasia, has been widely established as an exotic plantation tree in other countries. In north central USA, seed collected from natural stands in all parts of the trees range was planted as part of a forest tree improvement

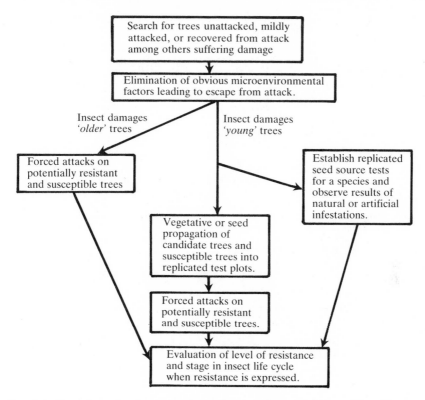

FIG. 6.4. Procedures for demonstrating resistance of trees to insects (from Hanover 1980).

study and provided an opportunity to examine susceptibility to several forest pests. When the trees were 7 to 12 years old, natural infestation levels of four insect species which attacked different parts of the tree were determined (Table 6.3). The larvae of the pine root collar weevil, *Hylobius radicis*, tunnel in the bark of young trees and can kill them. The pine sawfly, *Neodiprion sertifer*, a species introduced from Europe, defoliates both young and old trees but rarely kills them because only the old needles are attacked. The eastern pine shoot borer, *Eucosma gloriola*, kills twigs on the outside of the crown and, like other shoot moths, can cause stem deformation when the terminal shoot is attacked. Larvae of the Zimmermann pine moth, *Dioryctria zimmermanni*, feed on bark cambium of new shoots and around branch whorls on the main stem, and during heavy attack trees may be killed.

In general, trees from England and central Europe proved most susceptible to *H. radicis, N. sertifer*, and *D. zimmermanni*. Varieties from southern Europe and Eurasia were, however, preferred by *E. gloriola*, at least at

Table 6.1. *Examples of genetic variation in resistance in forest trees*

Insect	Host(s)	Reference
Adelges laricis	Larix decidua Larix leptolepis	Blada 1982
Adelges cooleyi	Pseudotsuga menziesii	Meinartowicz and Szmidt 1978
Mindarus abietinus	Abies balsamea	DeHayes 1981
Cryptococcus fagisuga	Fagus sylvatica	Wainhouse and Deeble 1980
Elatobium abietinum	Picea spp.	Nichols 1987
Hylobius radicis Neodiprion sertifer Eucosma gloriola Dioryctria zimmermani	Pinus sylvestris	Wright et al. 1975; Steiner 1974; Wright and Wilson 1972
Pristiphora erichsonii	Larix spp.	Genys and Harman 1976
Euura lasiolepis Phyllocalpa spp.	Salix lasiolepis	Fritz and Price 1988

Table 6.2. *Differences in resistance of spruces to Elatobium abietinum (see text)*

Species of *Picea*	Natural infestation levels (aphids $8.5\,\mathrm{cm}^{-1}$ of shoot)	Mean relative growth rate ($\mu g\,\mu g^{-1}\,d^{-1}$)
American		
P. engelmanni	36	135
P. glauca	97	104
P. mexicana	Not measured	129
P. sitchensis	113	123
Europe and Asia		
P. abies	Not measured	133
P. brachytyla	0	99
P. glehnii	0	82
P. omorika	0	96
P. orientalis	0	96

Data from Nichols 1987.

moderate densities of attack; at higher attack densities the distinctions are blurred. Results from individual varieties also show notable variation in resistance to the different pests; compare for example attack by *N. sertifer* and *D. zimmermanni* on variety *mongolica* (Table 6.3).

Although some interesting varietal differences in susceptibility, which are quite likely to be genetic in origin were demonstrated in this study, some were probably due to other causes. For example there were differences in size between the northern and southern varieties which grew at

Table 6.3 *Relative susceptibility of Scots pine varieties to four insect species*

Variety of *Pinus sylvestris*	Per cent of trees attacked or killed[a]					
	Hylobius radicis	*Neodiprion sertifer*	*Eucosma gloriola*[b]		*Dioryctria zimmermanni*	
Scandinavia and Scotland	[a]		M	H		[a]
lapponica	14	0	5	50	15	7
septentrionalis	38	2	21	87	38	18
rigensis	45	6	31	90	47	22
scotica	18	6	41	100	57	26
Russia						
mongolica	30	1	19	83	55	29
uralensis	40	3	19	82	61	31
England and Central Europe						
polonica	67	19	37	88	62	25
hercynica	43	20	41	89	57	22
carpatica	53	19	41	86	62	26
haguenensis	65	26	38	85	74	35
pannonica	45	20	47	93	62	19
'East Anglia'	55	26	36	79	75	37
Southern Europe and Eurasia						
iberica	17	11	58	96	33	3
aquitania	12	10	49	96	29	7
subillyrica	11	12	56	97	48	7
illyrica	10	19	44	93	43	9
modopaea	19	9	53	97	41	6
armena	12	7	51	97	29	3

[b]Figures for years of moderate (M) and high (H) attack.

Seedlots were collected from natural stands and planted in a replicated randomized block design in north central USA. Data from Wright and Wilson 1972, Steiner 1974, and Wright *et al.* 1975.

different rates. The variety *laponnica*, for example, was only around half the height of other trees, and this probably affected attack rates by most of the insect species. Similarly, there were differences in phenology between the different varieties, and this could have affected attack by the bud feeding species. Thus, even with replicated field trials it may be difficult to demonstrate a genetic basis to resistance and of course such trials do depend on natural levels of infestation which can vary from year to year, so that levels of attack may not always be high enough to expose differences in susceptibility between the plots of trees.

Differences in susceptibility of individual trees has also been shown to have a genetic basis. In a study of isoenzyme variation in ponderosa pine, Linhart *et al.* (1981) compared trees with or without infestations of woolly aphids (*Adelges* spp.) and found a significant difference between the two groups. Similarly in Norway spruce trees, chemical differences have been detected between individual trees which differ in susceptibility to the woolly aphid, *Adelges abietis*. Both 'resistant' and 'susceptible' trees support infestations of immature insects but they fail to mature on resistant trees. Analysis of phenolic compounds in the foliage revealed an unidentified phenol in all the resistant trees studied (Fig. 6.5). Further work is needed to determine whether this compound is active in resistance or is a chemical marker linked with it. In either case, however, it could be used for screening large numbers of trees in a selection and breeding programme.

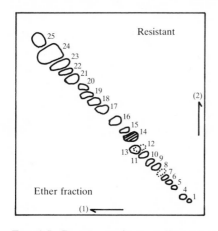 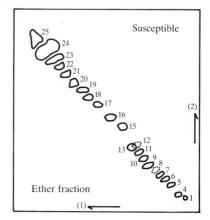

FIG. 6.5. Representative two-dimensional chromatograms of ether-soluble phenolics of Norway spruce foliage from trees susceptible or resistant to *Adelges abietis*. Resistant trees contain an unidentified phenolic no. 14. (from Tjia and Houston 1975).

6.5 BREEDING FOR INCREASED PEST RESISTANCE

Natural levels of resistance can be exploited in the management of forest insects (section 6.6), but breeding varieties with increased resistance to particular pests could potentially be much more valuable. There is clearly much raw material on which to base resistance breeding programmes because, as the previous examples show, trees often exhibit considerable variation in resistance. Furthermore, interspecific crosses are also relatively successful in many tree genera, considerably widening the scope for breeding programmes (Hanover 1980). It is perhaps surprising therefore that there are no examples where trees have been bred for resistance against a major insect pest of commercial forestry. Several factors have contributed to this situation. An important one is that the forest manager may be able to choose among several tree species or varieties for planting, and by manipulating the species composition of the forest could avoid chronic pest problems while having relatively little effect on the wood product that is eventually harvested.

But there are also formidable practical difficulties to breeding trees resistant to insect pests, especially those that only attack older trees. Bark beetles, for example, require bark which is thick enough for adults to excavate a brood chamber so that mature trees are more vulnerable to attack. To test directly for resistance to bark beetles through field bioassay of a series of progeny in a breeding programme would obviously require several generations of entomologists! Thus for these and other pests of mature trees, indirect methods of selection and testing, involving traits which are apparent early in life, would have to be developed before progress could be made (Hanover 1980). Terpenes have been suggested as possible markers for indirect selection for insect resistance in pines, spruces, and other conifers (Bridgen and Hanover 1982). These chemicals of course may actually be part of the resistance mechanism itself because they are known to affect insect behaviour and survival (Tables 3.1, 3.3, 9.1, and 9.2). They have several useful attributes as potential markers for insect resistance. For example, terpenes have been shown in several studies to be under strong genetic control (Hanover 1966, 1967; Squillace 1971); they can be sampled in young seedlings and can be measured accurately and quickly. In fact, terpenes have been used as markers for resistance of loblolly and slash pine to the fusiform rust, *Cronartium fusiforme* (Rockwood 1973, 1974).

In Scots pine, the percentage of cones infested by the pine cone weevil, *Pissodes validirostris*, has been related to the composition of monoterpenes extracted from the needles. α-Pinene which was the most abundant monoterpene, was negatively correlated with the intensity of damage (Fig. 6.6), and so might be a useful index of susceptibility in young trees before they have reached the cone bearing stage. Also in Scots pine, there is some evidence that diterpenoid resin acids could be indicators of resistance to the insects studied in Table 6.3 (Bridgen and Hanover 1982).

A further problem in breeding insect resistant trees, which was hinted at in the previous section (see Table 6.3), is that when trees are attacked by several important pests, it may be difficult to achieve increases in resistance to all of them. Indeed it is possible that increasing resistance to one pest may actually decrease resistance to another.

The development of co-operative studies involving geneticists, entomologists, and pathologists, and the increasing sophistication of plant breeding may overcome some of these problems. Before breeding programmes are initiated it is important to identify the key pest or pests against which resistance is required (Ortman and Peters 1980), and to obtain evidence for genetically determined variation in resistance in the forest which can be confirmed by procedures similar to those previously

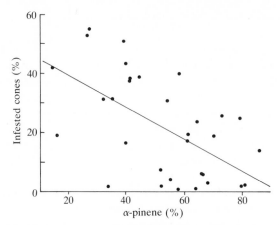

FIG. 6.6 Relationship between attacks on cones of Scots pine by *Pissodes validirostris* and the α-pinene concentration in monoterpenes extracted from needles (from Annila and Hiltunen 1977).

outlined (Fig. 6.4). Although it is not essential to know the exact cause of resistance before it can be developed in breeding programmes, it is essential to demonstrate its heritability because, even where differences in attack have a genetic basis, it could be due to a specific combination of non-additive genes and so have low heritability (DeHayes 1983). Because environmental factors can modify the genetic expression of resistance it is essential to test progeny under a range of different site conditions.

Some of the problems of breeding for resistance can be overcome by using vegetative propagation, which as well as providing a short cut to obtaining large numbers of resistant individuals, also takes advantage of non-additive as well as additive genetic variance (Zobel and Talbert 1984; John and Mason 1987). The development of methods of obtaining vigorous rooted cuttings from resistant 'mature' trees that have survived insect attack over many years and which are presumably well suited to local conditions, may allow fuller exploitation of natural resistance (Gibson *et al.* 1980). Unlike breeding programmes, however, no new combinations of genes are produced by vegetative propagation so that further gains in resistance are impossible using this technique.

6.6 HOST RESISTANCE AND INTEGRATED PEST MANAGEMENT

In the management of insect pests, natural variation in resistance is exploited in the choice of species for planting, selection of vigorous pest-free nursery stock, and in the silvicultural management of the forest during which susceptible individuals are removed in thinning operations (Chapter 5). When forests are replanted with seed collected from superior trees, or where natural regeneration is encouraged by leaving such trees on site following clear-felling, the tree population can become well adapted to local site conditions within 2 or 3 rotations (Gibson *et al*. 1982). This process, which has no real parallel in agriculture (Gibson *et al*. 1980), is likely to continue to be the main method of exploiting host resistance in the immediate future, largely because of the many practical and economic limitations to breeding pest resistant trees.

Nevertheless it is important to emphasize that even small increases in the level of resistance to significant pests could be useful in the context of integrated pest management, especially since trees can often compensate to some extent for insect damage. As outlined in Chapter 3, chemical defences in trees may prolong the development of insect herbivores. This can increase the risk of attack by natural enemies and so enhance their effectiveness in biological control programmes. Low levels of resistance together with natural enemies may in fact provide acceptable levels of control where neither method alone is effective in reducing the pest population (van Emden and Wearing 1965; van Emden 1986). High levels of resistance on the other hand, can have negative affects on natural enemies. For example, physical defences like hairy leaves may impede them so that levels of predation or parasitism are reduced (Obrycki 1986). Also, toxic secondary chemicals, sequestered from the host plant by herbivorous insects, can effectively protect them from natural enemies (Chapter 3) (Duffey *et al*. 1986).

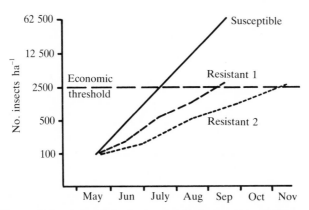

FIG. 6.7. Theoretical trends of an insect population on susceptible and resistant plants. Both resistant varieties reduce the pest population size by 50% in each generation but in addition, resistant variety no. 2 increases the development time of the survivors by 50%. A 5-fold increase in pest numbers per generation is assumed (from Adkisson and Dyck 1980).

Moderate levels of resistance could also be integrated with chemical control. By slowing the rate of insect population growth (Fig. 6.7), the use of resistant trees should reduce the need for insecticide applications. This could be especially useful in high value crops such as seed orchards where insecticides are more likely to be used.

Current tree improvement programmes aimed at increasing growth and productivity (Faulkner 1987) will reduce the natural variability between trees. Since natural variability in resistance is so important in silvicultural management of insect pests, this could make plantations of such trees more vulnerable to attack especially where clonal material is used. These aspects are discussed by Heybroek (1982) and Libby (1982).

7
Management 3: biological control

In the previous two chapters, we considered how pest populations can be manipulated 'from below' by reducing the abundance or favourability of their food supply through forest practices or host plant resistance. In this chapter, we consider control 'from above' by manipulation of natural enemies. Biological control is classically defined as the regulation of one organism by its natural enemies at a lower average population density than would otherwise occur (DeBach 1974). Although biological control is associated mainly with natural enemies, such as insect predators and parasitoids, insect pathogens are also important in this respect. It is significant that the term 'regulation' appears in the above definition; Chapter 2 describes the importance of regulation in insect population dynamics and illustrates some of the limitations of natural enemies in this context. This chapter concentrates mainly on the practical aspects of biological control of forest pests, but these basic ecological limitations should be borne in mind. Whilst many examples from forestry involve the release of natural enemies in an attempt to achieve long-term control, some disease organisms such as bacteria can only be used in 'one off' applications for short-term control and so in a sense are 'biological insecticides'. Because living disease organisms are employed in most cases, the general term of biological control can still be applied to this important technique.

7.1 THE ORIGIN AND DEVELOPMENT OF BIOLOGICAL CONTROL IN FORESTRY

Trees may have been the first plants to have been protected by deliberately applied biological control, for in thirteenth-century China nests of predatory ants were put in orchards to control insect pests and later, in the Yemen, ants were also used against date palm pests (Simmonds *et al.* 1976). Clearly, predation has long been considered important in reducing insect populations. The recognition that insects could parasitize other insects, however, came much later, in the seventeenth century, and it wasn't until the nineteenth century that their potential as natural control agents for insect pests was first considered. These early European applied biologists often studied forest insects and proposed the collection and release of native parasitoids to enhance natural control (van den Bosch and Messenger 1973; Schwerdtfeger 1973). We can only guess at the effectiveness of these early attempts at reducing infestations but the idea was established and later generations of forest entomologists were to emphasize the importance of parasitoids in the natural control of insects.

The first successful use of biological control in modern times came in the 1880s when the predatory Vedalia beetle, *Rodolia cardinalis*, was imported from Australia to control the cottony cushion scale, *Iceryia purchasi*, which had been introduced into the USA. This exotic pest was causing widespread damage to citrus trees in California when the predator was introduced and the subsequent dramatic reduction in scale populations saved the citrus industry from collapse. It was probably no accident that this first success should have been with a pest of trees, because trees provide a more 'apparent' and predictable environment for natural enemies than is found in other kinds of crops (Chapter 2). Also, scale insects themselves being largely sessile are highly predictable in time and space and this certainly contributed to the outstanding success of this project.

7.2 THE POTENTIAL FOR BIOLOGICAL CONTROL IN FORESTRY

There is no doubt that the characteristics of different crop systems determine not only the applicability of biological control but also its likely success (Table 7.1). Agricultural systems producing high value food crops are vulnerable to relatively small amounts of pest damage and, in general, pest density cannot be maintained at sufficiently low levels by biological control. In addition such systems occupy relatively small, intensively managed areas with a high input of insecticide and annual or semi-annual harvest during which the whole crop is removed and these cultural conditions are inimical to biological control. In protected cultivation such as horticultural crops under glass, quality standards are also very high but the impetus provided by resistance problems from the intensive use of insecticides as well as the ability to manipulate the environment, including pest and natural enemy density, have produced a number of notable successes with biological control (Hussey and Bravenboer 1971). In less disturbed perennial crops such as orchards, natural enemies can be established more easily but biological control of one pest may be disrupted by the use of broad-spectrum insecticides against other pests in the orchard. There are, nevertheless, several outstanding examples of biological control in orchards, particularly in North America, of such insects as *I. purchasi* (Doutt 1958) already referred to, olive scale, *Parlatoria oleae*, (Huffaker

Table 7.1. *The characteristics of different crop systems in relation to the potential for biological control*

Characteristics	Agriculture	Horticulture		Forestry	
		Glasshouses	Orchards	Plantations	Natural
Plant diversity	Low	Low	Low–Med	Low–Med	Med–High
Animal diversity	Low	Low	Low–Med	Low–Med	Med–High
Permanence	Low	Low	Medium	Med–High	High
Area	Small	Small	Small–Med	Med–Large	Large
Disturbance (management intensity)	High	High	Medium	Low–Med	Low
Manipulation of environmental conditions	Low	High	Low	Low	Low
Harvest	Annual	Semi annual	Annual	Periodic	Periodic
Pesticide use	High	High	Med–High	Low	Low
Value/unit area	High	High	Medium	Low	Low
Prospects for biological control	Low	Med–High	Medium	Medium	Medium

and Kennett 1966) and the walnut aphid, *Chromaphis juglandicola*, (DeBach 1974).

Forests grow in large contiguous areas, produce a relatively low value product and are relatively undisturbed by harvesting and insecticide applications and therefore appear to be an ideal environment for the establishment of biological control. But although there have been some important successes, there are fewer examples than might be expected given the apparent advantages of the forest environment (Caltagirone 1981). This can be partly explained by the fact that forest pests are, on the whole, still relatively localized geographically (Chapter 5) and there have been fewer opportunities for the introduction of natural enemies against exotic pests (classical biological control), a technique that has been outstandingly successful against pests of other crops.

7.3 BIOLOGICAL CONTROL IN THEORY AND PRACTICE

Figure 7.1 is a schematic illustration of the probability of death of gypsy moth, *Lymantria dispar*, at different population densities due to vertebrate predators, insect parasitoids, viral pathogens, and competition for food. The response of invertebrate and vertebrate natural enemies to changes in prey density and the characteristics which they should have, in theory, to be effective in biological control are discussed in Chapter 2 and further details can be found in Price (1984) and Huffaker and Rabb (1984). Competition for food is most likely to occur at high population densities although food can be limiting even when density is relatively low (see

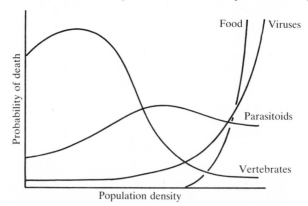

FIG. 7.1. The effect of population density of *Lymantria dispar* on the probability of death from vertebrate predators, insect parasitoids, viral pathogens, and food shortage (from Berryman *et al.* 1987, after Campbell 1975).

Chapters 2 and 3). In general, diseases caused by viruses and other micro-organisms occur at high insect population densities and, like competition for food, can cause outbreaks to collapse.

The relative importance of different mortality factors in the ecology of insect pests will largely determine the potential for biological control. *Lymantria dispar*, for example, is an eruptive pest (Chapter 1) but natural enemies are important in maintaining a low population density during non-outbreak periods, suggesting that there is considerable potential for biological control of this pest. However, when outbreaks occur, perhaps triggered by favourable weather or an increase in availability of susceptible hosts, natural enemies are overwhelmed by the rapid rise in population density and outbreaks are then terminated by the effects of competition for food or disease epizootics (or of course insecticide treatments). Other pests that have eruptive outbreaks such as 'aggressive' bark beetles whose population dynamics are largely determined by the availability of suitable host trees are not likely to be amenable to control by natural enemies. Similarly for many gradient pests, natural enemies may be unable to prevent increases in population density when key environmental conditions are favourable or where, for example, silvicultural practices increase the availability of some limiting resource such as breeding or feeding sites (Chapter 5). The situation is more complex for cyclic pests where interactions between the host tree, the environment and natural enemies and diseases contribute to the cyclic changes in population density. Thus the different life-history and outbreak characteristics of pests are important factors determining the potential for biological control.

The importance of natural enemies in maintaining some pests below outbreak levels is often revealed when their effectiveness is impaired by man's activities. For example, outbreaks of a diaspine scale insect on pine in California occurred after natural enemy numbers were reduced by insecticide fogging to control adult mosquitoes in residential areas. When the insecticide treatments were stopped, predator and parasitoid numbers increased again and the scale was brought under control (Luck and Dahlsten 1975). Similarly, biological control of the European spruce sawfly, *Gilpinia hercyniae*, in Canada was disrupted by applications of DDT against the spruce budworm, *Choristoneura fumiferana*, which reduced the non-target sawfly populations to such low levels that its virus disease and parasitoids were practically eliminated. When DDT treatments were discontinued, sawfly populations rebounded to damaging levels which were only reduced when the disease and the parasitoids were re-established (Neilson *et al.* 1971). There are examples, however, where the effectiveness of natural enemies has been impaired through natural rather than artificial processes. Successful control of the larch sawfly, *Pristiphora erichsonii*, by the parasitoid, *Mesoleius tenthredinis*, in parts of North

America was jeopardized when strains of the sawfly appeared which were able to encapsulate and kill the parasitoid eggs inside their body (Muldrew 1953, 1964). The situation was retrieved by use of a Bavarian strain of the parasitoid which could overcome the hosts' defensive mechanisms and, fortunately, progeny of crosses of the Bavarian and Canadian strains also inherited this ability (Turnock and Muldrew 1971).

The success of natural enemies used in biological control programmes is judged by their ability to reduce damage caused by the pest and if possible to constrain their populations below some 'economic threshold' level. The hypothetical example in Fig. 7.2 shows how the introduction of a natural enemy lowers the equilibrium population density of the pest so that satisfactory control is achieved within forests where the economic threshold is 'high'. But in more valuable crops such as Christmas tree plantations which are harvested after only a few years of growth and sold to a market where appearance of the trees is very important, only slight insect damage can reduce the value of individual trees. In this example the average pest density following the introduction of the natural enemy is still above the economic threshold for such crops, so that alternative controls will be needed in this situation.

Natural enemies may be utilized in a number of different ways in biological control depending on their origin and that of their host or prey (Table 7.2). The control of an introduced pest by its introduced natural enemy is known as classical biological control because of the outstanding early successes of this method. Introduced natural enemies may also be effective against native pests. This may occur by chance (fortuitous control) when releases are made against unrelated pests or when natural enemies of

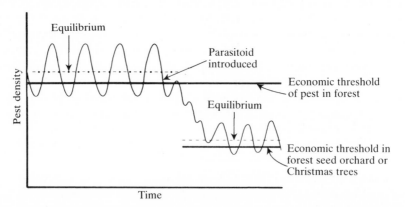

FIG. 7.2. A hypothetical example of biological control in relation to the economic threshold in a forest and in specialized forest crops. Control is achieved in the forest but not in the other crops where the economic threshold is lower (after Smith and van den Bosch 1967).

Table 7.2. *The ways in which natural enemies may be used in biological control programmes against insects (see text)*

Host or prey	Natural enemy	
	Introduced	Native
Introduced	Classical biological control	Fortuitous control
Native	Fortuitous control From related hosts 'Adaptation importation'	Augmentation Conservation Inundation Intra-areal transfer

insects related to the native pests are imported (Hokkanen and Pimentel 1984). Similarly, native natural enemies may occasionally be effective against an introduced pest and where such fortuitous control occurs these natural enemies may be suitable candidates for introduction into the pest's native habitat in what Franz and Kreig (1982) call 'adaptation importation'. The abundance or distribution of native natural enemies can also be manipulated in a number of ways in order to increase their effectiveness against native pests.

From the earliest days of biological control, there has been considerable debate over the merits of making single releases or introducing several natural enemies into pest populations (DeBach 1964). The main argument against multiple releases is the risk of increased competition, for example, through multiple parasitism so that the overall effectiveness of natural enemies is reduced. However, the alternative, that of selecting the 'best' natural enemy is unrealistic because it is difficult if not impossible to predict the impact of natural enemies on the prey population in a new environment (Chapter 2). Although some recent evidence suggests that the more natural enemy species there are in the environment the more difficult it is to establish new and perhaps more effective ones (Ehler and Hall 1982), on the whole, multiple releases appear to have given a greater degree of control when compared to programmes involving single releases (Huffaker *et al.* 1971).

7.4 THE CHARACTERISTICS AND USE OF BIOLOGICAL CONTROL AGENTS

7.4.1 Invertebrate predators and parasitoids

Important predators occur in several insect orders and include such diverse insects as ladybirds, ground and rove beetles (Coleoptera), lacewings (Neuroptera), true bugs (Hemiptera: Heteroptera), syrphid larvae (Diptera) and ants (Hymenoptera). Predators are usually polyphagous and can feed on a number of different prey species and typically consume many prey individuals both as larvae and adults. Although predators have on occasion been used successfully in biological control their lack of specificity generally limits their potential. Parasitoids, which are found in the Hymenoptera and Diptera (Fig. 7.3), are usually much more specific than predators and attack only one or a few related host species and have been used more successfully in biological control. Only the larvae of parasitoid species consume the hosts which are located by the searching adult females. Although adults do not usually feed on the host, many of them feeding only on nectar or pollen, some species may imbibe host fluids through punctures made with their ovipositor. The larvae of parasitoids may feed externally on the host (ectoparasitic) or feed within it (endoparasitic) with one (solitary) or several (gregarious) progeny of an individual parasitoid developing on an individual host. Parasitoids are characterized by the particular stage in their host's life cycle that they attack and it is possible to find egg, larval, and pupal parasitoids causing successive mortalities during a single host generation.

Although many parasitoids can detect and avoid hosts that are already parasitized, some hosts may be parasitized more than once, either by the same species (superparasitism) or different species (multiparasitism) and in either case this leads to competition and death of some of the parasitoid larvae. Hyperparasitoids on the other hand develop within the larvae of primary parasitoids and so have the potential to reduce their effectiveness. For this reason careful screening is necessary to avoid the possibility of releasing them along with their hosts in biological control programmes.

The use of exotic natural enemies

One of the most interesting cases of classical biological control in forests is that of the winter moth, *Operophtera brumata*, in Canada. This insect was introduced into Nova Scotia around 1930 where it attacked a number of broad-leaved trees but caused most damage to oak forests and apple orchards (Embree 1965; MacPhee 1967). Of the six parasitoids that were introduced from Europe and released in the mid-1950s (Graham 1958), only two became established, the tachinid, *Cyzenis albicans*, and the ichneumonid, *Agrypon flaveolatum*, and within 10 years they had spread throughout the province. Female *A. flaveolatum* oviposit directly into host larvae but *C. albicans* oviposits at the margins of damaged oak leaves in response to the sap flux and larvae become parasitized after ingesting the eggs (Hassell 1968). The response of *C. albicans* to damaged leaves causes it to aggregate in areas of high host density and this results in spatial density-dependent parasitism (Embree 1966; Hassell 1980; Roland 1986; Chapter 2).

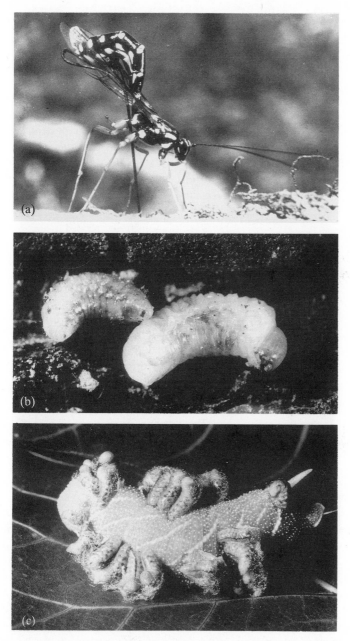

FIG. 7.3. (a) *Rhyssa persuasoria*, an ichneumonid parasitoid of siricid larvae, ovipositing through the bark of a felled log; (b) Ectoparasitic larva of a braconid parasitoid attacking a scolytid larva; (c) Larvae of a gregarious parasitic hymenopteran emerged from a lepidopteran host.

Following release of the parasitoids, populations of *O. brumata* on oak gradually declined and they now fluctuate at low density (Fig. 7.4). Although both parasitoids probably contribute to the high level of control achieved, parasitism by *C. albicans* is by far the most important. And yet *C. albicans* has an insignificant effect on *O. brumata* in Britain where populations of the moth are regulated by a complex of pupal predators in the soil (Chapter 2). These predators, which cause an average of 72 per cent mortality of *O. brumata* pupae in the soil also destroy many *C. albicans* pupae. Studies by Hassell (1980) suggest that the absence of the density-dependent soil mortality in Nova Scotia not only allowed moth populations to increase to outbreak levels but enabled *C. albicans* to display its full potential to regulate *O. brumata* populations at a low density.

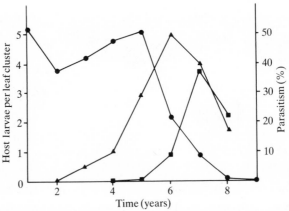

Fig. 7.4. The decline of populations of *Operophtera brumata* (circles) due to the activities of *Cyzenis albicans* (triangles) and *Agrypon flaveolatum* (squares). The data are from seven different areas of Nova Scotia, and show the course of the outbreak relative to the time of first appearance of *C. albicans* (from Embree 1966).

Operophtera brumata is now present in several parts of Canada and it is clear that successful control is not achieved in apple orchards where serious defoliation still occurs. The reasons for this are not entirely clear although some differences in the behaviour of *C. albicans* on infested oak and apple have recently been identified (Roland 1986). For example, female *C. albicans* do not appear to use feeding damage on apple leaves as a stimulus for oviposition, perhaps due to the absence of the oviposition stimulants present in oak leaf sap and, as a result, eggs are distributed more randomly on apple foliage. Nevertheless, no obvious differences in the distribution and extent of mortality from parasitism on oak and apple were found in this study and further work is needed to clarify the picture.

Two important points emerge from the biological control of *O. brumata* in Canada which have been emphasized in earlier chapters; the difficulty of predicting which natural enemies will be most effective in suppressing pest populations when introduced into a new environment and the importance of the host plant in influencing the interaction between insect herbivores and their natural enemies.

Fortuitous control by an introduced natural enemy (Table 7.2) occurs when it attacks other pests, related to its normal prey, that may be causing damage to trees. For example, seven of the parasitoids released against the spruce sawfly, *Gilpinia hercyniae*, and the European pine sawfly, *Neodiprion sertifer*, both of which are exotic pests in Canada, have been found to attack several native conifer-feeding sawflies and, in particular, a cocoon parasitoid appears to exert some degree of control of the Swaine jack pine sawfly, *Neodiprion swainei* (McGugan and Coppel 1962; Price 1970).

Native natural enemies that successfully attack exotic pests may be considered for introduction into the pests' native habitat ('adaptation importation'—Table 7.2). This was tried with two natural enemies of the pine shoot moth, *Rhyacionia buoliana*, which in North America is attacked by a pupal parasitoid, *Itoplectis conquisitor*, and a larval ectoparasitoid, *Hyssopus thymus*. During the 1970s they were introduced into Germany where *R. buoliana* is a native pest of young pine plantations. Only limited establishment followed from these introductions and more studies on their suitability are required before further releases are made, particularly since *I. conquisitor* has been recorded as a hyperparasitoid in cocoons of other parasitic wasps (Mertins and Coppel 1971).

The use of native natural enemies

Many of the principal attempts at biological control in Europe, where there are relatively few exotic forest pests, have involved the movement of native natural enemies from one area to another. Table 7.3 shows the restricted

Table 7.3. *The number of parasitoids associated with some forest insects that are native to mainland Europe and native or long established in Britain*

Species	Number of parasitoids	
	Britain	Mainland Europe
Pristiphora erichsonii	3	11 (in Alps)
Coleophora lariciphila	9	20 (in Alps)
Rhyacionia buoliana	9	15
Neodiprion sertifer	3	12
Gilpinia hercyniae	0?	12+
Zeiraphera diniana	29	76 (in Engadine)

After Greathead 1976 and Wainhouse 1987.

parasitoid fauna associated with some native or long-established forest insects in Britain compared with that at the centre of the distribution of the host tree in mainland Europe. It suggests that there is considerable scope for the transfer of native natural enemies from the centre to the edges of their hosts' range within Europe. When natural enemies are absent altogether from certain areas, it is important to determine whether this is because the environment is locally unsuitable or arises simply from the separation of pest and natural enemy as could occur, for example, during the establishment of plantations. In southern Sweden infestations of adelgids occurred on silver fir planted several hundred kilometres from the nearest natural stands of the tree in southern Germany. Transfer of the coccinellid, *Scymnus impexus*, from the Black Forest led to successful establishment, but it is too early to say whether the pest has been successfully controlled in the long term (Eidmann and Ehnström 1975; Eidmann 1976).

The bark beetle, *Dendroctonus micans*, is an important pest of spruce that probably originated in Siberia but by a process of natural spread and transport by man it can now be found in most parts of Europe where spruce is grown (Fig. 7.5). The spread of this insect has been characterized by the development of outbreaks in newly-colonized areas often resulting in the death of tens of thousands of trees (Grégoire 1988). Living trees are attacked by this solitary bark beetle and the larvae feed together within a large contiguous gallery. Trees may survive attack by a few beetles and in fact manual debarking of these brood areas formed the basis of an early control method (Fig. 7.6). Some outbreaks, however, were observed to decline spontaneously, apparently as a result of predation by *Rhizophagus grandis* (Fig. 7.7), a highly specific predatory beetle that had followed

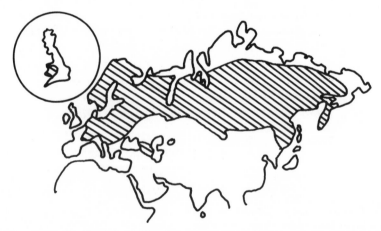

FIG. 7.5. The distribution of *Dendroctonus micans* in Europe (from Bevan and King 1983).

FIG. 7.6. Hand removal of *Dendroctonus micans* galleries on spruce. An early method of control!

its prey as it spread westward across Europe. In Belgium, where outbreaks first occurred at the turn of the century, *D. micans* is now at endemic levels and the predator is present in over 80 per cent of galleries (Tondeur and Grégoire 1979). The effectiveness of this predator appears to be due to its monophagous habit and ability to locate its prey, even when present at low density, by responding to the odour of frass produced by the bark beetle larvae.

In two areas of Europe recently colonized by *D. micans* (the Massif Central in southern France and western Britain) the predator was found to be absent and a programme of breeding and release was initiated in the two areas (Bevan and King 1983; Grégoire *et al*. 1985). The predator was unlikely to arrive in Britain by a process of natural spread and since both pest and natural enemy are introduced it could be considered as an example of classical biological control.

In Britain, *D. micans* became established in Wales and the border counties in the early 1970s and when first detected in the early 1980s, had

FIG. 7.7. *Dendroctonus micans* larvae being eaten by the smaller larvae of the predator *Rhizophagus grandis*.

already caused widespread damage (Chapters 5 and 10). Adult *R. grandis* were imported from Belgium and a breeding programme initiated which resulted in the release of 95 000 predators into infested forests in 1984–1987 (C. J. King, personal communication). In France, thousands of beetles were distributed at relatively few release sites whereas in Britain, relatively small numbers (10–100 pairs) were released in over 2400 sites. This release policy was adopted partly because of the 'demand' for predators from both state and private sectors, so that available beetles had to be released within a large area containing many separate sites. The fact that good establishment followed from these small releases was probably due to the predators kairomone response to the frass of its prey. Although the predator is now widely established in both France and Britain it may be several years before the success of these projects can be judged.

Ants have long been recognized as effective predators of forest insects, and wood ants are protected by law in parts of Europe. They are undoubtedly voracious and aggressive predators and can reduce numbers of several important defoliators such as *Lymantria* spp., *Panolis flammea*, *Bupalus piniaria* and *Dendrolimus pini* as well as some sawfly species, and 'green islands' are often left around nests during outbreaks (Wellenstein 1959; Greathead 1976; Laine and Niemela 1980; Warrington and Whittaker 1985*a, b*). However, like many generalist predators, they have little impact on their prey populations once numbers have risen to outbreak levels. The presence of ants may actually increase densities of aphids which are tended for their honeydew and protected from natural enemies (Wellenstein 1973). Although aphids can damage the trees, an interesting beneficial side-effect is that honeybees are able to utilize surplus honeydew and this can double the production of 'forest' honey which is an important local product in parts of Europe (Wellenstein 1965).

During the 1950s a great deal of work was done on the transfer of nests of red wood ants of the *Formica rufa* group between forests in Germany and Italy and subsequently, nests were imported into Canada. In Europe, the objective was to try and establish ants in areas where they were not abundant or were absent altogether. In managed forests, there are considerable practical difficulties to establishing and maintaining the uniform distribution of about four nests per hectare that are needed for the overall protection of forests (Greathead 1976). We must conclude from these studies that the transfer of ant nests between forests is not practical for modern intensive forestry.

An apparently successful transfer of a parasitoid within the UK was made during the 1970s when populations of the web-spinning larch sawfly, *Cephalcia lariciphila*, caused widespread defoliation in Wales. Defoliated trees were not killed and no chemical control was applied. In part of the outbreak area a previously unrecorded ichneumonid parasitoid, *Olesicampe monticola*, appeared and although its initial distribution was patchy, parasitism rates in some areas ranged from 4 per cent to 64 per cent (Brown and Billany 1976). In 1976 the parasitoid was introduced into a forest from which it was absent and by 1979 parasitism rates had reached 30 per cent (Billany 1979). Within the outbreak area as a whole, parasitism rates of up to 90 per cent occurred by 1979 (Fig. 7.8) with population collapse attributed in part to the parasitoid (Billany 1981; Billany *et al.* 1985).

There have been some impressive attempts to influence the levels of parasitism in forest insect populations by mass-release of their parasitoids. In Spain, Ceballos and Zarco (1952) described the collection of two tonnes of pine sawfly, *Diprion pini*, cocoons from which millions of parasitoids were obtained for release. They achieved only limited success in a localized area and their efforts serve to emphasize that the mass rearing and inundative release of parasitoids is likely to be an impractical method of control for most pests, especially for outbreaks covering extensive areas of forest. Experimental releases on a small scale, however, suggest that the method may have some potential in small blocks of forest and isolated plantations. In Italy, Rossi (1966) collected buds infested with the pine shoot moth, *Rhyacionia buoliana*, and the large number of ichneumonid parasitoids that emerged were released in a 10 ha nursery of infested maritime and stone pine, with notable improvement in control. In Poland, releases of the indigenous parasitic wasp, *Trichogramma* spp., were highly effective in destroying the eggs of *R. buoliana* (Koehler 1970).

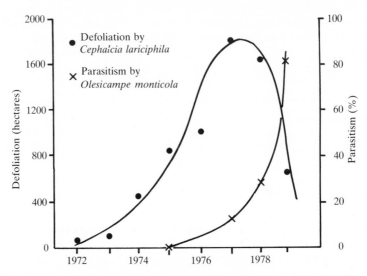

FIG. 7.8. The area of larch defoliated by *Cephalcia lariciphila* in South Wales and the percent parasitism by *Olesicampe monticola* (Anon 1981).

7.4.2 Vertebrate predators

Small mammals such as voles and shrews that inhabit the forest floor are occasionally important predators of forest insects, significantly reducing numbers of the overwintering stages of Lepidoptera and sawflies. In the forest canopy, birds are more conspicuous predators feeding on a wide range of insects, sometimes aggregating in flocks where prey is abundant. Recognition that birds are important predators of insect pests has a long history and in parts of Switzerland they were protected by law as early as the fourteenth century (Otvos 1979). Evidence of the importance of predation by insectivorous birds can be found in the many examples of cryptic or warning coloration, urticating hairs, or alarm reactions among foliage-feeding caterpillars. Woodpeckers, which search for insects on the branches and trunk of trees, are effective predators of bark beetles, particularly those that overwinter under bark. In a study of predation of the southern pine beetle, *Dendroctonus frontalis*, Kroll and Fleet (1979) demonstrated a significant reduction in within-tree populations of pupae and brood adults in trees exposed to woodpecker predation, and also found evidence that the feeding activity of the woodpeckers exposes the insects to invertebrate predators (Table 7.4).

Birds, like many invertebrate predators, feed on a wide variety of prey and there is no simple relationship between the abundance of a species and its frequency in the diet. As well as feeding on pest and non-pest species,

Table 7.4. *Mean within-tree population densities of Dendroctonus frontalis and natural enemies in trees protected from (screened) and exposed to (unscreened) woodpecker predation[a]*

	Mean density (no. dm^{-2})	
	Screened	Unscreened
Larvae	23.9	22.4
Pupae	15.3	1.0[b]
Brood adults	14.2	11.6[b]
Insect predators	0.2	0.6
Insect parasitoids	0.2	0.3

[a]Reduction in population on unscreened trees includes losses from predation and dislodging of brood in bark flakes.
[b]Significantly different from screened trees ($P < 0.05$).
From Kroll and Fleet 1979.

their diet may also include parasitized larvae and even adult parasitoids as well as other natural enemies. Interestingly, diseased larvae are also eaten and this may contribute to the spread of disease epizootics as discussed in the following section. The contribution of birds to the natural control of insect populations is probably most important when insects are at endemic levels, and they may well reduce the likelihood of outbreaks occurring because predation can be density-dependent at low densities (Chapter 2). Birds may also speed-up the collapse of pest outbreaks (Greathead 1976).

The augmentation of insectivorous birds in forests has been practised in Europe for 80 years or so, principally through provision of nest boxes and is based on the assumption that nesting sites are limited (Greathead 1976). While this may be true for some hole-nesting birds, because suitable dead and dying trees are removed from managed forest, there is no certainty that an increase in bird density increases mortality of important pest species. Where food supply is the limiting factor in bird population dynamics, as it appears to be for tits and tree creepers (Gibb 1960; Dornbusch 1964), then attempting to increase densities of birds at endemic population levels of the pest seems doomed to failure.

There have been few attempts to manipulate populations of small mammals for forest insect control. One apparently successful attempt, however, was the introduction of the masked shrew from New Brunswick to Newfoundland to increase predation of cocoons of sawfly larvae (Buckner 1966).

7.4.3 Microbial control

From the earliest days of forest entomology, biologists were aware of the importance of diseases, observing, for example, outbreaks or epizootics of fungal infection in insect populations. Viral and bacterial infections also occur in insects especially in the larvae of many Lepidoptera and sawfly species and these microbial diseases appear to have the potential to cause cyclic changes in the abundance of some important forest pests (Anderson and May 1980, 1981).

Mortality from viral and other infectious diseases is density-dependent because the pathogens are able to spread more quickly through high density populations (Fig. 7.1). Furthermore, unlike insect parasitoids or predators, pathogens do not suffer the restrictions of satiation or a finite fecundity. By the time populations collapse, however, some damage to the trees has usually occurred, although this can be tolerated more readily in forestry than in other crop systems. Spontaneously-occurring epizootics, therefore, can make a significant contribution to the natural control of some forest pests. However, the principal aim of applied microbial control is to introduce disease organisms into populations before outbreaks occur or, more commonly, to induce disease over wide areas by spraying the active disease organisms onto trees as a 'microbial insecticide'. Both viruses and bacteria have been used in this way and they have a number of obvious advantages over chemical insecticides since they are natural products that leave no toxic residues and, in general, are highly selective. However, an important practical consideration is that micro-organisms are much more sensitive than chemical sprays to a range of environmental factors. Viruses, for example, are rapidly inactivated by the ultraviolet radiation in strong sunlight and temperature and humidity conditions can affect the success of spraying operations, though appropriate formulation of microbial sprays can help to reduce their sensitivity to environmental conditions (Young and Yearian 1986). A further restriction on their use is an economic one. Their highly selective action means that they cannot be used in areas where more than one pest is damaging trees and so the market for each virus is relatively restricted. Thus although they are much cheaper to develop than chemical insecticides (Table 7.5), they are at present more expensive to buy and so costs per unit area may be higher.

Viruses

Epizootics caused by virus diseases have often been seen in insect populations, perhaps the earliest observation being that of 'tree top disease' named after the characteristic position of diseased and dead larvae of the nun moth, *Lymantria monacha,* (Evans 1986). Several groups of viruses

Table 7.5. *Comparative costs in the development of chemical and microbial pesticides*

Aspects of development	Costs (£)	
	Chemical	Microbial
Research and development	12 000 000	400 000
Market size for profitability	30 000 000 per year to recoup investment, i.e. limited to major crops	≤ 600 000 per year
Product safety—toxicological testing	3 000 000 lengthy	40 000

From Wainhouse 1987, after Lisansky 1984.

are capable of causing diseases in insects (Entwistle 1983) but the baculo-viridae is the only group whose host range is restricted entirely to arthropods. Baculoviruses replicate in the nuclei of insect cells of which the nuclear polyhedrosis viruses (NPV) are by far the most common type. They can be distinguished by their characteristic structure, in which the individual virus particles called virions are contained within a proteinaceous matrix, the polyhedron (Fig. 7.9). In granulosis viruses, which are less common and found only in Lepidoptera, the virions are individually encapsulated and are not grouped together in polyhedra. Cytoplasmic polyhedrosis viruses (CPV) are similar to NPVs except in their site of action but belong to a different group, the Reoviridae, which also includes viruses capable of infecting vertebrates and plants. In spite of this, the CPV of the pine processionary moth, *Thaumetopoea pityocampa*, has been used for control in the forest (Grison 1969). To cause disease, virus particles need to be ingested by the juvenile stages to gain entry through the mid-gut cells, after which virus multiplication and death of the host follows fairly rapidly. Young larvae are the most susceptible and very much larger doses are required to achieve the same infection level in later instars (Entwistle and Evans 1985). This makes the timing of application more critical than is usual for conventional insecticides, which can be a problem in large-scale control operations. In addition, larvae of pests such as the spruce budworm, *Choristoneura fumiferana*, and the pine beauty moth, *Panolis flammea*, which feed in protected situations during early instars, may not come into contact with virus-contaminated surfaces during this vulnerable stage.

The Lepidoptera and sawflies are particularly susceptible to baculovirus diseases (Fig. 7.10) and a number of forest insects suffer from periodic baculovirus epizootics (Table 7.6). Viruses are the most promising of the disease-causing organisms for insect control because they usually have effective mechanisms of spread throughout the population (horizontal

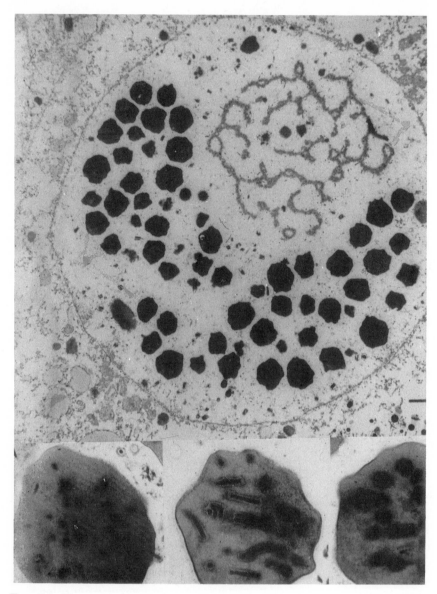

FIG. 7.9. Electron micrograph of the nucleus of a cell from the mid-gut of a lepidopteran larva (low magnification, top), showing the polyhedral inclusion bodies (PIBs) of a nuclear polyhedrosis virus (NPV). The virions are packed inside the polyhedron (high magnification, bottom).

FIG. 7.10. *Euproctis chrysorrhoea* larva killed by a nuclear polyhedrosis virus (NPV).

transmission) and persist abundantly in the environment, ensuring transmission from one generation to the next (vertical transmission).

For direct application to insect populations, standard ultra-low volume aerial application technology can be used after appropriate formulation (Young and Yearian 1986, Chapter 8). The particulate nature of the sprays, however, may require the development of new application techniques to ensure maximum efficiency (H. F. Evans, personal communication). A detailed discussion of various trials of the use of viruses for insect

Table 7.6. *Periodic baculovirus epizootics, some of which are cyclic*

Insect species	Host tree	Virus	Country	Period between outbreaks (years)
Bupalus piniaria	Pine	NPV	Netherlands	5–8
Gilpinia hercyniae	Spruce	NPV	N. America	>40
Lymantria dispar	Oak and other broad-leaves	NPV	Bulgaria	5–11
Lymantria fumida	Japanese fir	NPV (+ CPV)	Japan	5–7
Lymantria monacha	Conifers	NPV	Denmark	8–69
Orgyia pseudotsugata	Douglas fir	NPV	USA	7–10
Zeiraphera diniana	Larch/pine	GV	Switzerland	9–10

NPV = nuclear polyhedrosis virus; CPV = cytoplasmic polyhedrosis virus; GV = granulosis virus.
After Zethner 1976, Entwistle and Evans 1985, and Evans 1986.

control is given by Cunningham (1982). In most of these trials viruses were used as microbial insecticides, but inoculative releases can also be made by spraying small areas and allowing the disease to spread naturally through the population. This method avoids the costs of virus mass production and large-scale spraying operations but it can only be used where there is no immediate threat of damage, since there is an inevitable time delay between virus ingestion and disease and death during which some defoliation will occur. A compromise between large-scale application and inoculative release is suggested by Entwistle and Evans (1985) who propose spot applications on a grid system covering the infested area, the spacing between treatment centres determining the rapidity of control. A hypothetical example is given in Fig. 7.11 for the spread of NPV in a uni-voltine population of the spruce sawfly, *Gilpinia hercyniae*.

Although there are many forest insects that could potentially be controlled with viruses (Table 7.7), only six of them, all NPVs, have so far been registered worldwide. These are the viruses of Douglas fir tussock moth, *Orgyia pseudotsugata*(2), the gypsy moth, *Lymantria dispar*(1), the European pine sawfly, *Neodiprion sertifer*(2), and the redheaded pine sawfly, *Neodiprion lecontei*(1). Commercial registration of other viruses, for example that of *P. flammea* are expected in the near future. The NPV of *N. sertifer* which often causes natural epizootics, is the most widely used of these viruses and has been applied to thousands of hectares of forest in Europe over the last 25 years.

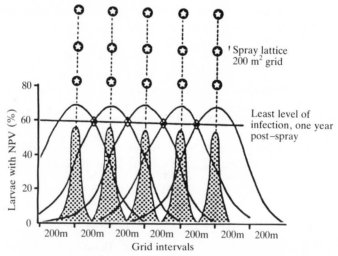

FIG. 7.11. The theoretical distribution of infection by *Gilpinia hercyniae* nuclear polyhedrosis virus (solid line) 1 year after spot application on a 200 m spray lattice. The presumed infection levels of the treated generation are also shown (stippled area) (from Entwistle and Evans 1985).

Table 7.7 *Examples of forest insects potentially controllable (>85% kill) with baculoviruses*

Insect species	Baculovirus	Host tree
Lepidoptera		
Choristoneura fumiferana	NPV	Spruce
Choristoneura muriana	GV	Spruce
Hyphantria cunea	NPV	Broad-leaves
Lymantria dispar	NPV	Broad-leaves
Lymantria fumida	NPV	Japanese fir
Lymantria monacha	NPV	Conifers
Malacosoma disstria	NPV	Aspen
Orgyia pseudotsugata	NPV	Douglas fir
Hymenoptera		
Gilpinia hercyniae	NPV	Spruce
Neodiprion lecontei	NPV	Pines
Neodiprion pratti pratti	NPV	Pines
Neodiprion sertifer	NPV	Pines
Neodiprion swainei	NPV	Jack pine

NPV = nuclear polyhedrosis virus; GV = granulosis virus.
From Entwistle and Evans 1985.

One of the best studied examples of virus control of a forest pest involves the European spruce sawfly, *Gilpinia hercyniae*. This pest was accidentally introduced into Canada in the 1930s where it caused extensive and damaging outbreaks (Balch and Bird 1944). During a programme of classical biological control it seems that an NPV was introduced along with some of the parasitoids. The subsequent extensive virus epizootics plus the activities of two parasitoids, *Drino bohemica* and *Exenterus vellicatus*, are believed to be responsible for the decline of this sawfly to non-outbreak levels. Although either the virus or the parasitoids acting alone give satisfactory control, the sawfly populations are maintained at even lower levels by both of them acting together (Reeks and Cameron 1971).

Like its spruce host plant, *G. hercyniae* is also an introduced species in Britain being first recorded around 1906 (Billany and Brown 1977). It remained at endemic levels, however, until outbreaks occurred in localized areas in Wales during the late 1960s. Within two or three years, a discrete epizootic of NPV occurred in the sawfly population which gradually spread within and between infestations eventually bringing them under complete control. Spread of the disease from an isolated epicentre (Fig. 7.12) followed a characteristic pattern, with disease incidence initially falling off rapidly with distance from the epicentre but forming an outward spreading wave in the second and subsequent years as host larvae died out at the original disease centre (Entwistle *et al.* 1983). Local spread occurred in a number of ways. Rain splash, wind, and the movement of predators which are able to pass infective NPV through the gut, were important

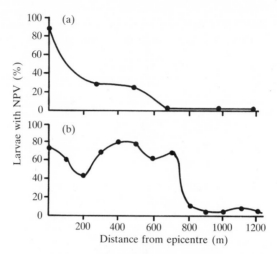

F‌IG. 7.12. The pattern of spread of the nuclear polyhedrosis virus of *Gilpinia hercyniae* from an epicentre at Afon Biga in Wales (a) October 1971, (b) September 1972 (after Entwistle *et al*. 1983).

mechanisms, but sublethally-infected adult sawflies can carry virus with them and deposit it conveniently near the oviposition site. Birds also played an important part in the process of virus dispersal (Entwistle *et al*. 1977*a*, *b*, but see Buse 1977). They feed on the corpses of diseased larvae and infective virus is returned to the foliage through contaminated droppings, perhaps many kilometres from the feeding site. This discontinuous dispersal of disease to form new epicentres resulted in a complex pattern of disease intensity in the later stages of the epizootic. Clearly the extent and speed of discontinuous spread has an important bearing on the efficacy of control in natural epizootics or following inoculative release.

Bacteria

The spore-forming bacterium, *Bacillus thuringiensis* (Bt), is one of the most common causes of bacterial disease in insects and it appears to have been first noted in Japan as causing a 'limp' disease of the domestic silkworm, *Bombyx mori* (Dulmage and Aizawa 1982). Unlike viruses, Bt is not highly infective in insects and rarely causes epizootics in nature. In fact Bt is not an obligate pathogen but when vegetative cells sporulate in response to sub-optimal conditions, which can be artificially created in fermentation chambers, they produce a crystal containing toxic proteins (the so-called δ endo-toxin) and once these cells are ingested the toxin is liberated into the insect gut causing disruption of the epithelial cells and ultimately death by septicaemia. The toxin thus acts as a very effective narrow-spectrum insecticide which, after suitable formulation, can be artificially applied to insect populations.

Several varieties or strains of Bt have now been isolated that show their optimal activity against particular insects. This variability between and even within strains of Bt can result in failure to control the target insect if the wrong isolate is used (Dulmage *et al.* 1981). Several forest Lepidoptera are susceptible and a number of applications have been made in experimental and operational trials giving acceptable levels of population reduction in about 75 per cent of cases (Morris 1982). Although further improvements in formulation and application technology are required to use Bt most effectively over large forest areas (Dulmage and Aizawa 1982), it has nevertheless been used on a wider scale than any other microbial insecticide. In the USA and Canada where environmental and socio-political constraints have halted or restricted the use of synthetic insecticides, it is often the only 'insecticide' that can be used. It is also quite widely used in various parts of Europe; in Spain for example, Bt is frequently applied against gypsy moth, *Lymantria dispar*.

Fungi

Fungal epizootics resulting in extensive mortality within populations are not uncommon in nature and have been observed in a number of forest insects, for example, the spruce budworm, *Choristoneura fumiferana* (Vandenberg and Soper 1978; Perry and Whitfield 1985). All the major groups of fungi contain forms that are lethal to insects and most insect groups are susceptible. There is, therefore, within the fungi, a wide range of reproductive and ecological characteristics that would seem to confer on them great flexibility as biocontrol agents (Ferron 1978) but this has not, in general, been translated into practice. Like viruses and bacteria, fungi can infect through the gut but most species enter through the integument; thus, both larval stages and adults can be attacked. Also, aphids and other sap-feeding insects that do not ingest disease organisms that occur on the surfaces of leaves can be readily infected by fungi. One disadvantage of this less specific method of infection, however, is that predators and parasitoids may be at some risk.

Various types of fungi have been used in insect control trials. The muscardine fungi, *Beauveria* spp. and *Metarrhizium* spp., have both been used in trials against agricultural pests, and *Beauveria* spp. has been used in limited trials against teak and mahogany pests in the tropics (Speight unpublished). Four species of fungi are now commercially available for use in control programmes and have been most successfully used in greenhouses, e.g. *Verticillium lecanii* in the UK. In these areas of protected cultivation, environmental conditions such as humidity can be carefully controlled so that fungi have the best chance of survival. Within the forest, environmental conditions are much more variable and often unsuitable for fungal development. However, some insects such as weevils and bark beetles that feed under bark on stumps or moribund trees occupy niches that appear to provide more favourable conditions. It may be possible to develop practical methods for the control of these insects especially since beetles seem to be relatively more susceptible to fungal diseases than other insect groups (Carruthers and Soper 1987). In general, however, the need for water for spore germination and the temperature-dependent rate of mycelial growth suggests that fungi are not suitable for widespread application in forest insect control, and they seem unlikely to contribute to practical control programmes in the near future.

Nematodes

Although an entirely distinct group of parasitic organisms, nematodes are usually considered under microbial control, but there is little information on the extent of parasitism by nematodes in nature or on their impact on host populations. There are, however, several groups of nematodes that are parasitic on insects either killing them directly or causing sublethal effects such as reduced fecundity (Fig. 7.13).

Most nematodes rely to some extent on bacteria in order to utilize fully their host as a food source and in *Neoaplectana carpocapsae* there is a

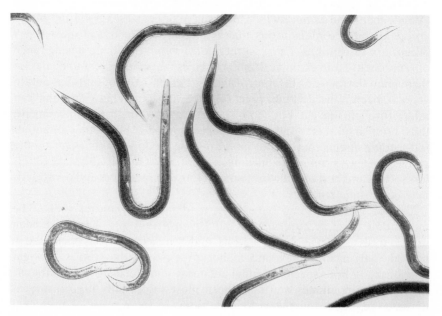

FIG. 7.13. Infective larvae of the insect-pathogenic nematode, *Heterorhabditis heliothidis*.

mutualistic relationship with a specific bacterium so that infected hosts are rapidly killed (Poinar 1972). This ability has made them the natural focus of attention for use in biological control. Deseo (1986) summarizes a number of experimental applications of *Neoaplectana* spp., against insects that attack trees but although some success is reported there are several important constraints on the use of nematodes in large-scale control programmes. Like fungi, the free-living nematodes are sensitive to environmental conditions and in most cases they are difficult to produce in large numbers. There is, however, one outstanding example of the control of an insect population with nematodes, that of *Sirex* woodwasps in Australasia, but this owes its success to a number of special features concerning the relationship of the nematode and its host.

Sirex noctilio is a native European insect attacking moribund or damaged trees. It was accidentally introduced into New Zealand but during the early 1950s it spread to Tasmania and was subsequently discovered in mainland Australia. In these countries, it attacked and killed apparently healthy trees of the introduced radiata pine, *Pinus radiata*, a tree which forms the main source of commercial softwoods yielding over $250 million (Australian) annually (Bedding 1984).

Following the early outbreaks of *S. noctilio* in New Zealand, populations collapsed naturally apparently due to parasitism by the nematode, *Deladenus siricidicola*, that must have originally been introduced along with its host (Zondag 1969). The interaction between the woodwasp and its nematode parasite is a complex one. Detailed studies of the nematode revealed that there were two morphologically distinct stages in its life cycle, one of which was mycetophagous and free living and the other parasitic (Bedding 1984). Female woodwasps parasitized by the nematode insert their ovipositors into the xylem of trees and deposit their eggs together with a phytotoxic mucus and spores of the fungus, *Amylostereum areolatum*. The fungal spores germinate and grow into the wood, normally providing food for the woodwasp larvae but now sustaining the nematodes which emerge from the eggs. This mycetophagous cycle is broken, however, when the nematodes develop in the proximity of the progeny of unparasitized females ovipositing in the same tree. The nematodes now develop into infectives which penetrate the larval cuticle and parasitize them. The host's reproductive organs, and eventually the eggs, become parasitized, and the cycle is repeated as new trees are attacked by the sterilized female woodwasps.

These extraordinary features of the nematode life cycle were crucial to the success of the subsequent culture and release programme. In particular, the free-living mycetophagous form of the nematode, which can survive in the environment in the absence of hosts, can be readily cultured on artificial medium. This dispenses with the need for insects which have a life cycle of 1–3 years. Although the parasitic form of the nematode sterilizes females, they nevertheless continue to oviposit and so disperse both nematodes and fungus throughout the forest.

During control programmes the nematodes are established in the wood-wasp population by felling and inoculating *S. noctilio* infested trees. Ninety-nine per cent of the adults emerging from these trees are parasitized (Bedding and Akhurst 1974). Alternatively, nematodes may be distributed by the transfer of infested logs between forests. In Tasmania, an extensive inoculation programme was undertaken in a plot of about 400 ha in which several thousand trees were being killed annually. This programme produced about 90 per cent parasitism of *S. noctilio* adults within two years and eventually prevented further tree mortality (Bedding 1984). Further success followed releases in Victoria and, subsequently, releases have been made in South Australia and New South Wales.

7.5 THE SAFETY OF BIOLOGICAL CONTROL AGENTS

There is little risk from the use of introduced natural enemies for biological control provided they are carefully screened before release and quarantine arrangements minimize the danger of introducing hyperparasitoids which could attack native natural enemies. The specificity of natural enemies is important in minimizing risks to non-target species but the results of the dynamic interaction between the host, introduced natural enemies and those already present in the environment is largely unpredictable and may very occasionally exacerbate or even create pest problems. A predatory mite which was accidentally introduced into Fiji, was found to attack the coconut leaf-mining beetle, *Promecotheca reichei*, an inocuous insect held at low density by effective natural enemies. The mite was capable of rapidly destroying all beetle larvae and pupae (but not eggs and adults) in a region before its own populations collapsed. Outbreaks of the beetle followed because native parasitoids attacking larvae were adversely affected and because the predatory mite was ineffective during the wet season (DeBach 1974). Control was, however, eventually re-established following the introduction of another parasitoid.

With microbial control the risk to non-target organisms is relatively small since most of the disease agents are fairly specific. However, risks to humans include the possibility of infection, toxicity and hypersensitive reactions and these need to be carefully assessed prior to registration (Rogoff 1982; Betz 1986). In the UK, for example, all formulations of microbial insecticides have to be tested for mammalian infectivity, as well as for cross-infectivity to other non-target organisms such as beneficial insects. The possibility that micro-organisms could change their character through mutation is another potential hazard that needs to be considered, although, of course, insect pathogens are a normal component of natural ecosystems to which we and other organisms have always been exposed and this emphasizes their essential difference from chemical insecticides.

In the future, however, it may prove possible to manipulate viruses genetically and hence to change the virulence or host range characteristics of the pathogens and such experiments would need to be carefully controlled. Research on these aspects of 'genetic engineering' are currently in progress in the UK and elsewhere (Newmark 1987).

8

Management 4: insecticides

8.1 HISTORICAL ASPECTS OF INSECTICIDE USE

Of all the insect pest control systems developed by man, chemical poisons are the most widely used. They are, however, the least discriminating and the excessive use of highly toxic and persistent insecticides can kill non-target organisms and also allow residues to build-up in the environment. From the first use of chemical insecticides well over a hundred years ago, insecticides have progressed from inorganic poisons such as arsenical compounds which are highly toxic to mammals, to synthetic chemicals some of which are much more selective in their action or remain toxic for as little as a few hours after application. These modern insecticides include the pyrethroids and the moulting inhibitor diflubenzuron discussed in section 8.5.1. The major developments in the discovery of insecticides are listed in Table 8.1. Coupled with increasing chemical sophistication have come new developments in the timing and technology of insecticide applications and this improved efficiency has also contributed to greater selectivity of insecticides.

The development of modern insecticides began in earnest in the 1940s with the production and widespread use of the organochlorine insecticide DDT. This chemical was first used during the Second World War to control public health pests in southern Europe and was later adopted by farmers as a 'cure-all' in pest control in the 1950s. It has also been widely used to control some forest insects and massive quantities have been applied in

Table 8.1. *Some milestones in the discovery of chemical pesticides*

Approximate year of introduction	Pesticide
1942	DDT
1945	BHC (HCH)
1945	Systemic organophosphorus insecticides
1948	Cyclodiene insecticides
1956	Carbamate insecticides
1975	Juvenile hormone analogues
1975	Photostable pyrethroids

From Graham-Bryce 1987.

North America where by the late 1950s millions of hectares of forest were being sprayed annually with the chemical. In European forestry, however, it has been less widely used and in countries such as Norway it has never been applied to forests from the air (Bakke 1970). During the period of intensive use of persistent broad-spectrum insecticides in the USA, there were alarming reports of side-effects on all kinds of wildlife as vividly described in Rachel Carson's *Silent Spring* (1962) (see also Pimentel *et al.* 1980). As well as damaging the environment, it became clear that pest outbreaks could be made worse by the use of DDT and related insecticides such as aldrin and dieldrin. These effects were due largely to the fact that natural enemies were affected more by the insecticide than the target insects so that after spraying, pest populations were able to build up rapidly in the absence of natural controls. This effect has been convincingly demonstrated by DeBach (1974) who sprayed lemon trees at regular intervals with sufficient DDT to kill natural enemies. Populations of Californian red scale, *Aonidiella aurantii*, on some trees increased by more than 1200-fold over a period of several years, whereas populations on unsprayed trees in the same grove remained under effective biological control (Fig. 8.1).

Although the widespread application of broad-spectrum insecticides is now considered unacceptable and will lead to problems of pest resistance and resurgence (Metcalf 1980), there are considerable economic constraints on the development of new, narrow-spectrum insecticides. Costs of insecticide development in real terms have more than doubled to over $25 million in the last 20 years (Kinoshita 1985), due in part to the new health

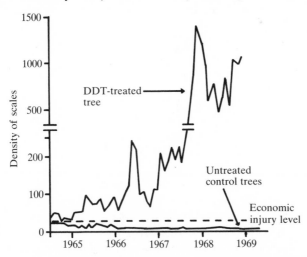

FIG. 8.1. Increases in *Aonidiella aurantii* caused by light applications of DDT, as compared with nearby untreated trees under biological control in the same grove (from DeBach 1974).

and environmental legislation which requires stringent testing of all new products before they can be cleared for commercial use (section 8.6). Thus the development of new narrow-spectrum insecticides with a limited market is unfortunately commercially unattractive. For the immediate future, therefore, chemical control in forestry will be characterized by the increasingly sophisticated use of existing insecticides aimed at maximizing control of target pests while minimizing environmental hazards.

8.2 THE SCALE OF CONTROL OPERATIONS WITH INSECTICIDES

Insecticides have been less widely used in European forests than in North American ones, partly because of the different scale of forest pest problems in the two regions. This difference can be seen in the extensive campaigns in North America against the spruce budworm, *Choristoneura fumiferana* (Armstrong 1985), and the gypsy moth, *Lymantria dispar* (White *et al.* 1981). In the USA about 12 million ha of forest was sprayed from the air between 1945 and 1974, mostly against these two pests (Jones 1985). DDT was used initially but was eventually replaced with the less persistent carbamate insecticide carbaryl from 1967 onwards. In Canada, spraying against *C. fumiferana* was much more extensive and in the 1950s and 60s as much as 2.7 million ha was sprayed in some years in New Brunswick alone.

Data on the extent of insecticide use in European forests are somewhat fragmentary. In Scandinavian countries, there has been considerable emphasis on the minimum use of insecticides and elsewhere the proportion of the forest estate treated each year is, on the whole, relatively small, although there are notable exceptions. In East and West Germany taken together, an average of about 21 000 ha per year (5 per cent of the total forest) were treated between 1925 and 1968 (Wellenstein 1978). In the USSR about 1 million ha of forest are treated annually but this represents only about 0.1 per cent of the forested area (Zakordonets 1975). Occasionally, extensive outbreaks can distort such national averages, a good example being the campaign against the nun moth, *Lymantria monacha*, in Poland during 1978–83 (Table 8.2). During the outbreak 2.5 million ha, representing over 25 per cent of Poland's forests were sprayed. These extensive areas of mainly Scots pine were planted on extremely poor sandy soils and so were highly vulnerable to stress-induced insect outbreaks. Forest planning and other silvicultural considerations (Chapter 5) could clearly make an important contribution to the integrated control of this pest.

Within the UK, aerial spraying of insecticides has increased considerably

Table 8.2. *Area of forest sprayed against Lymantria monacha, in Poland*

Year	Area sprayed (ha)
1978	20 000
1979	180 000
1980	500 000
1981	1 800 000
1982	2 500 000
1983	1 300 000
1984	150 000
Total	6 450 000

From Schönherr 1985.

following outbreaks of the pine beauty moth, *Panolis flammea*, which began in the 1970s (Stoakley 1977) (Table 8.3). Although the areas treated are relatively small in national terms, they represent a significant proportion of the new plantings of lodgepole pine in northern Scotland.

8.3 INSECTICIDES AND PEST BIOLOGY

Forest pests attack many different parts of the tree, feeding both on and in tissues (Table 8.4) (Chapter 4). These life-history characteristics, together with the size of the tree attacked determine whether chemical control is a realistic option for particular pests and where appropriate, how and when insecticides are applied.

Table 8.3. *Area of forest sprayed in the UK against Panolis flammea*

Year	Area sprayed (ha)
1978	4800
1979	3600
1980	1800
1981	60
1982	—
1983	—
1984	—
1985	4860
1986	1758
1987	1315
Total	18 193

From Stoakley, personal communication

Table 8.4. *Some examples of chemical control in relation to feeding habit of forest insects*

Habitat	Insect group	Feeding stage	Examples	Chemical control
Leaves	Lepidoptera Hymenoptera	Larval defoliators	*Bupalus piniaria* *Diprion pini*	Aerial spraying; may require regional organization
		Leafminers	*Coleophora laricella*	
		Sap feeders	*Elatobium abietinum*	Ground spraying in Christmas tree crops
Cones and seeds	Lepidoptera Hymenoptera	Larval borers	*Dioryctria abietella* *Megastigmus spermatrophus*	May be required in seed orchards; timing critical
Shoots	Lepidoptera Coleoptera	Larval moths and adult beetles boring in leaders and laterals	*Rhyacionia buoliana* *Tomicus piniperda*	Not really practical on forest scale; timing critical; logs may be protected against adult beetles
Bark	Coleoptera	Larval borers	*Ips typographus* *Tetropium gabrieli*	Not practical on forest scale; logs may be protected against adults
Wood	Lepidoptera Hymenoptera Coleoptera	Larval borers in sap and heartwood	*Cossus cossus* *Sirex noctilio* *Trypodendron lineatum*	Not practical on forest scale; logs may be protected against adult beetles

8.3.1 Methods of application

Pests that attack young trees, especially where small areas are involved, can be controlled by ground-based operations and in forest nurseries, for example, insecticide application systems appropriate for small-scale agriculture and horticulture can be used. In arboriculture and seed orchards individual trees can be treated using mist blowers until they are around 10 metres high.

The treatment of young conifers to protect them from the pine weevil, *Hylobius abietis*, is carried out prophylactically in many countries. The logistical problems of treating individual trees over large areas are overcome in this case by bulk dipping of transplants in centralized dipping tanks before planting out. Protection may be needed over two or even three seasons so that a fairly persistent insecticide must be employed. In the UK, gamma HCH is used but in Sweden, for example, only the pyrethroid permethrin is registered for protection of transplants (H. H. Eidmann, personal communication) (section 8.6). Although the use of centralized dipping areas is usually considered environmentally acceptable, local contamination does occur and, in particular, the problems of human exposure during dipping and planting-out are likely to result in a shift to the environmentally more acceptable pyrethroids such as cypermethrin.

For larger trees growing in the forest, stem-feeding insects such as bark beetles can only be treated in ground-based operations but in general such individual tree treatments are neither practical nor economic. Bark beetle larvae are well protected within the bark and treatments aimed at adults are difficult to apply to the whole trunk area. Despite these problems stem treatments have been used with apparent success against the spruce bark beetle, *Dendroctonus micans*, in the USSR. Insecticidal preparations that are absorbed into the bark and kill larvae were applied to some 10 million trees over a 15-year period (Targamadze *et al.* 1975). Bark and ambrosia beetles can be more readily controlled on felled timber because high volume topical applications of fairly persistent insecticides can be used to treat log stacks which occupy relatively small areas in the forest or in sawmills. The need for such measures though, can be largely avoided by appropriate forest practices (Chapter 5).

Aerial application of insecticides, is the only practical method of dealing with large-scale outbreaks and is used almost exclusively for lepidopteran and sawfly defoliators, many of which feed in exposed positions in the canopy. In Europe the gypsy moth, *Lymantria dispar*, and the nun moth, *L. monacha*, the pine processionary moth, *Thaumetopoea pityocampa*, the Siberian silk moth, *Dendrolimus sibiricus*, and the pine sawfly, *Diprion pini*, are among the defoliators most frequently controlled in this way. The methods of aerial application of insecticides are discussed more fully in section 8.5 and details of the chemical control of a range of forest pests can be found in Carter and Gibbs (1983), Hobart (1977), and Hamel (1983).

8.3.2 Timing of applications

Accurate timing of aerial applications of insecticide is important because the very young larvae may feed in protected situations in opening buds or at the base of needles whereas the older larger larvae cause more damage and are usually more resistant to insecticides. This problem is illustrated in Fig. 8.2 which shows that the optimum time for insecticide application to control *T. pityocampa*, occurs when most of the eggs have hatched but before larvae have developed to the relatively resistant third instar stage. The optimum period for application is only likely to last for 4 or 5 days (Buxton 1983).

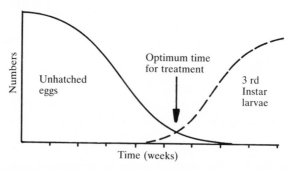

FIG. 8.2. The optimum time for insecticide application to control *Thaumetopoea pityocampa*. This occurs when the greatest number of eggs have hatched but before larvae have developed to the more resistant third instar (from Buxton 1983).

For insects that spend some or all of their larval period within the host tissues (Table 8.5) control is usually directed against adults prior to oviposition or the larval stage before it enters the host's tissues and timing is very important. Stoakley (1985) gives an example of the ineffective control of the winter moth, *Operophtera brumata*, on Sitka spruce in southern Scotland. The organophosphorus insecticide fenitrothion was applied 7 to 10 days after egg hatch by which time many larvae had tunnelled into young buds and so avoided direct contact with the insecticide.

Timing of spray applications is also important in situations where there is potential for some control by natural enemies since they are especially vulnerable to insecticides. In Spain, local or seasonal variations in egg hatch of *T. pityocampa* in relation to emergence of adults of the parasitic

Table 8.5. *Insect groups protected from insecticides*

Insect group	Habitat	Type of protection
Sap feeders (aphids, scales, adelgids)	On leaves, in rolls or under wax	Partial; but good exposure of many species
Gall formers (gall wasps and adelgids)	In plant growths on leaves and stems	Usually complete, except from some systemics
Leafminers (Coleoptera and Lepidoptera)	Between leaf epidermises	Usually complete, except for some systemics
Cone borers (Lepidoptera, Coleoptera, and Hymenoptera)	In seeds and/or cones	Usually complete, except for some systemics
Shoot borers (Lepidoptera and Coleoptera)	In leading and lateral young shoots and twigs	Usually complete, except for some systemics, and during very early external stages
Bark borers (Lepidoptera and Coleoptera)	In inner bark cambium/phloem	Complete, except during external stages
Wood borers (Lepidoptera, Coleoptera and Hymenoptera)	In sap and heart-wood	Usually complete
Soil dwellers (Coleoptera and Lepidoptera)	In soil around roots	Usually complete except for some soil drenches
Dead wood borers (Coleoptera and Isoptera)	In felled logs or planks	Complete except for some fumigants

wasp, *Phryxe caudata*, determines the impact of insecticide applications on these natural enemies. Where egg hatch and parasitoid emergence are closely synchronized (Fig. 8.3a), many parasitoids will be destroyed when insecticides are applied at the optimum time. In other localities or in different years the parasitoids may emerge later and be virtually unaffected (Fig. 8.3b).

8.4 THE IMPACT OF INSECTICIDES: PESTS, NATURAL ENEMIES, AND THE ENVIRONMENT

8.4.1 Pest resurgence

The resurgence of pest populations to outbreak levels following spraying has been commonly associated with the widespread use of persistent insecticides and largely results from destruction of natural enemies. The vulnerability of natural enemies to insecticides stems partly from the fact that they are highly mobile and thus more exposed to deposits of contact insecticides, and predators can build-up a toxic dose when they consume several prey individuals. As well as these behavioural aspects, natural enemies are often inherently more susceptible to insecticides (Mullin and Croft 1985). For

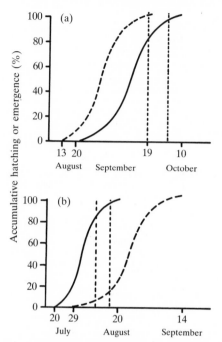

FIG. 8.3. Accumulative percentage of egg hatch of *Thaumetopoea pityocampa* (solid line), and of adult emergence of the larval parasitoid, *Phryxe caudata* (dotted line) in two localities in Spain during 1969. (a) Parasitoids are killed when insecticides are applied at the optimum time (indicated between vertical lines) (b) Parasitoids are relatively unaffected by spraying (from Dafauce 1972).

the gypsy moth, *Lymantria dispar*, in the USA, the LD_{50} of the carbamate insecticide carbaryl (the dose that will kill 50 per cent of the test organisms) is between 0.3 and 0.9 μg per larva, depending on instar. Two important larval parasitoids of this insect, a braconid wasp (*Apanteles* spp.) and a chalcid wasp (*Brachymeria* spp.) are much more vulnerable, with LD_{50} values of between 0.01 and 0.05 μg per adult insect. In other words a dose of insecticide sufficient to kill one pest larva would theoretically be able to kill up to twenty natural enemies (Tomlin and Forgash 1972).

Sometimes outbreaks may be perpetuated by the use of insecticides when the underlying conditions remain favourable for the insect pests. Chemical control of outbreaks of the spruce budworm, *Choristoneura fumiferana*, in New Brunswick kept the highly susceptible mature fir trees alive, preventing the natural collapse of the outbreaks through the eventual death of the host trees (Fig. 8.4).

Secondary pest problems can sometimes arise when insects, previously

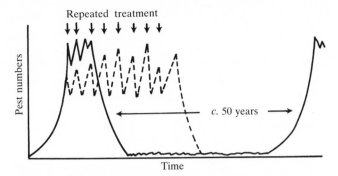

FIG. 8.4. Diagrammatic representation of the outbreak patterns of *Choristoneura fumiferana* in New Brunswick. Outbreaks occur on average every 50 years, and continue until trees are killed (solid line). Annual insecticide treatments keep trees alive, but semi-epidemic conditions persist (dotted line) (from Way and Bevan 1977).

at a low population density, increase to damaging levels following chemical control aimed at other insects. These induced pest problems, which are largely caused by the destruction of natural enemies, are usually associated with the intensive use of insecticides in agriculture (Coaker 1974) and are not in general an important feature of forest insect control.

8.4.2 Pest resistance

As well as possibly perpetuating some outbreaks, repeated applications of insecticides can select for resistance in the treated population by removing susceptible individuals (see Oppenoorth 1985 for review). Resistance is most likely to occur when a particular insecticide is applied at frequent intervals to relatively isolated populations with little insect movement into or out of the population (Matthews 1979). In contrast to the situation for agricultural and horticultural crops, the development of resistance has not so far been a significant problem in forest insect control and this is un-doubtedly due to the much less frequent use of insecticides (but see Robertson and Stock 1984). Nevertheless, reductions in insecticide use, especially of the more persistent compounds should be an important objec-tive in forest insect control.

8.4.3 The fate of insecticides in the forest

What happens to an insecticide once it has been sprayed onto the forest depends on a number of factors including the proportion of the insecticide that impacts onto the target leaves and insects, how much penetrates through the canopy to the forest floor and the persistence of the insecticide on leaves and in the soil. The main pathways of insecticide movement in the forest are shown in Fig. 8.5. The method of application and characteristics of the host foliage are two of the most important factors affecting collection of spray droplets by the targets. Balsam fir needles for example which differ in shape from those of spruce can collect around 75 per cent more insecticide (Sundaram 1975). Other aspects of the targeting of insecticides are discussed in section 8.5.3.

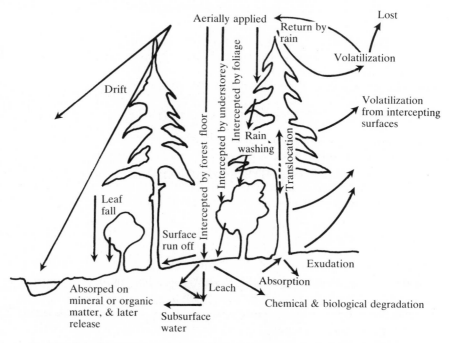

FIG. 8.5. The movement of pesticides in forests (from Hobart 1977).

Losses of insecticide from the surface of the foliage are initially fairly rapid, largely due to wash-off by rain followed by weathering and breakdown by light and biotic agencies but some insecticide may be absorbed by the leaves (Armstrong 1984). The way in which insecticides are formulated (section 8.5.2) is an important factor influencing their movement through the ecosystem. Water-based formulations, for example, are particularly susceptible to leaching and are readily lost from treated surfaces during rainfall, and enter soil, ground water, and streams. Trials with water-based sprays of fenitrothion have demonstrated that 50 per cent of the initial deposit on leaves is lost within 4 days of spraying with up to 85 per cent lost after 2 weeks (Armstrong 1984).

Insecticide in spray droplets that penetrate directly to the forest floor, together with that washed from the foliage, becomes incorporated into the litter layer. The fate of these residues is complex and not yet well understood but there are evidently large differences in the extent to which different insecticides are retained in the forest litter. DDT can persist for several years in temperate climates but the organophosphate phosphamidon and the carbamate aminocarb, for example, have been found to disappear very quickly; 75 per cent of low initial doses of aminocarb having been lost within a week (Armstrong 1984).

8.5 INSECTICIDE TECHNOLOGY

8.5.1 The characteristics and use of insecticides

The characteristics of the major groups of insecticides are summarized in Table 8.6. Most insecticides poison insects on contact or after they are ingested with their normal food and this difference in mode of action influences the way in which they are used to control insects. A contact insecticide, which enters the insect either through the cuticle or the spiracles, will be most successful when applied directly onto the surface of the target insect. Insecticides deposited in the immediate vicinity can, however, be picked up as insects move around and this mechanism is especially effective for insecticides with a significant residual activity. Insecticides belonging to the cyclodiene group of the organochlorines such as aldrin, dieldrin, and heptachlor can remain active for years and their persistence is so extreme that their use has been banned in many countries.

Insecticides that work only after ingestion must be deposited on the insect's normal food and a lethal dose is acquired during feeding. These kinds of insecticides are, therefore, most appropriate for insects that are active on the surface of leaves or bark. Like contact insecticides, they are not usually effective against the many forest insects that are concealed within the host plant tissues or, like some aphids and scales, that are sheltered underneath leaves or by waxy secretions and which feed on internal tissues from the outside (Table 8.5). Systemic insecticides that enter and move through plant tissues can be effective alternatives to contact insecticides for control of these pests.

Systemic insecticides are absorbed and translocated to physiologically active tissues when applied to different parts of the tree such as roots, bark, or leaves. Some systemics have only a relatively weak contact effect but become more poisonous as a result of changes that occur within the plant. They are thus relatively safe to natural enemies when sprayed onto plant surfaces. The extent of movement within the tree depends on a number of factors, particularly the part treated and the size of the tree. They are most

Table 8.6. *Characteristics of insecticides*

Insecticide	Approximate mammalian LD_{50} mg/kg	Mode of action	Residual activity	Uses and environmental impact
Organochlorines				
DDT	115	Contact, stomach	Very long	Banned in many countries, largely replaced by fenitrothion
gamma HCH	88–270	Contact, stomach some fumigant	Moderate	Banned in Scandinavia Protection of logs and transplants in UK. Broad spectrum, danger to non-target invertebrates
Organophosphates				
Malathion	2800	Contact	Fairly short	Treatment of Christmas trees against aphids
Fenitrothion	800	Contact	Fairly short	Aerial application against many lepidopteran defoliators. Environmentally safe when used in ULV formulation
Carbamates				
Pirimicarb	147	Foliar systemic, some fumigant	Short	Selective aphidicide used in nurseries and amenity trees. Said not to affect beneficial insects
Aldicarb	0.9	Systemic, some contact	Fairly short	Applied as granules to soil against sap-feeders and nematodes. Very toxic to wildlife
Synthetic pyrethroids				
Bioresmethrin	7070	Contact	Short	Wide pest range. Very safe to mammals; very toxic to fish and bees
Permethrin	430–4000	Contact	Short to moderate	Wide pest range, including protection of transplants against weevils. Very toxic to fish and bees
Insect growth regulators				
(1) *Urea insecticides*				
Diflubenzuron	>4640	Contact/ ingestion	Fairly short	Aerial application against lepidopteran defoliators. Fairly safe for beneficial insects.
(2) *Juvenile hormone analogues*				
Methoprene	>34 500	Contact/ ingestion	Short	Not generally suitable for forest insect control

effectively utilized when uptake occurs through roots or basal parts of the trunk and from direct injection into the vascular tissues (Norris 1981). Specialized treatments such as stem injection are not appropriate for forest use but can be of value for treatment of town trees and perhaps those in seed orchards where some success against seed-feeding insects has been reported (Fogal and Lopushanski 1984; Wiersma and Nordlander 1985).

Insecticides with a fumigant action are mainly used against soil pests and are of value in forest nurseries for treating soil before planting.

Detailed discussion of the properties of different classes of insecticides can be found in a number of publications including Hassall (1982), Kerkut and Gilbert (1985) and Graham-Bryce (1987). The organochlorine insecticides poison insects through stomach or contact action. Because of their residual activity on the treated surfaces they are effective against defoliators but are less effective against aphids. Gamma HCH, which is still widely used in forestry has a broad spectrum of activity and, under some conditions, can have moderate fumigant and systemic activity. Organophosphorus insecticides, which have largely replaced the organochlorines, are a versatile group and display a range of characteristics useful in pest control. They include contact insecticides (e.g. malathion, diazinon), systemics (e.g. phorate) and fumigants (e.g. dichlorvos). They do, however, exhibit a range of toxicity to mammals and a few are very poisonous. The carbamates include insecticides such as carbaryl, which has a broad-spectrum activity and aldicarb which has some systemic properties.

The newest major group of insecticides now being widely used as contact poisons against defoliators are the pyrethroids, some of which are among the most potent of insecticides. Derived from pyrethrins which occur naturally in some plants, these insecticides are usually much safer to mammals than organophosphorus and organochlorine insecticides. Some of the earliest pyrethroids such as resmethrin were shown to have very low residual toxicity which, together with their rapid knockdown effects, made them ideal for use in domestic pest control situations. Later compounds, like permethrin and cypermethrin, are more photostable and so have a more prolonged residual toxicity. They do have some disadvantages, however, being relatively expensive to produce and, although mammalian toxicity is low, they can be lethal to fish and invertebrates such as bees that may be present in treated areas (Ruigt 1985). They have, nevertheless, been used both in small and large-scale control operations. In Dutch poplar orchards, for example, permethrin has been used to control larvae of the clear-wing moth, *Sciapteron tabaniformis* (Wouters 1979), and in Poland aerial application of pyrethroids has been used to control the nun moth, *Lymantria monacha* (Bychawska and Sliwa 1982). In Czechoslovakia, sub-lethal doses of a pyrethroid have been mixed with formulations of the insect pathogenic bacterium, *Bacillus thuringiensis*, to control winter moth, *Operophtera brumata*, and the oak leaf roller moth, *Tortrix viridana* (Svestka 1980).

So far we have only considered conventional insecticides, most of which affect the insect nervous system (see Lund 1985 for discussion). The lack of specificity of these insecticides arises largely from their ability to damage the nervous system of other animals but an important new group of insecticides, the insect growth regulators affect physiological processes unique to insects and so are highly specific. There are two major groups of insect growth regulators (Chen and Mayer 1985; Retnakaran *et al*. 1985); the benzoylphenyl ureas or urea insecticides which inhibit chitin synthesis and disrupt the moulting process and the juvenile hormone analogues that are functionally similar to natural juvenile hormones and control the normal metamorphic changes in insects.

Diflubenzuron belongs to the first group of growth regulators and when ingested can have dramatic effects on insect development. Its effects on sixth instar larvae of the spruce budworm, *Choristoneura fumiferana*, are shown in Fig. 8.6. In this case the moult from larva to pupa is disrupted, resulting in the formation of larval/pupal hybrids in which the cuticle contains little chitin. Despite these experimentally-induced effects, *C. fumiferana* and several other tortricids are in fact relatively tolerant of this insecticide but the lymantrids (e.g. the gypsy moth *L. dispar*) have proved to be highly susceptible (Rappaport and Robertson (1981) in Retnakaran *et al*. 1985). Different larval stages also vary in their susceptibility but all are most vulnerable to treatment just before each moult. Once in the adult stage, however, insects are relatively resistant although the viability of eggs from treated adults can be reduced. For example, when treated bark was fed to the pine weevil, *Hylobius abietis*, subsequent egg hatch was reduced by 70 per cent or so (Kolbe and Hartwig 1982). The eggs themselves can also be killed by direct treatment.

Because diflubenzuron must be ingested it is not generally effective against concealed pests or sap-feeding insects but it has been widely used against defoliators, notably the pine processionary moth, *Thaumetopoea pityocampa*, and related species. These insects are particularly difficult to control with contact insecticides because the larvae aggregate in silken tents during the day. Trials with diflubenzuron in Israel (Halperin 1980), Greece (Georgevits 1980) and France (Demolin and Millet 1983) resulted in up to 100 per cent mortality of larvae and it persisted on foliage for around 27 days even after heavy rain. In Spain, effective control of *T. pityocampa* was obtained over 15 000 ha of pine forests without adverse effects on parasitoids, predators, or other non-target organisms (Robredo 1980).

Several studies have indicated that the effects of diflubenzuron on natural

FIG. 8.6. Abnormalities in *Choristoneura fumiferana* pupae induced by feeding the larvae on the insect growth regulator diflubenzuron, (a) pupa has larval head and thorax, (b) partially formed pupa with various larval features, (c) normal pupa (from Retnakaran and Smith 1975).

enemies are insignificant even when large areas are treated (Robredo 1980; Tsankov and Mirchev 1983). This is mainly because adult insects are inherently less susceptible and, in any case, would not normally ingest residues. Larval stages of natural enemies, however, may be as susceptible as host larvae. Treatment of young larvae of *L. dispar*, for example, reduces percent emergence of the larval parasitoid, *Apanteles melanoscelus* (Granett *et al.* 1976; Madrid and Stewart 1981). Appropriate timing of applications may minimize these adverse effects.

The second group of insect growth regulators, the juvenile hormone analogues (JHA) or juvenoids are chemicals that have been discovered to have effects on insects more or less identical to those of the natural juvenile hormone. Juvenile hormone analogues occur naturally in some trees, for example *Abies balsamea* (Bowers *et al.* 1966) and also in other plants. Because they are usually much more active and more stable than the natural hormone they have the potential for use in insect control. During larval development, relatively high concentrations of natural juvenile hormone occur in the early instars but concentrations decline during the last instar, preparatory to the pupal moult. Thus, to be effective, applications of juvenile hormone analogues must be made to older larvae in which natural levels of hormone are declining. Following treatment, high levels of the hormone mimic cause abnormal pupation or in some cases the formation of additional or supernumery larval instars. Thus as with chitin synthesis inhibitors, activity of JHA is relatively slow and larvae may continue to feed for some time after treatment.

A number of trials against forest insects have been made with JHA. In Russia, methoprene and the related hydroprene were reported to affect populations of *L. dispar* for two generations following an application to third and fourth instar larvae (Ben'kovskaya and Idrisova 1985). Tests with various juvenile hormone analogues against the spruce bark beetle, *Ips typographus*, and *H. abietis* in Europe have demonstrated clear insecticidal activity but the concealed habit of the larvae makes effective application difficult (Novak *et al.* 1976). Despite their many desirable characteristics JHA are not, in general, suitable for control of forest insects but they have found some success against a number of Diptera which are pests as adults and where slow activity against the larvae is not a problem (Bowers 1984). As with other insecticides, JHA can induce resistance in treated populations (Retnakaran *et al.* 1985).

New developments in the use of insect growth regulators for insect control may follow the discovery of compounds with anti-juvenile hormone properties. The precocenes, so called because they cause precocious development in insects resulting in undersized and non-viable adults, have been isolated from some plants (Bowers *et al.* 1976) and could form the basis of more effective hormonal insecticides.

8.5.2 The formulation of insecticides

So far we have only considered the characteristics of the insecticides themselves, the so-called 'active ingredients' (a.i.). However, the a.i. must be mixed or formulated with carrier substances so that the small quantities of a.i. used can be handled effectively and applied evenly over the treated area (Matthews 1979; Hassall 1982). Insecticidal compounds are normally insoluble in water, but an appropriate formulation, usually as wettable powders or emulsifiable concentrates, can allow them to be applied in water-based delivery systems. Wettable powders consist of finely-ground solids of inert diluent, together with the a.i. which may be solid or liquid. They are dispersed into the water carrier as a fine suspension, an agitation system often being needed to prevent sedimentation. In emulsifiable concentrates, a.i. is dissolved in certain kinds of oil or other organic solvent which is itself immiscible with water. When added to a larger volume of water, often with surfactants, tiny droplets of the solvent still containing the dissolved insecticide appear as a colloidal suspension. Formulations designed specifically for ultra-low volume application, discussed below, are normally applied in oil-based or oil/water mixtures containing special additives to prevent too rapid evaporation of the tiny spray droplets.

In very specialized situations such as direct injection of systemic insecticides into the trunks of trees, the correct formulation is essential to ensure rapid translocation within the plant whilst minimizing phytotoxic effects. Implanting capsules into tree trunks or branches is another method of using systemic insecticides in trees and the a.i. must be formulated with a carrier that releases it over an extended period. Acephate has been used in this way to control the processionary moth, *Thaumetopoea wilkinsoni*, on urban trees in Israel (Halperin 1985) but trials with this technique for control of the horse chestnut scale, *Pulvinaria regalis*, in the UK have met with little success.

Micro-encapsulation of insecticides is a way of achieving slow release of the a.i. for topically applied sprays. In this sophisticated formulation, the a.i. is enclosed in a gelatin or polymer coating which, as well as regulating the release rate, may also protect sensitive chemicals from UV light (Matthews 1979). In forestry, this technique has been used for the application of pheromones in trials of the mating-disruption technique (Chapter 9).

Finally, dry granular formulations avoid the need for liquid delivery systems. Systemic insecticides such as phorate can be incorporated with inert solids such as china clay and the resulting granules placed around the bases of young trees. The a.i. is slowly released into a localized area over a period of several weeks and taken up by the tree and this minimizes contamination of the soil and the likelihood of acute phytotoxic effects. Some examples of the use of granules are given by Hobart (1977).

8.5.3 The application of insecticides

No other branch of the science of insecticides has seen more research and increased sophistication in recent years than the technology of application. These developments stem from an urgent need to improve the efficiency with which insecticides are used so that pests can be controlled more cost-effectively with minimum pollution of the surrounding environment. Efficiency can be measured as the fraction of the applied dose that is received by or is required to kill pests during spraying operations (Graham-Bryce 1983). The extremely low efficiency of spray programmes in agriculture is illustrated in Table 8.7 and that of conventional spray systems in forestry is likely to be equally low. In liquid-based delivery systems, the key to explaining this low efficiency lies with a consideration of the spray droplets themselves and how they behave once released into the air.

Table 8.7. *Examples of the efficiency of insecticide use*

Compound	System	Method of application	Efficiency of utilization
Dimethoate	Aphids on beans	Foliar spray	0.03%
Gamma HCH	Capsid bugs on cocoa	Foliar spray	0.02%
Disulfoton	Aphids on wheat	Soil incorporation	2.90%
Gamma HCH	Flying locust swarms	Aerial spray	6.00%

From Graham-Bryce 1977.

Several factors influence the deposition of droplets on both foliage and insects, the most important being droplet size, target shape and size, density and type of foliage, the velocity of falling drops and windspeed (Barry 1984). Table 8.8 shows the relationship between droplet diameter, volume and the number of droplets from a unit volume of spray. A 10-fold increase in droplet diameter from 100 μm to 1000 μm (=1 mm) represents a 1000-fold increase in volume so that much of the volume of an insecticide spray can be contained within relatively few large drops. This is clearly shown from the droplet distribution of a typical fan nozzle that might be mounted on an aircraft boom system (Fig. 8.7). It has, however, been shown in a number of studies, contrary to previous assumptions, that very small droplets are in fact the most important ones for impacting on to the target and ultimately killing insects. The size distribution of droplets collected by budworm, *Choristoneura* spp., larvae is shown in Table 8.9. Ninety-three per cent of larvae had collected droplets no larger than 50 μm so that in conventional sprays the biologically effective portion

Table 8.8. *Droplet size relationships*
(*approximate*)

Droplet diameter (μm)	Droplet volume (cm^3)	Number of drops from 1 cm^3
1000	5×10^{-4}	2×10^3
500	6.5×10^{-5}	1.5×10^4
100	5×10^{-7}	2×10^6
50	6.5×10^{-8}	1.5×10^7
10	5×10^{-10}	2×10^9

constitutes only a few percent of the emitted spray volume because the bulk of the insecticide is contained within large droplets (Himel and Moore 1967).

It appears on current evidence that droplets in the range 20–50 μm cause most of the mortality in aerial applications of insecticide against forest insects but for other applications other sizes are optimal (Table 8.10). Very small droplets may fail to impact or contain insufficient insecticide to kill insects and larger droplets do not reach the target. Small droplets also give better coverage of the target and allow considerable economy in the volume of insecticide needed; for example, the same droplet density on a surface can be achieved with one-eighth of the volume of insecticide if the diameter of the droplets is halved (Matthews 1983).

The problem of drift

Although important in impacting on the target and killing insects, small droplets appear to be particularly susceptible to drift out of the treated

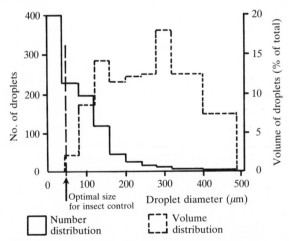

FIG. 8.7. Droplet distribution from a typical fan (hydraulic) nozzle (from Matthews 1979).

Table 8.9. *Maximum droplet size found on larvae of Choristoneura* spp.

Estimated droplet diameter (μm)	Percent of 1113 larvae
<21	23
21–26	53.5
27–30	6.2
31–33	2.4
34–36	1.6
37–38	2.2
39–40	0.7
41–42	0.5
43–44	0.7
45–46	0.6
47–50	2.0
51–68	4.4
69–95	2.0
96–107	0.2

From Himel and Moore 1967.

Table 8.10. *Optimum droplet size ranges for selected targets*

Target	Droplet diameter (μm)
Flying insects (e.g. locust swarms)	10–50
Insects on foliage (e.g. many forest pests)	30–50
Soil (e.g. nursery pests in soil or sap-feeders on small trees)	250–500

From Matthews 1979.

area and so they can contaminate the surroundings. The fate of the droplets, however, is largely dependent on movements of the surrounding air. In stable air conditions, small drops settle out of the air more slowly than large ones and tiny ones may be carried in and out of the foliage canopy in relatively slow moving air currents. In turbulent winds, however, small drops are impacted onto foliage and turbulent eddies immediately above the canopy ensure that small droplets penetrate into it (Joyce and Spillman 1979). Figure 8.8 shows the concentration of fenitrothion in balsam fir needles at different distances from the point of application in stable and unstable air conditions. Drift was more evident in stable air conditions which have previously been considered to be most suitable for aerial spraying.

Controlling droplet size

Conventional types of spray equipment produce a wide spectrum of droplet sizes due to the irregular break-up of liquid from the nozzle. But

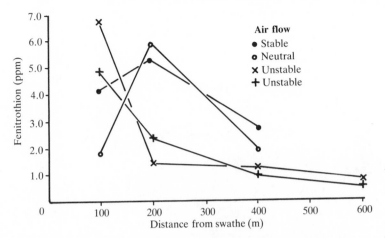

Fig. 8.8. Fenitrothion concentration in balsam fir needles as determined by gas chromatography. Each point is an average of upwind and downwind concentrations (from Wiesner 1984).

to be optimally efficient at killing insects with minimum waste, many more smaller drops need to be produced, preferably in the range 20–50 μm (Table 8.10). This has been achieved by the development of controlled droplet application (CDA) technology which has reduced the volume of insecticide needed in spraying operations considerably and promoted the use of ultra-low volume (ULV) techniques.

The most widely used form of CDA employs centrifugal-energy nozzles, more conveniently known as spinning disc or spinning cage atomizers (Matthews 1979). These mechanisms, revolving at high speed, are fed with insecticide which flows to the edge and is thrown off as filaments of liquid that fragment into droplets, the size of which is predominantly a function of the speed of rotation and the flow rate of the insecticide. Several kinds of spray machine employ these systems. Simple hand-held, battery-powered devices such as the Mini- or Micron-Ulva (Micron Sprayers Ltd.) are appropriate for use in forest nurseries whereas hand-held, petrol driven machines like the Turbair Fox (Turbair Ltd.) can be used in small-scale arboriculture or in seed orchards. Aircraft mounted systems for large-scale forest operations may employ spinning cage atomizers (Micronair Ltd) or the X15 multiple spinning disc systems (Micron Sprayers Ltd.). Based on a similar principle to that of the X15, the X30 spinning disc system has recently been developed jointly by the NERC Institute of Virology and the UK Forestry Commission to produce high droplet density and flexible control of droplet size. This system has been tested successfully from helicopters using diflubenzuron, fenitrothion and nuclear polyhedro-

FIG. 8.9. Aerial spraying of virus in Scotland against *Panolis flammea*, using a multiple spinning disc system mounted on a helicopter.

sis viruses of the pine beauty moth, *Panolis flammea*, and the pine sawfly, *Neodiprion sertifer* (P. F. Entwistle, personal communication) (Fig. 8.9).

The validation of CDA/ULV in European forestry

The technique of ULV application of insecticide was first used in the UK to control *P. flammea* in Sutherland during the late 1970s (Holden and Bevan 1979, 1981). ULV application of fenitrothion replaced the conventional LV spraying only after detailed comparison between the two methods had been made in order to get the necessary clearance from the regulating agency (J. T. Stoakley, personal communication) (section 8.6).

During these comparative studies, contamination of the soil, streams, birds, and other wildlife as well as that of operators was measured in one of the most intensively studied spray operations of its kind. In general, contamination in and around the target area was found to be at a low level for both application methods (Holden and Bevan 1979, 1981; Spray *et al.* 1987). But the fate of the insecticide during LV (20 dm^3 ha^{-1}) and ULV (1 dm^3 ha^{-1}) spraying was clearly different (Table 8.11). Both methods of application gave successful control (around 97.5 per cent mortality) but in the ULV-treated plots, the target surfaces collected over twice as much insecticide whereas only about one-tenth as much was lost to the ground. It was estimated in this study that the larvae collected from 2 to 8 times the LD_{50} dose suggesting that adjustments to the rate of application could lead to further improvements in efficiency. These results are a striking demon-

Table 8.11. *Aerial spraying against Panolis flammea, in Scotland, 1978*

	Ultra low volume	Low volume
Insecticide applied (g a.i. ha^{-1})	300	300
Amount lost outside target area	3	60
Amount lost to ground	13.5	115
Amount collected by target surfaces	283.5	125
Percentage of insecticide applied and collected by targets	94.5%	41.7%

The fate of fenitrothion—data expressed as g a.i. ha^{-1} (from Joyce and Beaumont 1979).

stration of the importance of improvements in aerial spraying technology in contributing to the efficient control of insect outbreaks.

Because ULV spraying requires a much smaller volume of insecticide and does not depend on access to large volumes of water, it is much more appropriate than LV methods for treating large remote areas. In this example, differences in the volume needed for the two application methods meant that the area treated per plane load could be increased from 40 to 800 ha.

8.5.4 The practicalities of aerial spraying

The often irregular topography of forest land presents major problems in trying to ensure even cover of insecticide over large tracts of forest. Steep slopes and valleys in forested mountainous areas not only make it virtually impossible to fly at constant altitude and speed above the canopy but local meteorological conditions also affect the pattern of spray deposit (Ekblad and Barry 1984; Akessen and Yates 1984). Airflows on mountain slopes and in deep valleys are markedly different and other meteorological conditions such as temperature inversions (Chapter 2) can influence the rate of sedimentation and the concentration of airborne droplets (Akessen and Yates 1984). It may be possible to avoid some adverse conditions such as temperature inversions during CDA for example (J. T. Stoakley, personal communication), but where timing is crucial, delay may affect the level of control. Other factors such as the size of the aircraft and the canopy characteristics of different tree species will vary from operation to operation and will influence both the method of application and its efficiency.

In general, fixed wing aircraft are used for large aerial spraying operations but smaller areas may be more easily treated from helicopters because they are more manoeuvrable and can fly more slowly over clearly defined target areas. Although the helicopter rotors produce a strong downdraft this apparently only improves canopy penetration at very low speeds, i.e. below 25 km h^{-1} and so is of no value at economic operational speeds (Matthews 1979). The speed of flying in both helicopters and fixed wing planes affects droplet behaviour in the air wake, and at faster speeds the released spray cloud is initially carried upwards so producing a wider swath and less concentrated deposit of insecticide (Akesson and Yates 1984).

Regulation of aircraft tracks by ground-based guidance systems greatly improves spraying accuracy and minimizes gaps or overspraying between swathes (Michie *et al.* 1979). Inertial guidance systems can lock the plane's flight track onto a predetermined spray grid over a forest thus removing the need for the pilot to keep a constant check on his direction and position in the grid (Matthews 1979). In remote forest areas, helicopters may be required to position track guidance beacons on the ground. Such systems may increase the cost of aerial spraying but make for accurate and verifiable applications.

8.6 REGULATION OF INSECTICIDE USE

Most countries have government agencies responsible for regulating the use of insecticides (Young 1983). The Environmental Protection Agency (EPA) in the USA and the Pesticides Registration and Surveillance Department (PRSD) in the UK are two examples of such bodies and they play an important role in ensuring that only approved chemicals and application methods are used. At present in the UK, specific approval has to be sought from PRSD for each insecticide control operation in forests (J. T. Stoakley, personal communication) and when treatment is by aerial application, approval is also required from the Civil Aviation Authority (Stell 1983).

8.7 THE COST OF INSECTICIDES AND THE ECONOMICS OF THEIR USE IN FORESTRY

Some of the earliest synthetic insecticides such as DDT and gamma HCH are relatively easy to manufacture and large quantities can be produced cheaply. The newer, less persistent insecticides, however, like some of the pyrethroids and diflubenzuron are much more expensive (Metcalf 1980) (Table 8.12), so there is a price to pay for using safer modern insecticides. This cost is more readily borne in the cultivation of high value agricultural and horticultural crops than in forests where the costs of control may not be recouped for several decades. The economics of large-scale chemical control operations in forests needs, therefore, to be carefully considered.

Table 8.12. *Number of manufacturing stages and relative costs of some insecticides*

Compound	Group	No. stages in manufacture	Approximate cost ($ kg^{-1})
Gamma HCH	Organochlorine	1	0.04
DDT	Organochlorine	1	0.75
Malathion	Organophosphate	3	2.26
Allethrin	Synthetic pyrethroid	13	88–110
Diflubenzuron	Insect growth regulator	Not available	88–110

From Metcalf 1980.

The idea of discounted revenue for determining the economic effectiveness of control operations is discussed in Chapter 10. It is most readily determined when trees are killed during outbreaks because losses in the absence of control measures can be calculated quite accurately. Stoakley (1977) estimated that death of lodgepole pine trees during outbreaks of the pine beauty moth, *Panolis flammea*, resulted in lost revenue of around £540 per hectare. With the cost of control at around £40 per hectare even trees of low yield class could if necessary be cost-effectively treated several times during a single rotation.

9
Management 5: behaviour-modifying chemicals

9.1 THE ROLE OF CHEMICALS IN INSECT BEHAVIOUR

Trees are the primary source of many complex chemicals and the main groups and their metabolic relationships are illustrated in Fig. 9.1. Many of these chemicals are of considerable importance in the interaction between insects and trees and, as described in Chapter 3, secondary chemicals such as terpenes and phenolics defend trees against insects and other herbivores, acting as direct poisons or reducing the quality of food. Specialized insects, however, have not only evolved mechanisms for minimizing the deleterious effects of secondary chemicals but may now depend on them to identify their hosts and may even use them directly or indirectly as chemical signals to communicate with other individuals. In this chapter we discuss the ways in which chemical signals between plants and insects and between insects can be used to manipulate insect behaviour and ultimately reduce damage to trees. In this discussion, it is important to remember that insect behaviour in the field, whether in host-location or mate-finding, is often complex and rarely controlled by response to single chemicals. More

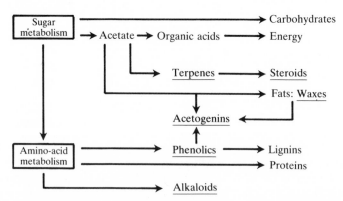

FIG. 9.1. The metabolic relationship of the major groups of chemicals in trees. Secondary chemicals are underlined (from Hanover 1975, after Whittaker and Feeny 1971).

commonly, the full behavioural repertoire occurs in response to a sequence of chemical stimuli which may act only at short or long range or at particular concentrations.

9.1.1 Finding and accepting hosts

Secondary chemicals are often attractive to specialized insects and used as 'token' stimuli in the process of host identification. The 'haloes' of volatile chemicals around trees can be detected by some insects so that suitable hosts may be located before actual contact is made. Although host odour detection may often occur during flight, the pine weevil, *Hylobius abietis*, for example, can detect odours diffusing through the soil from roots, and adults will burrow into the soil directly above the main roots of suitable hosts (Nordlander *et al.* 1986). Some examples of secondary chemicals as olfactory attractants are given in Table 9.1. Most of the examples are provided by bark beetles which have been widely studied because of the importance of host odours in their multicomponent pheromone communication systems as discussed below (Wood 1982).

Table 9.1. *Some examples of host tree secondary chemicals that are olfactory attractants for forest insects*

Insect	Host	Chemical
Scolytus scolytus	Elm	α-cubebene
Ips grandicollis	Pine	geraniol
		limonene
		methyl chavicol
		myrcene
Dendroctonus frontalis	Pine	3-carene
		α-pinene
Tomicus piniperda	Pine	α-pinene
		α-terpineol
Hylobius abietis	Pine	α-pinene
		α-terpineol
		3-carene
Pissodes strobi	Pine	limonene

From Visser 1986 and references in Hsiao 1985.
(See also Table 3.3.)

As well as attracting insects to their hosts, many secondary chemicals are also involved in host acceptance once contact is made and feeding or oviposition begins. Single chemicals may either stimulate feeding (phagostimulants) or oviposition, or deter it (inhibitors or deterrents) depending on concentration and the insect species involved (Table 9.2). Alkaloids and terpenoids are especially potent feeding deterrents and can influence the

Table 9.2. *Some examples of host tree secondary chemicals as phagostimulants or deterrents*

Insect	Host	Secondary chemical	Phagostimulant or deterrent
Choristoneura fumiferana	Fir and other conifers	Caffeic acid Pungenin	Phagostimulant Deterrent
Operophtera brumata	Oak	Tannic acid Tannins (high concentration)	Phagostimulant Deterrent
Hylastes ater	Pine and other conifers	α-pinene (high concentration)	Phagostimulant
Pissodes strobi	Pine	+ camphor Limonene	Phagostimulant Phagostimulant
Scolytus multistriatus	Elm	p-hydroquinone	Phagostimulant
		Juglone and other 1, 4-napthoquinones in non-hosts	Deterrent

From Gilbert and Norris 1968, Feeny 1970, and references in Hsiao 1985.

distribution of damage on trees. Larvae of the pine sawfly, *Neodiprion sertifer*, feed only on old foliage of pines, avoiding the current foliage which is distasteful to them. Similarly, larvae of the larch sawfly, *Pristiphora erichsonii*, feed on tufted needles on short shoots and reject single needles on long shoots because they contain several resin acids which are highly effective feeding deterrents (Ohigashi *et al.* 1981). These kinds of observation suggest that the identification of deterrent compounds and their application to foliage might protect it from insect feeding damage or oviposition (section 9.5).

Hormone mimics are another class of secondary chemicals that occur in plants. They are often powerful feeding deterrents but if ingested they can disrupt insect development. The leaves of yew, for example, contain high concentrations of the moulting hormone ecdysone and few insects attack this tree (Chapter 2). Analogues of juvenile hormone, which influences early larval development, are produced in the wood of grand fir in response to attack by the balsam woolly aphid, *Adelges piceae*, and this gives the trees some protection against subsequent attack (Puritch and Nijholt 1974). Since the discovery of chemicals in plants with juvenile hormone activity there has been considerable interest in the development of synthetic hormones that could be used to control insect pests. This has led to the development of the insect growth regulators discussed in the previous chapter.

9.1.2 Semiochemicals and insect communication

The many different kinds of chemicals that transmit information between organisms are called semiochemicals, with perhaps the best known being pheromones which mediate interactions between individuals of the same species as in the sex pheromones of Lepidoptera. Interspecific communication on the other hand takes two main forms depending on whether the sender or receiver of the message is able to benefit from it. Allomones mediate a response which is of advantage to the sender of the signal as in the case of defensive secretions. Larvae of sawflies in the genus *Neodiprion* store terpenoid compounds in the gut diverticulum and these are regurgitated by the larvae when disturbed by natural enemies and are often effective in repelling attack (Eisner *et al.* 1974). Kairomones on the other hand induce a response which is of benefit to the receiver, as when natural enemies detect chemicals from their prey. Pheromones released by an insect for intraspecific communication are often detected by natural enemies and so the same chemical may act as both pheromone and kairomone.

Many of these semiochemicals are of dietary origin and insects can sequester secondary chemicals present in the host and deposit them in specialized tissues or glands (Duffey 1980). These chemicals may then be used directly or may be modified in various ways either by the insect itself or by micro-organisms associated with it (Brand *et al.* 1975, 1976). Some species of *Dendroctonus* bark beetles can metabolize α-pinene to *trans*-verbenol and verbenone which are part of their multi-component aggregation pheromone (Hughes 1973*a,b*). *Ips paraconfusus* is able to utilize chemicals derived from myrcene and α-pinene which are present in the host tree (Jones 1985). The relatively small chemical changes required in these transformations are illustrated in Fig. 9.2.

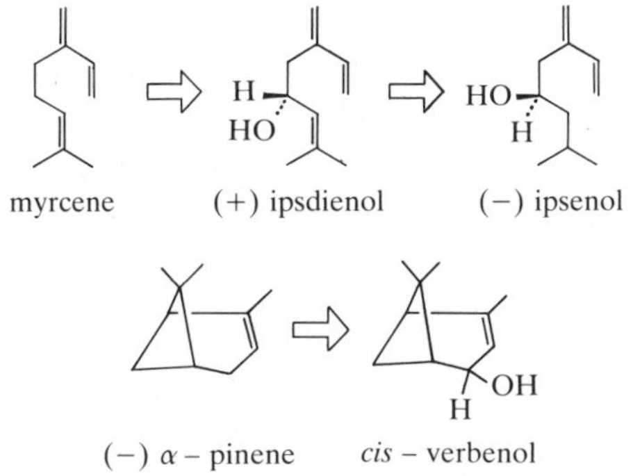

myrcene   (+) ipsdienol   (−) ipsenol

(−) α − pinene   *cis* − verbenol

FIG. 9.2. Conversion of host tree monoterpenes, myrcene and α-pinene, to chemicals used in bark beetle aggregation pheromones (from Jones 1985).

9.2 THE CHARACTERISTICS OF PHEROMONES

Of all the chemical interactions between insects and plants and amongst insects, pheromones have shown the most potential for use in insect control programmes. The most important ones are the sex pheromones of Lepidoptera, emitted by the calling female to attract a mate and the aggregation pheromones of bark beetles. The latter chemicals may be released by either sex and not only bring the sexes together on the host tree for mating but also synchronize a simultaneous attack on the tree which can overwhelm its defences (Chapter 4).

Within the last 20 years or so, through the close collaboration of biochemists and entomologists, the chemical identity of a number of pheromones of economically important forest insect pests has been determined, some examples of which are given in Table 9.3. Three-quarters of the pheromone chemicals isolated from Lepidoptera have proved to be straight chain 12, 14 or 16 carbon acetates and there are numerous examples where the same chemical is used by more than one species

Table 9.3. *Pheromones of some forest insects*

Species	Main pheromone components	Reference
Lepidoptera		
Rhyacionia buoliana	(E)-9-dodecenyl acetate	Smith *et al.* 1974
Panolis flammea	(Z)-9-tetradecenyl acetate (Z)-11-tetradecenyl acetate (Z)-11-hexadecenyl acetate	Baker *et al.* 1982
Lymantria dispar	(Z)-7, 8-epoxy-2 methyloctadecane (Disparlure)	Bierl *et al.* 1970, 1972 Yamada *et al.* 1976
Zeiraphera diniana	(E)-11-tetradecenyl acetate	Roelofs *et al.* 1971
Coleoptera		

Ips typographus	2-methyl-3-buten-2-ol
	2-methyl-6-methylene-2,
	    7-octadiene-4-ol
	    (Ipsdienol)
	cis-verbenol
		Vité *et al.* 1972
		Bakke 1976
		Bakke *et al.* 1977*b*

Scolytus scolytus	4-methyl-3-heptanol
	2, 3-dimethyl-5-ethyl-6,
	    8-dioxabicyclo (3.2.1.) octane
	    (Multistriatin)
		Blight *et al.* 1977, 1978

Gnathotrichus sulcatus	6-methyl-5-hepten-2-ol (Sulcatol)	Byrne *et al.* 1974
Trypodendron lineatum	3, 3, 7-trimethyl-2, 9-dioxatricyclo $(3.3.1.0^{4.7})$ nonane (Lineatin)	MacConnell *et al.* 1977 Borden *et al.* 1979

(Tamaki 1985). Although there are instances in which the pheromone message is based on a single chemical, the specificity of most sex pheromones and particularly aggregation pheromones results from mixtures of chemicals in precisely defined blends and also from the fact that many of the basic chemicals exist as geometrical or optical isomers and only one isomer or a precise mixture of isomers may be used in pheromones. Specificity of action may also be achieved through a particular time or rate of release and this may be important in preventing cross-attraction during release of a single component sex pheromone.

The blends of semiochemicals that promote aggregation by bark beetles are often very complex and may contain host tree kairomones as well as beetle-produced pheromones (Bordon *et al.* 1987). Both sexes may be attracted to the semiochemical blend, which may change in composition over time according to the density and sex ratio of beetles on the tree, and may eventually involve the release of anti-aggregation pheromones to mask or countermand the original attractive odour and prevent the over-exploitation of the tree. These aspects can be illustrated by the pheromone system of the southern pine beetle, *Dendroctonus frontalis* (Fig. 9.3) (Payne and Coulson 1985). The female 'pioneer' beetles release the chemical frontalin when they make contact with suitable host trees and this attracts flying male and female beetles, an effect which is enhanced both by host odour and by *trans*-verbenol which is released when females attack the tree. Both host odour and *trans*-verbenol appear to induce landing on vertical objects when perceived by flying beetles and together with the attractant frontalin, serve to initiate mass-attack. During this phase, newly arriving females continue to release more attractant, so their numbers build-up rapidly and males also release (+) *endo*-brevicomin (not shown) which apparently increases the response of females to frontalin. Males and to some extent boring females also release verbenone and the response to this depends on the amount released. In small quantities the number of males attracted is reduced but larger amounts also reduce the number of females attracted and it may play a role in switching attack to an adjacent tree. As the number of males builds up on the tree the amount of verbenone released increases. Males also release small amounts of (−) *endo*-brevicomin, which like verbenone in high concentrations reduces the number of males and females attracted, and eventually attack switches to nearby trees.

Although many aggregation pheromone systems appear to be simpler than that in *D. frontalis*, few have been investigated in full detail and it illustrates the level of complexity achieved in chemical communication and emphasizes the depth of understanding required before pheromones can be used effectively to manipulate their behaviour.

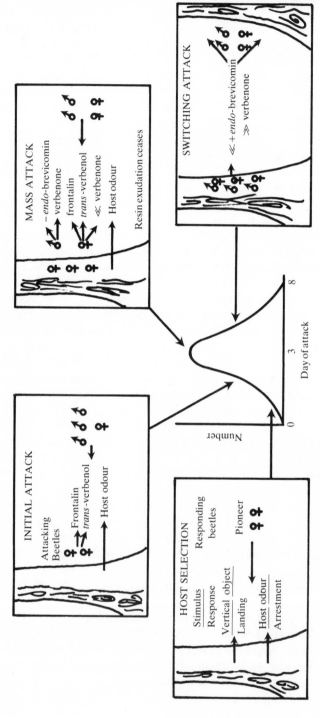

FIG. 9.3. The presumed role of visual and olfactory stimuli in the host selection and aggregation behaviour of *Dendroctonus frontalis* (from Payne and Coulson 1985, after Renwick and Vité 1969, Coster *et al.* 1977 and Payne *et al.* 1978).

9.3 THE USE OF INSECT PHEROMONES IN FOREST PEST MANAGEMENT

Pheromones have been used to manipulate insect behaviour in three main ways; (a) in traps to detect and monitor endemic populations, (b) to suffuse the atmosphere with pheromone and prevent mate location in male moths (the so-called mating-disruption or 'confusion' technique) and (c) in traps to catch large numbers of individuals to reduce population size (known as mass-trapping).

The potential of pheromones to attract adult insects to traps placed in forests and so allow monitoring of insect populations at non-outbreak densities was realized before their chemical identity was known. Many early studies with Lepidoptera relied on the attraction of males to live virgin females or solvent extracts of their abdomens which contain the sex pheromone producing glands. In Yugoslavia during the 1950s and 60s extracts of female gypsy moth, *Lymantria dispar*, were used in monitoring traps to identify incipient outbreaks by correlating trap catches of males with the density of egg masses (Maksimovic 1965). An example is given in Fig. 9.4 where a virgin female of the web-spinning larch sawfly, *Cephalcia lariciphila*, has attracted large numbers of males. Artificially synthesized pheromones are now available for many pest species. But before the appropriate pheromone can be used, it needs to be formulated so that it is not degraded by exposure to the elements and is released at the correct rate over the main period of insect activity.

9.3.1 The formulation and release of pheromones

Correct formulation to give the required release rate is difficult to achieve in practice. Field release rates often differ markedly from those determined in the laboratory under simulated field conditions and this can affect the efficacy of the monitoring and control methods. Figure 9.5 shows examples of the release rates for different kinds of formulations which vary from simple evaporation from a wick, hollow fibres or an impregnated rubber bung, to diffusion through multilayer polymeric materials. Microcapsule formulations (Chapter 8) which completely enclose the liquid pheromone may actually be sprayed onto trees with conventional insecticide spraying equipment either from the ground or from the air. The incorporation of chemical 'stickers' ensures retention of the broadcast pheromone by the forest canopy and ultraviolet light screens provide some protection from strong sunlight which can denature the pheromone.

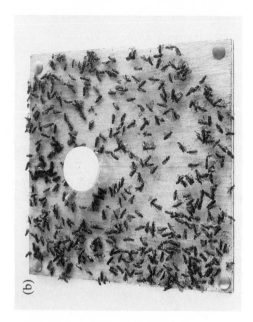

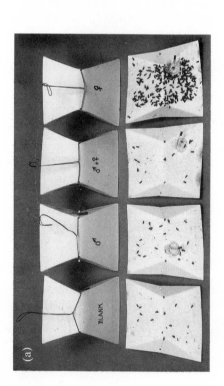

FIG. 9.4. (a) Male *Cephalcia lariciphila* caught in a Pherocon IC pheromone trap, and (b) a horizontal sticky trap using a virgin female sawfly as bait; (c) Bait chamber containing virgin female *C. lariciphila*, as used in (a) and (b) above (from Borden *et al.* 1978).

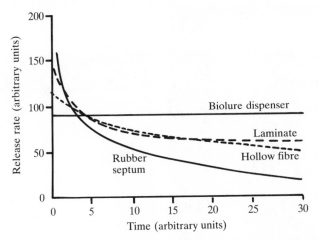

FIG. 9.5. Release rates of different kinds of pheromone dispenser (from Jones and Kelly 1986).

9.3.2 Pheromone traps

Baiting of traps to increase catches of insect pests is still the most common use of synthetic pheromones. Initially, both lures and traps were developed empirically and the size and cost of traps was an important consideration. A selection of trap types is shown in Fig. 9.6. Sticky traps such as the fin trap can be used for both Lepidoptera and Coleoptera and the pheromone lure is simply placed in the centre of a flat trapping surface. Alternatively, the trapping surface may be folded around the pheromone lure (Fig. 9.6b) so that attracted insects must enter the trap to be captured. Used principally for Lepidoptera this arrangement reduces considerably the number of non-target insects that are caught, simplifying assessment and reducing the possible effects of a large number of decomposing insects on attraction. Single enclosed funnel traps (not shown) also used for Lepidoptera, are highly selective and have a high capacity both for live trapping or, if strips of insecticide are placed inside, to kill their captives. The 'drainpipe' and slot-traps are used to capture bark beetles. The drainpipe traps present a dark vertical silhouette simulating a tree trunk and so provide a visual as well as an odour stimulus.

The 'catching power' required of traps depends on the way in which they will be used. Efficiency is not of overriding importance in survey and monitoring systems provided that some fairly constant proportion of the number approaching the trap is caught and that traps and lures are standardized to give results which are comparable from place to place and from year to year. Trapping at ports around imported timber is an important excep-

FIG. 9.6. Some different types of pheromone trap. (a) Sticky 'fin' (b) Delta[1], showing sticky insert removed for inspection, (c) Drainpipe[2], (d) slot[3].
[1]Biological Control Systems Ltd., Wales, [2]Borregaard Ind. Ltd, Norway, [3]Theysohn-Kuntstoff GMBH, West Germany

tion because efficient and highly attractive traps are needed to have the best chance of detecting alien species that may be present at very low density. In mass-trapping programmes efficiency is also very important so that the maximum number of insects are caught with the available traps. Having said this, it is very difficult to optimize the efficiency of a trap because the interaction between insect and trap is poorly understood, largely because of inadequate knowledge of insect behaviour close to the source of a pheromone and also because little is known of the way in which different components of a pheromone influence attraction, landing, and trap entry. *Lymantria dispar* males orient to vertical silhouettes and fly up and down close to trees in the presence of pheromone, presumably looking for females, and may not actually enter traps (Cardé *et al.* 1975; Richerson *et al.* 1976). In 'complex' traps such as the drainpipe trap the attracted beetles enter through small holes in the trap surface. These traps are thus selective in that natural enemies responding to the kairomone are often too big to enter the holes. However, since little is known about the stimulus for trap entry, many more beetles may approach and even land on the trap than actually enter it. The capture of male and female ambrosia beetles, *Trypodendron lineatum*, in sticky 'fin' traps and drainpipe traps baited with combinations of the aggregation pheromone lineatin and the primary attractants ethanol and α-pinene, demonstrate the interaction between attractants and trap type (Table 9.4). Lineatin alone was highly attractive in fin traps but in drainpipe traps it was no more attractive than ethanol plus α-pinene; clearly the addition of host volatiles is necessary to catch beetles in tree-trunk simulating traps.

In monitoring, it is important that traps are able to detect variations in abundance when insects are scarce as well as being big enough to hold large numbers of insects when population densities are high; how frequently traps can be visited will determine the capacity required. The life of the pheromone lure under ambient climatic conditions must also be considered.

9.3.3 Survey, detection and monitoring

Because insects are strongly attracted to suitable pheromone-baited traps they can be caught even when present at low density. Such traps can thus be used to provide information on the time of appearance, distribution and, possibly, abundance of endemic populations of forest pests. Surveys of large areas may be needed where the distribution of a potential pest species is unknown. The pine beauty moth, *Panolis flammea*, was until recently regarded as an harmless species in Britain until outbreaks occurred on exotic lodgepole pine in northern Scotland. In Norway, where lodgepole pine has been planted on a small scale, it was considered prudent to determine the distribution of this moth using pheromone traps. New distributional

Table 9.4. *Response of Trypodendron lineatum to two types of traps baited with lineatin, ethanol and α-pinene alone, or in various combinations*

Trap type	Treatment	No. beetles captured[a]		
		Male	Female	Total
Fin traps	Blank control	7a	4a	11a
	Ethanol	10a	14a	24a
	α-pinene	1a	6a	7a
	Ethanol + α-pinene	8a	10a	18a
	Lineatin	860b	473b	1333b
	Lineatin + ethanol	2361c	1884c	4245c
	Lineatin + α-pinene	184b	116b	300b
	Mixture of all three	554b	464b	1008b
Drainpipe traps	Blank control	1a	2a	3a
	Ethanol	1a	5a	7a
	α-pinene	2a	1a	3a
	Ethanol + α-pinene	123b	151c	274b
	Lineatin	134b	45b	179b
	Lineatin + ethanol	1102c	873d	1975c
	Lineatin + α-pinene	772c	219c	991c
	Mixture of all three	1199c	848d	2047c

[a] Numbers within a column followed by the same letter are not significantly different ($P<0.05$).
From Borden *et al*. 1982.

records were obtained when it was found in 25 per cent of 36 localities sampled (Austarå 1982). Knowledge of insect distribution may also be important where an introduced pest is extending its range into new forest areas. In the USA, disparlure, the synthetic sex-pheromone of *L. dispar*, is used in regular and widespread surveys to detect the presence of moths in susceptible forests (Table 9.5). Where possible, traps are set on a grid pattern of one trap per 7.8 km^2.

As well as allowing the survey and detection of pests, pheromone traps may be used to monitor population levels in areas known to be susceptible to outbreaks and can replace more labour-intensive methods such as soil sampling for pupae. In Czechoslovakia, *L. dispar* was monitored over an area of 3500 square miles, enabling local areas with increasing populations to be identified and appropriate control measures taken (Hochmut *et al*. 1977; Skuhravy and Hochmut 1980).

In France, a network of light traps is used to monitor the flight of the pine processionary moth, *Thaumetopoea pityocampa*. This is necessary because variation in hours of sunshine and minimum winter and maximum summer temperature affects the precise timing of the annual cycle and thus of control measures (Chapter 10). Pheromone traps may, ultimately, replace light traps, providing a more convenient system capable of monitoring very low density populations of this insect (Cuevas *et al*. 1983). Such low-density

Table 9.5. *Pheromone traps to survey populations of Lymantria dispar in the USA*

Year	No. traps	No. of states outside quarantine zone in which males captured
1972	120 000	11
1973	65 000	15
1974	70 000	10
1975	73 000	9
1976	84 000	10
1977	95 000	7

From Schwalbe (1981).

populations may be important because the larvae of *T. pityocampa* aggregate together and defoliate individual trees.

The main aim of many monitoring schemes is to detect increases in pest abundance so that appropriate control methods can be planned in advance and treatment restricted to areas of high pest density. When numbers of insects in traps approach some empirically determined threshold, intensive sampling can be carried out in localized high-risk areas.

In British Columbia, the Douglas fir tussock moth, *Orgyia pseudotsugata*, periodically defoliates conifers, often precipitating bark beetle outbreaks (Chapter 10). The populations are highly aggregated in both time and space and the location of outbreaks is difficult to predict. A pheromone-based monitoring system has, therefore, been developed to give warning of outbreaks (Shepherd *et al.* 1985). Experimental trapping to try to correlate catches with egg-mass density did not show a simple linear relationship although there was apparently a threshold effect at about 25 moths per trap above which egg masses were detected (Fig. 9.7). At permanent monitoring

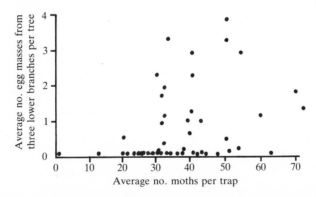

FIG. 9.7. The number of male *Orgyia pseudotsugata* caught in pheromone traps in relation to the density of egg masses laid by females of the same generation (from Shepherd *et al.* 1985).

sites, trap catches of about 25 moths usually occurred two years before defoliation was seen and so could be used to give warning of outbreaks. The most reliable method for predicting defoliation, however, appeared to be the trend of population density (Fig. 9.8) because *O. pseudotsugata* populations often exhibit cyclical patterns of population change making the trends easier to interpret. Two or three years of upward trends in the number of moths caught was taken as the signal for the implementation of egg-mass surveys and this system was able to give at least one year's advance warning of outbreaks.

Despite this and other successes with pheromone traps in monitoring insect populations, their wider adoption has been limited by problems in the interpretation of the catch data. In particular, it is often difficult to relate catch size to actual population size and, in Lepidoptera, the distribution of males caught in traps may not reflect the distribution of females which actually oviposit on trees. These aspects need to be considered when pheromone monitoring programmes are being developed. For the winter moth, *Operophtera brumata*, a good correlation was in fact established between catches of males in pheromone traps in Sitka spruce plantations in

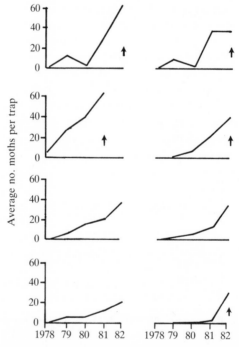

FIG. 9.8. Trends in abundance of *Orgyia pseudotsugata* determined from catches in traps baited with 0.01% pheromone. Moths were caught at 8 sites over 4–5 years. Five sites suffered defoliation in the years indicated by arrows (from Shepherd *et al.* 1985).

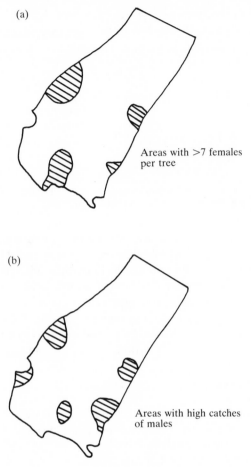

(a)

Areas with >7 females
per tree

(b)

Areas with high catches
of males

Fig. 9.9. The distribution of (a) egg-laying female *Operophtera brumata* and (b) catches of male moths in pheromone traps, within 720 ha of Sitka spruce (from Stoakley 1985).

Scotland and numbers of flightless females which were caught on sticky bands around tree trunks (Fig. 9.9). So for this insect, monitoring of males can clearly be used to locate 'hot spots' of infestation within large plantations (Stoakley 1985). Pheromone trap catches of the pine beauty moth, *Panolis flammea*, in various European countries are given in Table 9.6. Although there is clearly a relationship between trap catch and pupal density, whether it is precise enough to reflect variations in density within a given region remains to be seen. Other unresolved difficulties are that the insect's response to the trap may change with population density, perhaps due to an increase in the number of competing natural pheromone sources.

Table 9.6. *Number of Panolis flammea in the soil and in standard pheromone traps in some European countries*

Country		Pupal density m^{-2}	Critical density m^{-2}	Males/trap
Scotland:	Eastern Highlands	10.8	15	80.1
	Sutherland	7.2	15	92.8
Poland:	Masuren	0.7	4	13.7
Germany:	Bayern	0.2	1	3.5
	Baden-Wurttemberg	0	1	0.2
	Niedersachsen	0	1	1.1
Austria:	Niederoesterreich	0	1	0.2

From Bogenschutz 1980, Trofimova and Trofimov 1981, and J. T. Stoakley and H. Schmutzenhofer, personal communication.

Thus a different proportion of the population may be trapped at different densities. The proportion trapped may also be influenced by the density of traps themselves (Elkinton and Cardé 1980; Schwalbe 1981).

Although monitoring has been most widely practised using the sex pheromones of Lepidoptera, the aggregation pheromones of bark beetles may also be used in monitoring programmes (Bakke 1985). When monitoring bark beetles, traps should not be placed too near to healthy trees since they may be attacked by beetles that 'overshoot' the traps.

9.3.4 Mating-disruption

The survey and monitoring methods discussed in the previous section only provide information on the distribution and abundance of insect pests but pheromones can also be used directly to control insect populations. Mating-disruption is one such method in which the objective is to prevent successful mating of the target insects by interrupting or disrupting communication beween the sexes. This is achieved by introducing many artificial sources of pheromone into the environment either as discrete point source dispensers such as impregnated bungs or strips of hollow fibres distributed systematically throughout the area, or by broadcast spraying with micro-capsules, pheromone-impregnated fibres, or flakes.

There have been many empirical trials of mating-disruption. Most have drawn attention to gaps in our knowledge of the natural behaviour of insects during mate-finding, a deficiency which has contributed to the failure of some mating-disruption programmes. It is not clear how mate-finding is disrupted in the presence of multiple sources of pheromone, but the inability to locate calling females against the competing artificial pheromone sources or habituation to high background concentrations are possible mechanisms (Cardé 1981a). However, the attraction of mates by a sex pheromone is only one stage in a complex sequence of events that eventually leads to successful mating. Male *L. dispar*, for example, show a range of behaviour close to a pheromone source such as vertical flight near vertical silhouettes and landing followed by walking and wing fanning (Cardé 1981*b*). In dense natural populations where there are many calling females, pheromone-stimulated males may use other cues, for example, visual or tactile, to locate females. These conditions are in fact simulated in mating-disruption by the use of multiple sources of synthetic pheromone. It is for these reasons that mating-disruption is most likely to be successful at low population densities where visual contact and chance encounters between male and female are less likely. By treating small isolated areas such as seed orchards, migration of mated females into the treated area should be minimized (Sartwell *et al.* 1980; Overhulser *et al.* 1980).

In the USA a pheromone formulation is now commercially available to disrupt mating in the western pine shoot borer, *Eucosma sonomana*, (Daterman *et al.* 1980; Coulson and Witter 1984). As for other shoot moths, precise timing of insecticidal application is necessary for effective control because the larvae spend much of their life feeding within the buds or shoots of attacked trees (Chapter 8). Typical damage results in multiple leader development and loss of height growth which is particularly noticeable in even-aged plantations before canopy closure. High value trees in seed orchards are especially at risk and here even relatively low population densities can be damaging. In large-scale experiments with aerially applied pheromone dispensers, up to 88 per cent reduction in damage levels has been achieved (Table 9.7). Dispensers applied from the ground on a grid pattern also gave good results so that treatment of small areas with point sources of pheromone may prove to be effective.

Although mating-disruption has been used with success against relatively few species, there are a number of candidate forest insect species such as those Lepidoptera which have flightless females; these occur mainly in the families Lymantriidae, Tortricidae and some Geometridae.

9.3.5 Mass-trapping

Mass-trapping is another method of directly controlling pest populations and it has been used against both Lepidoptera and Coleoptera. In Lepidoptera where only males are caught, the aim is to reduce their density so that a significant proportion of the female population remains unmated. As with mating-disruption the method is most likely to be successful against moths at low population densities (Knipling and McGuire 1966; Beroza and Knipling 1972). Many trials of mass-trapping have been made with the gypsy moth, *Lymantria dispar*, in both North America and Europe, but results have been inconclusive (Webb 1982). However, all the major ex-

Table 9.7. *Mating-disruption in Eucosma sonomana—reduction in terminal shoot damage to ponderosa pine plantations treated with aerial applications of pheromone*

Area treated (ha)	Pheromone (g ha^{-1})	Pheromone treatment	No. Plots	Damage reduction (%)
20	15	Conrel fibres	3	67
800	10	Conrel fibres	3	76
100	20	Hercon flakes	3	88

From Daterman 1982.

perimental work done during the 1970s was with racemic disparlure but it is now known that +disparlure is about 10 times more attractive (Yamada *et al.* 1976; Plimmer *et al.* 1977), so it may well be worth repeating some of the earlier experiments.

In bark beetles, both males and females are attracted to the aggregation pheromone and the aim is to reduce the population below the outbreak threshold so that there are too few beetles to attack and overwhelm living trees (Chapter 4). This threshold value will depend on stand vigour and in healthy unstressed forests the outbreak threshold will be high (Fig. 9.10). A characteristic of bark beetle outbreaks is that they develop during periods when host vigour is low or following physical damage by fire, wind-throw, drought and so on (Chapter 4). On theoretical grounds at least, mass-trapping would seem unlikely to reduce populations to sufficiently low levels while the forest remains highly susceptible (Fig. 9.10). Bark beetles are also highly mobile and able to increase local population

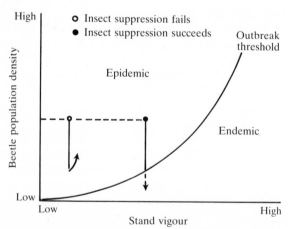

FIG. 9.10. The relationship between suppression of bark beetle populations by mass-trapping and the outbreak threshold as related to stand vigour (from Berryman 1978 and personal communication).

densities by aggregation so the area over which population reduction is required is likely to be large. Borden and McLean (1981) were able to circumvent some of these problems in their study of mass-trapping of the ambrosia beetle, *Gnathotrichus sulcatus*, which attacks cut timber in saw-mills in British Columbia. Because the product was of high value, intensive control could be justified economically and in the restricted area at risk they were able to reduce attacks on stored timber to acceptable levels.

The best example of an operational scale trial of mass-trapping in the forest is that of the spruce bark beetle, *Ips typographus*, during outbreaks that occurred in west-central Sweden and south-east Norway from 1978–82. The outbreak which had two foci was precipitated by a combination of windthrow and drought in areas where beetle populations were already high as a result of poor forest hygiene (Fig. 10.11) (Bakke 1982a; Worrell 1983). During this outbreak, mass-trapping was used as part of an integrated approach to control (Chapter 10).

A total of about 1 million pheromone-baited 'drainpipe' traps (Fig. 9.6c) were deployed in Norway and Sweden at the height of the campaign, about 70 per cent of which were in Norway (Bakke 1982a; Eidmann 1983). In heavily infested areas where it was necessary to clearfell the trees, traps were used at high density (20–30 ha^{-1}) to reduce dispersal of beetles emerging from the soil. In other areas where attack was less severe, one trap was deployed for every 3–5 trees killed in the previous year. To illustrate the scale of this enormous programme, between 1979–82 it cost an estimated £5 million, one-third of which was funded by the government. At its peak, it involved 1 per cent of the total population of Norway (A. Bakke, personal communication; Quisumbing and Kydonieus 1982).

In Norway 2.9×10^9 beetles were trapped in 1979 and 4.5×10^9 in 1980 (Bakke 1982b), but in order to determine the likely effect of this on population density, we need to know what proportion of the population was trapped and, ideally, the outbreak threshold density of beetles. There are no published data on population densities in the outbreak area, but Bakke (in Wainhouse 1987) estimated that about 50 000 beetles were produced from each cubic metre of the 1 million cubic metres of timber (about 3 million trees) killed by beetle attack in 1979. This analysis suggests a total beetle population of about 5×10^{10} of which overall, about 10 per cent was trapped in 1980 although local suppression may have been much higher.

It is difficult to assess the overall effectiveness of this extensive programme in contributing to the eventual decline of the outbreak (see Fig. 10.11). In the narrow terms of the objective of reducing beetle populations in an attempt to suppress the outbreak, the programme was of only limited success. Nevertheless the beetles trapped in 1980 were, in theory, capable of killing over 2 million trees.

9.4 OTHER USES OF PHEROMONES

There are a number of other ways in which pheromones can be used to manipulate forest insect populations. In Sweden, spruce trees in the *Ips typographus* outbreak areas were baited with pheromone prior to felling so that they were attacked by flying beetles. The trees were felled and removed before broods completed development and the baits moved to the next area due for felling (Eidmann 1983). This is an extension of the trap-tree method of bark beetle management discussed in Chapter 5. Similar experiments have been done in Canada by Borden *et al.* (1983) and Borden and Lacey (1985). By baiting trees with pheromone they were able to shift the locus of an infestation of mountain pine beetle, *Dendroctonus ponderosae*, from one site to another, separated from it by a clear cut area of 50 m. This suggests that it may be possible to concentrate attacks by this bark beetle into areas due for felling. They also considered that the residual population of beetles following harvesting of attacked trees could be 'mopped-up' by baiting and then felling selected trees. It may be, however, that new attacks on individual trees are being artificially created by concentrating beetles with pheromone baits in areas where the natural population density of beetles would have been too low or host resistance too high to allow perpetuation of the epidemic following removal of the naturally-attacked trees.

9.5 ANTI-FEEDANTS AND REPELLENTS

Anti-feedants have been used fairly widely to protect young trees from deer browsing in multiple-use forests (Pepper 1978, and personal communication) but although many chemicals inhibit insect feeding, the prospects for their use to protect forest trees appear limited, not least because of the different effects that the same chemical can have on different insect species. Chapman (1974) and Schoonhoven (1982) have reviewed the properties required of anti-feedant compounds if they are to have practical value. They need to be persistent, able to be translocated in the plant, and innocuous to non-target insects. Translocation is important because topical applications are quickly weathered and without it new growth would not be protected. Another problem with the application of anti-feedants is that since the insects are not killed, some may simply disperse to feed in adjacent untreated areas and those left behind may be more inclined to feed as starvation becomes more acute.

A number of experiments with repellents and anti-feedants have, however, been reported. Richmond (1985) used 'pine oil' consisting of oleoresins and terpene hydrocarbons to protect trees from the mountain pine beetle, *Dendroctonus ponderosae*. The oil, which may act as a repellent or simply mask the attractive host odour, was as effective as insecticides for the protection of high value trees in urban areas (see also Nijholt *et al.* 1981; Alfaro *et al.* 1984).

10

Management 6: integrated pest management

10.1 INTEGRATED PEST MANAGEMENT IN FORESTRY

The essence of integrated pest management (IPM) lies in the use of a number of alternative or complementary control procedures in a co-ordinated way to prevent damage by insect pests. The ideas and practice of IPM were first developed to provide an alternative to the unilateral application of insecticides to solve pest problems in agriculture. In forestry, insecticides have usually been much less intensively used so that problems of pest resistance and resurgence have been largely avoided. The main reasons for this difference, as we emphasized in Chapter 8 is that forests have a low value per unit area so the costs of applying insecticide to large and often remote forested areas cannot be justified. But an equally important factor is that many forest pests cannot be satisfactorily controlled with insecticides. Thus modern methods for the control of forest pests have necessarily been based on the principles of IPM, often using techniques that were developed in Europe during the nineteenth century, long before chemical insecticides were available for pest control. These control methods grew out of a developing insight into the ecology of forest insects and the factors contributing to outbreaks. In the late 1700s, for example, the importance of recently cut logs and stressed or dying trees in the life history of bark beetles was realized, so that the notion of forest hygiene led directly to improvements in the control of these insects (Chapters 4 and 5). For other pests, methods were developed to try and predict in advance the time and location of outbreaks by taking annual samples of overwintering stages in the forest litter. The ability to be forewarned about incipient pest outbreaks is an important aspect of IPM and many of these early methods have survived into modern practice and are used alongside recently developed monitoring techniques such as the use of pheromone-baited traps as described in Chapter 9.

In previous chapters, we considered the various ways of suppressing insect populations but the choice of method and the decision to apply it can only be made by integrating a range of information on pest biology, distribution and abundance, and the likelihood of damage to the trees. In this chapter, we discuss some of the ways in which this is done and give some examples where an integrated approach to control has been or is being developed.

10.1.1 Survey and detection, monitoring and prediction

The use of pheromones in survey, detection, and monitoring of Lepidoptera is discussed in Chapter 9. Regular surveying of the overwintering stages of some forest insects has been done since the late nineteenth century and this important tradition is now a legal requirement in several central European countries (Bogenschutz 1980). In practice, many monitoring systems sample a particular insect developmental stage over a fairly large area but where 'critical densities' are detected, i.e. those indicating the likelihood of an outbreak, additional more intensive sampling of later stages can be restricted to a smaller area around the epicentre of the potential outbreak. For example, when the pupae of lepidopteran or sawfly defoliators in forest-wide surveys exceeds the critical density, egg samples in areas of high pupal density may be taken before the decision to apply insecticide is made. Even with such intensive sampling, however, if key mortality factors operate on early instar larvae then in some years control may be applied when it is actually unnecessary.

The determination of critical densities is often based on knowledge of the course of previous outbreaks and it is important that such thresholds are determined locally because fecundity, mortality, and host plant resistance may vary from place to place. Critical densities for two defoliators in different parts of Europe are shown in Table 10.1. These densities can be estimated from field observations of pupal abundance prior to outbreaks,

Table 10.1. *Critical densities for two forest insects in different localities*

Insect	Locality	Critical density (Total pupae m^{-2})
Bupalus piniaria	Central Germany	6
	N. E. Germany	12
	England	50
Panolis flammea	G.D.R.	1
	Poland	4
	Czechoslovakia	8
	England	15
	Russia	23–54[a]

[a] Critical density depends on the stage of the outbreak.
From Schwerdtfeger 1941, Ebert and Otto 1969, Scott and Brown 1973, Trofimova and Trofimov 1981, and J. T. Stoakley personal communication.

FIG. 10.1. Clearfelling of lodgepole pine stands attacked by *Dendroctonus ponderosae*

but they may also be determined experimentally. This can be done by measuring the amount of foliage eaten by individual larvae and relating it to the total amount of foliage on trees at risk. Provided larval density can be predicted from pupal density, critical values can be determined for forest stands of different ages and obviously those for young trees will be much lower than for large mature ones. Critical densities may also vary with the 'stage' of an outbreak. Densities for control later in an outbreak can be higher than those used earlier on because the leaves of previously defoliated trees can be unpalatable to insects (Chapter 3) and natural enemies may be more abundant, causing higher mortality.

One of the main advantages of the detection of incipient outbreaks is that it allows for the efficient planning of direct control measures. For example, the gypsy moth, *Lymantria dispar*, causes extensive damage to trees in some parts of the mountains of southern Siberia every 10 years or so. Ground surveys can map dense concentrations of egg masses so that in the spring when the webbing of the young larvae is visible from the air, helicopters may be used for spot insecticide treatments rather than spraying the whole area at risk and this can reduce the area treated by as much as 90 per cent (Kolomiets 1980).

10.1.2 Hazard or risk-rating systems

Some knowledge of the vulnerability of stands to insect outbreaks can help to define which forests need to be included in monitoring programmes. A history of past outbreaks on particular sites or prior knowledge of the factors likely to precipitate an outbreak may allow the development of an index of risk or hazard for particular forests. In some cases it may then be possible to reduce that risk by appropriate silvicultural measures such as

Table 10.2. *Examples of the range of characteristics that can be used in risk-rating systems for forest insects*

Insect species	Host tree	Country	High risk feature(s)	Reference
Dendroctonus frontalis	Loblolly pine	USA	Dense stands of trees	Hicks 1980
Dendroctonus ponderosae	Lodgepole pine	USA	Large diameter trees with thick phloem	Amman *et al.* 1977
Dendroctonus rufipennis	Spruce	North America	Well drained creek bottoms	Schmid and Frye 1976
Phyllobius spp.	Birch	Finland	Sandy or morainic soils with specific plants in herb layer	Annila 1979
Pissodes validirostris	Pine seed orchards	Finland	Hilly terrain, exotic clones, proximity to plantations	Annila 1976
Pissodes validirostris	Scots pine	Russia	Drained bogs	Smetanin 1980
Sirex noctilio	Pine	Australia	Dense stands (1770 to 2440 trees ha^{-1})	Neumann and Minko 1981
Ips typographus	Norway spruce	Norway	Below average summer rainfall	Worrell 1983
Choristoneura fumiferana	Balsam fir and other conifers	Canada	High proportion of mature balsam fir	Blais 1983

fertilization or selective thinning (Mitchell *et al.* 1983; Waring and Pitman 1985). Where such methods cannot reduce the risk, areas vulnerable to repeated attack may need to be clearfelled (Fig. 10.1) and replanted with a different tree species where appropriate (Chapter 5).

The characteristics used to determine risk, some examples of which are given in Table 10.2, may not actually be those that directly affect the pest population but are simply correlated variables. For example, drought is one of the factors determining risk of bark beetle attack for many conifers because resin flow in the trees is reduced during dry periods and so they are less well defended against attack. Other systems may relate more directly to the life history of the insects. Houston and Valentine (1977) studying *L. dispar*, were able to show that, as well as stand composition, factors such as deep fissures or flaps on the bark and dead branches which provided protected oviposition and pupation sites were important in determining susceptibility of oak forests. Principal components analysis of 118 stands (Fig. 10.2) showed that in most cases it was possible to distinguish rarely infested stands from those with a history of defoliation.

Practical risk-rating systems should be easy to use, species specific and rely only on a few tree characteristics that are easy to see or measure and

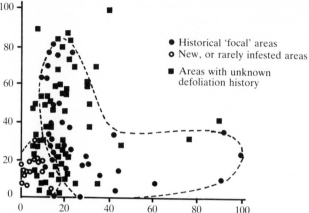

Fig. 10.2. The separation of broadleaved stands susceptible or resistant to defoliation by *Lymantria dispar* using principal components analysis of six structural features of trees. Features included fissures, bark flaps and dead branches that provide resting or pupation sites for the moth. Oak was the predominant species in all 118 stands. The axes describe the relativized co-ordinates of each stand generated by the analysis (from Houston and Valentine 1977).

which are reliable risk predictors (Ferrell 1980). Ferrell developed a risk-rating system for red fir in northern California which estimated the probability of death of mature trees from a complex of insects and diseases. Although several different organisms could contribute to mortality in this study, it provides a good example of the selection of risk predictors and their incorporation into an assessment system for use in the forest. From an examination of a number of different characters, the best risk-predicting parameters for individual red firs were found to be crown position in the canopy (C), percent live crown (L), shape and condition of the top (T) and the percentage of the crown missing, dying or dead (D). The probability of death within one year $(P1)$ was determined from:

$$P1 = 1/(1 + e^x)$$

where $x = 3.096 + 0.159\ C + 0.049\ L - 0.01\ T - 0.036\ D$.

The more useful statistic of probability of death within five years $(P5)$ was estimated from:

$$P5 = 1 - (1 - P1)^5.$$

For use in the forest, the risk equations were translated into an award–penalty points system in which the tree is awarded points when estimates of risk predictors have positive coefficients in the equations and penalized points when predictors have negative coefficients (Table 10.3) (see Ferrell 1980 for details). Using the risk equations, the risk point total obtained in the assessment could be translated into a percentage of trees expected to die within five years (bottom of Table 10.3 and Fig. 10.3).

Table 10.3. *An award–penalty risk system used to de-termine probability of death of mature red fir*

CROWN CLASS (=C)	AWARD
Suppressed	0
Intermediate	2
Co-dominant	4
Dominant	6
LIVE CROWN % (=L)	
5 points for each 10%	_____
TOTAL AWARD	_____

TOP CONDITION (=T)	PENALTY
Recent topkill	1
CROWN MISSING, DEAD OR DYING % (=D)	
4 points for each 10%	_____
TOTAL PENALTY	_____

RISK POINT TOTAL

(a) Enter total award or penalty, whichever larger
(b) Subtract smaller total   _____

(c) RISK POINT TOTAL   _____

PERCENT MORTALITY (within 5 years)			
(a) Award equals or exceeds Penalty			0 to 20%
(b) Penalty exceeds Award			
POINTS	%	POINTS	%
1 to 4	21 to 30	15 to 17	60 to 70
5 to 8	30 to 40	18 to 21	70 to 80
9 to 11	40 to 50	22 to 25	80 to 90
12 to 14	50 to 60	over 26	over 90

Individual trees are assessed for each category itemized above and total award or penalty used to assess risk of mortality within 5 years (see Fig. 10.3) (from Ferrell 1980).

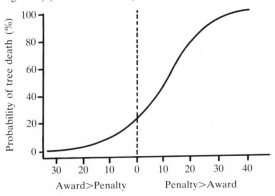

FIG. 10.3. Percentage of mature red fir expected to die within 5 years based on the award–penalty risk system (see text and Table 10.3) (from Ferrell 1980).

Obviously a great deal of effort is required in large stands to provide information of this sort for individual trees but other methods are available where estimates of risk to the whole forest stand can be obtained from measurements on a sample of individual trees. One such approach that has been widely used is based on estimates of stand 'vigour' from measurements of tree growth. Two main methods have been developed, the periodic growth ratio (Mahoney 1978) and stem growth efficiency (Waring and Pitman 1980, 1983) and they have been used almost exclusively to determine risk of attack by bark beetles. The periodic growth ratio (*PGR*) was developed in lodgepole pine stands as an aid to determining susceptibility to mountain pine beetle, *Dendroctonus ponderosae*. It is determined from the ratio of radial increment over the last 5 years to increment over the previous 5 years on a sample of dominant and co-dominant trees in the stand. Values above 1 indicate that stand growth and vigour is high whereas those less than around 0.9 indicate that the stand is becoming very susceptible to beetle attack.

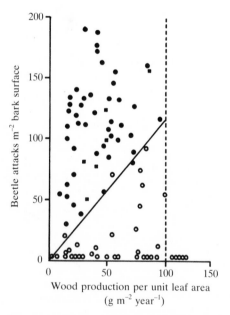

FIG. 10.4. The number of attacks by *Dendroctonus ponderosae* in relation to the stem growth efficiency of plots of lodgepole pine. Solid dots indicate 100% mortality, solid squares—death of strips of bark, circles with white centre—surviving trees, and the solid line—the level of attack predicted to kill trees of a given level of vigour. The dotted line indicates the threshold above which beetle attacks are unlikely to cause mortality (from Waring and Pitman 1983).

Stem growth efficiency (*SGE*) as a measure of vigour is based on the premise that stemwood production has less priority than root and shoot growth, so that the proportion of carbon allocated to stemwood production reflects the extent to which these important demands have been met (Chapter 3). Stem growth efficiency is determined from the amount of stem growth per unit leaf area (grams of stemwood m^{-2} foliage yr^{-1}). Since sapwood area and leaf area are linearly related, *SGE* can be calculated from the increase in basal area as a proportion of the sapwood area and can thus be determined entirely from measurements on the stem of individual trees (Grier and Waring 1974; Waring *et al.* 1980, 1982). Like *PGR*, this method has been used to predict mortality of lodgepole pines attacked by *D. ponderosae* (Fig. 10.4).

A synoptic model which uses several indicators of the susceptibility of stands to bark beetle attack has been developed by Berryman (1978) (Fig. 10.5). 'Stand resistance' is a combined estimate based on the *PGR*, the degree of crown competition (which increases with stand density) and the proportion of lodgepole pine in the stand. Stand resistance was related to the proportion of trees with thick phloem which is more suitable for beetle breeding than thin phloem. Large diameter lodgepole pine trees are, therefore, particularly at risk of attack by *D. ponderosae* especially during periods of drought. The relationship between the number of emerging

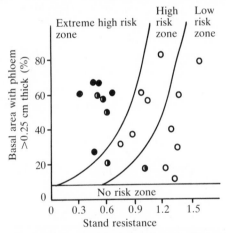

FIG. 10.5. The fit of the synoptic model to data from lodgepole pine stands below about 2000 m in Montana and Idaho, USA, in relation to attack by *Dendroctonus ponderosae*. Open circles = less than 10% basal area killed over 7 years, half circles = 11–40% basal area killed, closed circles = greater than 40% basal area killed. Phloem thickness was measured directly at breast height. Stand resistance for trees over 60 years old was determined from estimates of periodic growth ratio, competition among trees and the proportion of lodgepole pine in the stands (see text) (from Berryman 1978).

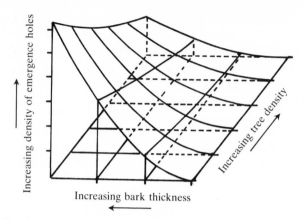

FIG. 10.6. The emergence density of *Dendroctonus ponderosae* in relation to bark thickness and stand density for lodgepole pine. In dense stands, trees have thinner bark which is unsuitable for beetle breeding (from Amman *et al.* 1977).

beetles, bark thickness and stand density, (Fig. 10.6) shows clearly that bark thickness provides a good measure of beetle productivity. Stands in which at least 40 per cent of the basal area of lodgepole pine had been killed by the beetle were correctly assigned to the 'extreme high risk zone' using the synoptic model (Berryman 1978) (Fig. 10.5).

As with the determination of critical densities discussed in the previous section, it may be unwise to apply risk-rating systems outside the forest areas in which they were developed. Amman (1985), for example, compared the efficacy of the *PGR* and *SGE* methods together with three others in predicting the risk of forest stands to *D. ponderosae* attack. The best methods correctly determined risk in only three out of five stands tested.

10.1.3 Economics and priorities of control

The concept of an economic damage threshold first introduced by Stern *et al.* (1959) is now widely taken to mean the point at which the cost of control can be offset by the reduction in damage to the crop. This break-even concept can thus be used as a decision rule in determining courses of action in IPM (Mumford and Norton 1984). In forestry, however, there is often a considerable time lag between expenditure on control and recovery of costs when the trees are eventually harvested so that use of the economic damage threshold is less straightforward. The importance of this time delay can be seen from the fact that £1000 spent now on control would be worth the equivalent of $1000 (1 + r)^n = £7040$ after 40 years ($n = 40$, $r =$ interest rate, e.g. 5 per cent). In determining the economic effectiveness of control, therefore, the current cost of control needs to be compared with the present value of economic benefits that accrue over the rotation age of the crop as a result of that control. This is usually referred to as discounted revenue (Johnston *et al*. 1967; Busby and Grayson 1981).

In general terms we can say that the economic threshold in forests is 'high' because they have a low value per unit area, although in special crops such as Christmas trees and seed orchards or where quality loss in valuable hardwood species is likely, the economic threshold may be considerably lower. But what that threshold is, i.e. how many insects cause how much damage at what economic cost, is unknown for most forest pests. A few detailed studies have been made, however, and some of them are discussed in Chapter 4. In general, direct control measures are only applied when trees are likely to be killed by pest outbreaks and in these situations a financial appraisal is more straightforward. But Hayes and Britton (1986) provide an example of the economic effectiveness of control to prevent growth loss from their study of the defoliation of lodgepole pine by the pine sawfly, *Neodiprion sertifer*. Defoliated trees were affected in a number of ways but the reduction in height growth was used to calculate the number of years delay in the economic rotation based on departure from general yield class curves (Hamilton and Christie 1971) (Chapter 1). In this study, defoliation by the sawfly resulted in a reduction in height growth of 0.8 m leading to a 3-year delay in the rotation. The decline in

Table 10.4. *The effect of rotation delay on the present value (discounted revenue in £'s) of lodgepole pine stands*

Delay in economic rotation (years)	Discounted revenue	Loss per ha	Discounted revenue	Loss per ha
	Yield class 6		Yield class 8	
0	140	0	260	0
1	133	7	248	12
2	127	13	236	24
3[a]	121	19	225	35
4	115	25	214	46
5	110	30	204	56
6	105	35	194	66

[a] This study

A 55-year non-thin rotation is assumed using a 5% discount rate at 1984/5 timber prices (from Hayes and Britton 1986.)

discounted revenue with increasing delay in rotation is shown in Table 10.4. The discounted cost of controlling an outbreak using a nuclear polyhedrosis virus preparation was estimated to be between £10 and £17 per hectare, so that control would be economically viable in this case.

However, the possible need for future control operations adding to the cost would need to be taken into account.

Although the economic injury level is essentially about profit and loss, there may be social and environmental costs as well and this can affect the decision to apply control measures. For example, chemical control of the pine processionary moth, *Thaumetopoea pityocampa*, in southern Europe and the gypsy moth, *Lymantria dispar*, in the USA is mainly undertaken at the rural/urban interface to protect people from the effects of the urticating hairs produced by the larvae.

10.1.4 Decision support systems

Decision support systems (DSS) are interactive computer-based systems that are able to utilize data and models to solve unstructured problems and so they are able to implement mathematically a forest manager's concept of an insect control problem (Rykiel *et al.* 1984; Sprague 1980). They can be used interactively to define a particular problem, and the information tree in Fig. 10.7 illustrates the range of information that can be incorporated in such systems.

Although DSS have been used in the USA, particularly in the management of bark beetles, they have not so far been developed in Europe. However, such systems are likely to become increasingly important in IPM as the volume and complexity of information on forest pests increases (Coulson and Saunders 1987).

10.2 DEVELOPING AN INTEGRATED APPROACH TO FOREST INSECT CONTROL

In Chapters 5–9 we discussed several alternative methods for preventing or controlling outbreaks of forest insects, considering them more or less in isolation as components of IPM. In order to build these components into IPM programmes they need to be linked together in a logical sequence such as that outlined in Table 10.5. The options selected for any particular pest will depend on a number of factors related to pest biology and the extent and severity of outbreaks and, in practice, will reflect a compromise between what is theoretically possible and what is economically viable.

The case histories discussed below show how the emphasis on different aspects of IPM relate to the ecology and pest status of the insects. Improvements in the efficiency or effectiveness of these and other programmes is, however, likely to come from an increase in the number of components in it (Table 10.5) rather than further increases in the precision

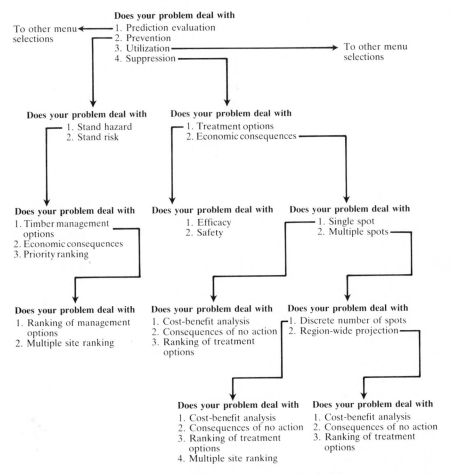

FIG. 10.7. Information tree for the *Dendroctonus frontalis* decision support system (from Rykiel *et al.* 1984).

of particular components. For example, increasingly accurate monitoring of changes in insect population density is of limited use if threshold values for economic damage to the trees are unknown. The case histories presented below should, therefore, be seen as evolving strategies of control rather than static examples of IPM.

Table 10.5. *Summary of procedures available for the integrated pest management of forest insects*

Suggested order of priority	Methods for preventing or minimizing pest problems	Discussed in chapter
1	Choose appropriate site, tree species or provenance, origin (exotic or native), planting regime (mixtures or monocultures)	1,5,6
2	Use good silvicultural practices, e.g. sanitation, hygiene, maintenance of tree vigour	5
	Establish quarantine measures against exotic pests; define internal quarantines for established ones	5
3	Survey for actual or potential pests, assess size and impact of problem	5,9,10
	Routinely monitor serious or potentially serious pest populations	10
4	Make control decisions based on all available information related to economic, silvicultural and entomological factors	10
	Methods to control pest outbreaks	
5	Silvicultural or ecological techniques, e.g. selective felling, hygiene, trap trees	5
6	Biological control with pathogens for lepidopteran and sawfly defoliators	7
	Biological control with parasitoids or predators where appropriate	7
7	Insecticidal control using selective chemicals applied efficiently	8

10.3 CASE HISTORIES OF INTEGRATED PEST MANAGEMENT IN FORESTRY

10.3.1 The pine processionary moth, *Thaumetopoea pityocampa*

Thaumetopoea pityocampa is widely distributed throughout Europe in countries with a Mediterranean climate and is a pest that causes social and environmental problems as well as economic damage. Social problems occur in urban areas because the later stage caterpillars are covered with urticating hairs which can be blown around in the wind and on contact may cause itching of skin and eyes and even allergic reactions. Infestations around seaside holiday resorts such as on the Atlantic coast of France may deter holidaymakers and so can have indirect economic consequences (Buxton 1983). Environmental aspects are particularly important in North Africa where pines, planted to stabilize sand dunes on the desert fringes, are frequently defoliated, so threatening the success of this important programme (Chararas 1977). Economic damage occurs in plantations through reduced growth or death of defoliated trees. In special crops such as the stone pine which has edible seeds, the damage threshold is lower than in plantations and even where insects occur at sub-outbreak densities, the presence of larval nests can disrupt harvesting. Most pine species, especially Corsican pine, appear to be susceptible although relative suscep- tibilities may vary between countries; cedars may also be attacked (Huchon and Demolin 1971). Details of the life history are given in Chapter 4.

Temperature is one of the most important factors affecting development. High summer temperatures may delay adult emergence and increase mortality of larvae whereas low winter temperatures delay larval develop- ment and may be lethal, so temperature variations in different parts of the insect's range can cause considerable differences in the timing of the life cycle (Demolin 1969; Huchon and Demolin 1971). In France, an example of how the life cycle varies in relation to differences in altitude and latitude is summarized in Fig. 10.8. This diagram is of considerable practical value because it can be used to determine the expected time of appearance of the different developmental stages in a normal year. A horizontal line drawn from the point of 50 per cent adult emergence, which is determined locally, indicates the approximate time of appearance of subsequent stages and this can be an important guide to the timing of control measures.

The time of adult emergence is usually determined from their appear- ance in light traps and these catches can also be a guide to the size of the population. This information is particularly useful because population size can vary unpredictably from year to year, largely because seasonal variations in temperature affect the proportion of pupae in prolonged diapause and in some years synchronized emergence of adults can give rise to unexpectedly high populations. The shape of the adult emergence curve, determined from light traps, can also provide important information on the likelihood of population build-up. Where the climate for development of T. pityocampa remains favourable for several consecutive years, emerg- ence is synchronized over a relatively short period (Fig. 10.9a) and under these conditions populations have the potential to increase to damaging levels. However, when emergence is spread out as in Fig. 10.9b, suggesting a disruptive influence of climate, the population is unlikely to increase to outbreak levels (Huchon and Demolin 1971; Dajoz 1980).

The choice of direct control measures against this pest depends on the size of the affected area. Where small areas of forest are affected or in parks and gardens, cutting and burning of well-formed winter nests or spot treatment with insecticide can be effective. For larger areas of forest, aerial spraying is the only practical method. Early use of persistent insecticides (DDT or trichlorfon) caused extensive mortality of natural enemies so that

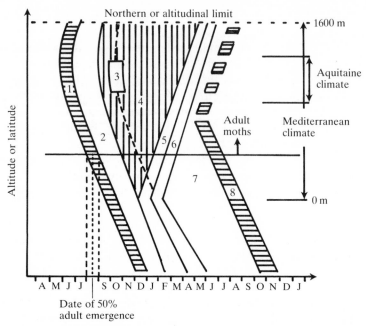

FIG. 10.8. The life cycle of *Thaumetopoea pityocampa* in France in relation to variations in altitude and latitude.
1. Adults.
2. Pre-hibernation eggs and young larvae.
3. Pre-hibernation processionary larvae moving to overwintering sites.
4. Hibernation in nests.
5. Post-hibernation development of larvae.
6. Post-hibernation processionary larvae moving to pupation sites.
7. Pupal diapause.
8. Adult development inside pupae.
Using the date of 50% adult emergence (in the example shown, 15 August), the horizontal line predicts the occurrence of the subsequent life stages for a particular altitude or latitude (from Dajoz 1980, after Demolin 1969).

some areas became re-infested within 3 or 4 years. Alternatives to DDT such as the insect growth regulator diflubenzuron are now widely used and because adult natural enemies are largely unaffected, re-infestations are now less common (Robredo 1980; F. R. Robredo, personal communication (Chapter 8).

10.3.2 The Douglas fir tussock moth, *Orgyia pseudotsugata*

This insect occurs widely throughout western North America but out-breaks only occur in the drier coniferous forests away from the coast. Many

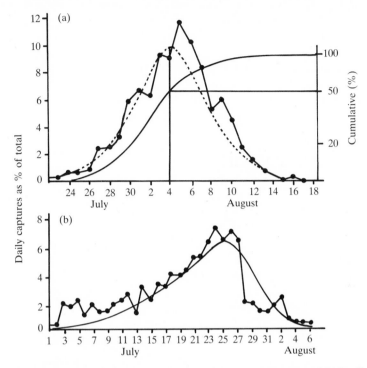

FIG. 10.9. Adult emergence curves for *Thaumetopoea pityocampa*, (a) distribution of captures following climatic conditions favourable for synchronized emergence, likely to be followed by pest outbreaks. 50% emergence point provides a reference date for subsequent appearance of development stages (Fig. 10.8). Data points represent daily captures as percentage of total; dotted line is a Gaussian distribution fitted to these data and solid line the cumulative sum of the daily captures. (b) Distribution of captures following variable and disruptive climatic conditions, unlikely to result in outbreak conditions (from Dajoz 1980).

aspects of the biology and control of this insect are discussed in Brookes *et al.* (1978). Its primary hosts are Douglas fir, grand fir and white fir although host preferences may vary in different parts of the insect's range. The first and second instar larvae are found in the upper crown which contains most of the new foliage on which they feed but later instars can feed on older foliage. During severe outbreaks, clumps of defoliated trees often occur throughout the forest and some of the trees, especially the smaller ones, may die. Because larval feeding is often most intense at the top of the tree, top-kill is characteristic of outbreaks and again is particularly damaging to small trees. Trees suffering up to 50 per cent defoliation lose about 30–40 per cent of their annual growth. Although the growth rate returns to normal after about six years, the loss of increment cannot be wholly compensated for by later growth so outbreaks have a considerable impact on productivity. Defoliated trees also run the risk of attack by the fir engraver beetle, *Scolytus ventralis*, which is able to colonize the weakened trees, and mortality from bark beetle attack may be higher than that caused by *O. pseudotsugata* alone.

Outbreaks can generally be classified into four stages, occurring in successive years (Fig. 10.10) and this typical behaviour is a useful guide to the planning of control measures. The release phase is characterized by rapid population growth and is followed by a peak phase where population density is at its highest. In the declining phase, population density decreases rapidly so that in the fourth year, i.e. the post-decline phase, populations are again at a low level. Natural mortality from a nuclear polyhedrosis virus and larval parasitoids are the main causes of population decline and egg parasitoids may be important in maintaining populations at low density. This outbreak sequence can occur synchronously in different areas and in some parts of its range *O. pseudotsugata* appears to show a cyclic variation in population density with outbreaks occurring every 8–9 years.

Because of the rapidity with which outbreaks can develop, monitoring is an important part of management. The use of a pheromone-based monitoring system is described in Chapter 9. Outbreaks can occur within a

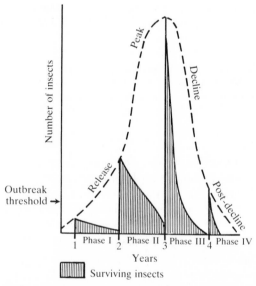

FIG. 10.10. The typical outbreak sequence of *Orgyia pseudotsugata* in the western USA. Idealized patterns of within-generation survivorship are also shown (from Mason and Luck 1978).

large geographical area but the development of a regional risk-rating system for stands has allowed monitoring to be confined to those areas most at risk. High risk is usually associated with competition between trees for moisture and nutrients and this is likely to occur on ridge tops and upper slopes and in mature (50 years old or more) multi-storeyed stands with a high density of host species. To some extent, past forest management practices have increased density and diversity within stands, resulting in increased competition and reduced host vigour. Highly susceptible mature stands should be harvested in such a way that site degradation is minimized while removing susceptible trees and encouraging natural regeneration of non-host or less preferred species.

In the past, outbreaks were often controlled with DDT which was applied to over 500 000 ha between 1947 and 1974. Forests were usually sprayed at the peak of the outbreak when defoliation was visible but as Fig. 10.10 makes clear, this was at a point when populations would collapse naturally. Less persistent insecticides are now used and are most effective when applied early in the outbreak. Other direct control measures include the use of a virus which was one of the first to be registered for use against a forest insect (Chapter 7).

10.3.3 The pine looper moth, *Bupalus piniaria*

The pine looper, *Bupalus piniaria*, has been one of the most intensively studied forest pests in Europe (Chapters 1, 2 and 4). In parts of central Europe and in Britain, outbreaks of this pest may be cyclic with a periodicity of 6–8 years (Barbour 1985, 1988). In Britain, an integrated approach to control of *B. piniaria* has been developed over the last 30 years.

As with many other forest pests, outbreaks are often associated with particular site conditions and susceptible pine stands are usually of low yield class, 25–70 years old and growing on poor sandy soils of intermediate xericity (500 to 600 mm p.a.) (Barbour 1988). Defoliation is assumed to cause incremental losses, but the major threat to trees temporarily stressed by defoliation comes from attacks of a secondary pest, the pine shoot beetle, *Tomicus piniperda*. Not only are attacked trees killed by this bark beetle but surrounding undefoliated trees may also be at risk as beetle population density rises. Chemical control of *B. piniaria* is, therefore, necessary to prevent death of trees and since outbreaks occur periodically on susceptible sites, monitoring forms an important part of the management of this pest.

About 50 different pine areas are surveyed annually to determine the density of overwintering pupae (Barbour 1987) and some examples of the temporal and spatial variation in density that this reveals are shown in

Table 10.6. *Results of the UK Forestry Commission annual survey for pupae of Bupalus piniaria*

Forest district	Unit	1977	1978	1979	1980	1981	1982	1983	1984	1985	1986	1987	1988
England													
Durham	Slaley	0.8	—	—	0.0	0.0	0.4	—	0.8	0.4	0.0	0.0	0.2
North York Moors	Cropton	1.2	4.8	0.4	0.0	0.0	0.8	1.6	3.6	2.4	0.4	0.4	0.8
	Langdale	14.9	21.6	3.2	4.0	1.2	1.6	2.8	3.2	3.6	0.8	1.2	0.5
	Wykeham	14.4	10.4	2.0	1.6	0.8	1.6	2.0	6.4	2.8	2.8	1.6	0.6
Cheshire	Delamere	4.4	4.4	4.0	2.4	0.8	1.2	2.8	2.0	1.6	1.2	0.8	0.5
Midlands	Cannock	17.2	34.9	10.8	2.8	3.2	5.6	10.8	11.2	12.0	1.6	2.8	2.2
	Swynnerton	3.2	5.6	2.4	0.8	0.4	1.2	—	11.6	11.2	2.0	0.8	1.0
Sherwood	Sherwood III	0.8	2.4	0.8	0.8	0.8	2.4	3.2	4.8	14.8	1.2	0.4	0.9
	Sherwood IV	3.6	27.2	3.2	2.0	1.6	3.2	4.8	10.0	9.6	24.4	4.4	1.4
	Sherwood V	1.6	1.6	1.2	1.2	1.6	1.2	1.2	2.4	2.0	0.4	0.4	0.3
Thetford	Croxton	0.4	0.0	0.0	0.8	0.0	0.0	0.0	—	0.4	0.0	0.0	0.0
	Feltwell	0.4	0.0	0.0	0.4	0.0	0.0	0.0	0.0	0.4	0.0	0.0	0.2
Scotland													
Easter Ross	Findon	0.8	1.6	0.8	0.8	0.4	0.4	4.4	3.2	2.0	0.4	0.8	0.1
Moray	Culbin	4.0	8.0	1.2	2.0	2.0	3.2	14.4	20.0	2.4	0.4	0.8	0.1
	Roseisle	0.4	1.2	2.8	12.0	2.8	2.4	16.0	45.6	3.6	0.0	0.4	0.4
Speyside	Speymouth	0.8	0.4	0.0	2.0	0.8	2.0	2.0	1.6	0.4	0.4	1.2	0.1
Angus	Montreathmont	3.2	5.2	1.2	0.8	0.4	2.0	—	15.6	0.4	0.0	0.4	0.5
Fife	Tentsmuir	57.2[a]	6.4	0.4	0.0	0.4	3.2	21.2	176.8[a]	22.4	0.8	0.8	0.3

[a] Aerial spraying carried out (see Table 10.7).
Data from selected units and forest districts, numbers expressed as mean pupae m^{-2} in compartment with highest count (Anon. 1983; Barbour 1987, and unpublished).

Table 10.6. Not only are there striking differences in pupal density between the different forests but there may also be considerable annual variations within forests and the data show that pupal densities can increase to high levels within 2 years. In the past, critical densities for some forests were considered to be as low as around 25 pupae m^{-2} (Fig. 1.5) but a figure of around 50 is now regarded as a more useful guide to the need for control measures in most forests (Table 10.1). Where densities approach this threshold, some indication of whether further increases can be expected in the following year can be obtained by more detailed examination of the pupal samples. Populations are likely to decline if mean pupal weights are significantly lower than in the previous year, if pupal parasitism exceeds 25 per cent or if cocoons of the parasitoid, *Dusona oxyacanthae*, are also present in the samples at a density of 2 or more m^{-2} (Barbour 1988). In areas supporting high numbers of pupae (around 35–40 m^{-2}), egg samples are sometimes taken on sample trees within the area at risk as an additional check on the population size.

Since the start of the *B. piniaria* monitoring system, several relatively small areas of forest have been sprayed with insecticide (Table 10.7).

Table 10.7. *Insecticide applications against Bupalus piniaria in the UK*

Year	Region	Area sprayed (ha)	Insecticide used
mid 1950s	Cannock and Culbin	*c.* 2430	DDT
1963	Cannock	*c.* 550	DDT
1969	North York Moors	540	Tetrachlorvinphos
1977	Tentsmuir	102	Tetrachlorvinphos
1979	Flanders Moss	72	Diflubenzuron
1984	Tentsmuir	1200	Diflubenzuron

From Stoakley, personal communication.

Although DDT was used in early spraying operations, the more selective diflubenzuron is now used and instead of spraying the whole area at risk, treatments are usually confined to the epicentre only. This change in tactics followed from the recognition that the pupal parasitoid, *Cratichneumon viator*, causes significant mortality at low host densities. Once *B. piniaria* populations have been reduced by spraying, therefore, parasitism levels often reach 60 to 100 per cent causing a further reduction in the density of this pest (D. Barbour, personal communication).

Where areas of defoliation occur in small untreated outbreaks, completely defoliated trees can be felled during the attack period of *T. piniperda* and the logs left in the forest. Beetle-infested logs should then be removed and the broods destroyed (Chapter 5). In this way, attack of surrounding partially defoliated trees can be avoided (Bevan 1974).

10.3.4 The spruce bark beetle, *Ips typographus*

This is probably the most destructive pest of spruce in Europe, with records of outbreaks dating from the eighteenth century. The losses that occurred during some of these outbreaks are shown in Table 10.8. Silviculture is important in the management of this and other bark beetles (Chapter 5) and enormous losses can occur if proper thinning practices and forest hygiene are not carried out consistently.

Table 10.8. *Estimated losses in timber volume caused by outbreaks of Ips typographus*

Country	Date	Losses million m³
Germany	1857–62	4.0
	1868–75	4.0
	1917–23	1.5
	1940–1	1.0
	1944–8	30.0
Sweden	1976–9	2.0
Norway	(1970)–82	5.0[a]

Data from Bakke and Riege 1982 and A. Bakke, personal communication[a].

The recent outbreak in west-central Sweden and south-east Norway (Table 10.8, see also Chapters 1 and 9) was intensively studied, resulting in the collection of much valuable information on the management of bark beetle outbreaks. The factors contributing to the initiation of this outbreak were slightly different in the two areas but the most important were drought, which was particularly severe during 1974–6, and windblow (Fig. 10.11). These natural disasters occurred at a time when endemic beetle population density was already high because of reductions in forest hygiene practices during the previous decade (Bakke 1982a). A further important factor was that over 25 per cent of the spruce forests were mature or over-mature and so were more susceptible to bark beetle attack. Once the outbreak was underway, populations were able to build up rapidly on the abundant breeding material of windblown and stressed trees and were then able to attack and kill standing trees.

In Norway, an integrated approach to control was adopted from the outset in a campaign that involved both government and national media. Co-ordination of the control effort over such a large heterogeneous area was complicated by the dissected nature of the forest estate: over 100 000 people owned about 80 per cent of the forests, most of them with holdings

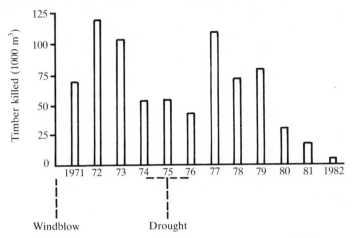

FIG. 10.11. Volume of spruce timber killed in southern Norway by *Ips typographus* (from Bakke 1983).

of less than 100 ha (Landmark 1976). To ensure concerted action the government provided subsidies to private owners for, among other things, construction of roads to inaccessible areas. In addition, laws were enacted to enforce the principle of forest hygiene. The national publicity campaign was so effective that a contemporary song appropriately called 'Bark beetle boogie' achieved national prominence on the radio (A. Bakke, personal communication) so there could have been few people who were unaware of the impact of this insect!

Removal of infested material from the forest was the main priority during the early part of the outbreak and silvicultural methods remained an important part of the control programme. Other direct control measures included the novel method of mass-trapping, details of which are discussed in Chapter 9 and also the limited use of pheromone-baited logs sprayed with insecticide. By surveying stands that had been killed from 1975 to 1980, a simple risk-rating index (R) was developed that should allow the identification of stands most at risk in future outbreaks. The index $R = S^2 (RD - 30)^3 \, SC$ was based on the percent spruce cover in the area (S), deviation from normal summer rainfall (RD) and the percent of the area occupied by higher site class forests (SC) and was significantly correlated with the percentage of the spruce killed in the area (Fig. 10.12).

10.3.5 The great spruce bark beetle, *Dendroctonus micans*

This European pest of spruce appears to have originally been confined to Siberia but it has been extending its range since the early part of this

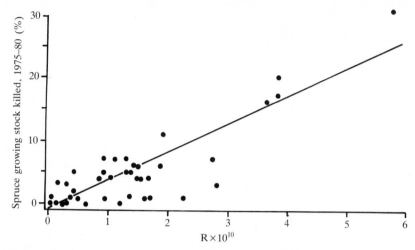

FIG. 10.12. Mortality of spruce in relation to the risk index (R) developed from surveys of stands killed by *Ips typographus* in south-east Norway (see text) (after Worrell 1983).

century through natural spread and accidental movement by man and is now widely distributed throughout Europe (Carle 1975; Grégoire 1988). The life cycle of *Dendroctonus micans* is unusual among bark beetles because living trees can be successfully attacked by single females without the need for an aggregation pheromone to co-ordinate a mass-attack as occurs in many other bark beetle species. The larvae, however, do produce an aggregation pheromone which causes them to feed together within single brood galleries in the living bark (Chapter 4).

Outbreaks of this insect tend to occur during colonization of spruce forests at the margins of its distribution and this has resulted in considerable damage to forests in several parts of Europe. The most recently colonized areas in which outbreaks have occurred include southern France, Turkey and Britain (Bevan and King 1983; Benz 1985; Grégoire 1988). In Belgium and other areas where outbreaks first occurred in the early part of this century, spontaneous biological control by the predatory beetle, *Rhizophagus grandis*, appears to have prevented further outbreaks. Subsequently, predators have been released in a number of areas in biological control programmes that are discussed in Chapter 7. In Britain a number of silvicultural methods were used to reduce population density, as well as to prevent further spread before predators were introduced. These methods are discussed in Chapter 5.

In Soviet Georgia, *D. micans* first appeared in the 1950s and within 10 years had spread through most of the area containing Oriental spruce, which amounts to about 8 per cent of the Republic's forests (Targamadze *et al.* 1975). A fully-integrated approach to the control of this insect was adopted, incorporating chemical, biological, and silvicultural methods to prevent mortality and increment loss in the highly susceptible Oriental spruce. This insect has caused considerable economic damage, but in the Caucasus mountains, the main aim of control was not to prevent loss of timber but rather to preserve the forest cover in watershed areas and on steep valley sides where forests are important in stabilizing the soil.

The main objective of direct control measures was to reduce the population density prior to the release of predators in biological control. Within the attacked stands, heavily infested trees were removed during salvage operations but lightly and moderately infested trees (less than 15 colonies per tree) recovered when the trunk was sprayed with HCH and an economic appraisal showed that the cost of control was offset by improved growth within 5 to 7 years (Targamadze *et al.* 1975). Some 10 million trees were individually treated in this way between 1957 and 1972. After populations had been reduced by sanitation felling and insecticide treatment, *R. grandis* which was introduced from central Europe and parts of the Soviet Union was released in the stands and is now widely distributed within spruce forests (Shavliashvili *et al.* 1976; Kolomiets and Bogdanova 1976).

In the long term, the main aim of IPM is to reduce the susceptibility of the forest through silvicultural means. Within the outbreak area it was clear that mixed stands of beech, fir and pine with less than 30 per cent spruce were least affected by *D. micans*, so in the reafforestation of previously heavily infested areas the more resistant mixed forests are established (Shavliashvili *et al.* 1976). At higher altitudes, however, where Oriental spruce is the climax species, it is not practical to change the species composition.

Bibliography

Aaron, J. R. (1976). Conifer bark; its properties and uses. *Forestry Commission Record* **110**, 1–31.

Adkisson, P. L. and Dyck, V. A. (1980). Resistant varieties in pest management systems. In *Breeding plants resistant to insects* (ed. F. G. Maxwell and P. R. Jennings), pp. 233–51. Wiley, New York.

Akessen, N. B. and Yates, W. E. (1984). Physical parameters affecting aircraft spray application. In *Chemical and biological control in forestry* (ed. W. Y. Garner and J. Harvey Jr.), pp. 95–115. American Chemical Society, Washington.

Alfaro, R. I., Van Sickle, G. A., Thomson, A. J., and Wegwitz, E. (1982). Tree mortality and radial growth losses caused by the western spruce budworm in a Douglas-fir stand in British Columbia. *Canadian Journal of Forest Research* **12**, 780–7.

Alfaro, R. I., Borden, J. H., Harris, L. J., Nijholt, W. W., and McMullen, L. H. (1984). Pine oil, a feeding deterrent for the white pine weevil, *Pissodes strobi* (Coleoptera: Curculionidae). *Canadian Entomologist* **116**, 41–4.

Alfaro, R. I., Thomson, A. J., and Van Sickle, G. A. (1985). Quantification of Douglas-fir growth losses caused by western spruce budworm defoliation using stem analysis. *Canadian Journal of Forest Research* **15**, 5–9.

Allsop, F. (1973). The first fifty years of New Zealand's forest service. *New Zealand forest service information series no. 59.*

Alma, P. J. (1970). A study of the activity and behaviour of the winter moth *Operophtera brumata* (L.) (Lep., Hydriomenidae). *Entomologists Monthly Magazine* **105**, 258–65.

Alstad, D. N., Edmunds, G. F. Jr., and Weinstein, L. H. (1982). Effects of air pollutants on insect populations. *Annual Review of Entomology* **27**, 369–84.

Amman, G. D. (1985). A test of lodgepole pine hazard rating methods for mountain pine beetle infestation in southeastern Idaho. In *The role of the host plant in the population dynamics of forest insects* (ed. L. Safrányik), pp. 186–200. Canusa.

Amman, G. D., McGregor, M. D., Cahill, D. B., and Klein, W. H. (1977). Guidelines for reducing losses of lodgepole pine to the mountain pine beetle in unmanaged stands in the rocky mountains. *USDA Forest Service General Technical Report INT-36.*

Anderbrant, O., Schlyter, F., and Birgersson, G. (1985). Intraspecific competition affecting parents and offspring in the bark beetle *Ips typographus*. *Oikos* **45**, 89–98.

Anderson, M. (1979). The development of plant habitats under exotic forest crops. In *Ecology and design in amenity land management* (ed. S. E. Wright and G. P. Buckley). Wye College and Recreation Ecology Research Group.

Anderson, R. M. and May, R. M. (1980). Infectious diseases and population cycles of forest insects. *Science* **210**, 658–61.

Anderson, R. M., and May, R. M. (1981). The population dynamics of microparasites and their invertebrate hosts. *Philosophical Transactions of the Royal Society of London* **291**, 451–524.

Anderson, W. W., Berisford, C. W., and Kimmich, R. H. (1979). Genetic differences among five populations of the southern pine beetle. *Annals of the Entomological Society of America* **72**, 323–7.

Annila, E. (1976). Cone and seed insect problems in seed orchards in Europe. *XVI IUFRO World Congress Div. 2*, pp. 369–80. Norway.

Annila, E. (1979). Damage by *Phyllobius* weevils (Coleoptera: Curculionidae) in birch plantations (in Finnish). *Metsantutkimuslaitoksen Julkaisuja Finland* **97**, 1–20.

Annila, E. and Hiltunen, R. (1977). Damage by *Pissodes validirostris* (Coleoptera, Curculionidae) studied in relation to the monoterpene composition in Scots pine and lodgepole pine. *Annales Entomologici Fennici* **43**, 87–92.

Anon. (1981). *Cephalcia lariciphila*. *Entopath News*, No. *83*, 4–6.

Anon. (1983). Annual pine looper survey 1982. *Entopath News*, No. *85*. 8–11.

Anon. (1985). *Insects of eastern forests*. USDA Forest Service Miscellaneous Publication No. 1426.

Anon. (1986). *World resources 1986*. A report by the world resources institute and the international institute for environment and development. Basic Books, Inc., New York.

Armstrong, J. A. (1984). Fate of chemical insecticides in foliage and forest litter. In *Chemical and biological control in forestry* (ed. W. Y. Garner and J. Harvey Jr.), pp. 241–51. American Chemical Society, Washington.

Armstrong, J. A. (1985). Tactics and strategies for larval suppression and prevention of damage using chemical insecticides. In *Recent advances in spruce budworms research* (ed. C. J. Sanders, R. W. Stark, E. J. Mullins and J. Murphy), pp. 301–19. Canadian Forestry Service and USDA Forest Service, Ottawa.

Askew, R. R. and Shaw, M. R. (1986). Parasitoid communities: their size, structure and development. In *Insect parasitoids*, 13th Symposium of the Royal Entomological Society, London (ed. J. Waage and D. Greathead), pp. 225–64. Academic Press, London.

Atkinson, D. J. (1953). The natural control of forest insects in the tropics. *Transactions of the International Congress of Entomology, Amsterdam, Vol. 2*, 220–3.

Austarå, Ø. (1982). Survey of the pine beauty moth *Panolis flammea* in Norway in 1980 and 1981 using traps with synthetic pheromone analogues. *Fauna Norwegia B* **29**, 105–9.

Austarå, Ø. (1984). Diameter growth and tree mortality of Norway spruce following mass attacks by *Epinotia nanana*. *Research paper from Norwegian Forest Research Institute 10/84*, 1–9.

Bailey, J. A. and Mansfield, J. W. (ed.) (1982). *Phytoalexins*. Blackie, Glasgow.

Bain, J. (1977). Overseas wood- and bark-boring insects intercepted at New Zealand ports. *Forest Research Institute, New Zealand Forest Service Technical Paper No. 63*, 1–28.

Baker, R., Bradshaw, J. W. S., and Speed, W. (1982). Methoxymercuration-demercuration and mass spectrometry in the identification of sex pheromones of *Panolis flammea*, the pine beauty moth. *Experimentia* **38**, 233–4.

Baker, W. L. (1948). Transmission by leafhoppers of the virus causing phloem necrosis of American elm. *Science* **108**, 307–8.

Baker, W. L. (1949). Studies on the transmission of the virus causing phloem necrosis of American elm, with notes on the biology of its vector. *Journal of Economic Entomology* **42**, 729–32.

Bakke, A. (1963). Studies on the spruce-cone insects *Laspeyresia strobilella* (L.) (Lepidoptera: Tortricidae), *Kaltenbachiola strobi* (Winn.) (Diptera: Itonidae) and their parasites (Hymenoptera) in Norway. Biology, distribution and diapause. *Reports of the Norwegian Forest Research Institute, No. 67* **19**, 1–151.

Bakke, A. (1968). Ecological studies on bark beetles (Coleoptera: Scolytidae) associated with Scots pine (*Pinus sylvestris* L.) in Norway with particular reference to the influence of temperature. *Meddelelser fra Det Norske Skogforsoksvesen, No. 83* **21**, 443–602.

Bakke, A. (1969). The effect of forest fertilisation on the larval weight and larval density of *Laspeyresia strobilella* (L.) (*Lepidoptera: Tortricidae*) in cones of Norway spruce. *Zeitschrift für angewandte Entomologie* **63**, 451–3.

Bakke, A. (1970). The use of DDT in Norwegian forestry. Review and present situation (in Norwegian). *Tidsskrift for Skogbruk* **78**, 304–9.

Bakke, A. (1971). Distribution of prolonged diapausing larvae in populations of *Laspeyresia strobilella* L. (Lep., Tortricidae) from spruce cones. *Norsk Entomologisk Tidsskrift* **18**, 89–93.

Bakke, A. (1976). Spruce bark beetle *Ips typographus* pheromone production and field response to synthetic pheromones. *Naturwissenschaften* **63**, 92.

Bakke, A. (1982a). Mass trapping of the spruce bark beetle *Ips typographus* in Norway as part of an integrated control program. In *Insect suppression with controlled release pheromone systems*, Vol. II (ed. A. F. Kydonieus and M. Beroza), pp. 17–25. CRC Press, Boca Raton, Florida.

Bakke, A. (1982b). The utilisation of aggregation pheromone for the control of the spruce bark beetle. In *Insect Pheromone Technology: Chemistry and Application*. (ed. B. A. Leonhardt and M. Beroza), ACS Symposium Series No. 190, 219–29. American Chemical Society, Washington.

Bakke, A. (1983). Host tree and bark beetle interaction during a mass attack of *Ips typographus* in Norway. *Zeitschrift für angewandte Entomologie* **96**, 118–25.

Bakke, A. (1985). Deploying pheromone-baited traps for monitoring *Ips typographus* populations. *Zeitschrift für angewandte Entomologie* **99**, 33–9.

Bakke, A. and Lekander, B. (1965). Studies on *Hylobius abietis* L. II. The influence of exposure on the development and production of *Hylobius abietis*, illustrated through one Norwegian and one Swedish experiment. *Meddelelser fra Det Norske Skogforsoksvesen, No. 73* **20**, 117–35.

Bakke, A. and Riege, L. (1982). The pheromone of the spruce bark beetle *Ips typographus* and its potential use in the suppression of beetle populations. In *Insect suppression with controlled release pheromone systems*, Vol. II (ed. A. F. Kydonieus and M. Beroza) pp. 3–15. CRC Press, Boca Raton, Florida.

Bakke, A. Austarå, Ø., and Pettersen, H. (1977a). Seasonal flight activity and attack pattern of *Ips typographus* in Norway under epidemic conditions. *Meddelelser fra Norsk Institutt for Skogforsning* **33**, 253–68.

Bakke, A., Frøyen, P., and Skattebøl, L. (1977*b*). Field response to a new pheromonal compound isolated from *Ips typographus*. *Naturwissenschaften* **64**, 98.

Balch, R. E. and Bird, F. T. (1944). A disease of the European spruce sawfly *Gilpinia hercyniae* (Htg.) and its place in natural control. *Scientific Agriculture* **25**, 65–80.

Baltensweiler, W. (1968). The cyclic population dynamics of the grey larch tortrix *Zeiraphera griseana* Hubner (=*Semasia diniana* Guenee) (Lepidoptera: Tortricidae). In *Insect abundance* (ed. T. R. E. Southwood), pp. 88–97. Blackwell Scientific Publications, Oxford.

Baltensweiler, W. (1975). The importance of the larch bud moth (*Zeiraphera diniana* Gn.) in the biocoenosis of forests of larch and Swiss stone pine (in German). *Mitteilungen der Schweizerischen entomologischen Gesellschaft* **48**, 5–12.

Baltensweiler, W. (1984). The role of environment and reproduction in the population dynamics of the larch budmoth *Zeiraphera diniana* Gn. (Lepidoptera, Tortricidae). In *Advances in invertebrate reproduction*, Vol. 3 (ed. W. Engels, W. H. Clark, A. Fischer, P. J. W. Olive and D. F. Went), pp. 291–301. Elsevier Science Publishers B.V.

Baltensweiler, W. and Fischlin, A. (1979). The role of migration for the population dynamics of the larch bud moth, *Zeiraphera diniana* Gn. (Lep. Tortricidae). *Bulletin de la Société Entomologique Suisse* **52**, 259–71.

Baltensweiler, W., Benz, G., Bovey, P., and Delucchi, V. (1977). Dynamics of larch bud moth populations. *Annual Review of Entomology* **22**, 79–100.

Barbour, D. A. (1985). Patterns of population fluctuation in the pine looper moth *Bupalus piniaria* L. in Britain. In *Site characteristics and population dynamics of Lepidopteran and Hymenopteran forest pests* (ed. D. Bevan and J. T. Stoakley) pp. 8–20. *Forestry Commission Research and Development Paper 135*.

Barbour, D. A. (1987). Annual pine looper survey 1985–7. *Entopath News, No. 89*, 8–11.

Barbour, D. A. (1988). The pine looper in Britain and Europe. In *Dynamics of forest insect populations. Patterns, causes, implications* (ed. A. A. Berryman), pp. 291–308. Plenum, New York.

Barras, S. J. and Hodges, J. D. (1969). Carbohydrates of inner bark of *Pinus taeda* as affected by *Dendroctonus frontalis* and associated microorganisms. *Canadian Entomologist* **101**, 489–93.

Barrett, J. W. (ed.) (1980). *Regional silviculture of the United States*. 2nd edition. John Wiley, New York.

Barry, J. W. (1984). Deposition of chemical and biological agents in conifers. In *Chemical and biological control in forestry* (ed. W. Y. Garner and J. Harvey Jr.) pp. 117–37. American Chemical Society, Washington.

Bassman, J., Myers, W., Dickmann, D., and Wilson, L. (1982). Effects of simulated insect damage on early growth of nursery-grown hybrid poplars in northern Wisconsin. *Canadian Journal of Forest Research* **12**, 1–9.

Batra, L. R. and Batra, S. W. T. (1979). Termite-fungus mutualism. In *Insect-*

fungus symbiosis nutrition, mutualism and commensalism (ed. L. R. Batra), pp. 117–64. J. Wiley, New York.

Beaver, R. A. (1989). Insect-fungus relationships in the bark and ambrosia beetles. In *Insect-fungus interactions* (ed. N. Wilding, N. M. Collins, P. M. Hammond and J. F. Webber), pp. 121–43. Academic Press, London.

Beck, S. D. (1965). Resistance of plants to insects. *Annual Review of Entomology* **10**, 207–32.

Beck, S. D. (1968). *Insect photoperiodism*. Academic Press, New York.

Beck, S. D. and Reese, J. C. (1976). Insect-plant interactions: nutrition and metabolism. *Recent Advances in Phytochemistry* **10**, 41–92.

Bedding, R. A. (1984). Nematode parasites of Hymenoptera. In *Plant and insect nematodes* (ed. W. R. Nickle). Marcel Dekker, New York.

Bedding, R. A. and Akhurst, R. J. (1974). Use of the nematode *Deladenus siricidicola* in the biological control of *Sirex noctilio* in Australia. *Journal of the Australian Entomological Society* **13**, 129–35.

Beddington, J. R., Free, C. A., and Lawton, J. H. (1978). Characteristics of successful natural enemies in models of biological control of insect pests. *Nature* **273**, 513–19.

Begon, M., Harper, J. L., and Townsend, C. R. (1986). *Ecology: individuals, populations and communities*. Blackwell Scientific Publications, Oxford.

Bejer-Petersen, B. (1976). *Dendroctonus micans* Kug. in Denmark. The situation 25 years after a 'catastrophe'. *Journal of Plant Diseases and Protection* **83**, 16–21.

Belsky, A. J. (1986). Does herbivory benefit plants? A review of the evidence. *American Naturalist* **127**, 870–92.

Ben'kovskaya, G. V., and Idrisova, N. T. (1985). The continued effect of juvenoids in the ontogeny of *Lymantria dispar* (in Russian). *Lesnoe Khosyaistvo, No 2*, 63–5.

Benson, W. W. (1978). Resource partitioning in passion vine butterflies. *Evolution* **32**, 493–518.

Benz, G. (1985). *Dendroctonus micans* in Turkey: the situation today. In *Biological control of bark beetles (Dendroctonus micans)* (ed. J. C. Grégoire and J. M. Pasteels), pp. 43–7. Université Libre de Bruxelles, Brussels.

Bernays, E. A. (1978). Tannins: an alternative viewpoint. *Entomologia experimentalis et applicata* **24**, 44–53.

Bernays, E. A., Chamberlain, D. J., and Leather, E. M. (1981). Tolerance of acridids to ingested condensed tannin. *Journal of Chemical Ecology* **7**, 247–56.

Beroza, M. and Knipling, E. F. (1972). Gypsy moth control with the sex attractant pheromone. *Science* **177**, 19–27.

Berryman, A. A. (1969). Responses of *Abies grandis* to attack by *Scolytus ventralis* (Coleoptera: Scolytidae). *Canadian Entomologist* **101**, 1033–41.

Berryman, A. A. (1978). A synoptic model of the lodgepole pine/mountain pine beetle interaction and its potential application in forest management. In *Theory and practice of mountain pine beetle management in lodgepole pine forests* (ed. A. A. Berryman, G. D. Amman, and R. W. Stark), pp. 98–105. University of Idaho, Moscow, Idaho.

Berryman, A. A. (1979). Dynamics of bark beetle populations: analysis of dispersal and redistribution. *Mitteilungen der Schweizerischen Entomologischen Gesellschaft* **52**, 227–34.

Berryman, A. A. (1981). Effects of site characteristics on insect population dynamics. *XVII IUFRO World Congress, Div. 2, Japan 1981*, 541–9.

Berryman, A. A. (1982). Population dynamics of bark beetles. In *Bark beetles in North American conifers: a system for the study of evolutionary biology* (ed. J. B. Mitton and K. B. Sturgeon), 264–314. University of Texas Press, Austin.

Berryman, A. A. (1986). *Forest insects, principles and practice of population management.* Plenum Press, New York.

Berryman, A. A. (1987). The theory and classification of outbreaks. In *Insect outbreaks* (ed. P. Barbosa and J. C. Schultz), pp. 3–29. Academic Press, San Diego.

Berryman, A. A. (ed.) (1988). *Dynamics of forest insect populations. Patterns, causes, implications.* Plenum, New York.

Berryman, A. A. (1989). Adaptive pathways in Scolytid-fungus associations. In *Insect-fungus interactions* (ed. N. Wilding, N. M. Collins, P. M. Hammond and J. F. Webber), pp. 145–59. Academic Press, London.

Berryman, A. A. and Stark, R. W. (1985). Assessing the risk of forest insect outbreaks. *Zeitschrift für angewandte Entomologie* **99**, 199–208.

Berryman, A. A., Stenseth, N. Chr., and Isaev, A. S. (1987). Natural regulation of herbivorous forest insect populations. *Oecologia (Berlin)* **71**, 174–84.

Bethlahmy, N. (1975). A Colorado episode: beetle epidemic, ghost forest, more streamflow. *Northwest Science* **49**, 95–105.

Betz, F., (1986). Registration of baculoviruses as pesticides. In *The biology of baculoviruses*, Vol. II, *Practical application for insect control* (ed. R. R. Granados and B. A. Federici), pp. 203–22. CRC Press, Boca Raton, Florida.

Bevan, D. (1974). Control of forest insects: there is a porpoise close behind us. In *Biology of pest and disease control* (ed. D. Price Jones and M. E. Solomon), pp. 302–12. Blackwell Scientific Publications, Oxford.

Bevan, D. (1987). Forest insects. A guide to insects feeding on trees in Britain. *Forestry Commission Handbook 1.* HMSO London.

Bevan, D. and King, C. J. (1983). *Dendroctonus micans* Kug, – a new pest of spruce in UK. *Commonwealth Forestry Review* **62**, 41–51.

Bevan, D. and Stoakley, J. T. (ed.) (1985). Site characteristics and population dynamics of lepidopteran and hymenopteran forest pests. *Forestry Commission Research and Development Paper 135.*

Bierl, B. A., Beroza, M., and Collier, C. W. (1970). Potent sex attractant of the gypsy moth: its isolation, identification and synthesis. *Science* **170**, 87–9.

Bierl, B. A., Beroza, M., and Collier, C. W. (1972). Isolation, identification and synthesis of the gypsy moth sex attractant. *Journal of Economic Entomology* **65**, 659–64.

Billany, D. J. (1979). Biological control. *Cephalcia lariciphila. Report on Forest Research* 36.

Billany, D. J. (1981). Biological control. *Cephalcia lariciphila. Report on Forest Research* 40.

Billany, D. J. and Brown, R. M. (1977). The geographical distribution of *Gilpinia hercyniae* Hymenoptera: Diprionidae in the United Kingdom. *Forestry* **50**, 155–60.

Billany, D. J., Winter, T. G., and Gauld, I. D. (1985). *Olesicampe monticola* (Hedwig) (Hymenoptera: Ichneumonidae) redescribed together with notes on its biology as a parasite of *Cephalcia lariciphila* (Wachtl) (Hymenoptera: Pamphiliidae). *Bulletin of Entomological Research* **75**, 267–74.

Birch, M. C. and Wood, D. L. (1975). Mutual inhibition of the attractant pheromone response by two species of *Ips* (Coleoptera: Scolytidae). *Journal of Chemical Ecology* **1**, 101–13.

Birks, H. J. B. (1980). British trees and insects: a test of the time hypothesis over the last 13,000 years. *American Naturalist* **115**, 600–5.

Blada, I. (1982). Testing larch clones for *Adelges laricis* resistance. In *Resistance to diseases and pests in forest trees* (ed. H. M. Heybroek, B. R. Stephan and K. van Weissenberg), pp. 466–71. Centre for Agricultural Publishing and Documentation, Wageningen.

Blais, J. R. (1983). Trends in the frequency, extent and severity of spruce budworm outbreaks in eastern Canada. *Canadian Journal of Forest Research* **13**, 539–47.

Blight, M. M., Mellon, F. A., Wadhams, L. J., and Wenham, M. J. (1977). Volatiles associated with *Scolytus scolytus* beetles on English elm. *Experientia* **33**, 845–6.

Blight, M. M., Wadhams, L. J., and Wenham, M. J. (1978). Volatiles associated with unmated *Scolytus scolytus* beetles on English elm: differential production of alpha-multistriatin and 4-methyl-3-heptanol and their activities in a laboratory bioassay. *Insect Biochemistry* **8**, 135–42.

Bogenschutz, H. (1980). Survey of pine defoliators in central Europe using sex attractants. In *Dispersal of forest insects: evaluation, theory and management implications* (ed. A. A. Berryman and L. Safranyik), pp. 51–65. Canusa.

Bordasch, R. P. and Berryman, A. A. (1977). Host resistance to the fir engraver beetle *Scolytus ventralis* (Coleoptera: Scolytidae). 2 Repellency of *Abies grandis* resins and some monoterpenes. *Canadian Entomologist* **109**, 95–100.

Borden, J. H. and Lacey, T. E. (1985). Semiochemical-based manipulation of the mountain pine beetle, *Dendroctonus ponderosae* Hopkins: A component of lodgepole pine silviculture in the Merritt Timber Supply area of British Columbia. *Zeitschrift für angewandte Entomologie* **99**, 139–45.

Borden, J. H. and McLean, J. A. (1981). Pheromone-based suppression of ambrosia beetles in industrial timber processing areas. In *Management of insect pests with semiochemicals. Concepts and practice* (ed. E. R. Mitchell), pp. 133–54. Plenum Press, New York.

Borden, J. H., Billany, D. J., Bradshaw, J. W. S., Edwards, M., Baker, R., and Evans, D. A. (1978). Pheromone response and sexual behaviour of *Cephalcia lariciphila* Wachtl (Hymenoptera: Pamphiliidae). *Ecological Entomology* **3**, 13–23.

Borden, J. H., Handley, J. R., Johnson, B. D., MacConnell, J. G., Silverstein, R. M., Slessor, K. N., Swigar, A. A., and Wong, D. T. W. (1979). Synthesis and field testing of 4,6,6-lineatin, the aggregation pheromone of *Trypodendron lineatum* (Coleoptera: Scolytidae). *Journal of Chemical Ecology* **6**, 445–56.

Borden, J. H., King, C. J., Lindgren, S., Chong, L., Gray, D. R., Oehlschlager, A. C., Slessor, K. N., and Pierce, H. D. Jr. (1982). Variation in response of

Trypodendron lineatum from two continents to semiochemicals and trap form. *Environmental Entomology* **11**, 403–8.

Borden, J. H., Chong, L. J., and Fuchs, M. C. (1983). Application of semiochemicals in post-logging manipulation of the mountain pine beetle, *Dendroctonus ponderosae* (Coleoptera: Scolytidae). *Journal of Economic Entomology* **76**, 1428–32.

Borden, J. H., Ryker, L. C., Chong, L. J., Pierce, H. D. Jr., Johnston, B. D., and Oehlschlager, A. C. (1987). Response of the mountain pine beetle, *Dendroctonus ponderosae* Hopkins (Coleoptera: Scolytidae), to five semiochemicals in British Columbia lodgepole pine forests. *Canadian Journal of Forest Research* **17**, 118–28.

Botterweg, P. F. (1982). Dispersal and flight behaviour of the spruce bark beetle *Ips typographus* in relation to sex, size and fat content. *Zeitschrift für angewandte Entomologie* **94**, 466–89.

Bowers, W. S. (1984). Insect-plant interactions: endocrine defences. In *Origins and development of adaptation* (ed. D. Evered and G. M. Collins), pp. 119–37. Pitman Books, London.

Bowers, W. S., Fales, H. M., Thompson, M. J., and Uebel, E. C. (1966). Juvenile hormone: identification of an active compound from balsam fir. *Science* **154**, 1020–2.

Bowers, W. S., Ohta, T., Cleere, J. S., and Marsella, P. A. (1976). Discovery of anti-juvenile hormones in plants. *Science* **193**, 542–7.

Brand, J. M., Bracke, J. W., Markovetz, A. J., Wood, D. L., and Browne, L. E. (1975). Production of verbenol pheromone by bacterium isolated from bark beetles. *Nature* **254**, 136–7.

Brand, J. M., Brack, J. W., Britton, L. N., Markovetz, A. J., and Barras, S. J. (1976). Bark beetle pheromones: production of verbenone by a mycangial fungus of *Dendroctonus frontalis*. *Journal of Chemical Ecology* **2**, 195–9.

Bridgen, M. R. and Hanover, J. W. (1982). Indirect selection for pest resistance using terpenoid compounds. In *Resistance to diseases and pests in forest trees* (ed. H. M. Heybroek, B. R. Stephan and K. van Weissenberg), pp. 161–8. Centre for Agricultural Publishing and Documentation, Wageningen.

Brix, H. (1971). Effects of nitrogen fertilisation on photosynthesis and respiration in Douglas-fir. *Forest Science* **17**, 407–14.

Brookes, M. H., Stark, R. W., and Campbell, R. W. (ed.) (1978). *The Douglas-fir tussock moth: a synthesis*. USDA Forest Service Technical Bulletin 1585.

Brown, R. M. and Billany, D. J. (1976). Biological control. The web-spinning larch sawfly *Cephalcia alpina*. *Report on Forest Research*, p. 38.

Browne, F. G. (1968). Pests and diseases of forest plantation trees. Clarendon Press, Oxford.

Bryant, D. G. (1974). A review of the taxonomy, biology and importance of the adelgid pests of true firs. *Newfoundland Forest Research Centre Information Report N-X-III*.

Bryant, J. P., Chapin, F. S. III., and Klein, D. R. (1983). Carbon/nutrient balance of boreal plants in relation to vertebrate herbivory. *Oikos* **40**, 357–68.

Bryant, J. P., Chapin, F. S. III., Reichardt, P. B., and Clausen, T. P. (1987). Response of winter chemical defense in Alaska paper birch and green alder to manipulation of plant carbon/nutrient balance. *Oecologia* (Berlin) **72**, 510–4.

Buckner, C. H. (1966). The role of vertebrate predators in the biological control of forest insects. *Annual Review of Entomology* **11**, 449–70.

Bultman, T. L. and Faeth, S. H. (1985). Patterns of intra- and interspecific association in leaf-mining insects on three oak host species. *Ecological Entomology* **10**, 121–9.

Busby, R. J. N. and Grayson. A. J. (1981). *Investment appraisal in forestry with particular reference to conifers in Britain.* HMSO, London.

Buse, A. (1977). The importance of birds in the dispersal of nuclear polyhedrosis virus of European spruce sawfly, *Gilpinia hercyniae* (Hymenoptera: Diprionidae) in mid-Wales. *Entomologia experimentalis et applicata* **22**, 191–9.

Buxton, R. D. (1983). Forest management and the pine processionary moth. *Outlook on Agriculture* **12**, 34–9.

Bychawska, S. and Sliwa, E. (1982). The fight against *Lymantria monacha* in 1981 (in Polish). *Las Polski No. 2*, 25–8.

Byers, J. A. and Wood, D. L. (1980). Interspecific inhibition of the response of the bark beetles, *Dendroctonus brevicomis* and *Ips paraconfusus*, to their pheromones in the field. *Journal of Chemical Ecology* **6**, 149–64.

Byrne, K. J., Swiger, A. A., Silverstein, R. M., Borden, J. H., and Stokkink, E. (1974). Sulcatol: population aggregation pheromone in the scolytid beetle, *Gnathotrichus sulcatus. Journal of Insect Physiology* **20**, 1895–900.

Caltagirone, L. E. (1981). Landmark examples in classical biological control. *Annual Review of Entomology* **26**, 213–32.

Campbell, R. W. (1975). The gypsy moth and its natural enemies. *USDA Forest Service, Agricultural Information Bulletin 381.*

Cannell, M. G. R. (1984). Sitka spruce. *Biologist* **31**, 255–61.

Cannell, M. G. R. and Smith, R. I. (1980). Yields of minirotation closely spaced hardwoods in temperate regions: review and appraisal. *Forest Science* **26**, 415–28.

Cardé, R. T. (1981*a*). Disruption of long-distance pheromone communication in the oriental fruit moth: camouflaging the natural aerial trails from females? In *Management of insect pests with semiochemicals: concepts and practice* (ed. E. R. Mitchell), pp. 385–98. Plenum Press, New York.

Cardé, R. T. (1981*b*). Precopulatory sexual behaviour of the adult gypsy moth. In *The gypsy moth: research toward integrated pest management* (ed. C. C. Doane and M. L. McManus), pp. 572–87. USDA Forest Service Technical Bulletin 1584.

Cardé, R. T., Doane, C. C., Granett, J., and Roelofs, W. L. (1975). Disruption of pheromone communication in the gypsy moth: Some behavioural effects of disparlure and an attractant modifier. *Environmental Entomology* **4**, 793–6.

Carey, M. L. and O'Brien, D. (1979). Biomass nutrient content and distribution in a stand of Sitka spruce. *Irish Forestry* **36**, 25–35.

Carle, P. (1975). *Dendroctonus micans* (Col. Scolytidae), a pest of spruce (bibliographical note) (in French). *Revue Forestière Française* **27**, 115–28.

Carpenter, J. R. (1940). Insect outbreaks in Europe. *Journal of Animal Ecology* **9**, 108–47.

Carron, L. T. (1985). *A history of forestry in Australia*. Australian National University Press.

Carrow, J. R. and Betts, R. E. (1973). Effects of different foliar-applied nitrogen fertilisers on balsam woolly aphid. *Canadian Journal of Forest Research* **3**, 122–39.

Carruthers, R. I. and Soper, R. S. (1987). Fungal diseases. In *Epizootiology of insect diseases* (ed. J. R. Fuxa and Y. Tanada), pp. 357–416. John Wiley, New York.

Carson, R. (1962). *Silent Spring*. Houghton Mifflin Co., Boston.

Carter, C. I. (1971). Conifer woolly aphids (Adelgidae) in Britain. *Forestry Commission Bulletin No 42*. HMSO, London.

Carter, C. I. (1972). Winter temperatures and survival of the green spruce aphid. *Forestry Commission Forest Record 84*. HMSO, London.

Carter, C. I. (1977). Impact of green spruce aphid on growth. *Forestry Commission Research and Development Paper 116*. HMSO, London.

Carter, C. I. and Barson, G. (1973). Flight activity of alate Adelgids (Homoptera, Aphidoidea) in southern England. *Bulletin of Entomological Research* **62**, 507–16.

Carter, C. I. and Gibbs, J. N. (1983). Pests and diseases of forest crops. In *Pest and disease control handbook* (ed. N. Scopes and M. Ledieu), pp. 575–91. BCPC Publications.

Carter, C. I. and Nichols, J. F. A. (1988). The green spruce aphid and Sitka spruce provenances in Britain. *Forestry Commission Occasional Paper 19*. HMSO, London.

Cates, R. G., Redak, R. A., and Henderson, C. B. (1983). Patterns of defensive natural product chemistry: Douglas fir and western spruce budworm interactions. In *Plant resistance to insects* (ed. P. A. Hedin) pp. 3–19. *ACS symposium series 208*. American Chemical Society, Washington.

Ceballos, G. and Zarco, E. (1952). An experiment on the biological control of an outbreak of *Diprion pini* (L.) in stands of *Pinus silvestris* in the Sierra de Albarracin (in Spanish) *Instituto Espanol de Entomologia, Madrid*, 1–38.

Chapin, F. S. III., Johnson, D. A., and McKendrick, J. D. (1980). Seasonal movement of nutrients in plants of differing growth form in an Alaskan tundra ecosystem: implications for herbivory. *Journal of Ecology* **68**, 189–209.

Chapman, R. F. (1974). The chemical inhibition of feeding by phytophagous insects: a review. *Bulletin of Entomological Research* **64**, 339–63.

Chapman, V. J. (1958). The geographical status of New Zealand lowland forest vegetation. *New Zealand Geographer* **14**, 103–14.

Chararas, C. (1977). Problems presented in different Mediterranean countries by insect pests of forests. Insect pests of forests in Tunisia (in French). *Compte rendu des séances de l'Académie d'agriculture de France* **62**, 1236–42.

Chen, A. C. and Mayer, R. T. (1985). Insecticides: effects on the cuticle. In *Comprehensive insect physiology biochemistry and pharmacology*, Vol. 12, *Insect control* (ed. G. A. Kerkut, L. I. Gilbert), pp. 57–77. Pergamon Press, Oxford.

Cheng, L. (1970). Timing of attack by *Lypha dubia* Fall (Diptera: Tachinidae) on the winter moth *Operophtera brumata* (L.) (Lepidoptera: Geometridae) as a factor affecting parasite success. *Journal of Animal Ecology* **39**, 313–20.

Christiansen, E. (1985). *Ips/Ceratocystis* – infection of Norway spruce: what is a deadly dosage? *Zeitschrift für angewandte Entomologie* **99**, 6–11.

Christiansen, E. and Bakke, A. (1971). Feeding activity of the pine weevil *Hylobius abietis* L. (Col., Curculionidae) during a hot period. *Norsk Entomologisk Tidsskrift* **18**, 109–11.

Christiansen, E. and Ericsson, A. (1986). Starch reserves in *Picea abies* in relation to defence reaction against a bark beetle transmitted blue-stain fungus, *Ceratocystis polonica*. *Canadian Journal of Forest Research* **16**, 78–83.

Christiansen, E. and Horntvedt, R. (1983). Combined *Ips/Ceratocystis* attack on Norway spruce, and defensive mechanisms of the trees. *Zeitschrift für angewandte Entomologie* **96**, 110–18.

Claridge, M. F. and Wilson, M. R. (1981). Host plant associations, diversity and species-area relationships of mesophyll-feeding leafhoppers of trees and shrubs in Britain. *Ecological Entomology* **6**, 217–38.

Claridge, M. F. and Wilson, M. R. (1982). Insect herbivore guilds and species-area relationships: leafminers on British trees. *Ecological Entomology* **7**, 19–30.

Coaker, T. H. (1974). Crop pest problems resulting from chemical control. In *Origins of pest, parasite, disease and weed problems* (ed. J. M. Cherrett, G. R. Sagar), pp. 313–28. Blackwell Scientific Publications, Oxford.

Coley, P. D. (1983). Herbivory and defensive characteristics of tree species in a lowland tropical forest. *Ecological Monographs* **53**, 209–33.

Collins, B. M. and White, F. M. (1981) *Elementary forestry*. Reston Publishing Co. Inc., Reston.

Commins, H. N. and Hassell, M. P. (1979). The dynamics of optimally foraging predators and parasitoids. *Journal of Animal Ecology* **48**, 335–51.

Connell, J. H. and Slatyer, R. O. (1977). Mechanisms of succession in natural communities and their role in community stability and organisation. *American Naturalist* **111**, 1119–44.

Connor, E. F. and McCoy, E. D. (1979). The statistics and biology of the species-area relationship. *American Naturalist* **113**, 791–833.

Connor, E. F., Faeth, S. H., Simberloff, D., and Opler, P. A. (1980). Taxonomic isolation and the accumulation of herbivorous insects: a comparison of introduced and native trees. *Ecological Entomology* **5**, 205–11.

Cooper, A. N. (1976). Recreation and amenity in coniferous production forests: some overseas observations and some suggestions for New Zealand. *New Zealand Journal of Forestry* **21**, 43–57.

Cornell, H. V. and Washburn, J. O. (1979). Evolution of the richness-area correlation for cynipid gall wasps on oak trees: a comparison of two geographical areas. *Evolution* **33**, 257–74.

Coster, J. E., Payne, T. L., Hart, E. R., and Edson, L. J. (1977). Aggregation of the southern pine beetle in response to attractive host trees. *Environmental Entomology* **6**, 725–31.

Coulson, R. N. (1979). Population dynamics of bark beetles. *Annual Review of Entomology* **24**, 417–47.

Coulson, R. N. and Saunders, M. C. (1987). Computer-assisted decision-making as applied to entomology. *Annual Review of Entomology* **32**, 415–37.

Coulson, R. N. and Witter, J. A. (1984). *Forest entomology, ecology and management*. J. Wiley, New York.

Coulson, R. N., Mayyasi, A. M., Foltz, J. L., and Hain, F. P. (1976). Interspecific competition between *Monochamus titillator* and *Dendroctonus frontalis*. *Environmental Entomology* **5**, 235–47.

Coulson, R. N., Hennier, P. B., Flamm, R. O., Rykiel, E. J., Hu, L. C., and Payne, T. L. (1983). The role of lightning in the epidemiology of the southern pine beetle. *Zeitschrift für angewandte Entomologie* **96**, 182–93.

Coutts, M. P. (1970). The physiological effects of the mucus secretion of *Sirex noctilio* on *Pinus radiata*. *Australian Forest Research* **4**, 23–6.

Cowling, E. B. and Merrill, W. (1966). Nitrogen in wood and its role in wood deterioration. *Canadian Journal of Botany* **44**, 1539–54.

Crawley, M. J., (1983). *Herbivory. The dynamics of animal–plant interactions*. Blackwell Scientific Publications, Oxford.

Crawley, M. J. (1985). Reduction of oak-fecundity by low-density herbivore populations. *Nature* **314**, 163–4.

Crooke, M. (1979). The development of populations of insects. In *Ecology of even-aged forest plantations* (ed. E. D. Ford, D. C. Malcolm and J. Atterson), pp. 209–17. Institute of Terrestrial Ecology.

Cuevas, P., Montoya, R., Belles, X., Camps, F., Coll, J., Guerrero, A., and Riba, M. (1983). Initial field trials with the synthetic sex pheromone of the processionary moth *Thaumetopoea pityocampa* (Denis and Schiff). *Journal of Chemical Ecology* **9**, 85–93.

Cunningham, J. C. (1982). Field trials with baculoviruses: Control of forest insects. In *Microbial and viral pesticides* (ed. E. Kurstak), pp. 335–86. Marcel Dekker, New York.

Dadd, R. H. (1984). Nutrition: organisms. In *Comprehensive insect physiology biochemistry and pharmacology*, Vol. 4, *Regulation: digestion, nutrition, excretion* (ed. G. A. Kerkut and L. I. Gilbert), pp. 313–90. Pergamon Press, Oxford.

Dafauce, C. (1972). Synthesis of the current concept of integrated control (in Spanish). *Boletin de la Estacion Central de Ecologia* **1**, 5–13.

Dajoz, R. (1980). *Ecologie des insectes forestiers*. Gauthier-Villars, Paris.

Daterman, G. E. (1982). Control of western pine shoot borer damage by mating disruption – a reality. In *Insect suppression with controlled release pheromone systems*, Vol. II (ed. A. F. Kydonieus and M. Beroza), pp. 155–63. CRC Press, Boca Raton, Florida.

Daterman, G. E., Sartwell, C., and Sower, L. L. (1980). Prospects for controlling forest Lepidoptera with controlled release pheromone formulations. In *Controlled release of bioactive materials* (ed. R. Baker), pp. 213–26. Academic Press, London.

Day, K. (1984). The growth and decline of a population of the spruce aphid *Elatobium abietinum* during a three year study, and the changing pattern of fecundity, recruitment and alary polymorphism in a Northern Ireland forest. *Oecologia (Berlin)* **64**, 118–24.

DeBach, P. (ed.) (1964). *Biological control of insect pests and weeds*. Chapman and Hall, London.

DeBach, P. (1974). *Biological control by natural enemies*. Cambridge University Press, Cambridge.

DeHayes, D. H. (1981). Genetic variation in susceptibility of *Abies balsamea* to *Mindarus abietinus*. *Canadian Journal of Forest Research* **11**, 30–5.

DeHayes, D. H. (1983). Selection for insect resistance in forest trees. In *Proceedings, forest defoliator–host interactions: A comparison between gypsy moth and spruce budworms* (ed. R. L. Talerico and M. Montgomery) pp. 9–14. USDA General Technical Report NE 85.

Demolin, G. (1969). Bioecology of the pine processionary *Thaumetopoea pityocampa* Schiff. The incidence of climatic factors (in Spanish). *Boletin del Servicio de Plagas Forestales* **12**, 9–24.

Demolin, G. and Millet, A. (1983). Dimilin applied at three different concentrations to control the pine processionary caterpillar, *Thaumetopoea pityocampa* (in French). *Revue Forestière Française* **35**, 107–10.

Dempster, J. P. (1983). The natural control of populations of butterflies and moths. *Biological Reviews* **58**, 461–81.

Dempster, J. P. and Pollard, E. (1981). Fluctuations in resource availability and insect populations. *Oecologia* **50**, 412–6.

Dempster, J. P. and Pollard, E. (1986). Spatial heterogeneity, stochasticity and the detection of density dependence in animal populations. *Oikos* **46**, 413–16.

Denno, R. F., Raup, M. J., and Tallamy, D. W. (1981). Organisation of a guild of sap-feeding insects: Equilibrium vs non-equilibrium coexistence. In *Insect life history patterns: Habitat and geographic variation* (ed. R. F. Denno and H. Dingle), pp. 151–81. Springer-Verlag, New York.

Deseo, K. V. (1986). Control of tree- and stem-borer pests with insect-parasitic nematodes. In *Principles of fundamental and applied aspects of invertebrate pathology* (ed. R. A. Samson, J. M. Vlak and R. Peters), pp. 271–4. Proceedings from 4th international colloquium of invertebrate pathology. Veldhoven.

Dickison, R. B. B., Haggis, M. J., and Rainey, R. C. (1983). Spruce budworm moth flight and storms: case study of a cold front system. *Journal of Climate and Applied Meteorology* **22**, 278–86.

Dickison, R. B. B., Haggis, M. J., Rainey, R. C., and Burns, L. M. D. (1986). Spruce budworm moth flight and storms: further studies using aircraft and radar. *Journal of Climate and Applied Meteorology* **25**, 1600–8.

Dixon, A. F. G. (1970). Quality and availability of food for a sycamore aphid population. In *Animal populations in relation to their food resources* (ed. A. Watson), pp. 271–87. Blackwell Scientific Publications, Oxford.

Dixon, A. F. G. (1971). The role of aphids in wood formation II. The effect of the lime aphid, *Eucallipterus tiliae* L. (Aphididae), on the growth of lime, *Tilia × vulgaris* Hayne. *Journal of Applied Ecology* **8**, 393–9.

Dixon, A. F. G. (1979). Sycamore aphid numbers: the role of weather, host and aphid. In *Population dynamics*. The 20th Symposium of The British Ecological Society (ed. R. M. Anderson, B. D. Taylor and L. R. Taylor), pp. 105–21. Blackwell Scientific Publications, Oxford.

Dixon, A. F. G. (1985). *Aphid ecology*. Blackie, Glasgow.

Dixon, A. F. G. and McKay, S. (1970). Aggregation in the sycamore aphid *Drepanosiphum platanoides* (Schr.) (Hemiptera: Aphididae), and its relevence to the regulation of population growth. *Journal of Animal Ecology* **39**, 439–54.

Doane, C. C. and McManus, M. L. (ed.) (1981). *The gypsy moth: research toward integrated pest management*. USDA Forest Service Technical Bulletin 1584.

Doom, D. and Frenken, G. W. P. (1980). Postponement of replanting as a silvicultural method to prevent damage by the large pine weevil *Curculio abietis* (in Dutch). *Nederlands Bosbouwtijdschrift* **52**, 217–27.

Doom, D. and Luitjes, J. (1971). The influence of felled Scots pine on the population density of the pine shoot beetle (in Dutch). *Nederlands Bosbouwtijdschrift* **43**, 180–91.

Dornbusch, M. (1964). Bird enclosures in forestry, a forest protective and cultural measure (in German). *Aufsatz Vogelschutz und Vogelkunde Akademie Landwirtschaftwissenschaften*. DDR, Berlin No. 1, 11–5.

Doutt, R. L. (1958). Vice, virtue and the Vedalia. *Bulletin of the Entomological Society of America* **4**, 119–23.

Duff, G. H. and Nolan, N. J. (1953). Growth and morphogenesis in the Canadian forest species. I. The controls of cambial and apical activity in *Pinus resinosa* Ait. *Canadian Journal of Botany* **31**, 471–513.

Duffey, S. S. (1980). Sequestration of plant natural products by insects. *Annual Review of Entomology* **25**, 447–77.

Duffey, S. S., Bloem, K. A., and Campbell, B. C. (1986). Consequences of sequestration of plant natural products in plant-insect-parasitoid interactions. In *Interactions of plant resistance and parasitoids and predators of insects* (ed. D. J. Boethel and R. D. Eikenbarry), pp. 31–60. Ellis Horwood Ltd., Chichester.

Dulmage, H. T. and Cooperators (1981). Insecticidal activity of isolates of *Bacillus thuringiensis* and their potential for pest control. In *Microbial control of pests and plant diseases 1970–1980* (ed. H. D. Burges), pp. 193–222. Academic Press, London.

Dulmage, H. T. and Aizawa, K. (1982). Distribution of *Bacillus thuringiensis* in nature. In *Microbial and viral pesticides* (ed. E. Kurstak), pp. 209–38. Marcel Dekker, New York.

Dusaussoy, G. and Geri, C. (1971). Study of the residual populations of *Diprion pini* L. at Fontainebleu after the outbreak of 1963–1964 (in French). *Annales des Sciences Forestières* **28**, 297–322.

Ebert, W. and Otto, D. (1969). The population dynamics of pine looper moth (*Bupalus piniarius* Linne) in the north German lowland (in German). *Wanderversammlung deutscher Entomologen* **80**, 309–16.

Edmunds, G. F. and Alstad, D. N. (1978). Coevolution in insect herbivores and conifers. *Science* **199**, 941–5.

Edwards, P. J. and Wratten, S. D. (1983). Wound induced defences in plants and their consequences for patterns of insect grazing. *Oecologia (Berlin)* **59**, 88–93.

Ehler, L. E. and Hall, R. W. (1982). Evidence for competitive exclusion of introduced natural enemies in biological control. *Environmental Entomology* **11**, 1–4.

Ehrlich, P. R. and Raven, P. H. (1964). Butterflies and plants: a study in coevolution. *Evolution* **18**, 586–603.

Eichhorn, O. (1978). Prognosis of the seasonal flight periods and sequence of generations of the pine sawfly *Diprion pini* (Hym., Diprionidae) (in German). *Anzeiger für Schadlingskunde, Pflanzenschutz, Umweltschutz* **51**, 65–9.

Eichhorn, O. and Pausch, K. L. (1986). Studies on the spruce webspinning sawflies of the genus *Cephalcia* spp. Panz. (Hym., Pamphiliidae). I. Problems of the generation development of *C. abietis* L. (in German). *Journal of Applied Entomology* **101**, 101–11.

Eidmann, H. H. (1976). Aspects of biological control of forest insects in Sweden. *Ambio* **5**, 23–6.

Eidmann, H. H. (1979). Integrated management of pine weevil (*Hylobius abietis* L.) populations in Sweden. *USDA General Technical Report WO-8*, 103–9.

Eidmann, H. H. (1981). Pine weevil research for better reforestations. *XVII IUFRO World Congress, Japan Div. 2*, 441–7.

Eidmann, H. H. (1983). Management of spruce bark beetle *Ips typographus* in Scandinavia using pheromones. *10th International Congress of Plant Protection* **3**, 1042–50.

Eidmann, H. H. and Ehnstrom, B. (1975). Establishment of *Scymnus impexus* (Col., Coccinellidae) in Sweden (in German). *Entomologisk Tidskrift* **96**, 14–6.

Eikenbary, R. D. and Fox, R. C. (1968). Responses of Nantucket pine tip moth parasites to tree level, orientation, and hosts per pine tip. *Annals of the Entomological Society of America* **61**, 1380–4.

Eisner, T., Johanessee, J. S., Carrel, J., Hendry, L. B., and Meinwald, J. (1974). Defensive use by an insect of a plant resin. *Science* **184**, 996–9.

Ekblad, R. B. and Barry, J. W. (1984). Technological progress in aerial application of pesticides. In *Chemical and biological control in forestry* (ed. W. Y. Garner and J. Harvey Jr.), pp. 79–94. American Chemical Society, Washington.

Eldridge, R. H. and Simpson, J. A. (1987). Development of contingency plans for use against exotic pests and diseases of trees and timber 3. Histories of control measures against some introduced pests and diseases of forests and forest products in Australia. *Australian Forestry* **50**, 24–36.

Elkinton, J. S. and Cardé, R. T. (1980). Distribution, dispersal and apparent survival of male gypsy moths as determined by capture in pheromone baited traps. *Environmental Entomology* **9**, 729–37.

Embree, D. G. (1965). The population dynamics of the winter moth in Nova Scotia 1954–1962. *Memoirs of the Entomological Society of Canada* **46**, 1–57.

Embree, D. G. (1966). The role of introduced parasites in the control of the winter moth in Nova Scotia. *Canadian Entomologist* **98**, 1159–68.

Embree, D. G. (1971). The biological control of the winter moth in eastern Canada by introduced parasites. In *Biological control* (ed. C. B. Huffaker), pp. 217–26. Plenum Press, New York.

Entwistle, P. F. (1983). Control of insects by virus diseases. *Biocontrol news and information* **4**, 203–25.

Entwistle, P. F. and Evans, H. F. (1985). Viral control. In *Comprehensive insect physiology biochemistry and pharmacology*, Vol. 12, *Insect control* (ed. G. A. Kerkut and L. I. Gilbert), pp. 347–412. Pergamon Press, Oxford.

Entwistle, P. F., Adams, P. H. W., and Evans, H. F. (1977a). Epizootiology of a nuclear-polyhedrosis virus in European spruce sawfly (*Gilpinia hercyniae*): the status of birds as dispersal agents of the virus during the larval season. *Journal of Invertebrate Pathology* **29**, 354–60.

Entwistle, P. F., Adams, P. H. W., and Evans, H. F. (1977*b*). Epizootiology of a nuclear-polyhedrosis virus in European spruce sawfly, *Gilpinia hercyniae*: birds as dispersal agents of the virus during winter. *Journal of Invertebrate Pathology* **30**, 15–19.

Entwistle, P. F., Adams, P. H. W., Evans, H. F., and Rivers, C. F. (1983). Epizootiology of a nuclear polyhedrosis virus (Baculoviridae) in European spruce sawfly (*Gilpinia hercyniae*): spread of disease from small epicentres in comparison with spread of baculovirus diseases in other hosts. *Journal of Applied Ecology* **20**, 473–87.

Ericsson, E., Larsson, S., and Tenow, O. (1980). Effects of early and late season defoliation on growth and carbohydrate dynamics in Scots pine. *Journal of Applied Ecology* **17**, 747–69.

Escherich, K. (1923). *Die Forstinsekten Mitteleuropas*. Vol. 2. Paul Parey, Berlin.

Escherich, K. (1931). *Die Forstinsekten Mitteleuropas*. Vol. 3. Paul Parey, Berlin.

Evans, H. F. (1986). Ecology and epizootiology of baculoviruses. In *The biology of baculoviruses*, Vol. II, *Practical application for insect control* (ed. R. R. Granados and B. A. Federici), pp. 89–132. CRC Press, Boca Raton, Florida.

Evans, J. (1982). *Plantation forestry in the tropics*. Clarendon Press, Oxford.

Everard, J. E. (1974). *Fertilisers in the establishment of conifers in Wales and southern England*. Forestry Commission Booklet 41.

Faeth, S. H. and Simberloff, D. (1981). Experimental isolation of oak host plants: effects on mortality, survivorship, and abundances of leaf-mining insects. *Ecology* **62**, 625–35.

Fagerström, T., Larsson, S., Lohm, U., and Tenow, O. (1978). Growth in Scots pine (*Pinus silvestris* L.): a hypothesis on response to *Blastophagus piniperda* L. (Col., Scolytidae) attacks. *Forest Ecology and Management* **1**, 273–81.

Fagerström, T., Larsson, S., and Tenow, O. (1987). Optimal defence in plants. *Functional Ecology* **1**, 73–81.

Fares, Y., Sharpe, P. J. H., and Magnuson, C. E. (1980). Pheromone dispersion in forests. *Journal of Theoretical Biology* **84**, 335–59.

Faulkner, R. (1987). Genetics and breeding of Sitka spruce. *Proceedings of the Royal Society of Edinburgh* **98B**, 41–50.

Feeny, P. P. (1968). Effects of oak leaf tannins on larval growth of the winter oak moth *Operophtera brumata*. *Journal of Insect Physiology* **14**, 805–17.

Feeny, P. P. (1969). Inhibitory effect of oak leaf tannins on the hydrolysis of proteins by trypsin. *Phytochemistry* **8**, 2119–26.

Feeny, P. (1970). Seasonal changes in oak leaf tannins and nutrients as a cause of spring feeding by winter moth caterpillars. *Ecology* **51**, 565–81.

Feeny, P. P. (1975). Biochemical coevolution between plants and their insect herbivores. In *Coevolution of animals and plants* (ed. L. E. Gilbert and P. H. Raven), pp. 3–19. University of Texas Press, Austin.

Feeny, P. (1976). Plant apparency and chemical defence. In *Biochemical interactions between plants and insects* (ed. J. W. Wallace and R. L. Mansell). *Recent advances in phytochemistry*, Vol. 10, 1–40. Plenum Press, New York.

Ferrell, G. T. (1980). *Risk-rating systems for mature red fir and white fir in northern California*. General Technical Report PSW-39. USDA Forest Service, Pacific Southwest Forest and Range Experiment Station.

Ferron, P. (1978). Biological control of insect pests by entomogenous fungi. *Annual Review of Entomology* **23**, 409–42.

Fisher, M. and Dixon, A. F. G. (1986). Role of photoperiod in the timing of dispersal in the green spruce aphid *Elatobium abietinum*. *Journal of Animal Ecology* **55**, 657–67.

Fisher, R. A. and Greenbank, D. O. (1979). A case study of research into insect movement: spruce budworm in New Brunswick. In *Movement of highly mobile insects: concepts and methodology in research* (ed. R. L. Rabb and G. G. Kennedy), pp. 220–9. North Carolina State University, Raleigh, North Carolina.

Fogal, W. H. and Lopushanski, S. M. (1984). Stem injection of insecticides for control of white spruce seed and cone insects. In *Proceedings of the cone and seed insects working party conference. Working Party S2.07,01* (ed. H. O. Yates), pp. 157–67. Canadian Forestry Service, Ontario.

Forestry Commission (1984). *Forestry Commission 63rd annual report and accounts 1982–83*, 31. HMSO, London.

Forestry Commission (1987). *Forestry facts and figures 1986–87*. Forestry Commission, Edinburgh.

Forrest, G. I. (1980). Genotypic variation among native Scots pine plantations in Scotland based on monoterpene analysis. *Forestry* **53**, 101–28.

Fowler, S. V. (1984). Foliage value, apparency and defence investment in birch seedlings and trees. *Oecologia (Berlin)* **62**, 387–92.

Fowler, S. V. and Lawton, J. H. (1985). Rapidly induced defences and talking trees: the devil's advocate position. *American Naturalist* **126**, 181–95.

Fox, L. R. (1981). Defense and dynamics in plant-herbivore systems. *American Zoologist* **21**, 853–64.

Fox, L. R. and Macauley, B. J. (1977). Insect grazing on *Eucalyptus* in response to variation in leaf tannins and nitrogen. *Oecologia (Berl.)* **29**, 145–62.

Fraenkel, G. (1959). The raison d'etre of secondary plant substances. *Science* **129**, 1466–70.

Franz, J. M. (1958). The effectiveness of predators and food in limiting gradations of *Adelges (Dreyfusia) piceae* (Ratz.) in Europe. *10th International Congress in Entomology* **4**, 781–7.

Franz, J. M. and Krieg, A. (1982). *Biologische Schadlingsbekampfung*. Paul Parey, Berlin.

Fraval, R. (1986). Regulation of populations of *Lymantria dispar* (L.) (Lep., Lymantriidae) in the Atlantic coastal plains of Morocco: effects of climate, natural enemies and anthropeic factors (in French). *Journal of Applied Entomology* **102**, 38–52.

Fritz, R. S. and Price, P. W. (1988). Genetic variation among plants and insect community structure: willows and sawflies. *Ecology* **69**, 845–56.

Führer, E. (1985). Air pollution and the incidence of forest insect problems. *Zeitschrift für angewandte Entomologie* **99**, 371–7.

Furuta, K. (1982). Natural control of *Lymantria dispar* L. (Lep., Lymantriidae) population at low density levels in Hokkaido (Japan). *Zeitschrift für angewandte Entomologie* **93,** 513–22.

Gallun, R. L. and Khush, G. S. (1980). Genetic factors affecting expression and stability of resistance. In *Breeding plants resistant to insects* (ed. F. G. Maxwell and P. R. Jennings), pp. 63–85. J. Wiley, New York.

Genys, J. B. and Harman, D. M. (1976). Variation in larch sawfly attack of different species and geographic strains of larch, exhibiting diverse growth rates. *Journal of Economic Entomology* **69,** 573–8.

Georgevits, R. P. (1980). New perspectives for the control of the pine processionary (*Thaumetopoea pityocampa* Schiff.) with Dimilin (in Greek). *Anakoinoseis Idrumaton Dasikon Ereunon* **8,** 7–25.

Gershenzon, J. (1984). Changes in the level of plant secondary metabolites under water and nutrient stress. In *Phytochemical adaptation to stress* (ed. B. N. Timmermann, C. Steelink and F. A. Loewus), pp. 273–320. Plenum, New York.

Gibb, J. A. (1960). Populations of tits and goldcrests and their food supply in pine plantations. *Ibis* **102,** 163–208.

Gibbs, J. N. (1978). Intercontinental epidemiology of Dutch elm disease. *Annual Review of Phytopathology* **16,** 287–307.

Gibbs, J. N. and Wainhouse, D. (1986). Spread of forest pests and pathogens in the northern hemisphere. *Forestry* **59,** 141–53.

Gibson, I. A. S. and Jones, T. (1977). Monoculture as the origin of major forest pests and diseases. In *Origin of pest, parasite, disease and weed problems* (ed. J. M. Cherrett and G. R. Sagar), pp. 139–61. Blackwell Scientific Publications, Oxford.

Gibson, I. A. S., Burley, J., and Speight, M. R. (1980). The adoption of agricultural practices for the development of heritable resistance to pests and pathogens in forest crops. *Commonwealth Forestry Institute Occasional Papers, No. 18,* 1–24. Commonwealth Forestry Institute, Oxford.

Gibson, I. A. S., Burley, J., and Speight, M. R. (1982). The adoption of agricultural practices for the development of heritable resistance to pests and pathogens in forest crops. In *Resistance to diseases and pests in forest trees* (ed. H. M. Heybroek, B. R. Stephan, and K. von Weissenberg), pp. 9–21. Centre for Agricultural Publishing and Documentation (Pudoc), Wageningen.

Gilbert, B. L. and Norris, D. M. (1968). A chemical basis for bark beetle (*Scolytus*) distinction between host and non-host trees. *Journal of Insect Physiology* **14,** 1063–8.

Gould, F. (1983). Genetics of plant-herbivore systems: interactions between applied and basic study. In *Variable plants and herbivores in natural and managed systems* (ed. R. F. Denno and M. S. McClure), pp. 599–653. Academic Press, New York.

Goyer, R. A. and Benjamin, D. M. (1972). Influence of soil fertility on infestation of jack pine plantations by the pine root weevil. *Forest Science* **18,** 139–47.

Graham, A. R. (1958). Recoveries of introduced species of parasites of the winter moth, *Operophtera brumata* (L.) (Lepidoptera: Geometridae), in Nova Scotia. *Canadian Entomologist* **90,** 595–6.

Graham-Bryce, I. J. (1977). Recent developments in the chemical control of agricultural pests and diseases in relation to ecological effects. In *Ecological effects of pesticides* (ed. F. H. Perring and K. Mellanby), pp. 47–60. Academic Press, London.

Graham-Bryce, I. J. (1983). Formulation and application of biologically active chemicals in relation to efficacy and side effects. In *Natural products for innovative pest management* (ed. D. L. Whitehead and W. S. Bowers), pp. 463–73. Pergamon Press, Oxford.

Graham-Bryce, I. J. (1987). Chemical methods. In *Integrated pest management* (ed. A. J. Burn, T. H. Coaker and P. C. Jepson), pp. 113–59. Academic Press, London.

Granett, J., Dunbar, D. M., and Weseloh, R. M. (1976). Gypsy moth control with Dimilin sprays timed to minimise effects on the parasite *Apanteles melanoscelus*. *Journal of Economic Entomology* **69**, 403–4.

Gray, B. (1972). Economic tropical forest entomology. *Annual Review of Entomology* **17**, 313–54.

Greathead, D. J. (ed.) (1976). *A review of biological control in western and southern Europe*. Technical communication No. 7. Commonwealth Institute of Biological Control.

Greenbank, D. O. (1957). The role of climate and dispersal in the initiation of outbreaks of the spruce budworm in New Brunswick. II. The role of dispersal. *Canadian Journal of Zoology* **35**, 385–403.

Greenbank, D. O. (1963). The development of the outbreak. In *The dynamics of epidemic spruce budworm populations* (ed. R. F. Morris). *Memoirs of the Entomological Society of Canada* No. 31, 19–23.

Greenbank, D. O., Schaefer, G. W. and Rainey, R. C. (1980). Spruce budworm (Lepidoptera: Tortricidae) moth flight and dispersal: new understanding from canopy observations, radar, and aircraft. *Memoirs of the Entomological Society of Canada* **110**, 1–49.

Grégoire, J.-C. (1988). The greater European spruce bark beetle. In *Dynamics of forest insect populations. Patterns, causes, implications* (ed. A. A. Berryman), pp. 455–78. Plenum, New York.

Grégoire, J.-C., Merlin, J., Pasteels, J. M., Jaffuel, R., Vouland, G. and Schvester, D. (1985). Biocontrol of *Dendroctonus micans* by *Rhizophagus grandis* Gyll. (Col., Rhizophagidae) in the Massif Central (France). A first appraisal of the mass-rearing and release methods. Proceedings of the IUFRO conference on man-made outbreaks of forest pests and their control. Gottingen 1984. *Zeitschrift für angewandte Entomologie* **99**, 182–90.

Greig, B. J. W. and Gibbs, J. N. (1983). Control of Dutch elm disease in Britain. In *Research on Dutch elm disease in Europe* (ed. D. A. Burdekin). *Forestry Commission Bulletin* **60**, 10–16.

Grier, C. C. and Waring, R. H. (1974). Conifer foliage mass related to sapwood area. *Forest Science* **20**, 205–6.

Griffiths, K. J. (1969). The importance of coincidence in the functional and numerical responses of two parasites of the European pine sawfly, *Neodiprion sertifer*. *Canadian Entomologist* **101**, 673–713.

Grijpma, P. and Schuring, W. (1984). Development of the bark beetles *Ips typographus*, *Ips cembrae* and *Pityogenes chalcographus* in non-marketable thinning material (in Dutch). *Nederlands Bosbouwtijdschrift* **56**, 159–64.

Grison, P. (1969). Reflections on the use of *Smithiavirus pityocampae* Vago in the microbiological control of *Thaumetopoea pityocampa* Schiff (in Spanish). *Boletin del Servicio de Plagas Forestales* **12**, 105–12.

Grunwald, M. (1986). Ecological segregation of bark beetles (Coleoptera, Scolytidae) of spruce. *Journal of Applied Entomology* **101**, 176–87.

Györfi, J. (1951). Hymenopterous parasites and forest undergrowth (in German). *Zeitschrift für angewandte Entomologie* **33**, 32–47.

Hagen, K. S. (1986). Ecosystem analysis: Plant cultivars (HPR), entomophagous species and food supplements. In *Interactions of plant resistance and parasitoids and predators of insects* (ed. D. J. Boethel and R. D. Eikenbarry), pp. 151–97. Ellis Horwood Ltd., Chichester.

Hagen, K. S., Dadd, R. H., and Reese, J. (1984). The food of insects. In *Ecological entomology* (ed. C. B. Huffaker and R. L. Rabb), pp. 79–112. John Wiley, New York.

Hairston, N. G., Smith, F. E., and Slobodkin, L. B. (1960). Community structure, population control, and competition. *American Naturalist* **94**, 421–5.

Halperin, J. (1980). Control of the pine processionary caterpillar (*Thaumetopoea wilkinsoni* Tams) with diflubenzuron. *Phytoparasitica* **8**, 83–91.

Halperin, J. (1985). Control of the pine processionary caterpillar by acephate implants (preliminary trials). *International pest control* **27**, 70–1.

Hamilton, G. J. and Christie, J. M. (1971). *Forest management tables (metric).* Forestry Commission Booklet No. 34. HMSO, London.

Hamel, D. R. (1983). *Forest management chemicals. A guide to use when considering pesticides for forest management.* USDA Forest Service Agricultural Handbook No. 585.

Hamrick, J. L., Mitton, J. B., and Linhart, Y. B. (1981). Levels of genetic variation in trees: influence of life history characteristics. In *Isozymes of North American forest trees and forest insects* (ed. M. T. Conkle), pp. 1–64. USDA General Technical Report PSW-48.

Hanover, J. W. (1966). Environmental variation in the monoterpenes of *Pinus monticola* Dougl. *Phytochemistry* **5**, 713–7.

Hanover, J. W. (1967). Genetics of monoterpenes 1. Gene control of monoterpene levels in *Pinus monticola* Dougl. *Heredity* **21**, 73–84.

Hanover, J. W. (1975). Physiology of tree resistance to insects. *Annual Review of Entomology* **20**, 75–95.

Hanover, J. W. (1980). Breeding forest trees resistant to insects. In *Breeding plants resistant to insects* (ed. F. G. Maxwell and P. R. Jennings), pp. 487–511. J. Wiley, New York.

Hargrove, W. W., Crossley, D. A. Jr, and Seastedt, T. R. (1984). Shifts in insect herbivory in the canopy of black locust, *Robinia pseudacacia*, after fertilisation. *Oikos* **43**, 322–8.

Harris, K. M. (1970). Horse-chestnut scale. *The Arboricultural Association Journal* **1**, 257–62.

Harris, M. K. and Frederiksen, R. A. (1984). Concepts and methods regarding host plant resistance to arthropods and pathogens. *Annual Review of Phytopathology* **22**, 247–72.

Hassall, K. A. (1982). *The chemistry of pesticides. Their metabolism, mode of action and uses in crop protection.* Macmillan Press, London.

Hassell, M. P. (1968). The behavioural response of a tachinid fly (*Cyzenis albicans* (Fall.)) to its host, the winter moth (*Operophtera brumata* (L.)). *Journal of Animal Ecology* **37**, 627–39.

Hassell, M. P. (1978). *The dynamics of arthropod predator-prey systems.* Princeton University Press, Princeton, New Jersey.

Hassell, M. P. (1980). Foraging strategies, population models and biological control: a case study. *Journal of Animal Ecology* **49**, 603–28.

Hassell, M. P. (1982). Patterns of parasitism by insect parasitoids in patchy environments. *Ecological Entomology* **7**, 365–77.

Hassell, M. P. (1985). Insect natural enemies as regulating factors. *Journal of Animal Ecology* **54**, 323–34.

Hassell, M. P. and May, R. M. (1974). Aggregation of predators and insect parasites and its effect on stability. *Journal of Animal Ecology* **43**, 567–94.

Hassell, M. P., Lawton, J. H., and Beddington, J. R. (1977). Sigmoid functional responses by invertebrate predators and parasitoids. *Journal of Animal Ecology* **46**, 249–62.

Haukioja, E. (1980). On the role of plant defences in the fluctuation of herbivore populations. *Oikos* **35**, 202–13.

Haukioja, E. and Hanhimaki, S. (1985). Rapid wound-induced resistance in white birch (*Betula pubescens*) foliage to the geometrid *Epirrita autumnata*: a comparison of trees and moths within and outside the outbreak range of the moth. *Oecologia (Berlin)* **65**, 223–8.

Haukioja, E., Niemela, P., Iso-Iivari, L., Ojala, H., and Aro, E.-M. (1978). Birch leaves as a resource for herbivores I. Variation in the suitability of leaves. *Report of the Kevo Subarctic Research Station* **14**, 5–12.

Haukioja, E., Niemela, P., Iso-Iivari, L., Siren, S., Kapiainen, K., Laine, K. J., Hanhimaki, S., and Jokinen, M. (1981). The significance of birch in the population dynamics of the autumnal moth (in Finnish). *Luonnon Tutkija* **85**, 127–40.

Haukioja, E., Niemela, P., and Siren, S. (1985a). Foliage phenols and nitrogen in relation to growth, insect damage, and ability to recover after defoliation, in the mountain birch *Betula pubescens* ssp *tortuosa*. *Oecologia (Berlin)* **65**, 214–22.

Haukioja, E., Suomela, J., and Neuvonen, S. (1985b) Long-term inducible resistance in birch foliage: triggering cues and efficacy on a defoliator. *Oecologia (Berlin)* **65**, 363–69.

Hawkins, B. A. and Lawton, J. H. (1987). Species richness for parasitoids of British phytophagous insects. *Nature* **326**, 788–90.

Hayes, A. J. and Britton, R. J. (1986). Attacks of *Neodiprion sertifer* in *Pinus contorta*. *EPPO Bulletin* **16**, 613–20.

Heads, P. A. and Lawton, J. H. (1983). Studies of the natural enemy complex of the holly leaf-miner: the effects of scale on the detection of aggregative responses and the implications for biological control. *Oikos* **40**, 267–76.

Hedlin, A. F. (1964). Results of a six-year pilot study on Douglas-fir cone insect population fluctuations. *Forest Science* **10**, 124–8.

Hedlin, A. F., Yates, H. O., Tovar, D. C., Ebel, B. H., Koerber, T. W., and Merkel, E. P. (1981). *Cone and seed insects of North American conifers*. Canadian Forestry Service, United States Forest Service, Secretaria de Agricultura y Recursos Hidraulicos, Mexico.

Heliovaara, K., Terho, E., and Annila, E. (1983). The effect of nitrogen fertilisation and insecticides on the population density of the pine bark bug *Aradus cinnamomeus* (Heteroptera: Aradidae). *Silva Fennica* **17**, 351–7.

Heliovaara, K. and Vaisanen, R. (1986). Industrial air pollution and the pine bark bug, *Aradus cinnamomeus* Panz. (Het; Aradidae). *Journal of Applied Entomology* **101**, 469–78.

Hellqvist, C. and Lindström, A. (1982). Results from field experiments with a plastic collar against pine weevil attacks on forest tree seedlings (in Swedish). *Smaskogsnytt, Sveriges Lantbruksuniversitet No. 5*, 1–12.

Heybroek, H. M. (1982). Monoculture versus mixture: interactions between susceptible and resistant trees in a mixed stand. In *Resistance to diseases and pests in forest trees* (ed. H. M. Heybroek, B. R. Stephan and K. van Weissenberg), pp. 326–41. Centre for Agricultural Publishing and Documentation, Wageningen.

Hicks, R. R. Jr. (1980). Climatic, site and stand factors. In *The Southern pine beetle* (eds. R. C. Thatcher, J. L. Searcy, J. E. Coster, G. D. Hertel), pp. 55–68. USDA Forest Service Technical Bulletin 1631.

Himel, C. M. and Moore, A. D. (1967). Spruce budworm mortality as a function of aerial spray droplet size. *Science* **156**, 1250–1.

Hobart, J. (1977). Pesticides in forestry: an introduction. In *Ecological effects of pesticides* (ed. F. H. Perring and K. Mellanby), pp. 61–88. Academic Press, London.

Hochmut, R., Skuhravy, V., and Svestka, M. (1977). Monitoring the nun moth (*Lymantria monacha* L.) with pheromone traps during the latent period (in Czechoslovakian). *Lesnictvi* **23**, 265–86.

Hodges, J. D. and Lorio, P. L. (1969). Carbohydrate and nitrogen fractions of the inner bark of loblolly pines under moisture stress. *Canadian Journal of Botany* **47**, 1651–7.

Hodges, J. D. and Lorio, P. L. (1975). Moisture stress and composition of xylem oleoresin in loblolly pine. *Forest Science* **21**, 283–90.

Hokkanen, H. and Pimentel, D. (1984). New approach for selecting biological control agents. *Canadian Entomologist* **116**, 1109–21.

Holden, A. V. and Bevan, D. (ed.) (1979). *Control of the pine beauty moth by fenitrothion in Scotland 1978*. Forestry Commission, Edinburgh.

Holden, A. V. and Bevan, D. (ed.) (1981). *Aerial application of insecticide against pine beauty moth*. Forestry Commission, Edinburgh.

Holling, C. S. (1959). Some characteristics of simple types of predation and parasitism. *Canadian Entomologist* **91**, 385–98.

Holling, C. S. (1965). The functional response of predators to prey density and its role in mimicry and population regulation. *Memoirs of the Entomological Society of Canada* **45**, 1–60.

Holling, C. S. (1966). The functional response of invertebrate predators to prey density. *Memoirs of the Entomological Society of Canada* **48**, 1–86.

Hollinger, D. Y. (1986). Herbivory and the cycling of nitrogen and phosphorus in isolated California oak trees. *Oecologia (Berlin)* **70**, 291–7.

Hopkins, A. D. (1920). The bioclimatic law. *Journal of the Washington Academy of Science* **10**, 34–40.

Horber, E. (1980). Types and classification of resistance. In *Breeding plants resistant to insects* (ed. F. G. Maxwell and P. R. Jennings), pp. 15–21. J. Wiley, New York.

Horntvedt, R., Christiansen, E., Solheim, H., and Wang, S. (1983). Artificial inoculation with *Ips typographus* – associated blue-stain fungi can kill healthy Norway spruce trees. *Meddelelser fra Norsk Institutt for Skogforskning* **38**, 1–20.

Horsfall, J. G. and Cowling, E. B. (ed.) (1980). *Plant disease: an advanced treatise Vol. V. How plants defend themselves*. Academic Press, New York.

Houston, D. R. and Valentine, H. T. (1977). Comparing and predicting forest stand susceptibility to gypsy moth. *Canadian Journal of Forest Research* **7**, 447–61.

Hsiao, T. H. (1985). Feeding behaviour. In *Comprehensive insect physiology biochemistry and pharmacology*, Vol. 9, *Behaviour* (ed. G. A. Kerkut and L. I. Gilbert), pp. 471–512. Pergamon Press, Oxford.

Huchon, H. and Demolin, G. (1971). The bioecology of the pine processionary. Potential and current distribution (in French). *Phytoma* **23**, 11–20.

Huffaker, C. B. and Kennett, C. E. (1966). Studies of two parasites of olive scale, *Parlatoria oleae* (Colvee) IV Biological control of *Parlatoria oleae* (Colvee) through the compensatory action of two introduced parasites. *Hilgardia* **37**, 283–335.

Huffaker, C. B., Messenger, P. S., and DeBach, P. (1971). The natural enemy component in natural control and the theory of biological control. In *Biological control* (ed. C. B. Huffaker), pp. 16–67. Plenum Press, New York.

Huffaker, C. B. and Rabb, R. L. (ed.) (1984). *Ecological Entomology*. J. Wiley, New York.

Hughes, P. R. (1973a). *Dendroctonus*: production of pheromones and related compounds in response to host monoterpenes. *Zeitschrift für angewandte Entomologie* **73**, 294–312.

Hughes, P. R. (1973b). Effect of alpha-pinene exposure on *trans*-verbenol synthesis in *Dendroctonus ponderosae* Hopk. *Naturwissenschaften* **60**, 261–2.

Hussey, N. W. and Bravenboer, L. (1971). Control of pests in glass-house culture by the introduction of natural enemies. In *Biological control* (ed. C. B. Huffaker), pp. 195–216. Plenum, New York.

Ikeda, T., Matsumura, F., and Benjamin, D. M. (1977). Mechanism of feeding discrimination between matured and juvenile foliage by two species of pine sawflies. *Journal of Chemical Ecology* **3**, 677–94.

Innes, J. L. (1987). *Air pollution and forestry. Bulletin 70*. HMSO, London.

Ives, W. G. H. and Nairn, L. D. (1966). Effects of water levels on the overwintering survival and emergence of the larch sawfly in a bog habitat. *Canadian Entomologist* **98**, 768–77.

Jansen, D. H. (1968). Host plants as islands in evolutionary and contemporary time. *American Naturalist* **102**, 592–5.

Jansen, D. H. (1973). Host plants as islands. II. Competition in evolutionary and contemporary time. *American Naturalist* **107**, 786–90.

Jeffords, M. R. and Endress, A. G. (1984). Possible role of ozone in tree defoliation by the gypsy moth (Lepidoptera: Lymantriidae). *Environmental Entomology* **13**, 1249–52.

Jensen, T. S. and Nielsen, B. O. (1984). Evaluation of pheromone catches of the nun moth, *Lymantria monacha* L. Effect of habitat heterogeneity and weather conditions in the flight period. *Zeitschrift für angewandte Entomologie* **98**, 399–413.

John, A. and Mason, B. (1987). Vegetative propagation of Sitka spruce. *Proceedings of the Royal Entomological Society of Edinburgh* **93B**, 197–203.

Johnson, C. G. (1969). *Migration and dispersal of insects by flight.* Methuen, London.

Johnson, R. (1987). The challenge of disease resistance. In *Genetics and plant pathogenesis* (ed. P. R. Day and G. J. Jellis), pp. 311–23. Blackwell Scientific Publications, Oxford.

Johnston, D. R. (1975). Tree growth and wood production in Britain. *Philosophical Transactions of the Royal Society of London. B.* **271**, 101–14.

Johnston, D. R., Grayson, A. J., and Bradley, R. T. (1967). *Forest planning.* Faber and Faber, London.

Jones, F. G. W. and Jones, M. G. (1974). *Pests of field crops*, 2nd edn. Edward Arnold, London.

Jones, O. T. (1985). Chemical mediation of insect behaviour. In *Progress in pesticide biochemistry and toxicology*, Vol. 5, *Insecticides* (ed. D. H. Hutson and T. R. Roberts), pp. 311–73. J. Wiley, Chichester.

Jones, O. T. and Kelly, D. (1986). Biotechnological innovation in the use of behaviour modifying chemicals in crop protection. In *Biotechnology and Crop Improvement and Protection* (ed. P. R. Day), pp. 173–84. British Crop protection Council Monograph No 34. BCPC Publications, Thornton Heath.

Jones, T. (1985). Forest pests and diseases. In *Pesticide application: principles and practice* (ed. P. T. Haskell), pp. 249–72. Clarendon Press, Oxford.

Joyce, R. J. V. and Beaumont, J. (1979). Collection of spray droplets and chemical by larvae, foliage and ground deposition. In *Control of pine beauty moth by fenitrothion in Scotland 1978* (ed. A. V. Holden and D. Bevan), pp. 63–80. Forestry Commission, Edinburgh.

Joyce, R. J. V. and Spillman, J. J. (1979). Discussion of aerial spraying techniques. In *Control of pine beauty moth by fenitrothion in Scotland 1978* (ed. A. V. Holden and D. Bevan), pp. 13–24. Forestry Commission, Edinburgh.

Kamm, J. A., Morgan, P. D., Overhulser, D. L., McDonough, L. M., Triebwasser, M., and Kline, L. N. (1983). Management practices for cranberry girdler (Lepidoptera: Pyralidae) in Douglas-fir nursery stock. *Journal of Economic Entomology* **76**, 923–6.

Kareiva, P. (1987). Habitat fragmentation and the stability of predator-prey interactions. *Nature* **326**, 388–90.

Kellomaki, S., Puttonen, P., Tamminen, H., and Westman, C. J. (1982). Effect of nitrogen fertilisation on photosynthesis and growth in young Scots pines – preliminary results. *Silva Fennica* **16**, 363–71.

Kennedy, C. E. J. (1986). Attachment may be a basis for specialisation in oak aphids. *Ecological Entomology* **11**, 291–300.

Kennedy, C. E. J. and Southwood, T. R. E. (1984). The number of species of insects associated with British trees: a re-analysis. *Journal of Animal Ecology* **53**, 455–78.

Kerkut, G. A. and Gilbert, L. I. (ed.) (1985). *Comprehensive insect physiology biochemistry and pharmacology*, Vol. 12, *Insect control*. Pergamon Press, Oxford.

Kettlewell, H. B. D. (1973). *The evolution of melanism*. Clarendon Press, Oxford.

Kidd, N. A. C., Lewis, G. B., and Howell, C. A. (1985). An association between two species of pine aphid, *Schizolachnus pineti* and *Eulachnus agilis*. *Ecological Entomology* **10**, 427–32.

Kinoshita, G. B. (1985). The economics of entomological effort: viewpoint of the pesticide industry in Canada. *Canadian Entomologist* **117**, 909–21.

Klomp, H. (1966). The dynamics of a field population of the pine looper, *Bupalus piniaria* L. (Lep. Geom.). *Advances in Ecological Research* **3**, 207–305.

Klomp, H. (1968). A seventeen-year study of the abundance of the pine looper, *Bupalus piniaria* L. (Lepidoptera: Geometridae). In *Insect abundance* (ed. T. R. E. Southwood), pp. 98–108. Blackwell Scientific Publications, Oxford.

Knerer, G. and Atwood, C. E. (1973). Diprionid sawflies: polymorphism and speciation. *Science* **179**, 1090–9.

Knipling, E. F. and McGuire, J. U. (1966). *Population models to test theoretical effects of sex attractants used for insect control*. USDA Agricultural Information Bulletin No. 308, pp. 1–20.

Kobayashi, F., Yamane, A., and Ikeda, T. (1984). The Japanese pine sawyer beetles as the vector of pine wilt disease. *Annual Review of Entomology* **29**, 115–35.

Koehler, W. (1970). The role of *Trichogramma* in limiting populations of *Rhyacionia buoliana* Schiff. (in German). *Tagungsbericht-Akademie der Landwirtschaftswissenschaften de Deutschen Demokratischen Republik, Berlin* **110**, 177–83.

Kolbe, H. and Hartwig, I. (1982). Experiments with the chitin synthesis inhibitors Bayer SIR 8514 and dimilin 25 WP for reducing the hatching rate of *Hylobius abietis* larvae (in German). *Zeitschrift für Pflanzenkrankheiten und Pflanzenschutz* **89**, 715–9.

Kolomiets, N. G. (1980). Principles of using entomophages in the integrated protection of forests in Siberia (in Russian). *Izvestiya Sibirskogo Otdeleniya Akademii Nauk SSSR No. 10*, 48–51.

Kolomiets, N. G. and Bogdanova, D. A. (1976). Outbreak of *Dendroctonus micans* (in Russian). *Lesnoe Khozyaistvo No. 12*, 71–3.

Kozlowski, T. T. and Constantinidou, H. A. (1986). Responses of woody plants to environmental pollution I. Sources and types of pollutants and plant responses. *Forestry Abstracts* **47**, 5–51.

Kramer, P. J. (1983). *Water relations of plants*. Academic Press, New York.

Kramer, P. J. and Kozlowski, T. T. (1979). *Physiology of woody plants*. Academic Press, New York.

Kroll, J. C. and Fleet, R. R. (1979). Impact of woodpecker predation on overwintering within-tree populations of the southern pine beetle (*Dendroctonus frontalis*). In *The role of insectivorous birds in forest ecosystems* (ed. J. G. Dicksen, R. N. Conner, R. R. Fleet, J. C. Kroll, and J. A. Jackson), pp. 269–81. Academic Press, New York.

Kuc, J. (1984). Phytoalexins and disease resistance mechanisms from a perspective of evolution and adaptation. In *Origins and development of adaptation*. Pitman, London.

Kulman, H. M. (1971). Effects of insect defoliation on growth and mortality of trees. *Annual Review of Entomology* **16**, 289–324.

Kunkel, H. (1968). Investigations on *Cryptococcus fagisuga* Bar. (Insecta Coccina), a representative of the bark parenchyma suckers (in German). *Zeitschrift für angewandte Entomologie* **61**, 373–80.

la Bastide, J. G. A. and van Vredenburch, C. L. H. (1970). Factors affecting seed production of trees; analysis, forecasting and consequences for forestry practice (in Dutch). *Nederlands Bosbouwtijdschrift* **42**, 88–93.

Laine, K. J. and Niemela, P. (1980). The influence of ants on the survival of mountain birches during an *Oporinia autumnata* (Lep., Geometridae) outbreak. *Oecologia (Berl.)* **47**, 39–42.

Landmark, L. (1976). *Forestry in Norway*. Norwegian Forestry Society, Oslo. 30.

Långström, B. (1983). Life cycles and shoot-feeding of the pine shoot beetles. *Studia Forestalia Suecica, No. 163*, 1–29.

Lanier, G. N. and Burns, B. W. (1978). Barometric flux. Effects on the responsiveness of bark beetles to aggregation attractants. *Journal of Chemical Ecology* **4**, 139–47.

Larsen, J. A. (1980). *The boreal ecosystem*. Academic Press, New York.

Larsson, S. (1983). Effects of artificial defoliation on stem growth in *Salix smithiana* grown under intensive culture. *Acta Oecologia Oecologia Applicata* **4**, 343–9.

Larsson, S. (1985). Seasonal changes in the within-crown distribution of the aphid *Cinara pini* on Scots pine. *Oikos* **45**, 217–22.

Larsson, S. and Tenow, O. (1980). Needle-eating insects and grazing dynamics in a mature Scots pine forest in central Sweden. In *Structure and function of northern coniferous forests–an ecosystem study*. Ecological Bulletin (Stockholm) (ed. T. Persson) **32**, 269–306.

Larsson, S. and Tenow, O. (1984). Areal distribution of a *Neodiprion sertifer* (Hym., Diprionidae) outbreak on Scots pine as related to stand condition. *Holarctic Ecology* **7**, 81–90.

Lavery, P. B. (1986). *Plantation forestry with Pinus radiata—review papers*. Paper no. 12. School of Forestry, University of Canterbury, Christchurch, New Zealand.

Lawton, J. H. (1978). Host-plant influences on insect diversity: the effects of space and time. In *Diversity of insect faunas*. Symposium of the Royal Entomological Society of London, No. 9 (ed. L. A. Mound and N. Waloff), pp. 105–25. Blackwell Scientific Publications, Oxford.

Lawton, J. H. (1986). The effect of parasitoids on phytophagous insect communities. In *Insect parasitoids* (ed. J. Waage and D. Greathead), pp. 265–87. Academic Press, London.

Lawton, J. H. and Hassell, M. P. (1981). Asymmetrical competition in insects. *Nature* **289**, 793–5.

Lawton, J. H. and Hassell, M. P. (1984). Interspecific competition in insects. In *Ecological entomology* (ed. C. B. Huffaker and R. L. Rabb). John Wiley, New York.

Lawton, J. H. and McNeill, S. (1979). Between the devil and the deep blue sea: on the problem of being a herbivore. In *Population dynamics* (ed. R. M. Anderson, B. D. Turner and L. R. Taylor), pp. 223–44. Blackwell Scientific Publications, Oxford.

Lawton, J. H. and Strong, D. R. (1981). Community patterns and competition in folivorous insects. *American Naturalist* **118**, 317–38.

Leather, S. R. (1986). Insect species richness of the British Rosaceae: the importance of host range, plant architecture, age of establishment, taxonomic isolation and species-area relationships. *Journal of Animal Ecology* **55**, 841–60.

Leather, S. R. (1987). Pine monoterpenes stimulate oviposition in the pine beauty moth, *Panolis flammea*. *Entomologia experimentalis et applicata* **43**, 295–303.

Leather, S. R. and Barbour, D. A. (1987). Associations between soil type, lodgepole pine (*Pinus contorta* Douglas) provenance, and the abundance of the pine beauty moth, *Panolis flammea* (D&S). *Journal of Applied Ecology* **24**, 945–52.

Lechowicz, M. J. (1984). Why do temperate deciduous trees leaf out at different times? Adaptation and ecology of forest communities. *American Naturalist* **124**, 821–42.

Leonard, D. E. (1974). Recent developments in ecology and control of the gypsy moth. *Annual Review of Entomology* **19**, 197–229.

Levitt, J. (1972). *Responses of plants to environmental stresses*. Academic Press, New York.

Levitt, J. (1980). *Responses of plants to environmental stresses*, 2nd edn, Vol. 2. Academic Press, New York.

Libby, W. J. (1982). What is a safe number of clones in a plantation? In *Resistance to diseases and pests in forest trees* (ed. H. M. Heybroek, B. R. Stephan and K. van Weissenberg), pp. 342–60. Centre for Agricultural Publishing and Documentation, Wageningen.

Liese, W. (1984). Wet storage of windblown conifers in Germany. *New Zealand Journal of Forestry* **29**, 119–35.

Lindström, A. (1983). Collars against attack by *Hylobius abietis* on planting stock (in Swedish). *Skogsfakta, Skogsvetenskapliga Fakulteten Sveriges Lantbruksuniversitet, Biologi och Skogsskotsel, No. 5*, 1–4.

Lines, R. (1960). Common silver fir in Britain. *Scottish Forestry* **14**, 20–30.

Lines, R. and Mitchell, A. F. (1965). Differences in phenology of Sitka spruce provenances. *Report on Forest Research*, 173–88.

Linhart, Y. B., Mitton, J. B., Sturgeon, K. B., and Davies, M. L. (1981) An analysis of genetic architecture in populations of ponderosa pine. In *Isozymes of North American forest trees and forest insects* (ed. M. T. Conkle), pp. 53–9. USDA General Technical Report PSW-48.

Lisansky, S. G. (1984). Biological alternatives to chemical pesticides. *Proceedings of Biotech, 1984*, 455–66.

Loman, M. D. (1984). An assessment of techniques for measuring herbivory: is rainforest defoliation more intense than we thought? *Biotropica* **16**, 264–8.

Lonsdale, D. (1980). *Nectria* infection of beech bark: variations in disease in relation to predisposing factors. *Annales des Sciences Forestières* **37**, 307–17.

Lonsdale, D. (1983). Wood and bark anatomy of young beech in relation to *Cryptococcus* attack. In *Proceedings, IUFRO beech bark disease working party conference* (ed. D. Houston and D. Wainhouse), pp. 43–9. USDA Forest Service General Technical Report WO-37.

Lonsdale, D. and Wainhouse, D. (1987). Beech bark disease. *Forestry Commission Bulletin 69*. HMSO, London.

Lorio, P. L. (1986). Growth-differentiation balance: a basis for understanding southern pine beetle-tree interactions. *Forest Ecology and Management* **14**, 259–73.

Love, J. D. (1955). The effect on streamflow of the killing of spruce and pine by the Englemann spruce beetle. *Transactions American Geophysical Union* **36**, 113–18.

Loyttyniemi, K. and Uusvaara, O. (1977). Insect attack on pine and spruce sawlogs felled during the growing season. *Communicationes Instituti Forestalis Fenniae* **89**, 1–48.

Luck, R. F. and Dahlsten, D. L. (1975). Natural decline of a pine needle scale (*Chionaspis pinifoliae* (Fitch)), outbreak at South Lake Tahoe, California following cessation of adult mosquito control with malathion. *Ecology* **56**, 893–904.

Luitjes, J. (1958). On the economic significance of insect pests in forests (*C. alpina* and *D. pini*) (in Dutch). *Mededeling Instituut voor toegepast biologisch Onderzoek in de Natuur (Itbon)* No. 40, 1–56.

Lund, A. E. (1985). Insecticides: effects on the nervous system. In *Comprehensive insect physiology biochemistry and pharmacology*, Vol. 12, *Insect control* (ed. G. A. Kerkut and L. I. Gilbert), pp. 9–56. Pergamon Press, Oxford.

MacArthur, R. H. and Wilson, E. O. (1967). *The theory of island biogeography*. Princeton University Press, New Jersey.

MacConnell, J. G., Borden, J. H., Silverstein, R. M., and Stokkink, E. (1977). Isolation and tentative identification of lineatin, a pheromone from the frass of *Trypodendron lineatum* (Coleoptera: Scolytidae). *Journal of Chemical Ecology* **3**, 549–61.

MacLean, D. A. (1981). Impact of defoliation by spruce budworm populations on radial and volume growth of balsam fir: a review of present knowledge. *Mitteilungen der Forstlichen Bundesversuchsanstalt Wien* **142**, 293–306.

MacPhee, A. W. (1967). The winter moth *Operophtera brumata* (Lepidoptera: Geometridae), a new pest attacking apple orchards in Nova Scotia, and its coldhardiness. *Canadian Entomologist* **99**, 829–34.

Madrid, F. J. and Stewart, R. K. (1981). Impact of diflubenzuron spray on gypsy moth parasitoids in the field. *Journal of Economic Entomology* **74**, 1–2.

Mahoney, R. L. (1978). Lodgepole pine/mountain pine beetle risk classification methods and their application. In *Theory and practice of mountain pine beetle management in lodgepole pine forests*, pp. 106–13. Forest, Wildlife and Range Experiment Station, University of Idaho, Moscow, USDA Forest Service,

Forest Insect and Disease Research, Washington D.C. and the Intermountain Forest and Range Experiment Station, Ogden, Utah.

Maksimovic, M. (1965). Sex attractant traps with female odour of the gypsy moth used for forecasting the increase of population of the gypsy moth. *Proceedings 12ᵗʰ International Congress of Entomology 1964*, 398, London.

Mamiya, Y. (1983). Pathology of the pine wilt disease caused by *Bursaphelenchus xylophilus*. *Annual Review of Phytopathology* **21**, 201–20.

Martinat, P. J. (1987). The role of climatic variation and weather in forest-insect outbreaks. In *Insect outbreaks* (ed. P. Barbosa and J. C. Schultz), pp. 241–68. Academic Press, San Diego.

Martineau, R. (1984). *Insects harmful to forest trees*. Multiscience Publications Ltd and Canadian Forestry Service.

Mason, C. J. and McManus, M. L. (1981). Larval dispersal of the gypsy moth. In *The gypsy moth: research toward integrated pest management* (ed. C. C. Doane and M. L. McManus), pp. 161–202. Technical Bulletin 1584, USDA, Washington.

Mason, R. R. and Luck, R. F. (1978). Population growth and regulation. In *The Douglas-fir tussock moth: a synthesis* (ed. M. H. Brookes, R. W. Stark and R. W. Campbell), pp. 41–7. Forest Service Science and Education Agency, Technical Bulletin 1585, USDA, Washington D.C.

Matthews, G. A. (1979). *Pesticide application methods*, Longman, London.

Matthews, G. A. (1983). The application of pesticides. In *Pest and disease control handbook* (ed. N. Scopes and M. Ledieu), pp. 33–51. BCPC Publications, London.

Matthews, J. D. (1983). *The role of north-west American trees in western Europe*. H.R. MacMillan Lecture, March 17, 1983. University of British Columbia. 24 pp.

Mattson, W. J. Jr. (1971). Relationship between cone crop size and cone damage by insects in red pine seed-production areas. *Canadian Entomologist* **103**, 617–21.

Mattson, W. J. (1978). The role of insects in the dynamics of cone production of red pine. *Oecologia (Berl.)* **33**, 327–49.

Mattson, W. J. Jr. (1980). Herbivory in relation to plant nitrogen content. *Annual Review of Ecology and Systematics* **11**, 119–61.

Mattson, W. J. and Addy, N. D. (1975). Phytophagous insects as regulators of forest primary production. *Science* **190**, 515–22.

Mattson, W. J. and Haack, R. A. (1987). The role of drought in outbreaks of plant-eating insects. *BioScience* **37**, 110–18.

Mattson, W. J., Lawrence, R. K., Haack, R. A., Herms, D. A., and Charles, P.-J. (1988). Defensive strategies of woody plants against different insect-feeding guilds in relation to plant ecological strategies and intimacy of association with insects. In *Mechanisms of woody plant defenses against insects. Search for pattern* (ed. W. J. Mattson, J. Levieux, and C. Bernard-Dagan), pp. 3–38. Springer-Verlag, New York.

May, R. M. (1978). Host-parasitoid systems in patchy environments: a phenomenological model. *Journal of Animal Ecology* **47**, 833–44.

McClure, M. S. (1980a). Foliar nitrogen: a basis for host suitability for elongate hemlock scale, *Fiorinia externa* (Homoptera: Diaspididae). *Ecology* **61**, 72–9.

McClure, M. S. (1980*b*). Competition between exotic species: scale insects on hemlock. *Ecology* **61**, 1391–401.

McGugan, B. M. and Coppel, H. C. (1962). Biological control of forest insects 1910–1958. In *A review of the biological control attempts against insects and weeds in Canada*. CAB Technical communication No. 2, 35–216.

McNamee, P. J., McLeod, J. M., and Holling C. S. (1981). The structure and behaviour of defoliating insect/forest systems. *Researches on Population Ecology* **23**, 280–98.

McNeill, S. and Southwood, T. R. E. (1978). The role of nitrogen in the development of insect/plant relationships. In *Biochemical aspects of plant and animal coevolution* (ed. J. B. Harborne), pp. 77–95. Academic Press, New York.

Meinartowicz, L. E. and Szmidt, A. (1978). Investigations into the resistance of Douglas fir (*Pseudotsuga menziesii* (Mirb.) Franco) populations to the Douglas fir woolly aphid (*Gilletteella cooleyi* Gill.). *Silvae Genetica* **27**, 59–62.

Mertins, J. W. and Coppel, H. C. (1971). The insect parasites of the introduced pine sawfly, *Diprion similis* (Hartig) (Hymenoptera: Diprionidae), in Wisconsin with keys to the adults and mature larval remains. *Transactions of the Wisconsin Academy of Sciences Arts and Letters* **59**, 127–68.

Messenger, P. S. (1970). Bioclimatic inputs to biological control and pest management programs. In *Concepts of pest management* (ed. R. L. Rabb and F. E. Guthrie), pp. 84–102. North Carolina State University Press, Raleigh.

Metcalf, R. L. (1980). Changing role of insecticides in crop protection. *Annual Review of Entomology* **25**, 219–56.

Michie, E. J. S., Kinvig, N. R., and Neal, A. W. (1979). Getting off the ground. In *Control of pine beauty moth by fenitrothion in Scotland 1978* (ed. A. V. Holden and D. Bevan), pp. 13–24. Forestry Commission, Edinburgh.

Miller, C. A. (1977). The feeding impact of spruce budworm on balsam fir. *Canadian Journal of Forest Research* **7**, 76–84.

Miller, C. A., Greenbank, D. O., and Kettla, E. G. (1978). Estimated egg deposition by invading spruce budworm moths (Lepidoptera: Tortricidae). *Canadian Entomologist* **110**, 609–15.

Miller, H. G. (1979). The nutrient budgets of even-aged forests. In *The ecology of even-aged forest plantations* (ed. E. D. Ford, D. C. Malcolm and J. Atterson), pp. 221–56. Proceedings of IUFRO Div. 1, Institute of Terrestrial Ecology.

Miller, R. H. and Berryman, A. A. (1985). Energetics of conifer defence against bark beetles and associated fungi. In *Proceedings of the IUFRO conference on the role of the host in the population dynamics of forest insects* (ed. L. Safranyik), pp. 13–23. Canadian Forestry Service and USDA Forest Service, Victoria.

Mitchell, R. G., Waring, R. H., and Pitman, G. B. (1983). Thinning lodgepole pine increases tree vigour and resistance to mountain pine beetle. *Forest Science* **29**, 204–11.

Moran, N. and Hamilton, W. D. (1980). Low nutritive quality as defence against herbivores. *Journal of Theoretical Biology* **80**, 247–54.

Moran, V. C. and Southwood, T. R. E. (1982). The guild composition of arthropod communities in trees. *Journal of Animal Ecology* **51**, 289–306.

Morris, O. N. (1982). Bacteria as pesticides: Forest applications. In *Microbial and* viral pesticides (ed. E. Kurstak), pp. 239–88. Marcel Dekker, New York.

Morrow, P. A. (1977). The significance of phytophagous insects in the *Eucalyptus* forests in Australia. In *The role of arthropods in forest ecosystems* (ed. W. J. Mattson), pp. 19–29. Springer, New York.

Morrow, P. A. and Fox, L. R. (1980). Effects of variation in *Eucalyptus* essential oil yield on insect growth and grazing damage. *Oecologia* **45**, 209–19.

Morrow, P. A. and LaMarche, V. C. Jr. (1978). Tree ring evidence for chronic insect suppression of productivity in subalpine *Eucalyptus*. *Science* **201**, 1244–5.

Mott, D. G., Nairn, L. D., and Cook, J. A. (1957). Radial growth in forest trees and the effects of insect defoliation. *Forest Science* **3**, 286–304.

Muldrew, J. A. (1953). The natural immunity of the larch sawfly (*Pristiphora erichsonii* (Htg.)) to the introduced parasite *Mesoleius tenthredinis* Morley, in Manitoba and Saskatchewan. *Canadian Journal of Zoology* **31**, 313–32.

Muldrew, J. A. (1964). The biological control programme against the larch sawfly. *Proceedings of the Entomological Society of Manitoba* **20**, 63.

Mullin, C. A. and Croft, B. A. (1985). An update on development of selective pesticides favoring arthropod natural enemies. In *Biological control in agricultural IPM systems* (ed. M. A. Hoy and D. C. Herzog), pp. 123–50. Academic Press, New York.

Mulock, P. and Christiansen, E. (1986). The threshold of successful attack by *Ips typographus* on *Picea abies*: a field experiment. *Forest Ecology and Management* **14**, 125–32.

Mumford, J. D. and Norton, G. A. (1984). Economics of decision making in pest control. *Annual Review of Entomology* **29**, 157–74.

Murdoch, W. W., Chesson, J., and Chesson, P. L. (1985). Biological control in theory and practice. *American Naturalist* **125**, 344–66.

Murdoch, W. W. and Reeve, J. D. (1987). Aggregation of parasitoids and the detection of density dependence in field populations. *Oikos* **50**, 137–41.

NCC (1986). *Nature conservation and afforestation in Britain*. Nature Conservancy Council, Peterborough.

Neilson, M. M., Martineau, R., and Rose, A. H. (1971). *Diprion hercyniae* (Hartig), European spruce sawfly (Hymenoptera: Diprionidae). *Commonwealth Institute of Biological Control Technical Communication* **4**, 136–43.

Nelson, R. R. (1982). On genes for disease resistance in plants. In *Resistance to diseases and pests in forest trees* (ed. H. M. Heybroek, B. R. Stephan and K. van Weissenberg), pp. 84–93. Centre for Agricultural Publishing and Documentation, Wageningen.

Neumann, F. G. (1979). Insect pest management in Australian radiata pine plantations. *Australian Forestry* **42**, 30–8.

Neumann, F. G. and Minko, G. (1981). The *Sirex* wood wasp in Australian radiata pine plantations. *Australian Forestry* **44**, 46–63.

Neuvonen, S. and Niemela, P. (1981). Species richness of macrolepidoptera on Finnish trees and shrubs. *Oecologia (Berl)* **51**, 364–70.

Newmark, P. (1987). UK release of four genetically manipulated organisms planned. *Nature* **326**, 537.

Nichols, J. F. A. (1987). Damage and performance of the green spruce aphid,

Elatobium abietinum on twenty spruce species. *Entomologia experimentalis et applicata* **45**, 211–17.

Niemela, P. and Haukioja, E. (1982). Seasonal patterns in species richness of herbivores: Macrolepidopteran larvae on Finnish deciduous trees. *Ecological Entomology* **7**, 169–75.

Niemela, P., Aro, E-M., and Haukioja, E. (1979). Birch leaves as a resource for herbivores. Damage-induced increase in leaf phenolics with trypsin-inhibiting effects. *Report of the Kevo Subarctic Research Station* **15**, 37–40.

Nijholt, W. W., McMullen, L. H., and Safranyik, L. (1981). Pine oil protects living trees from attack by three bark beetle species, *Dendroctonus* spp. (Coleoptera: Scolytidae). *Canadian Entomologist* **113**, 337–40.

Nilssen, A. C. (1978). Development of a bark fauna in plantations of spruce (*Picea abies* (L.) Karst.) in North Norway. *Astarte* **11**, 151–69.

Nilsson, S. (1976). Rationalization of forest operations gives rise to insect attack and increment loss. *Ambio* **5**, 17–22.

Nimmo, M. (1971). *Nothofagus* plantations in Great Britain. *Forestry Commission Forest Record No 79*.

Nordlander, G., Eidmann, H. H., Jacobsson, U., Nordenhem, H., and Sjodin, K. (1986). Orientation of the pine weevil *Hylobius abietis* to underground sources of host volatiles. *Entomologia experimentalis et applicata* **41**, 91–100.

Norris, D. M. (1981). From theory to practice with systemic pesticides in trees. *XVII IUFRO World Congress, Div. 2 Japan 1981*, 587–90.

Nothnagle, P. J. and Schultz, J. C. (1987). What is a forest pest? In *Insect outbreaks* (ed. P. Barbosa and J. C. Schultz), pp. 59–80. Academic Press, London.

Novak, V., Sehnal, F., Romanuk, M., and Streinz, L. (1976). Responses and sensitivity of *Ips typographus* L. (Col., Scolytidae) and *Hylobius abietis* L. (Col., Curculionidae) to juvenoids. *Zeitschrift für angewandte Entomologie* **80**, 118–31.

Nyrop, J. P. and Simmons, G. A. (1986). Temporal and spatial activity patterns of an adult parasitoid, *Glypta fumiferanae* (Hymenoptera: Ichneumonidae), and their influence on parasitism. *Environmental Entomology* **15**, 481–7.

Obrycki, J. J. (1986). The influence of foliar pubescence on entomophagous species. In *Interactions of plant resistance and parasitoids and predators of insects* (ed. D. J. Boethel and R. D. Eikenbarry), pp. 61–83. Ellis Horwood Ltd., Chichester.

Ohigashi, H., Wagner, M. R., Matsumura, F., and Benjamin, D. M. (1981). Chemical basis of differential feeding behaviour of the larch sawfly *Pristiphora erichsonii* (Hartig). *Journal of Chemical Entomology* **7**, 599–614.

Oksanen, H., Perttunen, V., and Kangas, E. (1970). Studies on the chemical factors involved in the olfactory orientation of *Blastophagus piniperda* (Coleoptera: Scolytidae). *Contributions from Boyce Thompson Institute* **24**, 299–304.

Oliver, H. R. (1975). Ventilation in a forest. *Agricultural Meteorology* **14**, 347–55.

O'Neil, L. C. (1963). The suppression of growth rings in jack pine in relation to defoliation by the Swaine jack-pine sawfly. *Canadian Journal of Botany* **41**, 227–35.

Opler, P. A. (1974). Oaks as evolutionary islands for leaf-mining insects. *American Scientist* **62**, 67–73.

Oppenoorth, F. J. (1985). Biochemistry and genetics of insecticide resistance. In *Comprehensive insect physiology biochemistry and pharmacology*, Vol. 12, *Insect control* (ed. G. A. Kerkut and L. I. Gilbert), pp. 731–73. Pergamon Press, Oxford.

Ortman, E. E. and Peters, D. C. (1980). Introduction. In *Breeding plants resistant to insects* (ed. F. G. Maxwell and P. R. Jennings), pp. 3–13. J. Wiley, New York.

Otto, H. J. (1985). Sylviculture according to site conditions as a method of forest protection. *Zeitschrift für angewandte Entomologie* **99**, 190–8.

Otvos, I. S. (1979). The effects of insectivorous bird activities in forest ecosystems: an evaluation. In *The role of insectivorous birds in forest ecosystems* (ed. J. G. Dickson, R. N. Conner, R. R. Fleet, J. C. Kroll and J. A. Jackson), pp. 341–4. Academic Press, New York.

Overhulser, D. L., Daterman, G. E., Sower, L. L., Sartwell, C., and Koerber, T. W. (1980). Mating disruption with synthetic sex attractants controls damage by *Eucosma sonomana* (Lepidoptera: Tortricidae, Olethreutinae) in *Pinus ponderosa* plantations II. Aerially applied hollow fiber formulations. *Canadian Entomologist* **112**, 163–65.

Painter, R. H. (1951). *Insect resistance in crop plants*. Macmillan, New York.

Painter, R. H. (1958). Resistance of plants to insects. *Annual Review of Entomology* **3**, 267–90.

Payne, T. L. (1970). Electrophysiological investigations on response to pheromones in bark beetles. *Contributions from Boyce Thompson Institute* **24**, 275–82.

Payne, T. L. and Coulson, R. N. (1985). Role of visual and olfactory stimuli in host selection and aggregation behaviour by *Dendroctonus frontalis*. In *The role of the host in the population dynamics of forest insects* (ed. L. Safranyik), pp. 73–82. Canadian Forestry Service and USDA Forest Service.

Payne, T. L. and Richerson, J. V. (1985). Pheromone-mediated competitive replacement between two bark beetle populations: influence on infestation suppression. *Zeitschrift für angewandte Entomologie* **99**, 131–8.

Payne, T. L., Coster, J. E., Richerson, J, V., Edson, L. J., and Hart, E. R. (1978). Field response of the southern pine beetle to behavioural chemicals. *Environmental Entomology* **7**, 578–82.

Peek, R. D. and Liese, W. (1974). First experiences with sprinkling windthrown timber in lower Saxony (in German). *Forst- und Holzwirt* **29**, 261–3.

Pepper, H. W. (1978). Chemical repellents. Forestry Commission Leaflet 73. HMSO, London.

Perry, D. A. (1979). Variation between and within tree species. In *Ecology of even-aged forest plantations* (ed. E. D. Ford, D. C. Malcolm, and J. Atterson), pp. 71–98. Institute of Terrestrial Ecology.

Perry, D. F. and Whitfield, G. H. (1985). The interrelationships between microbial entomopathogens and insect hosts: a system study approach with particular reference to the Entomophthorales and the eastern spruce budworm. In *Animal-microbial interactions* (ed. J. M. Anderson, A. D. M. Rayner and D. Walton), pp. 307–17. Cambridge University Press, Cambridge.

Peterken, G. F. (1981). *Woodland conservation and management*. Chapman and Hall, London.

Phillips, D. H. (1978). *The EEC plant health directive and British forestry*. Forestry Commission Forest Record 116. HMSO, London.

Piene, H. (1980). Effects of insect defoliation on growth and foliar nutrients of young balsam fir. *Forest Science* **26**, 665–73.

Pimentel, D., Andow, D., Dyson-Hudson, R., Gallahan, D., Jacobson, S., Irish, M., Kroop, S., Moss, A., Schreiner, I., Shepard, M., Thompson, T., and Vinzant, B. (1980). Environmental and social costs of pesticides: a preliminary assessment. *Oikos* **34**, 126–40.

Plimmer, J. R., Schwalbe, C. P., Paszek, E. C., Bierl, B. A., Webb, R. A., Marumo, S., and Iwaki, S. (1977). Contrasting effectiveness of (+) and (−) enantiomers of disparlure for trapping native populations of gypsy moth in Massachusetts. *Environmental Entomology* **6**, 518–22.

Poinar, G. O. (1972). Nematodes as facultative parasites of insects. *Annual Review of Entomology* **17**, 103–22.

Price, P. W. (1970). Characteristics permitting coexistence among parasitoids of a sawfly in Quebec. *Ecology* **51**, 445–54.

Price, P. W. (1976). Colonisation of crops by arthropods: non-equilibrium communities in soybean fields. *Entomological Society of America* **5**, 605–11.

Price, P. W. (1984). *Insect ecology*, 2nd edn. John Wiley, New York.

Price, P. W. (1986). Ecological aspects of host plant resistance and biological control: interactions among three trophic levels. In *Interactions of plant resistance and parasitoids and predators of insects* (ed. D. J. Boethel and R. D. Eikenbarry), pp. 11–30. Ellis Horwood Ltd., Chichester.

Price, P. W., Bouton, C. E., Gross, P., McPheron, B. A., Thompson, J. N., and Weis, A. E. (1980). Interaction among three trophic levels: influence of plants on interactions between insect herbivores and natural enemies. *Annual Review of Ecology and Systematics* **11**, 41–65.

Puritch, G. S. and Nijholt, W. W. (1974). Occurrence of juvabione-related compounds in grand fir and Pacific silver fir infested by balsam woolly aphid. *Canadian Journal of Botany* **52**, 585–7.

Quisumbing, A. R. and Kydonieus, A. F. (1982). Laminated structure dispensers. In *Insect suppression with controlled release pheromone systems*, Vol. I (ed. A. F. Kydonieus and M. Beroza), pp. 213–35. CRC Press, Boca Raton, Florida.

Raffa, K. F. and Berryman, A. A. (1983). Physiological aspects of lodgepole pine wound responses to a fungal symbiont of the mountain pine beetle, *Dendroctonus ponderosae* (Coleoptera: Scolytidae). *Canadian Entomologist* **115**, 723–34.

Raffa, K. F. and Berryman, A. A. (1987). Interacting selective pressures in conifer-bark beetle systems: a basis for reciprocal adaptations? *American Naturalist* **129**, 234–62.

Rainey, R. C. (1979). Dispersal and distribution of some Orthoptera and Lepidoptera by flight. *Mitteilungen der Schweizerischen Entomologischen Gesellschaft* **52**, 125–32.

Rappaport, N. G. and Robertson, J. L. (1981). Lethal effects of five molt inhibitors fed to the western spruce budworm (*Choristoneura occidentalis* Freeman) (Lepidoptera: Tortricidae) and the Douglas-fir tussock moth (*Orgyia pseudo-*

tsugata [McDonnough]) (Lepidoptera: Lymantriidae). *Zeitschrift für angewandte Entomologie* **91**, 459–63.

Raupp, M. J. (1985). Effects of leaf toughness on mandibular wear of the leaf beetle, *Plagiodera versicolora*. *Ecological Entomology* **10**, 73–9.

Redfern, D. B., Stoakley, J. T., Steele, H., and Minter, D. W. (1987). Dieback and death of larch caused by *Ceratocystis laricicola* sp. nov. following attack by *Ips cembrae*. *Plant Pathology* **36**, 467–80.

Reeks, W. A. and Cameron, J. M. (1971). Current approach to biological control of forest insects. *Commonwealth Institute of Biological Control Technical Communication* **4**, 105–13.

Reeve, J. D. and Murdoch, W. W. (1985). Aggregation by parasitoids in the successful control of the California red scale: a test of theory. *Journal of Animal Ecology* **54**, 797–86.

Regnander, J. (1976). Sprinkling of insect attacked pulpwood – an important part of the control of bark beetles (in Swedish). *Sveriges Skogsvardsforbunds Tidskrift* **74**, 497–504.

Regnander, J. (1977). Better than insecticides (in Swedish). *Skogen* **64**, 278–81.

Reid, R. W., Whitney, H. S., and Watson, J. A. (1967). Reactions of lodgepole pine to attack by *Dendroctonus ponderosae* Hopkins and blue stain fungi. *Canadian Journal of Botany* **45**, 1115–26.

Renwick, J. A. A. and Vité, J. P. (1969). Bark beetle attractants: mechanisms of colonisation by *Dendroctonus frontalis*. *Nature* **244**, 1222–3.

Retnakaran, A. and Smith, L. (1975). Morphogenetic effects of an inhibitor of cuticle development of the spruce budworm, *Choristoneura fumiferana* (Lepidoptera: Tortricidae). *Canadian Entomologist* **107**, 883–6.

Retnakaran, A., Granett, J., and Ennis, T. (1985). Insect growth regulators. In *Comprehensive insect physiology biochemistry and pharmacology*, Vol. 12, *Insect control* (ed. G. A. Kerkut and L. I. Gilbert), pp. 529–601. Pergamon Press, Oxford.

Rhoades, D. F. (1979). Evolution of plant chemical defense against herbivores. In *Herbivores: Their interaction with secondary plant metabolites* (ed. G. A. Rosenthal and D. H. Janzen), pp. 3–54. Academic Press, New York.

Rhoades, D. F. (1983). Herbivore population dynamics and plant chemistry. In *Variable plants and herbivores in natural and managed systems* (ed. R. F. Denno and M. S. McClure), pp. 155–220. Academic Press, New York.

Rhoades, D. F. and Cates, R. G. (1976). Towards a general theory of plant anti-herbivore chemistry. In *Biochemical interactions between plants and insects* (ed. J. W. Wallace and R. L. Mansell). *Recent advances in phytochemistry*, Vol. 10, pp. 168–213. Plenum Press, New York.

Richerson, J. V., Cameron, E. A., and Brown, E. A. (1976). Sexual activity of the gypsy moth. *American Midland Naturalist* **95**, 299–312.

Richmond, C. E. (1985). Effectiveness of two pine oils for protecting lodgepole pine from attack by mountain pine beetle (Coleoptera: Scolytidae). *Canadian Entomologist* **117**, 1445–6.

Richmond, H. A. and Nijholt, W. W. (1972). Water misting for log protection from ambrosia beetles in British Columbia. *Canadian Forest Service, Council of Forest Industries Project Report*.

Robertson, J. L. and Stock, M. W. (1984). *Differential population characteristics of western spruce budworm.* USDA Forest Service General Technical Report. NE-90, 7-12.

Robredo, F. (1980). Large-scale treatments with diflubenzuron against the pine processionary in Spain (in Spanish). *Boletin del Servicio de Defensa Contra Plagas e Inspeccion Fitopatologica* **6**, 141–54.

Rockwood, D. L. (1973). Monoterpene-fusiform rust relationships in loblolly pine. *Phytopathology* **63**, 551–3.

Rockwood, D. L. (1974). Cortical monoterpene and fusiform rust resistance relationships in slash pine. *Phytopathology* **64**, 976–9.

Rodin, L. E. and Basilevic, N. I. (1967). *Production and mineral cycling in terrestrial vegetation.* Oliver and Boyd, Edinburgh and London.

Roelofs, W. L., Cardé, R. T., Benz, G., and Von Salis, G. (1971). Sex attractant of the larch bud moth found by electroantennogram method. *Experimentia* **27**, 1438–9.

Rogers, D. J. and Hubbard, S. F. (1974). How the behaviour of parasites and predators promotes population stability. In *Ecological stability* (ed. M. B. Usher and N. H. Williamson). Chapman and Hall, London.

Rogoff, M. H. (1982). Regulatory safety data requirements for registration of microbial pesticides. In *Microbial and viral pesticides* (ed. E. Kurstak), pp. 645–79. Marcel Dekker, New York.

Rohwer, G. G. (1979). Plant quarantine philosophy of the United States. In *Plant health. The scientific basis for administrative control of plant diseases and pests* (ed. D. L. Ebbels and J. E. King), pp. 23–34. Blackwell Scientific Publications, Oxford.

Roland, J. (1986). Parasitism of winter moth in British Columbia during build-up of its parasitoid *Cyzenis albicans:* attack rate on oak v. apple. *Journal of Animal Ecology* **55**, 215–34.

Roques, A. (1983). *Les insectes ravageurs des cônes et graines de conifères en France.* INRA, Paris.

Rossi, D. (1966). Biological control of *Evetria buoliana* Schiff. (in Italian). *Sperimentali di Entomologia Agraria Perugia* **11**, 1–14.

Royama, T. (1970). Factors governing the hunting behaviour and selection of food by the great tit (*Parus major* L.). *Journal of Animal Ecology* **39**, 619–68.

Ruigt, G. S. F. (1985). Pyrethroids. In *Comprehensive insect physiology biochemistry and pharmacology*, Vol. 12, *Insect control* (ed. G. A. Kerkut and L. I. Gilbert), pp. 183–262. Pergamon Press, Oxford.

Rudinsky, J. A. (1962). Ecology of Scolytidae. *Annual Review of Entomology* **7**, 327–48.

Russell, C. E. and Berryman, A. A. (1976). Host resistance to the fir engraver beetle. I. Monoterpene composition of *Abies grandis* pitch blisters and fungus-infected wounds. *Canadian Journal of Botany* **54**, 14–18.

Rykiel, E. J., Saunders, M. C., Wagner, T. L., Loh, D. K., Turnbow, R. H., Hu, L. C., Pulley, P. E., and Coulson, R. N. (1984). Computer-aided decision making and information accessing in pest management systems, with emphasis on the southern pine beetle (Coleoptera: Scolytidae). *Journal of Economic Entomology* **77**, 1073–82.

Saarenmaa, H. (1985). The role of temperature in the population dynamics of

Tomicus piniperda (L.) (Col., Scolytidae) in northern conditions. *Zeitschrift für angewandte Entomologie* **99**, 224–36.

Sanders, C. J., Stark, R. W., Mullins, E. J., and Murphy, J. (ed.) (1985). *Recent advances in spruce budworms research.* Canadian Forestry Service and USDA, Ottawa.

Sartwell, C. and Dolph, R. E. Jr. (1976). *Silvicultural and direct control of mountain pine beetle in second-growth ponderosa pine.* USDA Forest Service Research Note, Pacific Northwest Forest and Range Experiment Station PNW-268.

Sartwell, C., Daterman, G. E., Sower, L. L., Overhulser, D. L., and Koerber, T. W. (1980). Mating disruption with synthetic sex attractants controls damage by *Eucosma sonomana* (Lepidoptera: Tortricidae, Olethreutinae) in *Pinus ponderosa* plantations. I. Manually applied polyvinyl chloride formulations. *Canadian Entomologist* **112**, 159–62.

Savill, P. S. and Evans, J. (1986). *Plantation silviculture in temperature regions with special reference to the British Isles.* Clarendon Press, Oxford.

Schaefer, G. W. (1976). Radar observations of insect flight. In *Insect flight* (ed. R. C. Rainey), pp. 157–97. Symposia of the Royal Entomological Society, No. 7. Blackwell, Oxford.

Schaefer, G. W. (1979). An airborne radar system technique for the investigation and control of migrating pest insects. *Philosophical Transactions of the Royal Society B* **287**, 459–65.

Schmid, J. M. and Frye, R. H. (1976). *Stand ratings for spruce beetles.* USDA Forest Service Research Note RM-309, 1–4.

Schmutzenhofer, H. (1975). The course of the nun moth outbreak in the Waldviertel 1964–67. On the outbreak of the nun moth *Lymantria monacha* in the Waldviertel (Lower Austria) 1964–1967) and further development up to 1973 (in German). *Mitteilungen der Forstlichen Bundesversuchsanstalt,* Wien **110**, 5–24.

Schoeneweiss, D. F. (1975). Predisposition, stress, and plant disease. *Annual Review of Phytopathology* **13**, 193–211.

Schönherr, J. (1985). Nun moth outbreak in Poland in 1978–1984. *Zeitschrift für angewandte Entomologie* **99**, 73–6.

Schoonhoven, L. M. (1982). Biological aspects of antifeedants. *Entomologia experimentalis et applicata* **31**, 57–69.

Schowalter, T. D. (1981). Insect herbivore relationship to the state of the host plant: biotic regulation of ecosystem nutrient cycling through ecological succession. *Oikos* **37**, 126–30.

Schowalter, T. D., Hargrove, W. W., and Crossley, D. A. Jr. (1986). Herbivory in forested ecosystems. *Annual Review of Entomology* **31**, 177–96.

Schroeder, L. M. (1988). Attraction of the bark beetle *Tomicus piniperda* and some other bark- and wood-living beetles to the host volatiles α-pinene and ethanol. *Entomologia experimentalis et applicata* **46**, 203–10.

Schultz, J. C. (1983). Habitat selection and foraging tactics of caterpillars in heterogeneous trees. In *Variable plants and herbivores in natural and managed systems* (ed. R. F. Denno and M. S. McClure), pp. 61–70. Academic Press, New York.

Schwalbe, C. P. (1981). Disparlure-baited traps for survey and detection. In *The gypsy moth: research toward integrated pest management* (ed. C. C. Doane and M. L. McManus), pp. 542–8. USDA Forest Service Technical Bulletin 1584.

Schwerdtfeger, F. (1935). Studies on the variation in abundance of some forest pests. I. The climate of regions in Germany where *Bupalus piniarius, Panolis flammea* and *Diprion pini* are injurious (in German). *Zeitschrift für Forst-u. Jagdwesen* **67**, 15–38, 85–104.

Schwerdtfeger, F. (1941). On the causes of variation in abundance of insects (in German). *Zeitschrift für angewandte Entomologie* **28**, 254–303.

Schwerdtfeger, F. (1954). Forest insects in primaeval and commercial forests (in German). *Allgemeine Forstzeitung* **9**, 278–82.

Schwerdtfeger, F. (1973). Forest entomology. In *History of entomology* (ed. R. F. Smith, T. E. Mittler and C. N. Smith), pp. 361–86. Annual Reviews Inc.

Scott, T. M. and Brown, R. M. (1973). Insecticidal control of the pine looper moth in Great Britain. III. Aerial spraying with Tetrachlorvinphos. *Forestry* **46**, 81–93.

Scott, T. M. and King, C. J. (1974). *The large pine weevil and black pine beetles*. Forestry Commission Leaflet 58. HMSO, London.

Sharpe, P. J. H. and Wu, H. (1985). A preliminary model of host susceptibility to bark beetle attack. In *The role of the host plant in the population dynamics of forest insects* (ed. L. Safranyik), pp. 108–27. Canadian Forestry Service and the USDA.

Sharpe, P. J. H., Wu, H., Cates, R. G., and Goeschl, J. D. (1985). Energetics of pine defense systems to bark beetle attack. In *Integrated pest management research symposium: The proceedings* (ed. S. J. Branham and R. C. Thatcher), pp. 206–23. USDA Forest Service General Technical Report SO-56.

Shavliashvili, I. A., Mukhasavria, A. L., and Zharkov, D. G. (1976). *Dendroctonus micans* Kug.-populations and integrated control in Georgia. *XVI IUFRO World Congress, Norway, Div. 2*, 421–8.

Shepherd, R. F., Gray, T. G., Chorney, R. J., and Daterman, G. E. (1985). Pest management of Douglas-fir tussock moth, *Orgyia pseudotsugata* (Lepidoptera: Lymantriidae): monitoring endemic populations with pheromone traps to detect incipient outbreaks. *Canadian Entomologist* **117**, 839–48.

Simmonds, F. J., Franz, J. M., and Sailer, R. I. (1976). History of biological control. In *Theory and practice of biological control* (ed. C. B. Huffaker and P. S. Messenger), pp. 17–39. Academic Press, New York.

Skuhravy, V. and Hochmut, R. (1980). Monitoring the nun moth, *Lymantria monacha* in Czechoslovakia using pheromone traps (Lepidoptera, Lymantriidae). *Acta Entomologica Bohemoslovaca* **77**, 426–9.

Slansky, F. Jr. and Scriber, J. M. (1985). Food consumption and utilisation. In *Comprehensive insect physiology biochemistry and pharmacology*, Vol. 4, *Regulation: digestion, nutrition, excretion* (ed. G. A. Kerkut and L. I. Gilbert), pp. 87–163. Pergamon Press, Oxford.

Smetanin, G. M. (1980). Effect of forest drainage on the spread and numbers of *Pissodes validirostris* (in Russian). *Lesnoe Khozyaistvo No. 1*, 68–70.

Smirnoff, W. A. and Bernier, B. (1973). Increased mortality of the Swaine jack-pine sawfly, and foliar nitrogen concentrations after urea fertilisation. *Canadian Journal of Forest Research* **3**, 112–21.

Smirnoff, W. A. and Hutchison, P. M. (1965). Bacteriostatic and bacteriocidal effects of extracts of foliage from various plant species on *Bacillus thuringiensis* var *thuringiensis* Berliner. *Journal of Invertebrate Pathology* **7**, 273–80.

Smirnoff, W. A. and Valéro, J. (1975). The medium-term effects of applying urea or potassium fertilizer on *Pinus banksiana* and the behaviour of its insect pests *Neodiprion swainei* and *Toumeyella numismaticum* (in French). *Canadian Journal of Forest Research* **5**, 236–44.

Smith, A. D. M. and Maelzer, D. A. (1986). Aggregation of parasitoids and density-independence of parasitism of field populations of the wasp *Aphytis melinus* and its host, the red scale *Aonidiella aurantii*. *Ecological Entomology* **11**, 425–34.

Smith, I. M. (1979). EPPO: the work of a regional plant protection organisation, with particular reference to phyto-sanitary regulations. In *Plant health. The scientific basis for administrative control of plant diseases and pests* (ed. D. L. Ebbels and J. E. King), pp. 13–22. Blackwell Scientific Publications, Oxford.

Smith, R. F. and van den Bosch, R. (1967). Integrated control. In *Pest control – biological, physical, and selected chemical methods* (ed. W. W. Kilgore and R. L. Doutt), pp. 295–340. Academic Press, New York.

Smith, R. G., Daterman, G. E., Daves, G. D. Jr., McMurtrey, K. D., and Roelofs, W. L. (1974). Sex pheromone of the European pine shoot moth: chemical identification and field tests. *Journal of Insect Physiology* **20**, 661–8.

Smith, S. M., Hubbes, M., and Carrow, J. R. (1986). Factors affecting inundative releases of *Trichogramma minutum* Ril. against the spruce budworm. *Journal of Applied Entomology* **101**, 29–39.

Solomon, M. E. (1949). The natural control of animal populations. *Journal of Animal Ecology* **18**, 1–35.

Southey, J. F. (1979). Preventing the entry of alien diseases and pests into Great Britain. In *Plant health. The scientific basis for administrative control of plant diseases and pests* (ed. D. L. Ebbels and J. E. King), pp. 63–70. Blackwell Scientific Publications, Oxford.

Southwood, T. R. E. (1961). The number of species of insects associated with various trees. *Journal of Animal Ecology* **30**, 1–8.

Southwood, T. R. E. (1973). The insect/plant relationship – an evolutionary perspective. In *Insect/plant relationships* (ed. H. F. van Emden), pp. 3–30. Blackwell Scientific Publications, Oxford.

Southwood, T. R. E. (1977). Habitat, the templet for ecological strategies. *Journal of Animal Ecology* **46**, 337–65.

Southwood, T. R. E. (1978). *Ecological methods with particular reference to the study of insect populations*. Methuen, London.

Southwood, T. R. E. and Kennedy, C. E. J. (1983). Trees as islands. *Oikos* **41**, 359–71.

Speight, M. R. (1986). Environmental influences on host plant susceptibility to insect attack. In *Insects and the plant surface* (ed. B. E. Juniper and T. R. E. Southwood), pp. 309–16. Edward Arnold, London.

Speight, M. R. and Speechley, H. T. (1982). Pine shoot moth in S.E. Asia I. Distribution, biology and impact. *Commonwealth Forestry Review* **61**, 121–34.

Sprague, R. H. Jr. (1980). Guest editors introduction, selected papers on decision support systems from the 13th Hawaii international conference on system sciences. *Data Base* **12**, 2–7.

Spray, C. J., Crick, H. Q. P., and Hart, A. D. M. (1987). Effects of aerial applications of fenitrothion on bird populations of a Scottish pine plantation. *Journal of Applied Ecology* **24**, 29–47.

Spurr, S. H. and Barnes, B. V. (1980). *Forest ecology*, 3rd edn. John Wiley, New York.

Squillace, A. E. (1971). Inheritance of monoterpene composition in cortical oleoresin of slash pine. *Forest Science* **17**, 381–7.

Städler, E. (1974). Host plant stimuli affecting oviposition behaviour of the eastern spruce budworm. *Entomologia experimentalis et applicata* **17**, 176–88.

Stark, R. W. (1965). Recent trends in forest entomology. *Annual Review of Entomology* **10**, 303–24.

Steffan, A. W. (1972). Suborder Aphidina, aphids (in German). In *Die Forstschadlinge Europas*, Vol. I (ed. W. Schwenke), pp. 162–386. Paul Parey, Hamburg.

Steiner, K. (1974). Genetic differences in resistance of scotch pine to eastern pineshoot borer. *The Great Lakes Entomologist* **7**, 103–7.

Stell, G. (1983). The safe and efficient use of pesticides. In *Pest and disease control handbook* (ed. N. Scopes and M. Ledieu), pp. 15–32. BCPC Publications, London.

Sterling, P. H. (1983). Brown-tail: the invisible itch. *Antenna* **7**, 110–13.

Stern, V. M., Smith, R. F., van den Bosch, R. and Hagen, K. S. (1959). The integrated control concept. *Hilgardia* **29**, 81–101.

Stevens, G. C. (1986). Dissection of the species-area relationship among wood-boring insects and their host plants. *American Naturalist* **128**, 35–46.

Stoakley, J. T. (1977). A severe outbreak of the pine beauty moth on lodgepole pine in Sutherland. *Scottish Forestry* **31**, 113–25.

Stoakley, J. T. (1985). Outbreaks of winter moth, *Operophtera brumata* L. (Lep., Geometridae) in young plantations of Sitka spruce in Scotland. Insecticidal control and population assessment using the sex attractant pheromone. *Zeitschrift für angewandte Entomologie* **99**, 153–60.

Stock, M. W.. Guenther, J. D., and Pitman, G. B. (1978). Implications of genetic differences between mountain pine beetle populations to integrated pest management. In *Theory and practice of mountain pine beetle management in lodgepole pine forests* (ed. A. A. Berryman, G. D. Amman and R. W. Stark), pp. 197–201. University of Idaho, Moscow, Idaho.

Strong, D. R. (1974a). The insects of British trees: community equilibrium in ecological time. *Annals of Missouri Botanical Garden* **61**, 692–701.

Strong, D. R. (1974b). Nonasymptotic species richness models and the insects of British trees. *Proceedings of the National Academy of Science USA* **71**, 2766–9.

Strong, D. R. and Levin, D. A. (1979). Species richness of plant parasites and growth form of their hosts. *American Naturalist* **114**, 1–22.

Strong, D. R., Lawton, J. H., and Southwood, T. R. E. (1984). *Insects on plants*, *community patterns and mechanisms.* Blackwell Scientific Publications, Oxford.

Sturgeon, K. B. (1979). Monoterpene variation in ponderosa pine xylem resin related to western pine beetle predation. *Evolution* **33**, 803–14.

Sundaram, K. M. S. (1975). Phosphamidon isomers in coniferous foliage. *Chemical Control Research Institute Information Report CC-X-95.*

Svestka, M. (1980). Effect of the bacterium *Bacillus thuringiensis* Berl. (thuricide) and the pyrethroid ambush on *Operophtera brumata* L., *Tortrix viridana* L. and the entomofauna of an oak stand (in Czechoslovakian). *Lesnictvi* **26**, 643–54.

Svihra, P., Paine, T. D., and Birch, M. C. (1980). Interspecific olfactory communications in southern pine beetles. *Naturwissenschaften* **67**, 518.

Sweet, G. B. (1975). Flowering and seed production. In *Seed orchards* (ed. R. Faulkner), pp. 72–82. Forestry Commission Bulletin 54.

Szujecki, A. (1987). *Ecology of forest insects.* Dr W. Junk and PWN-Polish scientific publishers, Warsaw.

Tahvanainen, J., Julkunen-Tiitto, R., and Kettunen, J. (1985). Phenolic glycosides govern the food selection pattern of willow feeding leaf beetles. *Oecologia (Berlin)* **67**, 52–6.

Tamaki, Y. (1985). Sex pheromones. In *Comprehensive insect physiology biochemistry and pharmacology*, Vol. 9, *Behaviour* (ed. G. A. Kerkut and L. I. Gilbert), pp. 145–91. Pergamon Press, Oxford.

Targamadze, K. M., Shavliashvili, I. A., Mukhashavria, A. L., Murusidze, B. V., and Zedginidze, A. A. (1975). Determining the economic effectiveness of forest pest (European spruce beetle) control expenditure. *VIII International Plant Protection Congress, Moscow* **2**, 23–7.

Tauber, M. J., Tauber, C. A., and Masaki, S. (1986). *Seasonal adaptations of insects.* Oxford University Press, Oxford.

Tenow, O. (1972). The outbreaks of *Oporinia autumnata* Bkh. and *Operophtera* spp. (Lep., Geometridae) in the Scandinavian mountain chain and northern Finland 1862–1968. *Zoologiska Bidrag fran Uppsala, Suppl* **2**, 1–107.

Tenow, O. (1975). Topographical dependence of an outbreak of *Oporinia autumnata* Bkh. (Lep., Geometridae) in a mountain birch forest in northern Sweden. *Zoon* **3**, 85–110.

Thatcher, R. C. (1960). Bark beetles affecting southern pines: a review of current knowledge. *USDA Forest Service, South Forest Experiment Station Occasional Paper 180.*

Thomson, A. J. and Shrimpton, D. M. (1984). Weather associated with the start of mountain pine beetle outbreaks. *Canadian Journal of Forest Research* **14**, 255–8.

Thomson, A. J. and Van Sickle, G. A. (1980). Estimation of tree growth losses caused by pest activity. *Canadian Journal of Forest Research* **10**, 176–82.

Tinbergen, L. (1960). The natural control of insects in pinewoods. I Factors influencing the intensity of predation by songbirds. *Archives Neerlandaises de Zoologie* **13**, 265–343.

Tjia, B. and Houston, D. B. (1975). Phenolic constituents of Norway spruce resistant or susceptible to eastern spruce gall aphid. *Forest Science* **21**, 180–4.

Tomlin, A. D. and Forgash, A. J. (1972). Toxicity of insecticides to gypsy moth larvae. *Journal of Economic Entomology* **65**, 953–4.

Tondeur, A. and Grégoire, J-C. (1979). Chemical orientation of *Rhizophagus grandis* (Coleoptera: Rhizophagidae) towards mates and towards preys; *Dendroctonus micans* (Coleoptera: Scolytidae). In *Animals and environmental fitness* (ed. R. Gilles), pp. 93–4. Pergamon Press, Oxford.

Torrent, J. A. (1955). Oak tortrix and its control in Spain. *FAO Plant Protection Bulletin* **3**, 117–21.

Trofimova, O. V. and Trofimov, V. N. (1981). Predicting the degree of damage to stands by the pine noctuid *Panolis flammea* (in Russian). *Lesnoe Khozyaistvo* No. 10, 58–61.

Tsankov, G. and Mirchev, P. (1983). The effect of some plant protection measures on the egg parasite complex of the pine processionary (*Thaumetopoea pityocampa*) (in Bulgarian). *Gorskostopanska Nauka* **20**, 84–9.

Tuomi, J., Niemela, P., Haukioja, E., Siren, S., and Neuvonen, S. (1984). Nutrient stress: an explanation for plant anti-herbivore responses to defoliation. *Oecologia (Berlin)* **61**, 208–10.

Turnock, W. J. and Muldrew, J. A. (1971). *Pristiphora erichsonii* (Hartig), larch sawfly. *Commonwealth Institute of Biological Control Technical Communication* **4**, 113–27.

Valentine, H. T. and Houston, D. R. (1979). A discriminant function for identifying mixed-oak stand susceptibility to gypsy moth defoliation. *Forest Science* **25**, 468–74.

van den Bosch, R. and Messenger, P. S. (1973). *Biological control.* International Textbook Company Ltd., Aylesbury.

van der Plank, J. E. (1968). *Disease resistance in plants.* Academic Press, New York.

van Emden, H. F. (1969). Plant resistance to *Myzus persicae* induced by a plant regulator and measured by aphid relative growth rate. *Entomologia experimentalis et applicata* **12**, 125–31.

van Emden, H. F. (1978). Insects and secondary plant substances – an alternative viewpoint with special reference to aphids. In *Biochemical aspects of plant and animal coevolution* (ed. J. B. Harbourne), pp. 309–23. Academic Press, London.

van Emden, H. F. (1986). The interaction of plant resistance and natural enemies: effects on populations of sucking insects. In *Interactions of plant resistance and parasitoids and predators of insects* (ed. D. J. Boethel and R. D. Eikenbarry), pp. 138–50. Ellis Horwood Ltd, Chichester.

van Emden, H. F. and Bashford, M. A. (1971). The performance of *Brevicoryne brassicae* and *Myzus persicae* in relation to plant age and leaf amino acids. *Entomologia experimentalis et applicata* **14**, 349–60.

van Emden, H. F. and Wearing, C. H. (1965). The role of the aphid host plant in delaying economic damage levels in crops. *Annals of Applied Biology* **56**, 323–4.

van Emden, H. F., Eastop, V. F., Hughes, R. D., and Way, M. J. (1969). The ecology of *Myzus persicae*. *Annual Review of Entomology* **14**, 197–270.

van Sickle, G. A., Alfaro, R. I., and Thomson, A. J. (1983). Douglas-fir height growth affected by western spruce budworm. *Canadian Journal of Forest Research* **13**, 445–50.

Vandenberg, J. D. and Soper, R. S. (1978). Prevalence of Entomophthorales mycosis in populations of spruce budworm, *Choristoneura fumiferana*. *Environmental Entomology* **7**, 847–53.

Varley, G. C. (1949). Population changes in German forest pests. *Journal of Animal Ecology* **18**, 117–22.

Varley, G. C. and Gradwell, G. R. (1960). Key factors in population studies. *Journal of Animal Ecology* **29**, 399–401.

Varley, G. C. and Gradwell, G. R. (1968). Population models for the winter moth. In *Insect abundance* (ed. T. R. E. Southwood), pp. 132–42. Symposium of The Royal Entomological Society of London No. 4. Blackwell Scientific Publications, Oxford.

Varley, G. C., Gradwell, G. R., and Hassell, M. P. (1973). *Insect population ecology, an analytical approach*. Blackwell Scientific Publications, Oxford.

Varty, I. W. (1956). *Adelges insects of silver fir*. Forestry Commission Bulletin No. 26.

Vinson, S. B. (1976). Host selection by insect parasitoids. *Annual Review of Entomology* **21**, 109–33.

Visser, J. H. (1986). Host odor perception in phytophagous insects. *Annual Review of Entomology* **31**, 121–44.

Vité, J. P. (1961). The influence of water su;ply on oleoresin exudation pressure and resistance to bark beetle attack in *Pinus ponderosa*. *Contributions from Boyce Thompson Institute* **21**, 37–66.

Vité, J. P. and Wood, D. L. (1961). A study on the applicability of the measurement of oleoresin exudation pressure in determining susceptibility of second growth ponderosa pine to bark beetle infestation. *Contributions from Boyce Thompson Institute* **21**, 67–78.

Vité, J. P., Bakke, A., and Renwick, J. A. A. (1972). Pheromones in *Ips* (Coleoptera: Scolytidae): occurrence and production. *Canadian Entomologist* **104**, 1967–75.

Voûte, A. D. (1964). Harmonious control of forest insects. *International Review of Forest Research* **1**, 325–83.

Wagner, M. R. (1988). Induced defenses in ponderosa pine against defoliating insects. In *Mechanisms of woody plant defenses against insects. Search for pattern*. (ed. W. J. Mattson, J. Levieux, C. Bernard-Dagan), pp. 141–55. Springer-Verlag, New York.

Wainhouse, D. (1980). Dispersal of first instar larvae of the felted beech scale, *Cryptococcus fagisuga*. *Journal of Animal Ecology* **17**, 523–32.

Wainhouse, D. (1987). Forests. In *Integrated pest management* (ed. A. J. Burn, T. H. Coaker and P. C. Jepson), pp. 361–401. Academic Press, London.

Wainhouse, D. and Deeble, R. (1980). Variation in susceptibility of beech (*Fagus* spp) to beech scale (*Cryptococcus fagisuga*). *Annales des Sciences Forestières* **37**, 279–89.

Wainhouse, D. and Gate, I. M. (1988). The beech scale. In *Dynamics of forest insect populations. Patterns, causes, implications* (ed. A. A. Berryman), pp. 67–85. Plenum, New York.

Wainhouse, D. and Howell, R. S. (1983). Intraspecific variation in beech scale populations and in susceptibility of their host *Fagus sylvatica*. *Ecological Entomology* **8**, 351–9.

Wardle, J. A. (1984). *The New Zealand Beeches. Ecology, utilisation and management*. New Zealand Forest Service.

Wareing, P. F. and Patrick, J. (1975). Source-sink relations and the partition of assimilates in plants. In *Photosynthesis and productivity in different environments* (ed. H. P. Cooper), pp. 481–99. Cambridge University Press.

Waring, R. H. (1982). Coupling stress physiology with ecosystem analysis. In *Carbon uptake and allocation in subalpine ecosystems as a key to management* (ed. R. H. Waring), pp. 5–8. Forest Research Laboratory, Oregon State University, Corvallis.

Waring, R. H. (1983). Estimating forest growth and efficiency in relation to canopy leaf area. *Advances in Ecological Research* **13**, 327–54.

Waring, R. H. and Pitman, G. B. (1980). *A simple model of host resistance to bark beetles*. Forest Research Laboratory Research Note 65, Oregon State University, Corvallis.

Waring, R. H. and Pitman, G. B. (1983). Physiological stress in lodgepole pine as a precursor for mountain pine beetle attack. *Zeitschrift für angewandte Entomologie* **96**, 265–70.

Waring, R. H. and Pitman, G. B. (1985). Modifying lodgepole pine stands to change susceptibility to mountain pine beetle attack. *Ecology* **66**, 889–97.

Waring, R. H., Thies, W. G., and Muscato, D. (1980). Stem growth per unit of leaf area: a measure of tree vigor. *Forest Science* **26**, 112–7.

Waring, R. H., Schroeder, P. E. and Oren, R. (1982). Application of the pipe model theory to predict canopy leaf area. *Canadian Journal of Forest Research* **12**, 556–60.

Waring, R. H., M McDonald, A. J. S., Larsson, S., Ericsson, T., Wiren, A., Arwidsson, E., Ericsson, A., and Lohammar, T. (1985). Differences in chemical composition of plants grown at constant relative growth rates with stable mineral nutrition. *Oecologia (Berlin)* **66**, 157–60.

Warrington, S. and Whittaker, J. B. (1985a). An experimental field study of different levels of insect herbivory induced by *Formica rufa* predation on sycamore (*Acer pseudoplatanus*) I. Lepidoptera larvae. *Journal of Applied Ecology* **22**, 775–85.

Warrington, S. and Whittaker, J. B. (1985b). An experimental field study of different levels of insect herbivory induced by *Formica rufa* predation on sycamore (*Acer pseudoplatanus*) II. Aphidoidea. *Journal of Applied Ecology* **22**, 787–96.

Watt, A. D. and Leather, S. R. (1988). The pine beauty moth in Scottish lodgepole pine plantations. In *Dynamics of forest insect populations. Patterns, causes implications* (ed. A. A. Berryman), pp. 243–66. Plenum, New York.

Way, M. J. (1966). The natural environment and integrated methods of pest control. *Journal of Applied Ecology* **3** (suppl.), 29–32.

Way, M. J. and Bevan, D. (1977). Dilemmas in forest pest and disease management. In *Ecological effects of pesticides* (ed. F. H. Perring and K. Mellanby), pp. 95–110. Academic Press, London.

Webb, R. E. (1982). Mass trapping of the gypsy moth. In *Insect suppression with controlled release pheromone systems*, Vol. II (ed. A. F. Kydonieus and M. Beroza), pp. 27–56. CRC Press, Boca Raton, Florida.

Webber, J. F. and Gibbs, J. N. (1989). Insect dissemination of fungal pathogens of trees. In *Insect-fungus interactions* (ed. N. Wilding, N. M. Collins, P. M. Hammond and J. F. Webber) pp. 160–93. Academic Press, London.

Welch, R. C. (1981). The insect fauna of *Nothofagus*. *NERC Institute of Terrestrial Ecology Annual Report 1980*, 50–3.

Wellenstein, G. (1959). The scope and limits of the use of pathogenic agents, useful insects and birds in practical forest protection (in German). *Forstwirtschaft-liches Centralblatt* **78**, 150–66.

Wellenstein, G. (1965). Methods and results of research on the influence of ants of the *Formica rufa* group on the forest biocoenosis (in German). In *Research and practical experience in the biological protection of forests*. Collana Verde Ministry of Agriculture and Forestry, Rome **16**, 369–92.

Wellenstein, G. (1973). The development of artificially founded colonies of hill-building red wood ants of the *Formica rufa* – group in south-western Germany. *OEPP/EPPO Bulletin No. 9*, 23–34.

Wellenstein, G. (1978). Chemical forest pest control. In *Problems of insect and tick control. Biological medical and legal aspects* (in German), pp. 157–69. Erich Schmidt Verlag, Berlin.

Wellington, W. G. (1954). Weather and climate in forest entomology. *Meteoro-logical Monographs* **2**, 11–8.

West, C. (1985). Factors underlying the late seasonal appearance of the leipidop-terous leaf-mining guild on oak. *Ecological Entomology* **10**, 111–20.

White, J. and Strehl, C. E. (1978). Xylem feeding by periodical cicada nymphs on tree roots. *Ecological Entomology* **3**, 323–7.

White, T. C. R. (1969). An index to measure weather-induced stress of trees associated with outbreaks of psyllids in Australia. *Ecology* **50**, 905–9.

White, T. C. R. (1974). A hypothesis to explain outbreaks of looper caterpillars, with special reference to populations of *Selidosema suavis* in a plantation of *Pinus radiata* in New Zealand. *Oecologia (Berlin)* **16**, 279–301.

White, W. B., McLane, W. H., and Schneeberger, N. F. (1981). Pesticides. In *The gypsy moth: research toward integrated pest management* (ed. C. C. Doane and M. L. McManus), pp. 423–42. USDA Technical Bulletin 1584.

Whitham, T. G. and Mopper, S. (1985). Chronic herbivory: impacts on architec-ture and sex expression of pinyon pine. *Science* **228**, 1089–91.

Whittaker, R. H. (1975). *Communities and ecosystems*, 2nd edn. Macmillan, London.

Whittaker, R. H. and Feeny, P. P. (1971). Allelochemics: chemical interactions between species. *Science* **171**, 757–69.

Wiersma, N. and Nordlander, G. (1985). Testing of systemic insecticides against insects in Norway spruce cones (in Swedish). *Vaxtskyddsnotiser* **48**, 113–6.

Wiesner, C. J. (1984). Droplet deposition and drift in forest spraying. In *Chemical and biological control in forestry* (ed. W. Y. Garner and J. Harvey Jr.), pp. 139–51. American Chemical Society, Washington.

Williams, C. B. Jr. (1967). Spruce budworm damage symptoms related to radial growth of grand fir, Douglas-fir, and Engelmann spruce. *Forest Science* **13**, 274–85.

Wilson, J. W. (1972). Control of crop processes. In *Crop processes in controlled environments* (ed. A. R. Rees, K. E. Cockshull, D. W. Hand and R. G. Hurd), pp. 7–30. Academic Press, New York.

Wilson, L. F. (1976). Entomological problems of forest crops grown under intensive culture. *Iowa State Journal of Research* **50**, 277–86.

Wilson, L. F. and Millers, I. (1983). Pine root collar weevil – its ecology and management. *USDA Forest Service Technical Bulletin No. 1675*, 1–33.

Wingfield, M. J., Blanchette, R. A., and Nicholls, T. H. (1984). Is the pinewood nematode an important pathogen in the United States? *Journal of Forestry* **82**, 232–35.

Wint, G. R. W. (1983). The effect of foliar nutrients upon the growth and feeding of a lepidopteran larva. In *Nitrogen as an ecological factor* (ed. J. A. Lees, S. McNeill and I. H. Rorison), pp. 301–20. Blackwell Scientific Publications, Oxford.

Winter, T. G. (1974). New host plant records of Lepidoptera associated with conifer afforestation in Britain. *Entomologist's Gazette* **25**, 247–58.

Wood, D. L. (1982). The role of pheromones, kairomones, and allomones in the host selection and colonisation behaviour of bark beetles. *Annual Review of Entomology* **27**, 411–6.

Worrell, R. (1983). Damage by the spruce bark beetle in south Norway 1970–1980. A survey and factors affecting its occurrence. *Meddelelser fra Norsk Institutt for Skogforskning* **38**, (6), 1–34.

Wouters, L. A. (1979). Control of *Sciapteron [Paranthrene] tabaniformis* larvae in poplar nurseries (in Dutch). *Populier* **16**, 39–40.

Wright, J. W. and Wilson, L. F., (1972). Genetic differences in scotch pine resistance to pine root collar weevil. *Michigan State University Agricultural Experiment Station Research Report 159*, 5pp.

Wright, J. W., Wilson, L. F., and Bright, J. N. (1975). Genetic variation in resistance of scotch pine to Zimmerman pine moth. *The Great Lakes Entomologist* **8**, 231–6.

Wright, L. C., Berryman, A. A. and Wickman, B. E. (1984). Abundance of the fir engraver, *Scolytus ventralis*, and the Douglas-fir beetle, *Dendroctonus pseudotsugae*, following tree defoliation by the Douglas-fir tussock moth, *Orgyia pseudotsugata*. *Canadian Entomologist* **166**, 293–305.

Wylie, F. R. and Peters, B. C. (1987). Development of contingency plans for use against exotic pests and diseases of trees and timber. 2. Problems with the detection and identification of pest insect introductions into Australia, with special reference to Queensland. *Australian Forestry* **50**, 16–23.

Yamada, M., Saito, T., Katugiri, K., Iwaki, S., and Marumo, S. (1976). Electroantennogram and behavioural responses of the gypsy moth to enantiomers of disparlure and its trans analogues. *Journal of Insect Physiology* **22**, 755–61.

Young, J. W. (1983). Registration requirements for pesticides. In *Natural products for innovative pest management* (ed. D. L. Whitehead and W. S. Bowers), pp. 523–40. Pergamon Press, Oxford.

Young, R. A. (ed.) (1982). *Introduction to forest science*. J. Wiley, New York.

Young, S. Y. and Yearian, W. C. (1986). Formulation and application of baculo-viruses. In *The biology of baculoviruses*, Vol. II, *Practical application for insect control* (ed. R. R. Granados and B. A. Federici), pp. 157–79. CRC Press, Boca Raton, Florida.

Zakordonets, V. A. (1975). Hygienic requirements regarding chemical methods of forest protection. *VIII International Congress of Plant Protection. Vol. 2*, 158–62.

Zethner, O. (1976). Control experiments on the nun moth (*Lymantria monacha* L.) by nuclear-polyhedrosis virus in Danish coniferous forests. *Zeitschrift für angewandte Entomologie*, **81**, 192–207.

Zobel, B. J. and Talbert, J. (1984). *Applied forest tree improvement*. J. Wiley, New York.

Zobel, B. J., van Wyk, G., and Stahl, P. (1987). *Growing exotic forests*. J. Wiley, New York.

Zondag, R. (1969). A nematode infection of *Sirex noctilio* (F.) in New Zealand. *New Zealand Journal of Science* **17**, 732–47.

Zumr, V. (1982). The data for the prognosis of spring swarming of main species of bark beetles (Coleoptera, Scolytidae) on the spruce (*Picea excelsea* L.). *Zeitschrift für angewandte Entomologie* **93**, 305–20.

Zwolfer, H. (1971). The structure and effect of parasite complexes attacking phytophagous host insects. In *Proceedings of the advanced study institute on the dynamics of numbers of populations (Oosterbeek, 1970)* (ed. P. J. den Boer and G. R. Gradwell), pp. 405–18. Centre for Agricultural Publishing and Documentation (Pudoc), Wageningen.

Index